THE WELFARE STATE IN BRITAIN SINCE 1945

The Welfare State in Britain since 1945

Rodney Lowe

MACMILLAN

First published 1993 by
THE MACMILLAN PRESS LTD
Houndmills, Basingstoke, Hampshire RG21 2XS
and London
Companies and representatives
throughout the world

ISBN 0–333–44255–5 hardcover
ISBN 0–333–44256–3 paperback

A catalogue record for this book is available
from the British Library.

Printed in Great Britain by
Mackays of Chatham PLC
Chatham, Kent

Contents

Contents

List of Figures and Tables

Figures

Tables

Acknowledgements

My foremost debt is to all those who have written on the welfare state and whose work I have used. My foremost obligation, therefore, is to apologise to those whose views I have failed to acknowledge, have caricatured or, worse still, have ignored. I should also apologise to readers in Scotland and Northern Ireland who will immediately perceive, with resignation, that this is yet another book which focuses essentially on England and Wales. The reasons for this are twofold. I simply do not as yet have the necessary expertise to write on welfare policy in their countries; and the inclusion of such information would have made even more complex a book which many may feel is too long already. It is an omission which I hope to remedy in a second edition, should one be commissioned.

I should like to thank the University of Bristol, the Nuffield Foundation and the Economic and Social Research Council for their financial support over the past five years. The grant from the ESRC enabled me jointly to edit *The Development of the Welfare State, 1939–51: a guide to documents in the Public Record Office* (HMSO, 1992) which, it is hoped, will stimulate and facilitate research in this area. I should also like to thank my editor, Vanessa Graham, for her patience; Anne Griffiths, Penny Grigg, Jean Richards and Anita Hathway for wrestling with the manuscript; my wife, Sue, for her readiness to correct everything I have written (or indeed said); and Gini, Alex and the cat for coping, in their own peculiar ways, with my preoccupations.

RODNEY LOWE

1 Introduction

In the mid-1970s the welfare state in Britain was, or at least was widely considered to be, in crisis. With unemployment standing at just under one million, the Labour government in its budget of April 1975 chose not to reflate the economy and thus became the first postwar government, other than during a temporary balance of payments or sterling crisis, to abandon the goal of 'full' employment. The reasons for this decision were made explicit in the following year, when a serious sterling crisis had obliged the government to seek a loan from the International Monetary Fund. As the Prime Minister, James Callaghan, told his party conference in September 1976:

> We used to think that you could just spend your way out of a recession and increase employment by cutting taxes and boosting government spending. I tell you in all candour, that option no longer exists, and that in so far as it ever did exist, it worked by injecting inflation into the economy. And each time that happened the average level of unemployment has risen. Higher inflation was followed by higher unemployment. That is the history of the last twenty years.[1]

One of the original props of the welfare state – the confidence of Keynesian economists that governments could and should guarantee a high level of employment – was thereby kicked away.

This revolution in economic thinking and policy had immediate consequences for social policy. Most obviously, the monetary targets imposed upon all public expenditure checked a projected expansion of the social services. More fundamentally, it abandoned one of the major assumptions underlying the 1942 Beveridge Report, which has conventionally been regarded as a principal blueprint of the welfare state. The system of social security which it had proposed was dependent on the maintenance of a high level of employment. Administratively, how else could traditional fears about the consequences of state welfare, such as the undermining of the will to work, be laid to rest if jobs could not be offered to claimants to test their sincerity? Socially, was security of income alone – without the positive benefits of productive employment – an 'adequate provision for human happiness'? Economically, would not the cost of social security become

1

'insupportable' were mass unemployment simultaneously to increase expenditure on unemployment benefit and (by lowering economic activity) reduce government revenue?[2] The whole nature and practicality of Beveridge's proposal was, therefore, dependent on the elimination of mass unemployment.

The revolution in economic thinking and policy also destroyed a third prop of the welfare state which had been made explicit in another of its blueprints, the 1944 *Employment Policy* white paper. It had argued that the maintenance of employment would ultimately depend not so much on government action but on the 'understanding and support of the community as a whole – and especially of the efforts of employers and workers in industry'.[3] With the apparent inability of the government to manage the economy and the consequent disappointment of expectations about increased social welfare, however, this understanding and support started to be seriously eroded. The Conservative government in 1973 had already been branded as managerially incompetent following its clash with the miners and the resulting three-day week; and the Labour Party had won two elections in 1974 largely on the ground that it could maintain industrial cooperation. Its main weapon was the social contract, whereby trade unions agreed not to use the full market power which they derived from full employment (which by increasing wages and hence costs might eventually undermine Britain's industrial competitiveness and thereby create unemployment) on condition that an equivalent distribution of wealth and income would be provided by government through the social services and taxation. The monetary restrictions on the social services, combined with the introduction of an (albeit voluntary) prices and incomes policy, convinced the public sector unions in particular that such a contract was unlikely to be honoured; and they consequently used their full market power to demand wage increases of up to 35 per cent. The resulting 'winter of discontent' of 1978–9, in which rubbish piled up high in the streets and in certain instances (duly exploited by the press) the dead could not be buried, was the direct prelude to the election of a Conservative government in May 1979. The public sector unions, as one incensed insider noted, had in effect elected Margaret Thatcher.[4]

Margaret Thatcher, who had become leader of the Conservative Party in February 1975, just before Labour's tacit abandonment of 'full' employment, represented a major break in postwar political assumptions and attitudes. As she readily admitted, she felt none of the 'bourgeois guilt' for the mass unemployment of the interwar years, which had so coloured the planning and implementation of the welfare state during and after the Second World War.[5] Instead her philosophy and policies were shaped by the continued spectacle since 1945 of Britain's declining economy and rising ungovernability. In her view and that of the increasing section of the electorate to whom she appealed, the policies of full employment, expanding social services and corporatism which underlay the postwar welfare state had failed. They, and the attitudes which validated them, urgently needed to be replaced. As she informed *The Times* on 19 January 1984, she wanted her government to be remembered as the one 'which decisively broke with the debilitating consensus of a paternalistic government and a dependent people; which rejected the notion that the State is all powerful and the citizen is merely its beneficiary; which shattered the illusion that Government could somehow substitute for individual performance'.

This crisis in the welfare state was not peculiar to Britain but was experienced in all western industrialised countries. The world recession, exacerbated by the quadrupling of the price of oil in 1973–4, checked the economic growth which each country had enjoyed since 1945 and upon which each had depended for the increased revenue necessary to finance the expanding welfare services its electorate demanded. With projected revenue falling short of projected expenditure a 'fiscal crisis' occurred, which a rejuvenated body of Marxist analysts identified as the final and inevitable crisis of capitalism – last spotted in 1931 but then, in their opinion, temporarily postponed by war and the implementation of Keynesian economics. The popularity of all social democratic parties was eroded to the extent that even in Scandinavia, where they had governed since before the war, they were to lose power in the early 1980s. Everywhere Keynesian economics and welfare programmes, or at least projected increases in welfare programmes, were either abandoned or modified.

When the dust settled however, one remarkable fact was as true for Britain as for all other welfare states. Whatever the changes in economic and political assumptions, social spending in absolute terms had not decreased, but had continued to rise. This was partly due to technical factors: the changing age structure of the population (with an increasing number of elderly people, in particular, requiring greater expenditure on pensions and institutional care); the increasing burden of unemployment benefits (as predicted by Beveridge); and the increases in the relative cost of labour-intensive welfare services which could not match the savings achieved by increased industrial productivity (in the fashionable jargon of the day, 'the relative price effect'). It was also due, however, to the continuing popularity of welfare policy amongst the electorate. Public opinion, so far as it could be divined, may have wanted cuts in public expenditure but not at the expense of those welfare services from which the majority would benefit directly.[6] Governments, therefore, dared not make significant cuts but confined themselves to eliminating the more obvious cases of waste and checking the projected rise in expenditure. Did this in fact mean that the depth of the crisis facing the welfare state, both in Britain and abroad, in the 1970s was exaggerated at the time by both political rhetoric and academic analysis? Moreover is it true, as has been claimed, that in the 1980s 'the right-wing reaction' was 'only half successful'?[7] Had Keynes been repudiated but not Beveridge?

The purpose of this book is to answer such questions by examining in depth the period from the establishment of the welfare state in the mid-1940s to its perceived crisis in the mid-1970s; and then by looking more impressionistically at the years since 1976 to gauge the extent to which the welfare state has been abandoned or retained. The heart of the book is therefore Part II, an historical analysis of the 'classic' welfare state judged not just in hindsight but in the light of contemporary aspirations and constraints.[8] What exactly does the term 'welfare state' mean? What were its original objectives? How did they change over time? To what extent were they achieved? To what extent was any failure – if failure there was – the result of a lack of political will (individual or collective), unavoidable constraints (of an economic or international nature) or faulty logic and unrealistic assumptions?

The major chapters concentrate on the six traditional areas of welfare policy – employment policy, social security, education, health, housing and the personal social services. They are prefaced by an examination of the economic, social and political context in which policy was formulated and implemented, and succeeded by another analysing the combined impact (if any) of all policies on the distribution of power, income and wealth. Part III, on welfare policy since 1976, follows the same structure, if more briefly. Events are too recent for historical analysis and contemporary commentaries abound. Any fuller analysis could add little to such commentaries and would limit the space available for the book's central concern, the evolution of the classic welfare state between 1945 and 1975.

Such a concern underlines the fact that in many ways the book is a sequel to Derek Fraser's *The Evolution of the British Welfare State* (first published in 1973) which raised to new heights the study of social policy between 1800 and 1948. There are differences in approach, however, partly because of the shorter period covered and the greater concentration on the state, but mainly because of the greater use by historians in the past decade of theory. Fraser in his second edition (1980) acknowledged the need for more theoretical explicitness, but the range of possible interpretations identified in his foreword was not used to alter the text to any significant degree.

The use of theory by historians places them in an unresolvable dilemma. The time spent mastering the intricacies of one theory, let alone a set of theories, is time forfeited in the study of empirical evidence which must be their prime concern. Over the full range of their interests, therefore, no historian can afford to become an expert theorist.[9] Theoretical awareness is, nevertheless, indispensable. By clarifying implicit, and often confused, assumptions it can expedite research by clarifying how an argument should be structured and what sort of evidence should be sought. By helping to counterbalance the bias of contemporaries and of extant records, it can help in the task of both empathising with the past and assessing it critically. By opening horizons and suggesting new relationships, it can give meaning to evidence which might otherwise be overlooked. It can also, in supra-national developments such as the evolution of welfare states, provide the means by which international comparisons can be made as well as making available a wide range of literature written on an equally wide range of competing assumptions.

Similarly, in the assessment of welfare policy itself, it can provide a bridge between the competing academic disciplines of economics, political science and social administration. Why did welfare states develop simultaneously in a wide range of countries after the Second World War and then experience a simultaneous crisis in the mid-1970s? Beneath the surface, how similar is each welfare state? Why are welfare issues conceptualised in a particular way at a certain time and why are certain policy options politically acceptable at certain times but wholly ignored at others? Why does there appear to be so great a gap between the intentions of policymakers and the actual impact of policy? It is such questions which Part I addresses and, through the provision of a brief guide to the various competing theories of the state and of the policymaking process, it should also enable readers to develop their own solutions. At the same time, it is also designed to make explicit the actual assumptions on which the book itself is based.

The overall objective of the book is, therefore, to present an interpretation of the British welfare state since 1945 which others will find instructive and convincing. Any textbook worth its salt must, however, also aim to give its readers the interest and the ability to develop their own interpretations of the subject. This is the purpose behind the presentation of rival theoretical analyses and the deployment of evidence. Similar principles underlie the guidance on further reading. At present only the period up to 1951 has been adequately covered by historians. Commentaries on the period after 1975 are often repetitious and partial. In the limited space available, attention has been drawn to works of synthesis with good bibliographies and to more detailed monographs which both inform and inspire.

Part I

Theoretical Perspectives

2 The Nature of the Welfare State

The purpose of this chapter is to examine the competing definitions and theoretical interpretations of the welfare state before making explicit the assumptions on which this book is based – and thus its unavoidable bias. Such a theoretical approach can become very arid, so to minimise that danger the subject will be approached in two ways. First the welfare state will be defined and the three broad political strategies which have influenced its development in Britain will be examined. Then the more general theories, on which these assumptions and those of the more academic commentators have been based, will be analysed. Each of the latter will be related to the early history of the National Health Service (NHS) to illustrate how, from different theoretical assumptions, totally different and yet equally logical conclusions can be drawn from the same 'facts'.

The example of the NHS has been chosen for a number of reasons. It has always been one of the most popular services within the British welfare state and the two institutions have often been regarded by the public as synonymous. The political battle which it immediately provoked (over whether charges should be made for dental and ophthalmic care) illustrates the hard managerial and political decisions inseparable from the determination of priorities which, given the scarcity of resources in the real world, have to be made. It was also the occasion for a long-term split in the Labour Party which was to have serious consequences for the way in which the British welfare state was to develop. Finally, unlike other possible examples, a wide range of relevant public and private records are available and have already been extensively discussed and analysed.

2.1 THE DEFINITION OF THE WELFARE STATE

There is no agreement amongst historians and social scientists over when the first welfare states were established or what the term actually means. Some historians have identified their establishment in nineteenth-century Europe, others exclusively in the period after the Second World War. Some, inevitably, have done both. Many

9

social scientists (and politicians) have used the term as a mere synonym for the social services provided by government; others have used it broadly to describe the full range of powers exercised by government, or indeed of a whole society. One way to cut through this confusion and establish a working definition is to determine the time at which the term first became widely used and the reason for its public acceptance.

Changes in language suggest the recognition of a new phenomenon which no existing expression can adequately describe. The term was coined in the 1930s. It was used first in Germany as a term of abuse (*Wohlfahrstaat*) against the Weimar Republic, whose constitution was seen to have burdened the state with so many social responsibilities that it had undermined the country's political and economic viability.[1] With the subsequent rise of totalitarianism, the term was developed in Britain as an antonym for the 'warfare' or power state. A welfare state was conceived to be an organ of the community whose role was to serve the welfare of its citizens and respect international law, as opposed to the tyrannical 'warfare' state which imposed its will on both its citizens and its international neighbours. Such usage reached its apogee in a book, *Citizen and Churchman*, written in 1941 by the Archbishop of Canterbury, William Temple, but Temple did warn that the power assumed by a benevolent state to advance its citizens' welfare could lead to totalitarianism. Consequently he recommended that as many responsibilities as possible should be delegated to non-state agencies.

In the late 1940s, however, the term came to be used to describe just such a growth in the power of the state under the Labour government; and it was in this sense that it rapidly won international acceptance. British politicians were initially reluctant to use the phrase since in the USA, as in Germany in the 1930s, it was still a term of abuse and Britain was dependent at that time on American aid (not least to finance its welfare services); but by 1949 it was in regular use in both academic and political circles. In 1950 the Labour prime minister, Attlee, felt sufficiently confident to commend to his Party's by-election candidates the Government's achievement in laying the 'foundations of the Welfare State' and in 1952 *The Times* felt equally confident to inaugurate the first of many debates on 'The Crisis in the Welfare State'.[2]

Rapid international acceptance of the term signified the way in which the British welfare state reflected popular aspirations which had accompanied the growth of industrialisation and political democracy not just in Britain but in all Western countries. These aspirations were more specifically expressed in another term coined during the war, 'social security', which meant the freedom (or security) of all citizens from the fear of poverty; and it was by providing the means by which such security could be attained that the British welfare state, and more particularly the 1942 Beveridge Report, which was commonly regarded as its blueprint, gained its international reputation. The Report enjoyed a somewhat unusual fate for a government white paper. At home, it attracted on its day of publication a queue of purchasers one quarter of a mile long. Abroad, it was parachuted into occupied territories as an expression of the ideals for which the Allies were fighting. Thus it both attracted immense popularity and was seen, politically, to give substance to the vague aspirations of the Allies' first statement of war aims: the 1941 Atlantic Charter (into which Churchill had been obliged, by Labour ministers in his coalition, to insert the term social security).[3] It consequently found ready endorsement in many national reconstruction plans, such as the *Chartre de la Résistance* in France, as well as in many international conventions, culminating with the 1948 Universal Declaration of Human Rights by the United Nations.[4]

However the worldwide adoption of the term 'welfare state' threatens to confuse rather than to clarify its meaning because, in both their practices and objectives, welfare states have diverged as well as converged. For instance, in each country postwar reforms had to be welded onto existing services which had acquired over many years distinctive national peculiarities. They had also to be introduced in a variety of political circumstances, not least of which were the different speeds at which the dominant peacetime vested interests which had been disrupted by the war were able to regroup. Hence it was hardly surprising that individual services, such as the health service, continued to vary between countries in the range of individuals and problems covered and their methods of finance and administration.

The ultimate objectives of welfare states have also differed, because each has developed from and been forced to respond to different cultural traditions and attitudes, not least in relation to the role of the state in society. These differences have been so great that two social scientists, Furniss and Tilton, have distinguished between two very different types of welfare state, which they have termed 'the social security state' (such as Britain) and the 'social welfare state' (such as Sweden).[5] The former, in keeping with the British tradition of decentralisation, only requires the state to guarantee its citizens a national minimum of civilised life. The latter, in keeping with the stronger tradition of centralisation in Europe, requires the state actively to reduce inequalities of income (through the wage system), property (through environmental policies) and power (through genuinely joint decisions on the management of the economy).

Such distinctions also underline the fact that, even in particular countries, there can be no wholly static definition of a welfare state. Its definition will constantly evolve as a result of changing circumstances and political perspectives. In Britain for example, the Second World War left a curious legacy. The perceived economic efficiency of the wartime state (as compared to the perceived waste and inefficiency of the free market in the 1930s), and the common need of all classes in the blitz to rely on the social services, paved the way for a degree of state intervention and a centralisation of the social services which were strikingly at variance with the national tradition of individual freedom and decentralisation. As will be shown more fully in the next section, traditional liberal values did not fully reassert themselves until after 1975 but meanwhile, within the broad collectivist consensus, there was a fundamental conflict of purpose similar to that identified by Furniss and Tilton. On the one hand there were the 'reluctant collectivists' who after the economic dislocation and poverty of the 1930s were willing to accept increased state intervention as a 'mechanism for making good the failure of the market to control avoidable ills', but who did not wish to use it overtly as an 'instrument for economic change'.[6] On the other hand, there were others who wished to use welfare policy to engineer a new type of society in which income, wealth and power would be more equally distributed. Political influence oscillated between the adherents of these two strategies, before both were eventually challenged by the liberal traditionalists. There has consequently been no common or constant agreement over the ultimate objectives of even the British welfare state.

Despite the international adoption of the term 'welfare state' therefore, and despite also the widespread belief in the 1950s that a combination of social security and the mixed economy marked the final stage of the development of industrial society ('the end of ideology'), there has never in reality been within or between nations unanimity over the nature and ultimate purpose of a welfare state. This does not mean, however, that the term is meaningless; and even if certain commentators seeking academic purity (or obscurity) are tempted to abandon it, it is a term in common usage and so one that demands definition. Accordingly a welfare state, as pragmatically defined in this book, will be seen to have three immutable characteristics. The first is that the term refers not simply to a narrow range of social services but to a society in which government is expected to provide, and does provide, a wide range of services (economic as well as social) which affect the welfare of its citizens. The second and third characteristics concern its chronology and core functions, both of which require further elaboration.

Chronologically, welfare states were the unique creation of the 1940s – as indeed the origins of the term suggest. This is because it was in the 1940s that, across the range of industrialised countries, evolutionary changes in government policy reached a critical mass at which – consciously or unconsciously – they transformed the fundamental nature of the relationship between the state and its citizens. This revolution was reflected by, and acknowledged within, the Beveridge Report.[7] The Report's individual proposals may have been mere rationalisations or developments of past practice. Cumulatively, however, they had a totally different significance. For the first time in history all citizens were to be insured 'from the cradle to the grave' against every eventuality which might lead to the inadvertent loss of their income. At a stroke, therefore, they were released by the state from the fear of poverty – hitherto a predominant and constraining influence on their lives – and given a freedom which previously had been the exclusive privilege of the rich. This was, by any historic standard, a revolution – as was duly acknowledged in Britain by, amongst others, T. H. Marshall. Events, he concluded, transformed an 'evolutionary process' into a revolutionary change. 'We adopted the term "Welfare State" to denote this new entity composed of old elements.'[8]

What, however, were the core functions of this 'new entity'? In 1961 Asa Briggs produced a definition of the welfare state which has since been widely endorsed. He wrote:

A 'Welfare State' is a state in which organized power is deliberately used (through politics and administration) in an effort to modify the play of market forces in at least three directions – first, by guaranteeing individuals and families a minimum income irrespective of the market value of their work or property; second, by narrowing the extent of insecurity by enabling individuals and

families to meet certain social contingencies (for example, sickness, old age and unemployment) which lead otherwise to individual and family crises; and third, by ensuring that all citizens
without distinction of status or class are offered the best standards
available in relation to a certain agreed range of social services.[9]

The first two objectives, he admitted, were little different from those
of interwar social policy. It was the third, which embraced the concept of universalism and 'optimum' standards, which was the really
distinctive characteristic of a welfare state.

Such a definition has not wholly stood the test of time. Since
1975, for instance, the 'organised power' of the state has not been
deliberately used to 'modify the play of market forces'. The finite
resources of government compared to the infinite possibilities of
modern technology have also meant that many policies have had to
be curtailed well below their technical optimum. Nevertheless the
definition can still be satisfactorily modified to the effect that a
welfare state is a society in which government is expected to provide,
and does provide, for all its citizens not only social security but also
a range of other services at a standard well above the barest minimum. In so doing it consumes resources (through expenditure on
goods and the employment of manpower) on such a scale that it
cannot but affect the working of the economy. For this reason and
because – to minimise both its own expenditure and the possibility
of unrest – it has to be concerned with the underlying health of the
economy, it is obliged to play a more active role in the economy
than the mere fatalistic assurance that conditions are right for the
working of a self-regulating market.

The history of the NHS illustrates, in a British context, the forego-
ing characteristics of a welfare state. Its creation was in part, as
Beveridge claimed, a 'natural development from the past' for there
had long been concern over the existing hospital system and embarrassment over the fact that the most vulnerable members of poor
families (children, the majority of mothers and the retired) were not
covered by the state's health insurance scheme. On the other hand,
it also exemplified the revolutionary impact of the Second World
War. Bombs did not discriminate between rich and poor, with the
consequence that both required immediate access to free and uniform medical care. Hence the wartime Emergency Medical Service
set the precedent for a new universal service, with state intervention

no longer reserved for those deemed incapable of caring for themselves.

As will be shown later, universalism (or more particularly the permanent inclusion in the NHS of the middle classes, who had hitherto paid the full market cost of health care or health insurance) had certain detrimental effects, especially in relation to the degree of equality the service could achieve; but it also had a beneficial effect in making politically acceptable the provision of health care above a minimum standard, be it for altruistic reasons (universal provision spawned universal acceptance that everyone was entitled to the best possible treatment) or more cynical ones (the articulate middle classes wished to gain the best possible deal for themselves). However, the best was never the 'optimum' because, as the Guillebaud Report on the NHS explicitly acknowledged as early as 1956, public expectation and the possibilities of medical science were boundless whereas the economic resources of government were not.[10] The level at which health care was to be provided, therefore, was a political not a professional decision which inevitably fell below the technical optimum.

By this definition the welfare state in Britain has not been dismantled since 1975. The modification of market forces may not have been pursued so deliberately and the sense of community may have been questioned, but there has been no serious attempt to erode universal social security or to reduce standards of service to minimum prewar levels. This is because the welfare state is as much the creation of long-term political, economic and social forces as of temporary forces unleashed by the Second World War or of particular ambitions harboured by postwar social engineers. Between the wars successive governments had come to realise that, following the introduction of universal adult suffrage in 1918 and 1928, they would be under constant electoral pressure both to match equal political status with a more equal distribution of economic resources and (in defiance of classical economics) to increase rather than reduce public expenditure in the depression. Similarly the structural needs of an advanced industrial economy, working within a highly competitive international economy, obliged them first to intervene in and then to manage the economy.[11]

Not out of moral weakness or political venality therefore, but out of a pragmatic recognition of changing political and economic reality, the responsibilities and functions of government changed. It is this functional role of the state which has yet to be reversed by objections fundamentally aimed against the additional objectives to which post-war social engineers sought to direct state intervention. All that such objections have indeed achieved is a shift, at the margin, in the mix by which the state ensures its citizens' welfare either directly through its own services or more indirectly through the market and the family.[12] To achieve a more fundamental shift would require a further revolution in the relationship between the state and its citizens which at present would appear historically, politically and culturally unlikely.

2.2 THE THREE PRAGMATIC APPROACHES TO WELFARE IN BRITAIN

Allusion has already been made to the three broad political strategies which have directly influenced the development of the British welfare state: reluctant collectivism, democratic socialism and the New Right. The first is broadly synonymous with the policy of the moderate wing of the Conservative Party which, following the modernisation of Conservative policy by R. A. Butler in the 1940s, dominated the party until Margaret Thatcher's election as leader in 1975. The second was developed by the reformist wing of the Labour Party which reached its intellectual peak in the 1950s and early 1960s with the publication of Crosland's *The Future of Socialism* (1956) and the work, at the London School of Economics, of a group of social scientists led by R. M. Titmuss. The third steadily gained support within the Conservative Party throughout the 1960s and has been the inspiration behind Thatcherism. These strategies, while having much in common, differ fundamentally on the three critical issues of political freedom, economic efficiency and social justice.

2.2.1 Reluctant collectivism

Pre-eminent amongst the reluctant collectivists were the two intellectual founders of the British welfare state, Keynes and Beveridge. Both were essentially liberals, personally committed to the free market because, in their opinion, the minimisation of state intervention maximised the freedom of the individual and hence political freedom, economic efficiency and social variety. On reading Hayek's *The Road to Serfdom* (1943), the right-wing polemic which attacked the wartime consensus about the beneficence of state intervention upon which both the welfare state and Butler's 'new conservatism' were based, Keynes even acknowledged himself to be 'morally and philosophically . . . not only in agreement . . . but in deeply moved agreement'.[13] In practice however, reluctant collectivists such as he realised that, for a variety of economic and political reasons, the free market was no longer working in the ideal way assumed by classical economic theorists. It had after all been responsible in interwar Britain for an unacceptable level of economic waste and social distress. On technocratic and humanitarian grounds therefore, they accepted the need for greater state regulation. Politically too they realised that such intervention was essential. Beveridge, for example, argued that political freedom meant freedom not just from 'the arbitrary power of government' but also from 'economic servitude to want and squalor'.[14] The state alone could guarantee this freedom for everyone. Moreover, he acknowledged, were governments to permit economic waste and social inequality to continue, parliamentary democracy might be brought into disrepute and political stability threatened.

Beveridge's specific recommendations regarding the extent of state intervention varied greatly over time. In *Full Employment in a Free Society* (1944) he proposed the continuation of wartime planning and controls over many years in order to remedy the structural weakness of the British economy, which the market had appeared incapable of correcting in the interwar period. However, one of the three guiding principles of the Beveridge Report – despite later charges levelled against the social security system – was that 'the State in organising security should not stifle incentive, opportunity, responsibility'.[15] Consequently, in both the social insurance and assistance schemes, the state's role was to be strictly limited to guaranteeing each citizen a subsistence income. Individual living standards above that minimum should be determined not by the state but by personal effort and voluntary contributions to private insurance. Keynes envisaged a similarly limited role for the state. Like the classical economists, he sought to restrict its role to the provision of the conditions under which the free market could work efficiently. Where he disagreed with his predecessors was in his judgement of what those conditions were. It was his conviction that the market was no longer self-regulating and that state intervention was required to ensure that there was neither deficient nor excess demand in the economy; but once the state had performed that task, then the market should be left to function freely. Consequently the rate of

economic growth (and thereby living standards) should remain the
ultimate responsibility of industry, just as the nature of the goods
produced should continue to be determined by consumer choice.

Reluctant collectivism was, and is, therefore, grounded on firm
philosophical premises. The market is conceived as the best practical
mechanism for ensuring individual initiative and hence political freedom, economic efficiency and social justice; but its flaws are recognised and thus the need for a judicious degree of state intervention.
The critical question is just how much intervention is required; the
answer depends, at any given time, on a fine judgement about the
market's relative strengths and weaknesses. Such pragmatism identifies reluctant collectivism closely with the traditional Conservative
philosophy of conserving what is best in the old while adapting
constantly to the new; and indeed, under the initial inspiration of
Butler, it did provide the philosophical justification for the Conservative Party's defence of the welfare state after its return to power in
1951.[16]

Continual pragmatism, however, lays open the political exponents
of reluctant collectivism to the charge of unprincipled opportunism;
and this provided a double handicap for the Conservative party in
the 1950s and 1960s. On the one hand, by seeming merely to react
to weaknesses in the existing system and then to lament the moral
consequences of state intervention, it ceded the intellectual initiative
to the democratic socialists, who championed a more positive role
for the state. On the other hand the inherent tension between the
reluctant collectivists' recognition of the fundamental virtues of the
market and yet the need for its pragmatic reform led to considerable
hesitation in both the implementation of Butler's 'new conservatism'
and the deployment, let alone acceptance, of a new practical political
programme.[17] After January 1958, when the battle was temporarily
resolved in favour of the moderates – as symbolised by the resignation of Thorneycroft as chancellor of the exchequer – policy drifted
even further from the market with the commitment of Harold Macmillan to industrial planning and of Edward Heath to corporate
bargaining. This made it the more vulnerable to attack from the
ideologues of the New Right.

2.2.2 Democratic socialism

Despite the predominant influence of Beveridge and Keynes in the
early postwar years, it was the ideals of the democratic socialists

which gave the British welfare state its unique international reputation. At home these ideals also infused the welfare legislation of the 1945–51 Labour governments and provided the logic for further advances which Conservative ministers struggled to refute. To the social democrats, state intervention was not a mere corrective for market failings but the means of engineering a more equal and fair society. Like the reluctant collectivists, they condemned the unregulated market as economically inefficient. They attacked it also as undemocratic (because it concentrated economic, and thus effective political, power in a few hands), socially unjust (because it failed to reward people according to need) and unethical (because it encouraged self-interest and greed). They consequently sought to transform, by democratic means, the existing capitalist society into a socialist one in which production, through the utilisation of all available resources for the common good, would be efficient; in which the government, through the equalisation of economic power, would ensure political freedom for all; and in which social justice would be guaranteed by a predominant altruism.

The leading postwar social democratic thinkers were T. H. Marshall (Professor of Sociology, London School of Economics, 1930–56), Richard Titmuss (Professor of Social Administration, London School of Economics, 1950–1973) and Anthony Crosland. Marshall in 1948 developed a whig theory of history, whereby British citizens gained their civil rights between 1650 and 1832, their political rights between 1832 and 1918 and their social rights thereafter. The latter entailed the right to social services which, by increasing both the recipient's real income and the services that could be universally enjoyed (such as the health service), effectively minimised the inequality of living standards and 'legitimate expectations' which would otherwise have resulted from differences in money income. Thereby all citizens, despite their unequal money income, enjoyed equal status and an 'equal social worth'. The welfare state by institutionalising these social rights, Marshall argued, raised society onto a higher plane where the sense of community, which had been fleetingly experienced in the war, might become permanent. It also provided a temporary resolution to the fundamental conflict between the capitalist need for incentive (and hence unequal money incomes) and the democratic need for egalitarianism (and hence equal status). 'The conflict of principles', wrote Marshall, 'springs from the very roots of social order in the present phase of the development of democratic citizenship. Apparent inconsistencies are in fact a source of stability, achieved through a compromise which is not dictated by logic. This phase will not continue indefinitely.' Thus, the welfare state was a hybrid but not an unworkable hybrid. It was a pragmatic and constructive compromise between capitalism and socialism, from which a more socialist society would eventually emerge.[18]

Titmuss and his colleagues at the London School of Economics provided both a continuing critique of individual policies within the welfare state and a grand vision of its essential purpose. Their successes included the early dispelling of the myth that expenditure on the NHS was out of control and consuming a rapidly increasing proportion of GNP; the development of the concept of the 'social division of welfare', by which the existing welfare state could be exposed as surreptitiously transferring substantial resources not to the poor but to the rich by means of fiscal welfare (tax-relief) and the subsidising of occupational welfare (management's fringe benefits, such as private health insurance); and the rediscovery, through redefinition, of poverty in the 1960s. Titmuss' concern with the real-world impact of policy was reflected by his tenure of the deputy chairmanship of the Supplementary Benefit Commission, the agency responsible for ensuring that no-one's income fell below the official poverty line. He was also alive to the practical economic and political value of universal welfare services. Selectivity, he argued, wasted resources by demoralising the poor and lowering each service's standard. The potentially positive contribution that social expenditure could make to economic growth was thereby restricted. Selectivity also fostered political unrest by depriving society of a sense of fairness and unity. 'While means-testing seems to save money in the short-term by narrowing eligibility', one of Titmuss's colleagues has since argued, 'over the long-run it may add to the political and social costs of a . . . divided society'.[19] Such costs, of course, go unrecognised in the conventional cost-benefit analyses applied to social expenditure by economists.

Titmuss's overriding mission, however, was to emphasise the moral purpose of the welfare state – as was revealed by his ever-willingness to confront the frequent assertion, especially from the New Right, that economic growth would reduce poverty and inequality and thereby allow the welfare state to wither away. Not only could such an analysis be disproved empirically, he argued, but the purpose of welfare went far beyond the relief of a hard core of deprivation. Its purpose was to provide social justice, by providing compensation for the increasing social costs of economic change (such as illness arising from environmental pollution or unemployment arising from technological redundancy) which fell disproportionately on the poor and which traditionally went uncorrected by the market. It was also to elevate society by institutionalising a deeper sense of community and mutual care. Hence his singling out of the blood donor service (by which one citizen voluntarily gave a life-saving resource to another) as the epitome of the welfare state.

Crosland's *The Future of Socialism*, which was designed to redefine democratic socialism as the practical basis for Labour Party policy, built upon the work of academic social scientists such as Marshall and Titmuss. Crosland's ideal was to create a 'classless society' in which greater equality and fraternity would prove their economic worth – in contrast to the 'material inefficiency of capitalism' – by minimising both the waste of talent and the social antagonism which lay behind Britain's poor growth record and bad industrial relations (on which, incidentally, Crosland's main rival within the Party, Aneurin Bevan, was deemed to capitalise).[20] Crosland's particular target was the Marxist underpinnings of current Labour Party policy. Marxism, he argued, had 'little or nothing to offer the contemporary socialist either in respect of practical policy or of the correct analysis of our society, even of the right conceptual tools and framework'. Its predictions about the immiseration of the poor and capitalism's impending collapse had been constantly confounded, whereas its obsession with the economic power of the capitalist class had obscured the fact that political power, and hence effective economic power, had been transferred to the state. Capitalism, he maintained, had been peacefully transformed. Universal adult suffrage and full employment had given the workforce effective political and social power; and the welfare state had bestowed upon everyone a security and a range of services that had previously been the privilege of the rich. Simultaneously the transfer of power within industry from the owners to the managers had had a profound psychological impact which had made industry more socially responsible. In response to such changes, and armed with the new Keynesian techniques of demand management 'the passive state has given way to the active, or at least the ultimately responsible state; the political authority has emerged as the final arbiter of economic life; the brief, and historically exceptional, era of unfettered market relations is over'. It was incumbent on social democrats in general, and the Labour Party in particular, to use this enhanced power of the state to further economic growth and social justice. The means to those ends were not traditional policies, such as nationalisation, but a direct assault on the major remaining sources of inequality and waste, in particular the education system and inherited wealth.

Despite the defeat of the Labour Party in the elections of 1951, 1955, 1959 and 1970 it was these social democratic ideals which underpinned popular support for the welfare state. The basic assumptions underlining this consensus have been vividly summarised by David Donnison:

1. The growth of the economy and the population would continue. That, by itself, would not solve any problems; but it provided an optimistic setting for debate. The pursuit of social justice could be carried forward by engines of economic growth which would produce the resources to create a fairer society without anyone suffering on the way.
2. Although inequalities in incomes would persist, their harsher effects could be gradually softened by a 'social wage' (consisting of social services distributed with greater concern for human needs) and by the growing burden of progressive taxes, taking more from the rich than the poor, which were required to finance the social services.
3. Despite fierce conflicts about important issues (comprehensive schools, pensions, rent controls and so on) the people with middling skills and incomes – 'middle England' you might call them – would eventually support equalising social policies and programmes of this kind. Trade unions and the Labour movement would usually provide the political cutting edge for reform; and the Conservative governments which followed them would accept most of its results.
4. Therefore government and its social services, accountable to this central consensus, were the natural vehicles of progress. Among their generally trusted instruments were the doctors, teachers, town planners, nurses, social workers and other public service professions. The pretensions and powers of these professions should be critically watched, but progressive governments were expected to recruit more of these people. . . .
5. Although economic crises, political accidents and sheer ineptitude would often compel governments temporarily to abandon these aims, over the longer run they would all try to increase industrial investment and improve Britain's lagging productivity, to secure some broad agreement about the distribution of incomes, to get

unemployed people back into jobs, to free poorer people from means tests by giving them adequate benefits as of right, to give children a better start in life and more equal opportunities for the future, and to provide better care and support for the most vulnerable people and for families living on low or modest incomes. 'Middle England', we assumed, would not tolerate any radical departure from those aims. A government which allowed – let alone encouraged – a return to the high unemployment, the social conflicts and means tests of the 1930s could not survive.[21]

The social democratic consensus, therefore, assumed economic growth and, whilst recognising the danger of bureaucracy, regarded the growth of state intervention as both natural and beneficent. It even admitted the ratchet effect of party politics, later denounced by the New Right. On succeeding Labour, Conservative governments did not return policy to the 'common ground', upon which all parties were agreed in principle, but (because of the essential pragmatism of the reluctant collectivists) to an indeterminate 'middle ground' halfway between conservatism and socialism. Thus the 'middle ground' moved relentlessly further from the market. Social democracy had history on its side.

2.2.3 The New Right

While this consensus was at its height the old liberal values, which were later to be termed the New Right and which had last found expression in Hayek's *The Road to Serfdom* (1943), were exiled to an 'intellectual Siberia'.[22] In 1955 the Institute of Economic Affairs was tentatively established to propagate these values and throughout the 1960s, with encouragement from the USA, they gathered support to such effect that they temporarily influenced Conservative government policy between 1970 and 1972. Only after 1975, however, were they reintegrated into the main stream of political thought. By then the failure of Keynesian demand management, not only to sustain economic growth but also to resolve the combination (previously considered impossible) of high inflation and mass unemployment, had obliged both the Labour and Conservative Parties to reconsider their economic policy. Their common conclusion was that they should no longer actively manipulate demand but, more fatalistically, exercise a greater control over money supply. The market was thus to be given greater freedom to determine the country's fate.

This revival of faith in the market was sustained more naturally within the Conservative Party which, under Mrs Thatcher's leadership, argued with increasing conviction – and in direct defiance of reluctant collectivism and democratic socialism – that it was not the state but the market that was the best long-term guarantor of economic efficiency, social justice and political freedom. With regard to economic efficiency, Sir Keith Joseph argued that 'the blind, unplanned, uncoordinated wisdom of the market . . . is overwhelmingly superior to the well-researched, rational, systematic, well-meaning, cooperative, science-based, forward looking, statistically respectable plans of government'.[23] This was because individual producers, in order to maximise their profits in a competitive environment, had to satisfy speedily the ever-changing needs of individual consumers with goods of the highest possible quality at the lowest possible price. Consequently the market was the most efficient mechanism for the synchronisation of individual needs. The state might in the short term be able to correct the market's temporary failings but, however expert and benevolent, it could never in the longer term collect sufficient information to act efficiently – be efficiency defined either as the most economical use of resources or the speedy satisfaction of individual clients. Moreover, in the real world, the state could never achieve the disinterest and the altruism which both the reluctant collectivists and the democratic socialists naively believed to be possible. It would be subject to many insidious pressures, not least of which might be politicians' desire for short-term electoral advantage and bureaucrats' desire to extend their empires in order to enhance their own pay and career prospects. As the Institute of Economic Affairs concluded in 1965:

> Political priorities are established in response to such irrelevant pressures as the personalities of rival ministers, administrative convenience, the unequal power of organized lobbies, or simply short-term electoral calculations. Who will assert that the outcome of such crude, capricious pressures must necessarily prove superior to the dispersed preferences of consumers who know what they want and increasingly have money to pay their way?[24]

Such fallibility brings into question the paternalistic assumption that the state should define and thereafter engineer social justice. Even if there can be, at any given time, one incontrovertible definition of social justice, by what criteria are politicians and civil servants in the real world qualified to make it? Equally serious is the threat of state intervention to political freedom because if the democratic socialists sought through economic planning to impose a common morality on society they would run the risk of becoming, like their predecessors in the German Weimar Republic, 'the cultivated parents of a barbarous offspring'.[25] As Hayek argued in 1943, economic planning would set democracy on the road to serfdom because 'individual freedom cannot be reconciled with the supremacy of one single purpose to which the whole society must be entirely and permanently subordinated'. However much the electorate might request the rational planning of society, therefore, the temptation should be resisted. If it were acceded to, Parliament (faithfully reflecting the diversity of individual beliefs) would eventually find itself unable to draft a satisfactory, unitary plan and democracy would fall into disrepute (as it indeed had done in the 1930s through unfavourable comparison with the 'efficiency' of fascism and communism). Responsibility would consequently be transferred to technical experts or else to economic dictators and Parliament would be unable to challenge any part of the ensuing plan for fear of jeopardising the whole. 'The democratic statesman', concluded Hayek, 'who sets out to plan economic life will soon be confronted with the alternative of either assuming dictatorial powers or abandoning his plans.' This was indeed the experience of the Labour government in the 1940s. Democratic socialism was a chimera.

The New Right consequently maintains that it is the market and not the state that is the best guarantor of political stability and freedom. Negatively, it prevents a drift into dictatorship. Positively, by catering for minority interests and enabling mistakes to be speedily remedied, it ensures that there are no permanently frustrated minorities resentful of, and therefore unwilling to obey, coercive laws. More especially it permits people to act spontaneously, to determine their own morality and to be responsible for the satisfaction of their own objectives. This is, in Hayek's phrase, 'the freedom in economic affairs without which personal and political freedom have never existed'. Economic inequality, it is admitted, can deny individuals political freedom if it confines them below the subsistence level; but such inequality is essentially the consequence of scarce resources which the market, through encouraging economic efficiency, is best able to remedy. State planning not only constricts economic growth and thereby the opportunity for greater economic self-sufficiency, but also denies the freedom of choice which such self-sufficiency should bestow. By the same logic, the political power of the capitalist should be feared far less than that of the state for it is fragmented and flexible, whilst that of the state is centralised and rigid.

The New Right, except on its extreme libertarian wing, does not wholly reject state intervention. The government should be strong in order to set and enforce the rules by which the market can function freely – unimpeded, for example, by monopolies and cartels. With regard to welfare, Hayek in the 1940s acknowledged that Britain had accumulàted sufficient wealth to permit a certain collectivism without 'endangering general freedom'. This included state action to guarantee a minimum of physical efficiency (national assistance), to overcome common hazards (social insurance) and, rather surprisingly, to combat general fluctuations in economic activity.[26] The ideal, however, was to minimise state intervention by subjecting it to constant reappraisal; and, where state welfare was unavoidable, to provide it not directly but in the form of subsidies (or vouchers) to enable the recipient to choose freely in the market. This policy is deemed to be both efficient and potentially popular. For example the Institute of Economic Affairs, in a series of surveys of public attitudes towards welfare in the 1960s, discovered – like other pollsters – that 80 per cent of those questioned appeared to support the NHS; but such a response, it concluded, was biased by a 'widespread civic illiteracy' about the true costs of the service.[27] Once that cost had been explained and the possibility raised of vouchers, which might be exchanged for whatever mix of health care the individual wanted and topped up (if desired) by private payments, the popularity of the NHS dramatically declined.

2.2.4   The political divide

Each of the three strategies which have shaped the development of the British welfare state, therefore, shares a common belief in the need for the state to define and enforce the conditions under which the market can operate efficiently. The major difference between the reluctant collectivists and the New Right is in their pragmatic judgement about how extensive state intervention should be. The reluctant collectivists assume that as society grows more complex intervention must increase. In contrast the New Right seeks, by constant reappraisal, to minimise it. The fundamental ideological divide however is between the New Right and the democratic socialists. The New Right asserts that the market maximises efficiency in both the use of resources and the satisfaction of individual need, whereas democratic socialists maintain that the market wastes talent and resources and that economic efficiency is dependent on national planning. Such planning the New Right identified as a major threat to political freedom since it deprives all citizens of choice. Political freedom, retort the social democrats, can be provided only by the state because it alone can guarantee that no-one is condemned to exist at so low a standard of living that free choice ceases to be a reality. The state alone can create an altruistic society and thereby ensure social justice. The New Right questions the meaning of such a term, especially if it is to be defined and imposed by one agency, and sees the essence of a just society in the freedom of everyone to make – and accept the consequences of – their own choices.

Many issues remain unresolved in this confrontation. The New Right is still vulnerable to the charge that the market is imperfect (tending towards monopoly, which will stifle competition, and unable to identify and thereby compensate the social cost of economic change). This can undoubtedly alienate people and generate political conflict. The state's redistribution of resources to the middle class through fiscal and occupational welfare also demands attention. Democratic socialists, in their turn, have yet to confront the real-world fallibility of the state and the danger that a centralisation of power will result not in an altruistic society but in economic stagnation, lawlessness and the victimisation of the minority who are poor. Such unresolved issues lie at the heart of the continuing political battle over the nature and the future of the welfare state.

2.3 GENERAL THEORIES OF SOCIAL WELFARE

2.3.1 Pluralism, élitism and corporatism

The political theory which has underpinned these three approaches to welfare, and which has generally informed popular and academic reaction to them, is pluralism. Pluralism assumes that society is essentially stable and that power is widely diffused so that no-one is completely powerless and no group (or class) dominant. The role of the state is to mediate between the various interest groups in society in order to reconcile their differences. Thus, in the case of the NHS, the state mediates between the consumers of health care (the public) and its producers (the various branches of the medical profession) and the ultimate nature of the service represents the most acceptable compromise between their competing interests.

Certain objections can be raised to this theory. First, as the New Right has argued, the politicians and civil servants who constitute 'the state' may not be neutral arbiters but interested parties in their own right. The nature of the compromise they negotiate may, therefore, maximise their own interests rather than those of the public. Secondly, as élite theorists argue, certain groups with special contacts, expertise and knowledge may command unequal access to government and thereby permanently enjoy an unequal share of power which they can turn to their own selfish advantage. In health care, for example, it is argued that the medical profession has used its expertise and knowledge to dominate the NHS from its stormy inception under Bevan. The result has been the development of a 'medical model' of health care, which concentrates attention on the biological causes of illness in individual patients and thus directs a disproportionate amount of resources to hospitals and specialist surgery. Other models of health care, which lay equal stress on individual life-styles or the quality of the environment, have been relatively ignored with the consequence that health education (such as anti-smoking campaigns) and preventive medicine (such as stricter anti-pollution controls), which arguably offer better value for money, have been denied adequate resources. As in most Western countries, the reason for the predominance of the 'medical model' of health care in Britain is that it serves best the prejudices and the interests of the established medical profession. The public (as both patient and tax-payer) lacks the information and expertise to challenge its authority, which will continue to predominate until effectively challenged by another élite (such as health planners within government).[28]

A third deviation from pluralism is the theory of corporatism, which aroused particular interest in Britain in the late 1970s. Its essential premise is that, in advanced capitalist societies, pluralism declines and power is shared – usually covertly – between the state and several powerful interest groups to the exclusion of all others. As with most political theories there are many competing – and often conflicting – variations of corporatism. Its purpose can be either economic (to support technologically advanced and increasingly monopolistic industries) or political (to maintain stability). Corporatist institutions may be the creation of the state (as in fascist Germany and Italy where national organisations of employers and workers were created specifically to regiment their constituents) or spontaneous developments (as in Britain where employers' organisations and trade unions existed well before the major extension of state intervention).

One variation of corporatism, 'corporate bias', has been specifically applied to postwar Britain by Keith Middlemas.[29] He has argued that, particularly as a result of the two world wars, successive governments have increasingly shared power with institutions such as the CBI and TUC, which have thereby been transformed from ordinary pressure groups (as in a pluralistic society) to 'governing institutions'. In return for this exceptional power they have undertaken to control their own members and thereby minimise public unrest. The consequences have been an increase in the power of the civil service, which is instrumental in negotiating the covert deals; a decrease in the power of Parliament, which is powerless to overturn them; and an ineffectual policy of mere 'crisis avoidance', because any radical attempt to remedy Britain's underlying weaknesses – such as its bad industrial structure or industrial relations – would challenge the interests of the 'governing institutions', destroy the covert deals and thereby lift the constraints on public unrest. In the 1970s the New Right was especially aware, and critical, of corporatist trends within the welfare state. Rising unemployment, inflation and the seeming ungovernability of Britain were, for it, proof of the corruption of government that inevitably accompanies the release of the state from the discipline of both the market and of freely expressed political opinion.

2.3.2 Marxism

Marxism has had little direct impact on the development of welfare policy in Britain and, indeed, was rejected as obsolete by Crosland.[30] It has, however, underpinned both the 'fundamentalist' beliefs of the left wing of the Labour Party, with which Crosland was embattled, and many academic critiques of the welfare state. It is the complete antithesis of pluralism. It assumes that society is in fundamental conflict, with the pace of change being determined by a continual battle between those who own the means of production (the ruling class or the 'bourgeoisie') and those who do not (the working class). Any outburst of unrest is not regarded as wasteful and unnecessary, as it is by pluralists, but as 'creative' because it propels capitalism further along the road to the inevitable goal of

socialism and communism. A welfare state which contains such
unrest is therefore generally regarded by Marxists as neither a new
form of society nor a half-way house between capitalism and socialism (as democratic socialists maintain) but an advanced stage of
capitalism and, as Bismarck had intended all state welfare to be, a
bulwark against socialism.

There are three major variants of Marxism, each of which has
been as vigorously attacked by the others as they have been by
non-Marxists. The classical 'instrumentalist' variant assumes that a
coherent, class-conscious ruling class personally controls the
extended 'state', which includes not just the government and the
civil service but also other agencies of 'repression' such as the
judiciary, army and police force. The state is thus the instrument for
the furthering of the interests of the ruling class and the NHS, for
instance, does so because the leaders of the medical profession are
bound by close personal and cultural ties to that ruling class. This
interpretation has been applied most fully to Britain by Ralph
Miliband and has been attacked on the empirical grounds that –
despite some obvious personal interrelationships – the constant
battles within and between each agency of the 'extended state' provide little evidence of a coherent ruling class.[31]

In contrast the 'structuralists' argue that members of the 'extended'
state do not usually have close personal ties with the ruling class but
that the state is obliged to act in its long-term interests because of
certain structural constraints. The state is therefore only 'relatively
autonomous'.[32] One such constraint is the state's dependence for its
revenue on continuing economic growth and hence on the profitability of industry, which prevents it from attempting anything that
might permanently undermine the confidence of businessmen and
financiers either at home or abroad. This reticence has not only
affected welfare policy in times of emergency, such as in the 1940s
when Britain was dependent on US aid or in the 1970s when an IMF
loan was being sought, but throughout the whole postwar period
when the successful management of the economy was dependent on
the willingness of both business to invest and financiers to support
sterling. The perceived weakness of this theory is that the state is
depicted as being simultaneously strong and weak. On the one hand
it is sufficiently strong to implement reforms essential to the long-
term stability of capitalism (such as the NHS which helps to ensure
a healthy workforce), despite the well-documented objections of
capitalists to their short-term cost. On the other hand, despite the

ability to surmount such opposition, it is incapable of acting against capitalism's long-term interest. No logical explanation has been provided for this seeming contradiction and structuralists have consequently been condemned for excessive 'functionalism'. Their theory, it is claimed, rests on the crude assumption that because capitalism has survived, despite Marx's predictions, the function of the state must have been to support it.

The third 'neo-Marxist' variation is inspired by the writings of the Italian Marxist, Gramsci.[33] This explains the continuing dominance of capitalist values, despite conflicts within the ruling élite and the relative autonomy of the state, by admitting that the ruling class is fragmented (between for instance industrialists and financiers); and by arguing that capitalist 'hegemony' is maintained by a series of alliances forged – through the agency of the state – between the dominant 'fraction' of the élite and the other groups in society. By this means the short-sighted resistance to reform of certain fractions within the ruling class, which might eventually provoke unrest, can be overcome while capitalism's long-term interests are secured. Thus the creation of the welfare state can be represented as a 'passive revolution' whereby the most far-sighted fraction of the élite conceded, through the agency of the Labour Party, a series of reforms which in effect strengthened capitalism economically (by generating the demand for goods which had been lacking in the 1930s) and politically (by reconciling a majority of the electorate to capitalist values, as illustrated by successive Conservative victories between 1951 and 1959). As soon as the welfare state started to conflict with capitalism's long-term interest, as it did in the 1970s, it could be revoked and another series of alliances (as represented by Mrs Thatcher's populism) negotiated. Both the strength and the weakness of this theory lie in the concept of hegemony, the process by which capitalist values become so dominant – through, for example, formal education, the media and the social services' inculcation of the 'work ethic' – that other classes 'internalise' them and mistakenly believe them to serve their own interests. This self-delusion cannot, by its very nature, be empirically proven and its existence depends on the highly dangerous assumption that, for any given historical period, theorists are better able to judge than contemporary individuals or groups the nature of their true interests. Hard evidence of the state's negotiation of the necessary alliances is also, as yet, lacking.

From these general theories a specific critique of the welfare state has emerged from O'Connor in the USA and Gough in Britain.[34]

They classify welfare expenditure in capitalist societies as either social capital or social expenses. Social capital assists industrial profitability ('the process of capital accumulation') by providing services which will either increase productivity (for example improvements to the infrastructure, such as roads) or reduce the costs to industry of securing a healthy, well-educated workforce. All these services the market is itself incapable of providing profitably. Social expenses make politically acceptable ('legitimise') capitalism by eradicating the worst abuses which might provoke unrest and by creating a general impression of social justice. Expenditure on the NHS fulfils both functions, helping to create and maintain a healthy workforce and providing a free service according to need. Such expenditure, as the example of the NHS shows, does not serve the true interest of the working class. That class has paid its full share of the cost of 'free' service through direct and indirect taxation, and its vulnerable 'non-productive' members (such as pensioners and the mentally handicapped) receive a disproportionately low share of available resources. In contrast the careers of hospital doctors and the profits of drug companies, which had been threatened by the impending bankruptcy of the voluntary hospital system in the 1930s, have revived; and, through the 'medical model' of health care, industry has been able to disguise its responsibility – and thereby evade the payment of compensation – for ill health arising from its pollution of the environment. The 'medical model', therefore, serves not simply the interests of the medical profession (as maintained by élite theorists) but also, more significantly, the interests of the ruling class.

There is, argue O'Connor and Gough, an inherent contradiction in this dual role of capitalist welfare. There inevitably comes a time, as during the fiscal crisis of the 1970s, when the cost of social expenses starts to undermine, through rising taxation and inflation, the process of capital accumulation. To reduce it, however, is impossible because it risks the exposure of capitalist exploitation and thus social unrest. As Claus Offe has remarked: 'the contradiction is that while capitalism cannot coexist *with* the Welfare State, neither can it exist *without* the Welfare State'.[35]

Such a contradiction is welcome because it heralds capitalism's impending collapse. However there is also – as critics have been quick to point out – a parallel contradiction in the Marxists' own critique. Social reform is seen both as a concession from above consolidating capitalism (as in the concept of the 'passive revolution') and as the result of coercion from below forcing capitalism further towards a socialist society (resulting, for instance, from a 'creative' confrontation between the working class and the ruling élite, be it at an election or during a period of overt social unrest). If welfare cuts are threatened, as in the 1970s, should Marxists therefore welcome them as a relaxation of social control, which will increase the likelihood of confrontation, or should they oppose them as an attack on working-class living standards, painfully acquired? They cannot do both. The usual conclusion is that, despite their constant condemnation of welfare reform as a means of social control, they ultimately acknowledge – in conformity with the democratic socialists and indeed Marx's own interpretation of the 19th-century Factories Acts – that welfare reform presents a fundamental challenge to capitalism. 'The Welfare State', as Dearlove and Saunders have concluded, 'represents a "Trojan horse" within the citadels of capitalism in that it rests firmly on a set of values which are fundamentally opposed to those of capitalism.'[36] This inherent contradiction has been seen to weaken Marxism as a practical political philosophy, if not as a powerful critique of welfare policy in capitalist society.

2.3.3   Feminism

A final critique of the welfare state which has been gathering strength since the late 1960s is feminism. Arguing from both Marxist and non-Marxist premises, feminists maintain that the major purpose and the role of the welfare state has been to reinforce the dominance of men over women ('patriarchy'). Thus the Beveridge Report, rather than being a blueprint for beneficent reform, is seen as 'one of the most crudely ideological documents of its kind ever written'.[37] The explicit assumption underlying its proposals is that the majority of women who marry should enter into a 'partnership' with their husbands in which they should remain economically dependent upon them whilst, in the national interest, they breed and rear children. In one particularly notorious passage, for instance, Beveridge asserts: 'the attitude of the housewife to gainful employment outside the home is not and should not be the same as that of a single woman. She has other duties.'[38]

It is initially difficult, with historical perspective, to accept the feminist case. It has generally been acknowledged that in the inter-war years it was women's diet and health which suffered most severely from the loss of family income occasioned by unemployment; and, when unemployed themselves, women had no free access to medical care. In contrast the welfare state has provided the psychological and material advantages of a guaranteed income and free access to health care, as well as a foremost demand of interwar feminists – family allowances. In addition the maintenance of full employment has offered married women the opportunity of work and thus an independent income, not least in the expanded social services. It has even consolidated some of women's advantages over men. For example, as Titmuss argued in 1955, the average woman derives considerably more benefit than the average man from the state pension because of her earlier age of retirement (60 not 65) and her greater longevity (by four to five years).[39]

Such benefits were acknowledged and welcomed by women during and after the war.[40] For instance, the reaction of one ordinary, instinctively feminist housewife to the Beveridge Report was: 'His scheme will appeal more even to women than to men, for it is they who bear the real burden of unemployment, sickness, child-bearing and rearing and the ones who, up to now, have come off worse.' A survey of women's opinions on 'family needs and the social services' in the mid 1950s discovered general enthusiasm for the social services, especially the NHS. The impact of the welfare state on income, housing and health (together with other changes such as reduced working hours and reduced family size – again in defiance of Beveridge), was also seen by the mid 1950s to have altered fundamentally traditional relationships. As an early survey in the East End of London reported: 'In place of the old comes a new kind of companionship between man and woman, reflecting the rise in status of the young wife and children which is one of the great transformations of our time. There is now a nearer approach to equality between the sexes and, although each has a peculiar role, its boundaries are no longer so rigidly defined nor is it performed without consultation.'

However, these undeniable advances, feminists have argued persuasively, have been achieved at a very high cost.[41] Marxist feminists have argued that the welfare state has served only to reinforce women's traditional role in capitalist society: to reproduce an adequate, healthy and contented workforce through the unpaid care of children and husbands. Some have also argued that women are also a 'reserve army' of cheap labour to be welcomed into employment in periods of labour shortage but to be dismissed first in a recession. Other feminists also question the 'liberation' experienced by married women from increased job opportunities, owing to both the 'dual role' they have to play as wage-earners and housewives and the sexual stereotyping to which they are subjected at work. Most culpable here is the NHS, where dominant positions (such as doctors) are normally held by men and subordinate positions (such as nurses and ancillary workers) by women. The social services themselves also reinforce, overtly and covertly, the inferior position of women. The right to insurance benefit, for example, is established through contributions paid whilst in employment and because women on average are paid less and have more interrupted careers (owing in particular to childbirth and rearing) their rights are considerably less. The rights of non-working mothers are also established by their husband's contributions, so that the increasing number of divorcees and unmarried mothers are placed in a vulnerable position where their needs can only be met by means-tested supplementary benefit, with all the disadvantages that that entails. Other supposedly progressive policies (such as family allowances and community care) are also seen as being essentially designed not to help individual women as mothers and patients, but to encourage women in general to continue their traditional biological and unpaid caring role in order both to ensure the nation's future and to cut the escalating costs of institutional medicine.

The NHS itself is attacked not just because of its sexual division of labour but because it places women's health and most personal needs under the control of predominantly male doctors. Male standards of emotional and physical health are regarded as the norm and specifically female problems minimised. Reproduction is also regarded as central to women's personality, so that infertility is treated with far greater sympathy than abortion and family planning – although many women would regard the latter as vital for their control over their own bodies. Above all childbirth has been removed from the home, where it was the concern of female relatives and midwives, and (in the perceived medical interest of mother and child) removed to hospitals, where the greater use of impersonal machinery adds to the status of the doctor if not to the actual comfort of the mother.[42] In short, free access to the NHS has, like all welfare reform, reinforced male domination over women.

2.4 CONCLUSION

Each of the preceding theories, as indeed each of the three political approaches to welfare in postwar Britain, is highly persuasive when judged on its own assumptions. Each also appears somewhat fallible when judged against hard historical evidence. This fallibility has tempted many historians, initially sympathetic to the application of theory to historical analysis, to fall back on their profession's traditional assumption that each society in each age is unique. There can, they feel, be no general theory which can satisfactorily explain the simultaneous international development of welfare states after the Second World War by encompassing all their similarities and dissimilarities.

However, as argued in Chapter 1, no historical analysis can be atheoretical and so each should, as far as possible, admit its underlying bias. The assumptions upon which the structure of this book and its selection of evidence is based are essentially those of pluralism and reluctant collectivism. The traditional imperfections of pluralist analysis are admitted. In contrast to the bold Marxist theory of class conflict, it tends to ascribe historical change unheroically to 'broad, amorphous, evolutionary trends', whilst political analysis can descend into a myopic study of the 'immediate manoeuvrings of interest groups' which obscure the wider struggle for power which these manoeuvres represent.[43] There is also a tendency to underestimate the divergent strengths of the various competing interest groups, not least of whom are the politicians and administrators (who are far from neutral). However pluralism represents the values that were most prevalent in postwar Britain and, on that count alone, has considerable historical validity as an explanation of contemporary decisions. With hindsight it would also appear to accord most satisfactorily with the evidence.

Marxism is rejected not just for the technical reasons identified already, but because of its fundamental assumption that historical change is determined by the conflict between two economically determined classes. The central feminist assumption, that the main purpose of the welfare state is to reinforce patriarchy, is also adjudged too extreme. To succeed in a democratic society, any policy must reflect the general values of the time and the initial values which the welfare state reflected appear to have been as acceptable to women as to men. By institutionalising these values the welfare state inevitably tended to reinforce them; that, as the New Right would emphasise, is the inherent danger of centralisation. However, by remedying the deprivation from which women suffered in the interwar years, the welfare state has given women (and society as a whole) the strength to recognise these covert controls and to proceed to dismantle them. With regard to 'corporate bias', the accuracy of the evidence used to support its alleged evolution has been challenged elsewhere, and the conclusion appears inescapable that the most significant fact about corporatism in Britain is not that it has been attempted but that it has consistently failed.[44] Finally élitism seems eminently reconcilable with pluralism, once it is acknowledged that each élite is essentially transient, vulnerable at times to outside pressures and limited in power to particular areas of policy. These brief and perhaps over-simplistic conclusions are not to deny that each rejected theory has invaluable insights to offer, but merely to argue that a pluralistic perspective would appear to provide the most satisfactory premise on which to analyse the postwar British welfare state.

Reluctant collectivism similarly appears to be the most realistic of the three postwar welfare strategies. The idealistic objective of the democratic socialists to create an altruistic society is instantly attractive, but it is idealistic. It overlooks the real-world limitations of 'the state'. In its expressed wish to recreate the social solidarity and efficient central planning of the Second World War it would also seem to overlook the evidence of Titmuss himself. His account of wartime evacuation, for example, records – as do other commentaries – not social solidarity but frequent antagonism between the evacuees and their hosts. It also reveals the dislike of both for central planning, with large numbers of evacuees spontaneously returning home both in 1940 and at the end of the war. Titmuss concluded 'that people behaved in an unexpected way. By their behaviour they made planning difficult: they made a good plan look, in the end, like a bad plan.'[45] Such a conclusion hardly inspires faith in the practicality of social engineering. Likewise the New Right provides some acute criticisms of the many failings of the welfare state, but its strength lies essentially in its powers of criticism. Its own positive championing of the market, for both economic and political reasons, ignores the long-standing market failures which resulted in the depression of the interwar years. It turns a blind eye also to the fact that the market is inefficient in many technical ways, not least because imperfect knowledge results in a misallocation of resources and a degree of social inequality which is both economically disadvantageous and politically dangerous. In contrast reluctant collectivism, by endorsing the economic and political strength of the market while seeking simultaneously to correct its acknowledged weaknesses, offers an effective compromise. Between 1945 and 1975 this strategy may have revealed many of the conventional weaknesses of compromise but, as Marshall argued, there is no reason why such a compromise should not combine the strength of the two opposing ideologies and become a viable, principled philosophy. With greater private determination and public education it can, in other words, provide a positive programme for conviction politics.

2.5 FURTHER READING

The best introductions to general history, the practice of welfare in Britain and their interrelationships are V. George and P. Wilding, *Ideology and Social Welfare* (1985) and R. Mishra, *Society and Social Policy* (1977). A general introduction sympathetic to Marxist analysis is J. Dearlove and P. Saunders, *Introduction to British Politics* (1984), whilst a good feminist reader is C. Ungerson (ed.), *Women and Social Policy* (1985). The most noted 'New Right' attack on the welfare state is C. Barnett, *The Audit of War* (1986), and both its strengths and weaknesses are appraised in J. Harris, 'Enterprise and Welfare States: a comparative perspective', *Transactions of the Royal Historical Society*, vol. 40 (1990) pp. 175–95. The NHS is analysed in the light of competing theories by C. Ham, *Health Policy in Britain* (1982).

On the developing political strategies, there is really no substitute for the views of their original proponents: *The Collected Writings of John Maynard Keynes* (30 vols, 1971–89); the Beveridge Report (Cmd 6404); T. H. Marshall, *Citizenship and Social Class and other Essays* (1950); B. Abel-Smith and K. Titmuss (eds), *The Philosophy of Welfare* (1987); C. A. R. Crosland, *The Future of Socialism* (1956); and F. A. Hayek, *The Road to Serfdom* (1943). These works may be supplemented for reluctant collectivism by J. Harris, *William Beveridge* (1977) and A. Howard, *RAB: the life of R. A. Butler* (1987) and, for the New Right, by R. Harris and A. Seldon, *Over-ruled on Welfare* (1979).

3 The Nature of Policymaking

The historical analysis of the welfare state can benefit from theoretical insights into not just the distribution of power in society and the underlying objectives of state intervention but also the formulation of individual policies and the criteria for their effectiveness. This requires a change of focus from the general theories of sociology and political economy to the more technical disciplines of political science and economics. These disciplines are themselves concerned with broad issues such as the nature of power and the relative efficiency of state intervention and the market. Their main concern, however, is how political decisions are taken and implemented, and how policy objectives (once determined) can best be achieved. For instance, does state intervention – as its early proponents (such as Keynes and Beveridge) seemed to assume – really entail the taking of decisions by disinterested experts in command of the full range of relevant information; and are these decisions then automatically implemented in such a way that all citizens benefit, and only benefit, from them in the manner intended? Similarly, in a specific policy area, how can it be determined whether the use of scarce resources will be maximised, in general, by state intervention or the market and, in particular, by a given policy? Such theoretical questions as these have spawned a vast empirical literature, from which examples will again be largely selected from the early history of the NHS.

3.1 THE POLITICAL SCIENCE PERSPECTIVE

3.1.1 The three faces of power

One subject which political science has done much to illuminate is the nature of power. Three types (or 'faces') have been identified. The first, which is the easiest to recognise, is the power exercised by one individual or group over another in face-to-face confrontation. An obvious example is the conflict in 1951 between Bevan and Gaitskell over the introduction of dental and ophthalmic charges.

Gaitskell won the battle within Cabinet, the Labour government introduced charges and Bevan resigned.

The second type of power is the power to keep certain policy options off the political agenda and thereby stifle an unwelcome policy before an overt decision has to be taken ('the theory of non-decision making'). Examples here are the success of the medical profession and the Treasury in resisting, respectively, the extension of local authority health centres and community care in the 1950s. The former were wanted by the Labour Party as a local focus for all the health services provided by central and local government. The latter was recommended by the 1956 Guillebaud Report as a humane and cheap alternative to the institutional care of the old.[1] Neither was actively championed, however, because of the known hostility of the medical profession towards local authorities and of the Treasury towards any increase in annual expenditure – especially on grants to local authorities which it could not directly control. Because of the 'anticipated reaction' of powerful professional and bureaucratic interests, therefore, neither the Labour Party nor the Guillebaud Committee felt – or was – able to get the reforms debated seriously on their own merit.

The third type of power is the power so to shape people's ideas that they never conceive, let alone articulate, certain policy options which are in their interests. This type of power is synonymous with the neo-Marxist concept of hegemony and is therefore the hardest to identify. However, the rise of feminism exposed the power of male doctors in the 1950s – under the guise of 'scientific' medical expertise – to shape women's definition of their own needs. Similarly the Institute of Economic Affairs in the 1960s argued that the high degree of popular satisfaction with the NHS was maintained only because politicians and civil servants, for their own ends, deliberately fostered 'civic illiteracy' over its true cost and limitations.[2] Once that 'tacit conspiracy' was broken, so the IEA argued, the public would be the better able to identify its interests.

This distinction between the three faces of power has obvious implications for an understanding of policymaking and consequently for the identification and analysis of historical evidence. Policy-making must be defined by the historian not only as visible decisions between well-defined options, but also as the covert avoidance of other options and even the mere maintenance of the *status quo*. The history of welfare policy has therefore to recognise and explain not only what has happened in the past but what has not – a dangerous task made all the more difficult because evidence for non-decision making and hegemony is, by their very nature, sparse.

Such evidence, none the less, can be found. Government records, for instance, can reveal how certain policy options were quietly smothered. The failure of government to consider rationally novel ideas or perspectives, advanced either by public enquiries or social scientists, also provides prima-facie evidence of the second face of power. Moreover, the acceptance over time of new ideas should prompt the question of why these ideas had previously been deemed impractical. One striking example of the way in which this new type of evidence can heighten historical understanding is the light it casts on the official disdain with which the arguments of the New Right and Titmuss's concept of fiscal welfare (state handouts to the rich in tax relief) were originally treated. The welfare state between 1945 and 1975 enjoyed a reputation for rationality, reasonableness and pragmatism. This disdain suggests, on the contrary, that it was extremely intolerant of any idea which threatened the consensus on which it was based.

3.1.2 Bureaucracy and the formulation of policy

One institution which in all industrial countries has been involved in the exercise of all three faces of power, and which has accordingly been subject to extensive theoretical and empirical study, is the civil service (or 'bureaucracy', to use that term in its neutral sense).[3] Opinion is strongly divided over its beneficial or adverse effect on individual welfare. Bureaucracy's foremost theoretical champion is Max Weber, the German sociologist who helped to draft the constitution of the Weimar Republic after the First World War and whose ideas underpinned – if only unconsciously – the growth of the British civil service in the first half of the twentieth century. Weber argued that bureaucracy was the only rational means by which modern society could be organised, given society's increasing complexity and the greater equalisation of both economic and political power between its citizens. This was because of its efficiency (ensured by such organisational characteristics as a clear hierarchy and its adherence to rules) and its broad societal role (rising above sectional interest to define and act in the national interest). He was sufficiently realistic to acknowledge that there was an inherent tension between bureaucracy and political democracy. Officials might develop a specialist expertise against which ministers would appear as 'dilettantes'. To avoid criticism, they might favour secrecy and thus 'a poorly informed, and hence powerless parliament – at least insofar as ignorance is compatible with bureaucracy's own interest'. Officials' own interests might also intrude into and therefore bias their working definition of the 'by no means ambiguous' concept of the national interest.[4] Weber maintained, however, that an enlarged state bureaucracy was indispensable to good government; and he trusted that in each country its potential dangers would be checked by such countervailing forces as strong ministers, informed public opinion and industry's own bureaucracy.

Weber's theoretical assumptions have been attacked by both Marxists and the New Right. Given their fundamental belief in class conflict, Marxists (as has been seen) deny that there can be a single 'national interest' within capitalist society. Their basic assumption is, therefore, that bureaucracy can but serve the interest of the ruling class. In contrast the New Right denies the efficiency of bureaucracy in the allocation of scarce resources. This is in part because of bureaucratic self-interest. The nature of democratic politics (the need to win votes) biases politicians towards greater state expenditure, it is argued, and officials exploit this bias to maximise their budgets and hence their own salaries, power and prestige. However, even the most disinterested and public-spirited of bureaucrats can be guilty of serious economic misallocation. Zealous social reformers, for example, cannot have a complete understanding of what is in the public interest; and since the resources they obtain for one particular reform must inevitably be at the expense of another, they may well impede another policy which would have better served the public interest. Similarly, committed administrative reformers, in their determination to eliminate waste and promote honesty, can actually undermine good government both by removing the competition between rival departments (which had previously kept them responsive to changing public needs) and by displacing efficiency with honesty as the main criterion of official performance.[5] In short, the New Right argue, bureaucracy inherently discourages the very values which are needed to ensure a speedy response to conflicting and changing need. The more zealous and public-spirited the officials the greater the economic damage they can unwittingly cause.

Weber's assumptions about bureaucratic efficiency and the countervailing checks upon its political power have also been challenged empirically. In Britain the civil service's lack of specialist and managerial skills was officially condemned by the Fulton Committee on the Civil Service (1966–8), whilst its political power was first documented from within government by Richard Crossman, the publication of whose diaries after 1975 unleashed a torrent of ministerial, official and academic commentaries on the subject.[6] A good illustration of the civil service's perceived inefficiency is provided by the officials of the postwar Ministry of Health, whose serious underestimation of the demand for health care led to massive supplementary estimates in 1948 and 1949, which long tarred the NHS with a reputation for financial extravagance and mismanagement. Their continuing lack of statistical and administrative skills was exposed by the Guillebaud Committee in 1956; but there was no serious attempt to make good this deficiency until the appointment of a new permanent secretary and chief medical officer of health in 1960.[7]

The civil service's political power has conventionally been explained by the development of a 'departmental view' by permanent officials in each area of policy for which they are responsible and by its maintenance, even in the face of ministerial opposition. In health policy, for example, Barbara Castle (as secretary of state for social services between 1974 and 1976) found herself confronted by the concerted opposition of her senior staff when she sought to phase out pay beds in NHS hospitals in 1975. Similarly Crossman (as Minister of Housing) felt himself placed in a 'padded cell' where officials could insulate him from any information or pressure group that might challenge the 'departmental view'. Crossman's conviction was, however, that 'the key to the control by the civil service over politicians' was the official interdepartmental committee.[8] Such committees, under the guise of coordinating government policy, could be used by officials either to frustrate initiatives (which they may even have promised ministers to implement) or to construct complex packages of policies which could only be dismantled and reassembled by a very determined and united cabinet. As foreseen by the New Right, the increased emphasis on the planning of public expenditure after 1960 placed ministers even more firmly within a straitjacket of policies devised largely by officials.

The particular *bête noire* of Crossman, as it has been for most other critics of the British civil service, was the Treasury. The exceptional power of its officials springs from their three main responsibilities – economic policy (which determines the resources available for all other policies), the control of public expenditure (which makes their prior sanction necessary for all policy changes) and the management of the civil service (which ties the loyalty of civil servants, bent on promotion, to the Treasury rather than to their departmental minister). Such power has not been exercised with either noticeable expertise or disinterest. The Treasury's lack of specialist economic and managerial skills has been the source of constant criticism. Moreover, its officials have been perceived consistently to try to impose their own vested interests or 'departmental view', throughout the civil service, to the particular detriment of welfare policy. Treasury officials have, for instance, been reluctant to dispense with annual budgeting because of the strict control it permits over public expenditure, although the efficiency of economic management and of welfare expenditure requires a far longer perspective. Similarly they have been reluctant to increase grants to local authorities (which they cannot directly control) although, even by their own admission, long-term economies in areas such as health policy are dependent on their preventive services and community care.[9] Their dependence on financial markets both at home and abroad, to raise loans to fund the national debt and to maintain the value of sterling, has also given them a vested interest in minimising public, and especially welfare, expenditure. Consequently in both their routine work and in major crises (such as that over the 1976 IMF loan) Treasury officials have appeared to resort to every possible device to attack welfare expenditure. This has fostered the conviction – especially amongst democratic socialists – that the civil service has regularly frustrated the wishes of ministers, parliament and the electorate.

The power of the civil service, however, can be – and has been – greatly exaggerated; and the history of welfare policy is replete with examples of success for the three countervailing forces identified by Weber. The classic case of the strong spending minister imposing his will upon officials is Harold Macmillan as minister of housing and local government between 1951 and 1954. Backed by the Prime Minister and a clear manifesto commitment, he secured by 1953 the building of over 300 000 houses per year in the face of determined opposition from within both his own ministry and the Treasury.[10] The classic case of the power of public opinion is the acceptance of the Beveridge Report in 1943. Treasury officials had strenuously opposed the Report on philosophical, economic and administrative grounds. Universal social security, they argued, would undermine the incentive to work, divert scarce economic resources from more important policies (such as defence and the expansion of exports) and fail to target the poor.[11] However the popular reception of the Report, and the backbench revolt it provoked in Parliament against

Churchill's Coalition government, made such objections politically untenable. The Report's main principles were therefore immediately incorporated into postwar reconstruction plans. Finally the ability of pressure groups to defeat policies favoured by the civil service is well illustrated by the defeat, by the Confederation of British Industry (CBI) and Trades Union Congress (TUC), of successive prices and incomes policies and by the role of the British Medical Association (BMA) in the establishment and development of the NHS.

Such a catalogue of bureaucratic 'defeats' raises doubts about the real 'political' power of the civil service and indeed of the Treasury. The civil service is not, after all, a homogeneous body and battles both between and within departments can be easily exploited. Strong ministers who seek to reject or refine 'the departmental view', for example, are usually only opposed by senior staff and can rely upon the expertise and zeal of junior officials to win the necessary battles in Whitehall (and, especially, increased resources). When ministers are defeated, it is often not the result of any bureaucratic conspiracy but because they lack either the prime minister's support or a clearly defined party policy. A 'departmental view' may, moreover, be a sign not of bureaucratic power but simply of officials' desire to develop a non-partisan policy which (for the convenience of the public as well as the administrator) will ensure continuity of policy whichever party is in power, and to ensure that that policy is acceptable to those professions which will be responsible for its implementation. Official opposition to the reduction of pay beds in 1975 (which Barbara Castle admitted was confined largely to senior staff) was based, for example, on concern over the BMA's reaction and the future willingness of doctors to work within the NHS.[12] Indeed the considered opinion of two highly respected ministers of education in the 1960s was that, although the civil service inevitably had considerable influence over policy, the real constraints on ministers lay elsewhere: in the power of pressure groups, the need to respect local autonomy, the legacy of the past and the general economic climate.[13] In health policy these constraints have been duly represented by the power of the BMA, the autonomy of regional and local health authorities, the legacy of inadequate and unevenly distributed hospitals, and the impact of successive balance of payments crises.

The theoretical and empirical analysis of bureaucracy, therefore, highlights both its indispensability and its inherent weaknesses. A central bureaucracy is indispensable because traditional welfare agencies (such as the market, self help, charity and local government) have proved to be inadequate in an advanced industrial society. Its growth, however, also immensely complicates – and may over time actually impede – individual welfare. All three faces of power are exercised through and by bureaucracy. Direct confrontations have occurred between officials, ministers and pressure groups; certain policy options have been side-stepped by their having been labelled 'administratively impractical'; and certain values (such as, Marxists would argue, capitalism) have been reinforced to the exclusion of others by its actions. Such an exercise of power has usually been identified by political scientists in the formulation of policy, but it can also be located in the less publicised and analysed areas of policy implementation.

3.1.3 The implementation of policy

Increased concentration on the implementation of policy reflects political scientists' conviction not just that policy should be judged on its actual impact (rather than its intention) but that policy is actually made in the course of implementation, rather than by central 'decision-makers'. This conviction challenges the traditional 'top-down' model of policymaking by which, in the Weberian ideal, unambiguous central decisions are faithfully translated into action by well-disciplined officials working for a single agency and are untroubled by either economic constraints or social resistance. In its place there is now being substituted the more dynamic (and riskily entitled) 'bottom-up' approach which views policy as the constantly evolving interpretation of legislation – which has often been deliberately left ambiguous at the centre – by local officials ('street-level bureaucrats') who are heavily influenced by economic constraints, prevailing social prejudice and the actions of competing agencies. Policy, in this perspective, is not what Cabinets and senior officials plan but what lower-paid officials do.

Historical analysis has traditionally accorded some importance to policy-implementation. Problems encountered at a local level have been seen to be fed back to the centre and used to refine policy. It has also been recognised that Parliament and ministers have sufficient time only to debate the principles behind new legislation and that the authority to draft (and later to interpret and refine) policy has conventionally been delegated to officials. Indeed the increased resort to 'delegated legislation' was regarded by critics of the interwar British civil service as irrefutable evidence of the country's slide into bureaucracy.[14] Such traditional analysis, however, is essentially in accord with the 'top-down' model. In contrast the new 'bottom-up' approach begs three major new questions about the nature, and therefore the analysis, of policy.

First, what is the true nature of policy when – as in the case of the 1970 Chronically Sick and Disabled Persons Act – central government deliberately frustrates the specified objectives of a given item of legislation by apportioning to it insufficient finance? Is government policy to be judged by the declared objectives of its legislation or by its subsequent administrative action? Secondly, what is the true nature of national policy when (to permit adjustment according to local circumstances or professional judgement) discretion is specifically drafted into legislation that is to be implemented by local authorities or professional bodies? As a consequence of such discretion 'national' policy can vary considerably not only from area to area but also from the intentions of central policymakers. Local government, for example, is notorious for its ability to use its discretion (and such political and financial independence as it derives from local elections and rate finance) directly to frustrate central government policy. Within the NHS, regional and local health authorities have frequently used their professional expertise to diverge from central government policy – for instance the Leeds Regional Hospital Board in the 1960s developed its own mental health strategy in direct opposition to government guidelines.[15] Indeed the ultimate example of 'street-level' power is the 'clinical freedom' traditionally enjoyed by doctors because its corollary is that the size and structure of the NHS budget is finally determined by professional judgement (on such issues as the rate of admissions to hospitals and the prescription of drugs) rather than by any centralised plan.

Finally 'bottom-up' theorists have argued that policy is often effectively made by local officials, even when they are employed directly by central government. In the Weberian model this would be impossible because local officials working in a hierarchical institution and governed by clear rules would automatically implement the well-defined wishes of the legislators. However, this model is held not to be true for areas of policy such as national assistance, the forerunner of the present system of supplementary benefit. Here, as Michael Hill has argued, the intention of the original 1948 National Assistance Act – to eradicate the stigma of the Poor Law (and thus the low take-up of benefit) – has never been realised.[16] A major reason for this is that from the start insufficient funds were allocated to the service and that, in the absence of any clear criteria by which to ration benefit, local officials fell back on the traditional – but highly arbitrary and unscientific – distinction between the 'deserving' and 'undeserving' poor. Most of the 'special cases', in which circumstances did not conform neatly to the rules and qualification for benefit was therefore at the discretion of the official, were classified as 'undeserving'; and administrative discretion accordingly came to be used – and was seen to be used – illiberally.

There were many reasons for officials acting in this way. Such illiberality generally accorded with their own prejudices and those of a particularly articulate section of the public about 'scrounging'. It was a means not only of rationing scarce resources but also of simplifying the complex human problems with which they were faced. Moreover it helped some to secure acceptance, and possible promotion, in a system which openly professed its intention to eradicate not only stigma but also fraud and abuse. Whatever the reasons for the action of individual officials however, the history of national assistance makes it patently clear that local officials – when faced with conflicting signals from central policymakers – can play the major role in determining what the actual impact of policy should be on individual clients.

3.1.4 Incrementalism

The political science perspective thus reveals the full complexity of analysing welfare policy. Policy is revealed as being not a series of clear-cut decisions taken by ministers on the advice of disinterested civil servants, sanctioned by Parliament and automatically implemented. Rather it is a complex web of decisions and actions, resulting in both change and the avoidance of change, taken at every level within the government machine and often negotiated at length with outside pressure groups. Different parts of the state may act in a contradictory fashion at any one time. The purpose of policy is always shifting and its actual impact may often be very different from that originally intended. Temporary expedients may become entrenched as established principles.

Faced by such a bewildering array of potential evidence, historians may be tempted to assume – as does this book – that the only realistic approach to welfare policy is the incrementalist approach. Policy, in short, should be seen not as the outcome of some far-seeing rational plan but typically as a series of small adjustments, often governed by expedience and by limited objectives which have unforeseen consequences. Incrementalism does not deny that there may, at any given time, be some common assumptions shared by the majority of policymakers. Nor does it deny that, at certain critical points in history, far-seeing rational decisions may have the major effect on policy. Indeed the creation of the welfare state in Britain in the 1940s might be depicted as just such a time – although the gradual, uncertain evolution of the phrase would suggest that (for all the wartime planning) the overall consequences of reconstruction policy were not consciously predetermined. Rather, incrementalism stresses, over time and at all levels, the complex mixture of rationality and realism, short-term expediency and planned development that determines policy. The resulting tension has been most vividly summarised by an early adherent of planning, Karl Mannheim, who wrote in 1951:

> The last bitter decades have taught us that one can neither conceive of a Good Society without reference to the actual state of affairs nor reconstruct a whole social order by piecemeal administrative reforms . . . . In times of slow change one can proceed more or less by intuition without constantly consulting principles. But in a post-war social landslide, when greater upheaval takes place in a month than in normal decades, awareness of the social significance of events is a prerequisite to survival.[17]

3.2 THE ECONOMIC PERSPECTIVE

Since 1945 economics has become preeminent amongst the social sciences. In relation to more recently developed disciplines (such as sociology) it is seen to provide a more rigorous logic with which to analyse complex problems, whilst in relation to equally well-established sciences (such as philosophy) it is seen to be of more immediate relevance. Hence economists have been called upon not just to provide the theoretical criteria by which to judge the performance of the welfare state, but actually to participate in the formulation and implementation of policy. Their participation, moreover, has not been confined solely to the management of the economy but has also included the allocation of scarce resources to and within social policy.

The record of economists within government has not been particularly distinguished. Their advice has often been contradictory, as was
particularly apparent in the late 1970s with the open warfare between
Keynesians and monetarists. It has also frequently appeared ineffectual or positively harmful – so much so, in the 1960s for example,
that it became fashionable to chart the decline of the British economy
in direct relation to the number of economists employed at Whitehall. On one level such criticism was unjustified. Economists themselves rarely took major policy decisions and could justifiably argue
that those who did either ignored or misused their advice. On
another level, however, professional economic advice has increasingly revealed certain shortcomings which have raised questions
about both the applicability of economic theory to the real world
and the very assumptions upon which that theory is based.

A good example of such failings in macroeconomic policy is the
implementation of the Keynesian theory of demand management
(which was predominant between 1945 and 1975). It had been
opposed long before its implementation on practical as much as on
theoretical grounds, and such objections (as will be seen in Chapter
5.1) coloured the Treasury's contribution to the famous 1944
Employment Policy white paper. Subsequent events appear to have
justified the Treasury's misgivings. Successive problems over the
prompt collection of reliable data, the forecasting of future economic
trends and the devising of remedial action which would have its
desired (and full) effect within the requisite time span led many
commentators to conclude that – regardless of any 'unanticipated'
behaviour by the public – the economic techniques simply did not
exist to enable even the most disinterested chancellor of the
exchequer to 'fine-tune' the economy. Indeed, as the authoritative
Plowden Committee argued as early as 1961, demand management
as a 'remedy' for fluctuations within the economy could 'be even
worse than the disease'.[18] It could both destabilise the economy at the
macro level and at the micro level militate against the achievement of
'value for money' in public investment because such investment (such
as the building and staffing of a hospital) could not be accelerated
or retarded simply to counteract forecasted bouts of unemployment
or inflation. The practical failure of economists, in other words, lay
not just in the misuse of their advice by others but in the very nature
of that advice.

On the theoretical level, reservations have been voiced about
the objectivity of conventional economic theory and its technical

limitations, particularly in relation to social policy. Microeconomic analysis, for example, concentrates on the attainment of the maximum 'output' of welfare from a limited amount of resources (which cannot satisfy all need). On the demand side, it takes as its implicit standard the behaviour of 'economically rational' man making isolated decisions in a market where the price of each good is clearly signalled. Thus 'marginal analysis' assumes that people will always make choices that maximise their individual well-being (utility); and that when they are forced to make choices through limited resources, they will choose to purchase an object up to a point where the extra pleasure it brings (its marginal utility) is equal to the pleasure that has to be foregone through the non-purchase of an alternative object (its marginal opportunity cost). The price placed against each object facilitates their choice.

Such a standard is held by many, particularly democratic socialists, to be inherently flawed – if only because it replicates the values of the market which, in their opinion, has over time proved itself incapable of maximising welfare. There are three main objections. First, marginal analysis simultaneously underestimates and over-estimates human nature. People do not always seek to maximise their own material welfare but often choose, as Titmuss's blood donors illustrate, to act altruistically. Conversely, people (for reasons of either finance or personality) have different abilities to express and satisfy their needs which, consequently, the market will not accurately represent. Moreover, individual purchasers are generally unaware of the consequences to others of their choices (externalities). Therefore collective decisions, although smacking of paternalism, can maximise the *sum* of individual welfare more efficiently than individual decisions within a free market.

Secondly, marginal analysis would appear to condone the existing distribution of resources within society, however unequal it might be. The economist's classic definition of maximum welfare, or of the most efficient use of scarce resources, is the concept of Pareto optimality: the allocation of scarce resources in such a way that no one individual can be made better off without simultaneously making at least one other person worse off. The serious limitations of such a definition are well exposed by one commentator who has remarked that 'a socially efficient use of resources in the economist's sense of the term could . . . be one in which there was a great deal of poverty and hardship – providing the preferences of people with money to express themselves through the market were being met as fully as was possible'.[19] Consequently Pareto optimality is frequently contrasted unfavourably with Rawls' theory of social justice. This argues, *inter alia*, that social and economic inequality can be condoned only insofar as they benefit the least advantaged; and so there should be no reallocation of resources unless it is to the advantage of the least well-off.[20] Hence high salaries for hospital consultants, and further pay awards for them, are justified only so long as they serve to provide better medical treatment for (amongst others) the poorest members of society.

Finally there is the question of quantification. Some aspects of welfare, such as the quality of life, are simply unamenable to pricing. Therefore, in its costings, marginal analysis has either to ignore them or use surrogate measures. Both strategies can seriously bias its conclusions. Within the health service, for example, the relative cost of institutional and community care can be seriously misrepresented because the costs of the former can be calculated with relative ease whereas those of the latter (so far as it depends on 'unpaid' relatives or carers) cannot. One convention is to price the cost of the unpaid carers by the income foregone in the jobs they might otherwise have undertaken; but this ignores the possible decline in their quality of life (and therefore their welfare) resulting from the loss of their freedom to choose an alternative job and to have an independent income. The 'price' of human life is raised even more acutely with regard to the terminally ill. In seeking to maximise the 'output' of welfare from scarce resources, marginal analysis clearly focuses attention on relievable need. Logically this would deny treatment to the terminally ill, unless some price can be put on the value of the dying person's life and the peace of mind of both doctors and relatives ('vicarious' welfare). It is when such calculations come to be made that charges and countercharges of callousness and sentimentality between economists and non-economists become most virulent.

Such confrontations are largely unproductive. The better economists well recognise the limitations of their science. In macroeconomic policy, they accept that the successful management of the economy depends as much on political judgement and luck as on 'pure technique'.[21] In welfare policy they equally recognise that they are no more (and no less) qualified than anyone else to advise on the ideological and moral issues behind the allocation of scarce resources. Once a decision has been taken on these issues, however, they can offer a set of techniques backed by a body of theory which is better developed than those of most other social sciences. It is not, after all, amoral to attempt to identify the economic cost of 'social justice'; nor should such attempts be discouraged. Rather it is amoral to pretend that the humane treatment of a dying person has no cost and that (given scarce resources) certain other needs which could have been relieved will as a consequence be relieved less quickly. Within its acknowledged limitations, the strength of economics is that it has the means to confront such hard issues. As such it has much of value to say about the economic efficiency of both state intervention in general and of individual welfare policies in particular.

3.2.1 The economics of state intervention

State intervention in relation to welfare policy has traditionally been defended on ethical grounds. It has been argued for instance that all citizens should have certain social rights (such as freedom from poverty) which the market cannot automatically guarantee and that, on the grounds of social justice, there should be a more equitable distribution of income and wealth. Such ideals are not without their economic benefits. For example, more equitable income distribution has (as Keynesians recognise) consequences for consumer demand and hence production. It can also legitimise society and thereby contribute to political stability and social cohesion, which in their turn can facilitate economic growth. State intervention can, however, be defended on purely economic criteria, regardless of any ethical arguments. As one recent text has concluded: 'it does things which private markets for technical reasons either would not do at all, or would do inefficiently. We need a welfare state of some sort for efficiency reasons, and would continue to do so even if all distributional problems had been solved.'[22] What are these technical reasons and what sort of welfare state do they justify?

Four main reasons are usually advanced to justify state intervention: imperfect knowledge, imperfect competition, externalities and public goods. The first two are concerned with the absence in the real world of the theoretical preconditions for market efficiency. One of these preconditions is that everyone should be able to recognise both their own needs and the most efficient way of meeting them (perfect knowledge). Clearly this can rarely be the case. In health care for example it would actually diminish people's welfare if they spent most of their leisure time amassing sufficient knowledge about the range and price of treatment for all possible illnesses so that, when the due moment finally arrived (and assuming of course that they were conscious) they could make a rational choice. Moreover medical science is so complex that, however much leisure time they forfeited, most people would be unable to acquire sufficient knowledge to act rationally. Consequently independent consumer choice will always be inefficient and, if welfare is to be maximised, there is a prima-facie case for state intervention.

Exactly the same is true in the case of imperfect competition where one – or a few – producers have cornered the market for a given product. Although concentration of production can reduce costs ('economies of scale'), there is also the danger that it will lead to the charging of unnecessarily high prices (which will deny people the resources to buy other goods) or incur unnecessarily high costs (X-inefficiency), which will waste resources. In health care, elements of such monopolistic behaviour are most apparent in the multi-national drug companies. There is, however, also a tendency in the free market for doctors to exploit their privileged position and oversupply certain types of treatment. This is especially true when – unlike in the NHS – doctors are paid for each transaction or when an insurance policy disguises from the patient the actual cost of his treatment.

The other two economic justifications for state intervention relate to weaknesses inherent in the market. Externalities are the consequences to others, either beneficial or adverse, of actions by individuals or firms for which no direct reward or compensation is paid. Most actions have consequences for others, and so, if welfare is to be maximised, the benefits accruing to both those who take the decisions and those who are indirectly affected (its private and its 'external' benefits) must outweigh private and 'external' costs. Education, for example, produces beneficial externalities because an individual's education can benefit not only that individual but also others in terms of his or her increased socialisation or productivity. Conversely the drift of industry to the South East, for the quite legitimate reason of maximising private profit, can involve adverse externalities. By necessitating the replacement of such facilities as schools and hospitals which have been abandoned elsewhere, the relocation of industry consumes resources that could have been used more advantageously. The market, because it reflects largely individual (or private) costs and benefits, will inevitably tend to oversupply goods with adverse externalities whilst undersupplying those with beneficial externalities. Hence there is a prima-facie case for arguing that collective decisions, which can take into account all private and external costs and benefits, are more efficient in maximising welfare than individual market decisions.

The issue of externalities is closely related to that of public goods. Public goods are those, such as defence and public health, which are in everyone's interest but for which a market price cannot easily be charged. How, for example, could a private producer of defence or public health exclude a non-payer from enjoying these services? Because of people's reluctance to pay for goods they can enjoy at the expense of others, the market will tend to undersupply them. Consequently, if welfare is to be maximised and the 'responsible' citizen protected from the irresponsibilities of others (in relation, for example, to contagious diseases), state coercion is needed. It is because of these issues of externalities and public goods that economists, even in the heyday of nineteenth-century *laissez-faire*, were willing to advocate public expenditure on defence, education and, eventually, public health.

There are, therefore, sound theoretical justifications for state intervention; but they do not automatically determine how the state should provide welfare or indeed whether, in the real world, state provision will be any more efficient than the market. There are in fact four main methods of state intervention – cash transfers, regulation, finance and public production – and each may be illustrated in relation to health care. Cash benefits (such as old-age pensions) minimise calls upon the NHS by providing potential clients with an income which enables them either to maintain their own health or to be supported by relatives in their own homes. Regulations, such as those concerning food hygiene, minimise disease by protecting consumers from the consequences of their imperfect knowledge. Finance includes both taxation, which increases the price of goods which can damage health (such as cigarettes), and subsidies, which reduce the price of those which are beneficial (such as medicine). Finally, the NHS has largely brought medical care within the sphere of public production. Everyone in Britain is protected from the danger of their own imperfect knowledge by the provision, free at the point of access, of a full range of treatment by specialists who are paid by the state and consequently have no direct pecuniary interest in the choice of treatment they prescribe. Each of these interventionist policies entails a different degree of interference with the market. Cash benefits entail the least interference. They seek only to correct the market's weakness on the demand side, by distributing resources to those who would otherwise lack the ability to purchase a necessary minimum of goods. At the other extreme, public production largely supersedes the market.

The choice between the alternative means of intervention is controversial. Economists of the new right, who acknowledge the need for the state to correct the imperfections of the market, clearly advocate the least interference. They assert in particular that in the real world the state suffers from failings identical to those of the market. Officials lack the technical ability to measure over time the full social costs and benefits of individual actions (imperfect knowledge) and consequently the state is no more able than the market to resolve the problem of externalities. Indeed, because of its monopoly position, the state is under no competitive pressure either to keep consumers informed of the full range of opportunities open to them or to produce goods at the minimum possible cost. Thus the inherent danger of public production is, they conclude, the production of goods that satisfy the self-interest of politicians, bureaucrats or experts rather than maximise welfare.

Other economists disagree and stress, in contrast, the inherent real-world inefficiency of the market. An example frequently used is the financing of health care. Given its uncertain but potentially enormous cost to any one individual, the market solution to this problem is insurance, either on a voluntary basis (as in the USA) or under some degree of state regulation (as in interwar Britain and in many European countries today). Voluntary insurance, however, has innumerable imperfections. Many people may choose not to insure themselves, but if they fall ill this will impose externalities on others – such as the spread of contagious disease or the need ultimately for others to pay for their medical treatment. This is called the problem of the 'free rider'. Alternatively many people who are prepared to insure themselves, such as the chronically ill and the old, may find it impossible to find cover – at least at a cost which they can afford. This is either because they may be adjudged too great a risk (so the insurance company could not make a profit) or because the insurance company fears that relevant information about the degree of risk may not be disclosed (the problem of 'adverse selection'). Moreover certain contingencies, such as visits to the doctor or pregnancy, will usually not be covered since they are not random but within the power of the insured person to control (the problem of 'moral hazard'). Another type of moral hazard is the possible collusion between patient and doctor over the prescription of an unnecessarily expensive form of treatment since it is not they who will be paying (in increased charges or reduced profits) but the insurance company. Such collusion will nevertheless have high social costs because it will result in unnecessarily high consumption of scarce resources.

Many of these imperfections can be corrected by state regulation. For example, the state could make health insurance compulsory, require all insurance companies to take their fair share of high risk applicants and provide an inspectorate to monitor collusion. Such regulation would, however, be expensive to enforce and would increase the already considerable administrative costs involved in private companies estimating individual risks, issuing individual policies and paying individual claims. A far cheaper alternative (as is shown by the lower administrative costs of the NHS in relation to insurance-based schemes in the USA and in Europe) is for the principle of insurance to be superseded altogether by state finance and state production. Scarce resources can thereby by released for far more constructive purposes.[23]

There are, then, sound economic reasons for judging the market to be an inefficient mechanism for maximising welfare and for concluding that state intervention is functionally desirable. What form that intervention should take however raises as many controversial economic questions as it does philosophical ones (see Chapter 2.2). Those New Right economists who acknowledge the real-world failure of the market seek the minimum of remedial state intervention. To them the market alone has the potential to maximise welfare because it alone can provide the mechanism through which individuals can freely express their wishes and be made aware of the consequences (the marginal opportunity costs) of their choices. In contrast their opponents assert that, in advanced industrial countries, the state offers a potentially better mechanism not only for providing public goods but for minimising the dangers arising from imperfect knowledge, imperfect competition and externalities. They admit that in the real world state intervention can itself also be far from perfect; and they therefore acknowledge that it is incumbent upon them to develop the microeconomic concepts and techniques which will enable the state, in practice as well as in theory, to allocate resources more efficiently than the market.

3.2.2   The economics of individual welfare policies

The real-world failure of the state which microeconomists have particularly sought to rectify is the misallocation of scarce resources by
incrementalism, by élites and by misguided humanitarianism. Given
the political and administrative complexity of policy formulation and
implementation (summarised in the first half of this chapter), state
intervention tends to permit only the marginal adjustment of
resources over time between policies. Objective overviews of the
total allocation of resources, in order to determine whether the
overall mix of policies is correct, are discouraged. Similarly, where
the allocation of resources is entrusted to élites, there tends (as
argued in Chapter 2.3.1) to be misallocation because of either that
élite's self-interest or its inability to appreciate the full external costs
of its actions. Finally state intervention, by shielding voters from the
direct consequences of their choices, tends to encourage demands
for expenditure which, however laudable in humanitarian terms, may
actually reduce the eventual sum of individual welfare. After all,
given scarce resources, money spent on causes (however good)
cannot then be spent on other policies which might have benefited
more people over time. Money spent on short-term famine relief is
for instance money denied to projects to ensure that famine will not
recur in those areas.

The microeconomist's partial remedy for such government failure
is the concept of cost effectiveness: the evaluation of the total private
and external costs over time of a specific policy in relation to each
'unit' of welfare produced. This provides an immediate challenge to
the 'common sense' of bureaucratic managers or professional élites
who are concerned either with short-term considerations or with the
expenditure of resources within a given budget. The professional
training of doctors, for instance, encourages concentration on the
choice of treatment (however expensive) that will totally cure their
patient. The logic of cost effectiveness, on the other hand, requires
them to consider whether the sum of individual welfare would not
be increased if a similar amount of money were spent on a large
number of people, even if they were less seriously ill or if total cures
could not be effected.

Two of the major aids to the measurement of cost effectiveness
are marginal and cost-benefit analysis. The former again challenges
conventional 'common sense' by requiring the reallocation of
resources to be based on marginal rather than average costs. For

example, in the debate over community or institutional care for the elderly, community care would appear the cheaper option because the average cost of maintaining an individual at a given level of well-being in the community is less than the average institutional cost. However, the patients who will be affected (in other words those who would either leave institutional care or would not now enter it) are not average patients. They are generally less infirm than the average patient in institutional care (and therefore their cost should be less than average). Conversely they are more infirm than the average patient in the community (and therefore the cost of their community care should be higher than average). Reallocation of resources, therefore, should depend on whether the 'above average' cost of marginal patients in the community remains less than their 'below average' cost in institutional care. This need not always be the case. The apparently 'cheaper' option may in certain circumstances be the more expensive. Cost-benefit analysis is an even more sophisticated and complex attempt, particularly in relation to new policy initiatives, to quantify the full costs and benefits over time of a given policy. Its major benefit is that it places the immediate cost of a policy (which might appear prohibitive) in the context of future savings. Thus decisions can be made on criteria which are broader and more long term than is usual. It must, however, be admitted that its record in the real world – particularly over the location of London's third airport in the 1970s – has been far from encouraging.

A major reason for the ability of such microeconomic techniques to provide only a partial remedy for real-world government failure is their vulnerability to the weaknesses identified earlier in relation to marginal analysis. The problem of quantifying the unquantifiable is particularly acute when, to aid comparison between different policies, all individual well-being has to be reduced to a common 'unit' of welfare. How is the prolongation of the life of one individual to be weighed against the increased self sufficiency of another? Moreover, even in the simpler tasks of quantification, such as the construction of the 'points' system by which individual housing need is measured prior to the allocation of council housing, in-built prejudices and values are betrayed by the relative weighting given to different needs. Finally, cost-benefit analysis, like Pareto optimality, is coldly technocratic in that it is not concerned with the distribution of costs and benefits. All the costs might accrue to one group of people and all the benefits to another.

It might be argued that attempts to measure cost effectiveness,

however imperfect, are better than nothing. This is not necessarily
true. By placing undue weight, however unintentionally, on variables
that can be quantified, these variables can be given a spurious importance which may seriously prejudice subsequent analysis. Nevertheless it is reasonable to argue that – handled with due care – the
rationality of microeconomic analysis can provide an effective challenge to the assumptions underlying the decisions, or non-decisions,
of existing policymakers and thereby clear the ground for better
policymaking. Indeed in the NHS this happened in the 1970s and
1980s with, for example, the incorporation of marginal analysis into
the RAWP formula by which resources were allocated between
regional health authorities.[24]

3.2.3 Economic rationality

Economics, as is illustrated by the battle between Keynesians and
monetarists over the fundamental nature of economic relationships,
is a far from precise science. Nevertheless it does provide a reason-
ably rigorous set, or sets, of analytical criteria by which to judge the
relative efficiency of the welfare state in general and individual policies in particular. Economists of the New Right assign to the state
only the provision of public goods and a minimum of manipulation
and regulation to counteract the acknowledged real-world failures
of the market. This would so limit the role of government that, by
the definition provided earlier (in Chapter 2.1), the welfare state
would no longer exist. However other economists argue that, given
the problems of imperfect knowledge, imperfect competition and
externalities, the state should adopt a more interventionist role in the
interests of functional economic efficiency, let alone social justice. It
is admitted that in the real world there are as many potential government failures as market failures, but microeconomic techniques can
be developed to minimise them. Above all microeconomic analysis
– by concentrating attention both on the unavoidable scarcity of
resources and the 'output' of welfare – provides a rational approach
to the maximisation of welfare, which is itself a major factor in the
maximisation of social justice. To this extent economists can not only
provide a functional justification for the welfare state but also prove
themselves to be not the rivals but the allies of those who seek social
justice.

3.3 FURTHER READING

A compact introduction to political science theory is C. Ham and M. Hill, *The Policy Process in the Modern Capitalist State* (1984) which is particularly strong on the three faces of power and policy implementation. The two authors have applied general theory more simply, first to welfare policy in M. Hill, *Understanding Social Policy* (1980) and then to the NHS in C. Ham, *Health Policy in Britain* (1982). Another general introduction is J. Dearlove and P. Saunders, *Introduction to British Politics* (1984). The classic work on bureaucracy is M. Albrow, *Bureaucracy* (1970), whilst general criticism of the civil service is summarised in P. Kellner and Lord Crowther-Hunt, *The Civil Servants* (1980) and, considerably more wittily, in G. Kaufman, *How to be a Minister* (1980). The Treasury in the early post-war years is best analysed in S. Brittan, *Steering the Economy* (1969) and more recently, and conversationally, in H. Young and A. Sloman, *But Chancellor* (1984).

The standard work on the economics of welfare policy is A. J. Culyer, *The Political Economy of Social Policy* (1980). Two more accessible recent works are N. Barr, *The Economics of the Welfare State* (1987), which contains non-technical summaries to the theoretical chapters, and R. Levacic, *Economic Policy-Making* (1987). An interesting dialogue between an economist and a social administrator, with particular emphasis on microeconomic policy, is S. Charles and A. Webb, *The Economic Approach to Social Policy* (1986).

Part II

The Classic Welfare State, 1945–75

4 The Historical Context

The empirical analysis of welfare policy, as argued in Part I, needs to be informed by competing theoretical interpretations of the nature of both the welfare state and policymaking. It also needs to be placed in historical context. It is all too tempting to consider the overall development of policy – or to judge the relative success or failure of an individual policy – in isolation and according to some internal logic. Indeed a belief in incrementalism encourages this. However, it must be recognised that welfare policy was subject to external forces to which successive governments, distracted by other problems, responded within the constraints of what was deemed to be administratively and politically possible. The purpose of this chapter is to identify these various constraints and influences. What, in particular, was the economic context in which welfare policy developed and to what demographic pressures was it subject? Who held political power and how did this affect the priority accorded to welfare policy? How did the machinery of government, at central and local levels, adapt to the more positive welfare role which the state had assumed? How receptive was public opinion, as represented by vested interests and the electorate, to the duties as well as the rights imposed by state welfare?

The evolution of the NHS underlines the importance of such questions. The crisis which resulted in Bevan's resignation from the Labour Cabinet in 1951 was triggered not just by its own unexpectedly high costs but also by the restrictions placed on welfare expenditure by inflation and the trebling of defence expenditure occasioned by the outbreak of the Korean War in June 1950. The incoming Conservative government accorded the NHS a lower political priority, with the result that the minister of health did not sit in Cabinet for the rest of the 1950s. Its longer-term needs were not given serious consideration until the early 1960s when, in a new mood of planning, there was the coincidence of a new minister, a new permanent secretary to the ministry and a new chief medical officer. These needs revolved around the demographic problem of an ageing population but the most cost-effective response – community rather than institutional care – was rejected. This was in part because of the political power of hospital consultants, but also because of the perceived administrative and financial weakness of local government. It was this same perceived weakness which, as much as socialist ideology, had lain behind the original decision in 1948 to nationalise the hospital service. To understand fully, therefore, the nature and pace of change within the NHS, the historians must be alive to the economic, political, administrative and social contexts in which it developed.

4.1   THE ECONOMIC CONTEXT

The performance of the economy is clearly a major influence on both the development and the ultimate nature of welfare policy. A high level of employment, as Beveridge recognised, is the best guarantor of individual welfare. Also, by reducing the demand for cash benefits and simultaneously generating increased wealth, it provides the resources which can enable welfare policy to expand and diversify. Unemployment, conversely, by concentrating an increased proportion of diminishing resources on basic income support inhibits the development of other policies. Equally essential to the expansion and diversification of policy is economic growth. Financially it keeps government revenue buoyant as taxable income and profits increase. Politically it enables high levels of taxation to be levied with relative ease, because taxation is more likely to be resisted – and hence the financing of welfare policy jeopardised – when it threatens an anticipated rise, or even an absolute fall, in income. This was well recognised by the democratic socialists, one of whose basic assumptions (as summarised by Donnison) was that 'the pursuit of social justice' was dependent on the 'engines of economic growth which would produce the resources to create a fairer society without anyone suffering on the way'.[1]

The expansion of welfare policy was therefore greatly assisted by the unprecedented and consistently high levels of employment and economic growth throughout the period 1945–75. A definition of 'full employment' has never been universally agreed. In the 1940s Keynes suggested an ideal of 5 per cent unemployment whilst, between 1942 and 1944, Beveridge reduced his target from 8.5 per cent to 3 per cent. The latter figure alone was exceeded as an annual average, and then only marginally, on four occasions before 1975: in 1947, 1971–2 and 1975 when the highest figure (4.1 per cent) was recorded. By contrast the comparable figure for the interwar years had been 10.9 per cent with annual averages ranging from 7.4 to 17 per cent of the total workforce.[2] Equally impressive was the record of economic growth, with GDP doubling in real terms between 1948 and 1973 at an average annual rate of 2.8 per cent. The corresponding average for the 40 years before the First World War had been below 2.2 per cent and that for the years between 1924 and 1937 only 2.2 per cent. The detailed record was: 1950–5, 2.9 per cent; 1955–60, 2.5 per cent; 1960–4, 3.1 per cent; 1964–9, 2.5 per cent; 1969–73, 3.0 per cent. These figures reveal that growth was at its fastest in the first half of each decade.[3]

Such major achievements did not mean however, that welfare policy was unaffected by economic constraints of both a regular and a random nature. The aggregate figures cited above concealed certain disturbing trends. National figures for unemployment hide higher regional averages. Throughout the 1950s, for instance, unemployment averaged 7.7 per cent in Northern Ireland. Average economic growth was also half that of the EEC and so British governments had relatively fewer – and increasingly fewer – resources to devote to welfare policy. Of more immediate short-term importance were random shocks to the economy, such as the outbreak of the Korean War in June 1950 and the quadrupling of oil prices between 1972–4. Both fuelled inflation and required a reordering of expenditure priorities, with the result that ceilings had to be placed on public expenditure – such as that imposed on the NHS in 1951. There were also five major economic cycles between 1951 and 1972, during which governments sought to expand or contract public expenditure (in 'go' and 'stop' phases) in order to boost economic activity or to control it. Welfare expenditure was by no means the only component of public expenditure, and private consumption and investment were also constantly varied by budget changes to taxes and allowances; but welfare policy and, in particular, capital expenditure were frequently affected. The timing of the peaks and troughs in these respective economic cycles is therefore important to a full understanding of welfare policy and they are summarised in Table 4.1.

There were accordingly expansionary budgets in 1953, 1959, 1963 and 1972, the last two stimulating periods of economic growth known respectively as the Maudling and Barber booms, after the then Conservative chancellors.

There was no equivalent budget in 1968. Rather there was a severe deflationary package which included, amongst other things, the reintroduction of prescription charges (which the Labour government had withdrawn on its return to office in 1964). Retrenchment was

Table 4.1 Postwar economic cycles, 1951–73

Peak	Trough
1951 (i)	1952 (iii)
1955 (iv)	1958 (iii)
1960 (iii)	1963 (i)
1965 (i)	1967 (iii)
1969 (i)	1972 (i)
1973 (ii)	

Roman numerals identify the relevant quarter of the year.
Source: S. Pollard, *The Development of the British Economy* (1983) p. 422.

necessitated by the devaluation of the pound in November 1967; this underlines another constant check on welfare policy throughout this period – a series of interrelated balance of payments and sterling crises of which the devaluation of 1967 was merely an extreme example. Each crisis required government action to reduce domestic demand and thereby to discourage imports, encourage exports and reassure foreign bankers. Before 1964, as Table 4.2 illustrates, there had been isolated packages of economic cuts such as the September measures of 1957 and the Little Budget of 1961. What the table particularly highlights, however, are the annual crises which so constrained the Labour government in the 1960s.

The final major economic constraint on welfare expenditure was inflation. Before 1972 inflation was not particularly severe, although contemporary expectation – expecially in the 1950s – was that there should be no price increases at all. During the Korean War, admittedly, it was severe with prices rising by 20 per cent between 1949 and 1951; but between 1945 and 1963 prices rose on average by only 3.7 per cent per annum, and between 1964 and 1972 by only 5.4 per cent. Then inflation took off as the following price rises indicate: 1973–4, 16.1 per cent; 1974–5, 23.1 per cent; 1975–6, 16.3 per cent. Economists have identified many causes of inflation and prominent amongst them is welfare policy. The maintenance of full employment both strengthens the bargaining position of trade unions for increased wages and creates excess demand in the economy (cost-push and demand-pull inflation). Social security benefits provide an ever higher floor from which unions can start their negotiations. Finally, government borrowing to finance public expenditure can increase money supply. Before 1975, therefore, cuts in (or at least a slowing down in the rise of) public expenditure were recommended as an

Table 4.2 Major stimuli to economic expansion and contraction, 1947–74

	'Stop'	'Go'
1947 Aug.	Convertibility crisis	
1948–50		Marshall Aid
1949 Sept.	Devaluation	
1950 June	Korean War (to 1952)	
- - - - - - - - - -		
1953 April		Budget +£100–150m
1955 April		Budget +£156m
- - - - - - - - - -		
1955 Oct.	Autumn budget −£113m	
1956 Dec.	Suez	
1957 Sept.	Sterling crisis: September measures	
1959 April		Budget +£360m
1960 June	Balance of payments crisis	
1961 July	Sterling crisis: Little budget	
- - - - - - - - - -		
1962 Feb.	IMF loan	NEDC announces 4% growth target
1963 April		Budget +£450m: Maudling boom
━━━━━━━━		
1964 Nov.	Balance of payments crisis: IMF loan	
- - - - - - - - - -		
1965 June	Sterling crisis	
1965 Sept.		National Plan published
1966 July	Sterling crisis: July measures	
1967 Nov.	Devaluation	
1968 March	Budget −£923m	
- - - - - - - - - -		
1969 April	Budget −£340m	
1971 March		Budget +£256m
1972 April		Budget +£1211m: the Barber boom
1972 July		£ floated
- - - - - - - - - -		
1973 Oct.	OPEC oil price rises	
1973 Dec.	Public expenditure cuts	
━━━━━━━━		
1974 Feb.		Social Contract
1974 March	Healey budget	

Unbroken lines denote change of government, dotted lines peaks of the economic cycle. Figures for the budget specify the extent to which *The Economist* estimated it expanded or contracted the economy.

antidote to inflation, most significantly by Thorneycroft before his unprecedented resignation as chancellor in January 1958 and by Healey in his 1975 budget.

The broad economic climate was therefore highly favourable to the expansion and diversification of welfare expenditure between 1945 and 1955, although there were short-term constraints imposed by cyclical downturns in the economy, balance of payments crises and inflation. Because of the political difficulties that might be incurred, current expenditure on, for example, cash benefits was rarely cut, although its increase, in line with either public expectations or inflation, might be delayed. Capital expenditure (such as the building and equipment of hospitals) was more permanently affected because its contraction raised fewer immediate protests and its expansion took longer to plan and execute. Certainly short-term fluctuations may be seen to have hampered the stable development of welfare policy which the continuation of full employment and economic growth might have been expected to – and elsewhere in Europe did – facilitate.

4.2 THE DEMOGRAPHIC CONTEXT

If the performance of the economy ultimately determines the level of resources available to welfare policy, demographic change has a major influence on the level of demand – regardless of any improvements in the standard of service. All periods are 'victims' of the birth rate of some twenty and sixty years before, as those generations reach child-bearing and retirement age. Any variation in their own birthrates will also affect successively the cost of family support and of education, the demand for housing, the nature of the labour market and, ultimately, the cost of pensions and hospital care. The demand for all these services will also be progressively affected by improvements in the death rate. Consistency of trends of demographic change is therefore clearly desirable both to prevent fluctuations in demand for services with fixed costs, such as education, and to provide an even balance between those within the workforce (generating wealth) and those outside (consuming it). There was no such consistency between 1945 and 1975.

Given the consistently falling birth rate during the interwar period, an unexpected source of postwar instability was the annual variation

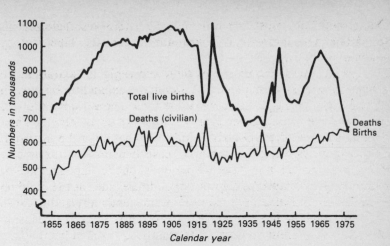

Source: J.F. Ermish, *The Political Economy of Demographic Change* (1983) p. 6.

Figure 4.1 Birth and death rates, 1855–1975

in the number of births – and in particular the baby booms of 1942–7 and 1955–65 (see Figure 4.1).

The unsettling consequence for education, for instance, was a sudden increase in demand for primary education in 1947, for secondary education in 1952 and for higher education in the late 1950s. Demand then fell away successively until the cycle was restarted in the 1960s, only to be halted once again in the early 1970s.

Many explanations have been advanced for the baby booms. Falls in the number of women never marrying, in the average age at marriage and in the mother's average age at the birth of her first child were common to both periods, and were especially important after 1955 to counteract the impact of the low interwar birthrate which had decreased the number of potential parents. In the 1940s parenthood was also encouraged by greater confidence in the future and a decrease in the economic disincentives to having children (such as rationing and tax changes which diverted resources to families). Between 1955 and 1965 increasing affluence again enabled couples to have children without seriously reducing their living standards. However, by the later 1960s slower economic growth was starting to disappoint people's increasing expectations. Childbirth also meant loss of income for women, who were becoming increasingly accustomed to working for relatively high wages. The economic disincentives of childbirth were therefore returning, and they helped to increase both the average age at marriage and (with the help of the newly introduced contraceptive pill) the age at which mothers had their first child. This trend did not necessarily indicate the desire for smaller families, merely their later conception; but in the short term it led to a dramatic fall in the annual birth rate.

A falling birth rate had been one of the great fears of the 1940s. Beveridge, for example, had advocated state support for children by such means as family allowances – and such policies had become politically acceptable – because it was projected that the population would go into absolute decline by the late 1960s. This danger was obviously averted. The population of Great Britain rose from 48.9 million to 60 million between the censuses of 1951 and 1971, with the number of children under fifteen rising to 12.9 million or 23.7 per cent of the population rather than Beveridge's estimate of 7.6 million or 16.5 per cent of the population. However the other main fear of the 1940s, the ageing of the population through a decrease in the death rate, did come to dominate policy. This was not so much because significantly more people were living into *advanced* old age, but rather because fewer people were dying at a younger age – life expectancy at birth for men rose from 66.5 years to 70 years between 1930 and 1977, whilst life expectancy at 65 remained almost constant at 77.[4]

This ageing of the population put an ever-increasing strain on the hospital and welfare services, for which the elderly (and in particular those over 75) were the major clients.[5] Most political concern how-ever was concentrated upon pensions, where the practice in Britain – as elsewhere – was that payments were financed not from a fund into which pensioners had paid throughout their lifetimes but directly from the contributions of those in work (pay as you go). The relative size of the labour force, however, was declining, because the large number of people born when the birth rate was high betwen 1890 and 1915 were retiring from employment, to be replaced by the smaller number born in the interwar period. This demographic shrinkage of the workforce clearly had serious implications; and one of the major reasons why earnings-related pensions became politically desirable in the late 1950s was that the higher earnings-related contributions could be collected from those in work, whilst earnings-related pensions would not have to be paid in full for a further twenty years – by which time the workforce would again be expanding as a result of the postwar baby booms.

The problem of pensions highlights the major impact of demographic change on welfare policy and economic growth: the variation in the number of 'non-productive' young and elderly people who are dependent on the wealth created by those of working age. The changing age structure of postwar Britain is summarised in Table 4.3, with the 'dependency ratio' expressed as a percentage both of those of working age (column 4) and, more significantly, of those actually working (column 5). Figures for 1911 have also been included to show that although the postwar dependency ratio was 'deteriorating', it was only reverting to that prevailing at the turn of the century. However, there was a dramatic change in the causes of dependency, with a relative decline in the number of children and a relative increase in those aged over 65. In 1911, for instance, there were 12.3 people of working age to support each person over 65; by 1971 there were only 3.6 (column 6). Such changes in the dependency ratio were clearly a major factor behind the increased need for welfare expenditure after 1945, although their potentially damaging consequences for economic growth could be countered by improvements both in the productivity of the workforce and in the employment ratio of those of working age. A major reservoir of untapped labour was indeed found in married women, whose participation in the labour market (often on a part-time basis only) rose from 10 per cent to 43 per cent between 1931 and 1971.

Two other demographic factors which had a significant impact on policy were changes in household structure and migration. A rise in the number of people living alone, especially amongst the elderly, is likely to increase demand for health and welfare services (although neighbours or nearby relations may be able to provide support when needed). Similarly a rise in the number of one-parent families is likely to increase demand for transfer payments. Both trends developed after 1945.[6] The number of people living alone rose from 1.8 per cent to 6.3 per cent of the population between 1931 and 1971. Meanwhile the number of divorces accelerated from an annual average of 7335 in 1936–40 to 32 168 in 1951–5 and 121 772 in 1971–5. This, in part, resulted from the introduction of legal aid in 1948 and the Divorce Act of 1969, which made divorce more financially and legally practicable. Rates of remarriage remained high, but by 1976 it was nevertheless estimated that 1.25 million (or 9 per cent) of all dependent children were living in one-parent families. A further

Table 4.3 Demographic change, 1911–71

	Age structure (%)			Dependency ratios		
	(1) 0–14	(2) 15–64	(3) 65+	(4) % of population of working age	(5) % of working population	(6) ratio of population of working age to pensioner
1911	30.6	64.2	5.2	55.8	60.2	12.3
1951	22.1	66.8	11.0	49.6	56.1	4.7
1961	23.0	65.1	11.9	53.6	60.9	4.2
1971	23.7	62.9	13.3	58.8	66.6	3.6

Figures for columns 1–4 and 6 are for England and Wales only. Column 5 refers to Britain as a whole.
Sources: A. H. Halsey (ed.), British Social Trends (1988) pp. 106, 127; J. Ermisch, The Political Economy of Demographic Change (1983) p. 14.

important change in household structure was a reduction in household size, from 4.1 in 1931 to 2.7 by 1971, as younger people sought – and were able to finance – a home of their own. To facilitate this change, the housing stock had to expand faster than the population.

Migration can also generate demand for welfare expenditure. The continuation of the interwar drift of the population to the South and the Midlands and then, from the 1960s, an accelerating exodus from urban areas made social services redundant in certain regions, whilst requiring their replacement elsewhere. Such movement had, for example, a greater impact than population change on the increase in house-building in the South and, by reducing the number of children in inner city areas, forced the closure of schools.

International migration was of less significance nationally, although of considerable political and local importance. Immigration from the West Indies peaked in the early 1960s and from the Indian sub-continent in 1968. Thereafter it was constrained by the Commonwealth Immigrants Acts of 1962, 1968 and 1971. Throughout the period it led to an increase in the aggregate population only in the late 1950s; and the net impact of emigration and immigration appears to have had little effect on either the gender or occupational balance of the population as a whole.[7] Increased coloured migration did however necessitate the introduction of race relations legislation in the 1960s, and in certain localities the concentration of immigrants with different languages and cultural values (such as the acceptance of large and one-parent families, respectively, amongst Asian and West Indian communities) created particular problems. The increased concentration of resources on the personal social services and on inner city areas by the Labour governments between 1964 and 1970 was one of the considered policy responses.

4.3 THE POLITICAL CONTEXT

The ultimate responsibility for the development of welfare policy in the face of such economic and demographic pressure fell not to disinterested experts (as Beveridge and Keynes appeared sometimes to assume) but to party politicians. The ideological differences between the Labour and Conservative Parties, which shared power after 1945, have already been discussed in Chapter 2.2. Welfare policy however was also shaped by personal and ideological tensions within both parties as well as by short-term electoral calculations and competition – for both attention and scarce resources – from other policies.

Six of the first ten postwar elections were won by the Labour Party, which was consequently in power for thirteen years between 1945 and 1975 (see Table 4.4). There was, as noted in Chapter 2.2.2, an underlying popular sympathy throughout the period with democratic socialist ideals concerning the welfare state, but this was not fully capitalised upon by successive Labour governments. To some extent this was due to sheer bad luck. Each of Labour's periods in office coincided with economic crises (not solely of the government's making) that were so severe that the pound had to be devalued in 1949 and 1968, and a loan sought from the IMF in 1976. Circumstances were therefore not favourable to the expansion of welfare expenditure. Moreover, in 1960 and 1963 there occurred the premature deaths of the party's deputy leader and leader, Bevan and Gaitskell. Both were passionately committed to the achievement of a more egalitarian society and had respectively the charisma and the technocratic expertise to consolidate, in the wake of the 'economic miracles' abroad, public acceptance for greater state intervention and to implement it successfully.

Earlier, however, both Bevan and Gaitskell had compounded Labour's misfortunes by exacerbating the ideological differences within the Party, which compromised its electoral image in the 1950s and were to do so again after 1970. The essence of the dispute was the speed and ultimate objective of socialist policy. Was socialism an ethical 'crusade' to ensure that those in power within a mixed economy acted with 'social responsibility' and thereby gradually achieved a more equal society; or was its objective the more direct and immediate transfer of economic, and hence political, power from the market to the state? The key policy-issue was nationalisation. The Attlee government between 1945 and 1951 had nationalised some 20 per cent of the economy; but neither the economic performance nor the managerial efficiency of the relevant industries had been noticeably improved and public opinion polls showed nationalisation to be electorally unpopular. The 'consolidationists' within the Party accordingly sought to postpone any further nationalisation. Then, after the publication in 1956 of Crosland's *The Future of Socialism*, the revisionists argued that nationalisation was only a means to an end and that the objective of egalitarianism could be better achieved by other means, such as educational reform. Such

Table 4.4 Election results, 1945–74

| | Labour | | Conservatives | | Others | Elected |
	Seats	% vote	Seats	% vote	Seats	prime minister
1945 July	393	47.8	213	39.8	34	Attlee
1950 Feb.	315	46.1	299	43.5	11	Attlee
1951 Oct.	295	48.8	321	48.0	9	Churchill
1955 May	277	46.4	345	49.7	8	Eden
1959 Oct.	258	43.8	365	49.4	7	Macmillan
1964 Oct.	317	44.1	304	43.4	9	Wilson
1966 Mar.	363	47.9	253	41.9	14	Wilson
1970 June	288	43.0	330	46.4	12	Heath
1974 Feb.	301	37.1	297	37.9	37	Wilson
1974 Oct.	319	39.2	277	35.8	39	Wilson

The dividing lines denote changes of government. The number of seats was reduced from 640 to 625 in 1950, but was increased by five in 1955 and 1974.
Source: D. and G. Butler, *British Political Facts, 1900–1985* (1986) pp. 226–7.

views were anathema to the 'fundamentalists' under Bevan and then to the various splinter groups of the New Left after 1957. On broad Marxist lines, they argued that without a direct transfer of economic power to the state there could be – in the words of the official 1973 *Labour Programme* – no 'fundamental shift in the balance of power and wealth to working people and their families'.

The dispute had serious consequences for the Labour Party. It totally disrupted, through the thirteen years the Party spent in opposition between 1951 and 1964, the serious planning of, and agreement with the trade unions on, a programme for the modernisation of Britain, for which the electorate was calling by the early 1960s. It also publicly discredited the Party at the very time it needed to reinforce the core of its 'working-class' support, which was being eroded by increasing affluence and the consequent shift, for example, from manual work and council tenancy to white-collar work and owner-occupancy. A disciplined programme of reform, extending state intervention over the economy and the distribution of wealth, could have won and retained new members. Instead, there was the spectacle of the bitter battles between Gaitskell and both the party's National Executive Committee (NEC) and Conference over the repeal of Clause 4 of the Party's constitution (the commitment to the 'common ownership of the means of production, distribution and exchange') and unilateral nuclear disarmament.[8] These battles revealed another key feature of the Labour Party: the deliberate location of the power to determine policy in the annual conference and, between conferences, in the NEC. Since the trade unions controlled, with their block votes, five-sixths of the votes at Conference and two-thirds of the seats on the NEC, this gave the public impression that the party leader was controlled by a powerful interest group – which appeared simultaneously to oppose economic growth and greater equality through its defence of 'restrictive practices' and the wage differentials of skilled workers.

It was factors such as these that prevented the Party from becoming, as many anticipated, the 'natural party of government' with the opportunity to develop the welfare state along social democratic – and possibly Swedish – lines. Indeed four of its election victories (in 1950, 1964 and twice in 1974) were so narrow that it was only between 1945 and 1950 and between 1966 and 1970 that Labour governments had a sufficiently comfortable parliamentary majority to pass controversial legislation. Nevertheless the welfare state bears the hallmarks of those two governments, especially the Attlee government of 1945–50. This government has been criticised, with some justice, for being conservative and backward looking. For instance, in his national broadcast on the Appointed Day of 5 July 1948 (the 'official birthday' of the welfare state, when both the NHS and the national insurance scheme came into operation) Attlee chose not to herald the dawn of a new egalitarian age, but to describe the reforms uncontroversially as

the culmination of effort made by all the people of this country over forty years or more to build together a social structure of mutual provision for contingencies, which if they were all left to face them alone, would overwhelm some and leave the confidence of others a prey to anxiety and fear.[9]

Nevertheless his government's incontrovertible achievement was to ensure the integrity of democratic institutions (when they came under genuine threat) and to pass an unprecedented range of economic and social legislation in the face of mounting economic crises and discouraging advice. Similar crises and advice had led in 1921 to the Geddes Axe and the abandonment of many reconstruction promises made during the First World War. With a different government that experience might well have been repeated. Instead the Attlee administration honoured the trust it felt it owed its pre-war supporters and the 1945 electors; and it established, in the words of Kenneth Morgan, 'the essential basis for future advance'.[10]

The 1966–70 Wilson government (which many expected to secure this advance) is widely considered, in contrast, to have betrayed the trust placed upon it to manage the economy more efficiently and to effect a greater measure of social equality. It inherited, as has been seen, an economic crisis and relentless demographic pressure on both the education system and pensions. It was also undermined by bitter personal rivalries, fomented in the 1950s, which the pragmatism – or short-term expediency – favoured by an increasingly paranoid Prime Minister did little to resolve. By taking the wrong strategic decisions (such as the unsuccessful three-year battle to avert devaluation) and, above all, by failing to ensure that increases in public expenditure achieved commensurate results, the government undoubtedly did much to discredit the efficacy of state intervention. Nevertheless it was essentially a humane government which passed much liberal legislation (on, for example, family planning, divorce and equal pay) and directed extra resources to the underprivileged (through increased expenditure on the personal social services and better publicised cash benefits). It was only an increase in the number of the underprivileged, largely for demographic reasons, and the exaggerated hopes of its supporters that have obscured this latter achievement.

The Wilson governments of 1974–6 were potentially even more important, with the formal agreement by the trade unions of a social contract in which increases in welfare benefits ('the social wage') were accepted as a *quid pro quo* for lower rises in industrial wages. Here indeed was the opportunity to forge an alliance on Swedish lines. However, the political stalemate arising from the inconclusive election of February 1974, and then from the Cabinet's unprecedented 'agreement to disagree' during the referendum on Britain's continuing membership of the EEC in 1975, paralysed the policy's implementation whilst inflation escalated.

The Conservative Party won only four elections before 1975 but each of its victories secured a working majority in relatively favourable economic circumstances. Consequently its seventeen years in office (uninterrupted from 1951 to 1964 and between 1970 and 1974) provided it with a major opportunity to influence welfare policy; but this influence was somewhat ambivalent because, as noted in Chapter 2.2.1, there was an inherent tension within the party between a fundamental belief in the virtues of the market and an awareness of its past failing. This tension was a source of internal political divisions which, although they did not match in either public or personal bitterness those within the Labour Party (at least until the mid-1970s), led to the unprecedented resignation of the chancellor of the exchequer in 1958 on the issue of 'excessive' welfare expenditure.

The essence of this dispute was the balance to be struck between the free market and state intervention. Most Conservatives sought to reduce taxation in order to maximise personal incentive and choice; but reduced taxation required reduced public expenditure and this, the moderates feared, would jeopardise both the Party's electoral support and the cooperation of the trade unions, which was essential for the achievement of higher production. The 'economic liberals' (who were increasingly in the 1960s to swell the ranks of the New Right) dismissed such arguments as unprincipled expediency but, in their own determination to restore market forces, they were in turn accused of acting on narrow class lines and of being politically naïve.[11] A balance was maintained between these opposing views until the mid-1950s, when the creation of the Institute of Economic

Affairs in 1955 and the chancellor's resignation in 1958 signified the economic liberals' defeat.

Thorneycroft's resignation well illustrated the crux of the dispute. In order to reassure foreign bankers and to control inflation, he wished to place a strict ceiling on public expenditure regardless of the political and social cost. His proposals included a £76 million package of cuts in welfare expenditure including, critically, the withdrawal of family allowance from the second child. This the Cabinet ultimately rejected on both political and practical grounds. Politically, as Macmillan argued, government 'in modern society' had an 'inescapable obligation to large sections of the community, the evasion of which would be both inequitable and unacceptable to public opinion'. In practice the proposals would be counter-productive – fuelling rather than reducing inflation because, in the real world of full employment, trade unions were likely to demand and secure compensatory wage increases. In 1949 all sections of the Party had combined to repudiate 'any suggestion that the deliberate creation of unemployment was necessary to maintain high production and industrial discipline'. This was the Achilles' heel of the economic liberals.[12]

The corresponding weakness of the moderates' policy, which was to remain predominant until the mid 1970s, was its inability to establish an incontrovertible link between state intervention and economic efficiency, which could both reassure the supporters and distinguish Conservative policy from that of Labour. There was no explicit statement of Conservative welfare policy after 1945. During the modernisation of policy under Butler in the late 1940s there was, for instance, no social services charter, only the famous *Industrial Charter* which committed the Party to both full employment and a code of good industrial practice in order to reinforce the security of industrial workers. Despite Butler's later preeminence, however, not even the *Industrial Charter* was implemented speedily. Little progress was made in either the voluntary or statutory implementation of this code until the early 1960s, when measures such as the Contracts of Employment Act (1963) and the Redundancy Payments Act (1965) were either enacted or planned.

The unofficial backbench One Nation group did seek to fill the void.[13] 'Economic and social policies must be so balanced', it argued, 'that they reinforce one another. The creation of more wealth must lead to better social conditions, and better social conditions to greater production.' More specifically, social security benefits were not condemned as demoralising but rather welcomed as providing a guaranteed minimum income and thereby enlarging freedom and security: 'such freedom and such security are the basis of a responsible society – and not its enemy'. Housing and education policy were also highlighted as particularly beneficial to economic growth through their potential to create a mobile and trained workforce. However, on its own admission the group never succeeded in fully squaring the circle of market economics and state welfare. This dilemma was nowhere more apparent than in the proposals of two of its original members, Macleod and Powell, to reduce and more effectively target social expenditure by abandoning universal benefits in favour of selectivity. Such a policy, both acknowledged, would require the extension of the means test which in the real world was both electorally unpopular and administratively inefficient.

Similar problems were encountered by another of the original members when, as party leader in the late 1960s and prime minister in the early 1970s, Heath sought to plan and implement a policy which could reconcile a return to 'market forces' with interventionist social policies. Consequently, just as the Labour Party had failed to take the hard decisions which had enabled the Swedish SDP to reach an accommodation with the unions on the creation of a more egalitarian society, so the Conservative Party failed – unlike the Christian Democrats in West Germany – to identify the means by which welfare policy could constructively support the market economy.

The Conservatives' terms in office can be divided into three phases. Following their traumatic defeat in 1945 and their failure to win any by-elections before 1951, the Party was convinced of – if not wholly converted to – the need to guarantee full employment and maintain the broad structure of the welfare state, as established by the Attlee government. The administrations headed by Churchill (1951 to April 1955) and Eden (1955 to January 1957) were largely content to confound the Labour Party's prediction that they would create mass unemployment, abandon the welfare state and antagonise the trade unions. Any distinctive innovations were the result not of a coherent strategy but of the initiative of individual ministers such as Macmillan and Eden who sought, respectively, to honour the election pledge to build 300 000 houses per annum and to expand technical education.

With a paramount need to rebuild party morale after the Suez debacle, Macmillan did not revert to market forces (as Thorneycroft's resignation testifies) but sought to develop an 'opportunity' as opposed to a 'welfare' state – in which state intervention encouraged individual responsibility and effort by such means as tax incentives for house ownership and earnings-related benefits. The realisation of Britain's relative decline also precipitated greater economic planning with, most notably, the creation of the National Economic Development Council at which government could meet with the two sides of industry to discuss the future rate of economic growth (and, by implication, the future boundaries of public expenditure). These attempts to revitalise Britain ended in disillusion and disarray. The 1960 balance of payments crisis tarnished the government's reputation for managerial efficiency, while France's rejection of Britain's application to join the EEC in 1963 halted the momentum of modernisation. Politically, Macmillan's dismissal of one-third of the Cabinet in July 1962 betrayed panic; and the scramble for the leadership after his resignation in 1963, amid various sex and spy scandals, was uncharacteristically undignified. His eventual replacement by the fourteenth Earl of Home, under whom Macleod and Powell refused to serve, also did little to further the image of a 'modern' party. Therefore, while many of the reforms inaugurated by Macmillan were highly appropriate for the 'developmental' state which – in the wake of the economic miracles abroad – he was trying to establish, their implementation ultimately lacked cohesion and conviction.

This was a weakness which Heath deliberately set out to remedy through the creation, while he was leader of the opposition between 1965 and 1970, of over thirty policy committees. As a result his government was one of the best prepared of all postwar governments; but the philosophy underlying its proposals had been neglected in favour of technocratic reform and no fall-back position had been prepared should unforeseen difficulties arise – as they certainly did with the rise in unemployment to over one million, the intransigence of the trade unions and finally the quadrupling of oil prices in October 1973. Consequently the government was characterised by spectacular 'U' turns in policy and ended with the miners' strike and the three-day week. Having sought to modernise every area of British society, from the reform of industrial relations to the restructuring of the health service and local government, it left possibly 'the fewest policy legacies of any post-war government'.[14]

Apart from the unresolved disputes and the shifting balance of power within each of the governing parties, welfare policy was fashioned by two other political factors. The first was elections.

During this period a 'political' cycle developed as a result of the manipulation of the economy to provide a climate favourable to the government during the run-up to a general election. The Labour government to their credit – but also to their cost – declined to act in such a way in 1950 and 1970; but during the Conservatives' terms of office there were expansionary budgets in 1955 and 1959, and a delay to deflation in 1964, which were not wholly justified by conventional economic indicators. Welfare policy could also be paralysed by inconclusive elections, such as those of 1974, and stimulated by by-elections or, more regularly, local government elections.

The second factor was the need for welfare policy to compete, for both the Cabinet's attention and scarce resources, with other areas of policy. This was especially true of foreign affairs and defence where, apart from the outbreak of actual hostilities such as the Korean War (1950–2) and the Suez campaign (November to December 1956), there were four predominant issues: the Cold War, decolonisation, entry into the EEC and Northern Ireland. The problem of Northern Ireland seriously distracted the Heath administration, whilst entry into the EEC created major divisions within both parties after 1960 and helped to paralyse the Wilson government in 1975. Over a longer period, the largely successful retreat from Empire (principally from the Indian sub-continent in the 1940s and from Africa and the Caribbean after 1960) also exhausted ministers and created particular problems for the Macmillan government when it had to seek support for its modernisation programme from irate backbenchers.

Throughout the whole period, however, the most serious demands on the Cabinet's time and on resources came from the escalation of the Cold War (from the Berlin blockade of 1948–9 to Russia's invasion of Czechoslovakia in 1968) and of the arms race. They diverted the attention of successive prime ministers, without whose involvement and encouragement no radical innovation in welfare policy could succeed. Attlee, for example, was involved in the creation of NATO, whilst Macmillan pioneered the concept of 'summit' meetings to reduce the threat of nuclear war. They also consumed scarce manpower and financial resources. To contain communism, as well as to protect essential supplies such as oil, Britain maintained sizeable forces in the Middle and Far East, as well as in Europe, until the withdrawal from East of Suez in 1968. It also developed its own independent nuclear deterrent. This was portrayed in the mid-1950s as a cheap alternative to conventional weapons; but it diverted highly skilled manpower from civilian production, became increasingly expensive with the greater sophistication of weaponry, and was unable in practice to replace conventional weapons in regionalised conflicts. It is true that defence expenditure (although higher than that of trading rivals such as Germany and Japan) did decline considerably as a percentage of GDP throughout the period, thus releasing resources for welfare policy. Individual policies such as social security and education came indeed to exceed defence in overall cost (see Appendix 1, Table A1.3).[15] The continuing competition for resources between defence and welfare policy, however, is a salutary reminder that, to achieve a full understanding, welfare policy should never be studied in isolation.

The period from 1945 to 1975 has been conventionally portrayed as one of political consensus. This is justified in relation to the basic framework of welfare policy, where there was a continuing all-party commitment to the mixed economy, the maintenance of full employment and a minimum standard of social security. However, there was bitter animosity between the two major parties (perhaps because their policies appeared so similar) as well as fundamental differences in their underlying philosophies even when, as in 1962, they appeared to be converging on a policy of modernisation.[16] Labour's priority was to engineer a more equal society through greater state intervention and, if necessary, higher taxation. The Conservatives were willing only to accept that degree of intervention and taxation which was compatible with market efficiency and personal initiative. Neither strategy, however, was developed to its logical conclusion – as in Sweden or West Germany. This was in part because of both parties' serious internal divisions and other distractions; but it was also, as will be seen, the result of advice emanating from the civil service and of the perceived wishes of the electorate.

4.4 THE ADMINISTRATIVE CONTEXT

Both political parties were dependent for the successful formulation and implementation of policy upon the administrative capability of the civil service and local government. As has been seen in Chapter 3.1, there are many ways in which bureaucracy can influence – and even determine – policy; and so it was of major significance for welfare policy that, in the early 1960s, both the traditional ethos of the civil service and the structure of local government were widely regarded as obsolete. This was, in particular, the view of two exhaustive enquiries appointed at the height of the campaign to 'modernise' Britain: the Fulton Committee on the Civil Service (1966–8) and the Redcliffe-Maud Royal Commission on Local Government in England (1966–9).

The conviction of the Fulton Committee was that the civil service had singularly failed to adapt to the transfer of the state's responsibilities from the 'passive and regulatory' to the 'active and positive'. As it argued:

> To meet these new tasks of government the modern Civil Service must be able to handle the social, economic, scientific and technical problems of our time, in an international setting. Because the solutions to complex problems need long preparation, the Service must be far-sighted; from its accumulated knowledge and experience, it must show initiative in working out what are the needs of the future and how they might be met. A special responsibility now rests upon the Civil Service because one Parliament or even one Government often cannot see the process through.[17]

Instead the civil service was an introverted, poorly-managed, badly-structured and essentially amateur institution which was unable efficiently to discharge its existing responsibilities – let alone plan and execute new ones. In particular, officials lacked the essential economic, statistical and accountancy skills to manage efficiently the economy or major spending programmes such as the NHS. They lacked also the training and the vision, instilled into French civil servants by the École Nationale d'Administration, to plan and implement bold initiatives. They sought rather to maintain political consensus by preserving the *status quo*.

All these failings, as noted in Chapter 3.1.2, were characterised by the Treasury which had overall responsibility for the management of the civil service. Until the 1960s it employed few economists or statisticians. Its strategic vision was limited by the demands of an annual budget. It preferred to advise others rather than take any direct responsibility for the implementation of policy – ultimately welcoming demand management, for instance, because it required officials only to manipulate (as Marquand has observed) 'the controls on the economic dashboard' and not to 'lift the bonnet and dirty their hands in the engine'. Finally, its characteristic response to new economic initiatives – from the implementation of demand management in the 1940s to the programme analysis review in the 1970s –

was to give responsibility to officials who were sceptical of, rather than committed to, their success.[18]

The administrative failings identified by Fulton were all the more culpable because, as a result of the reforms forced upon it during the Second World War, the postwar civil service potentially had the skill and dynamism to respond immediately to the state's adoption of a more positive role. There was an effective blend of regular and irregular civil servants. Specialists had become accustomed to reporting directly to ministers. Management skills had been encouraged. A new generation of talented officials, who considered 'everything was achievable', was also vying for permanent appointment. 'Postwar Whitehall', as Hennessy has remarked, 'was *the* place to be for the young and clever with a high personal charge of public duty'.[19] However, by the early 1950s the irregulars had either left or lost their independence; specialists had been made subordinate to generalists; and the new generation was being trained, as policy-advisers, in the art of crisis avoidance rather than, as executive managers, in risk-taking.

The failings of the postwar civil service admittedly may not have been as comprehensive as its detractors averred. Ironically the appointment of the Fulton Committee itself delayed reforms that were already being implemented by the Treasury as the result of the more restrained yet equally radical recommendations of the 1961 Plowden Report.[20] Nor were any failings the sole responsibility of the civil service. Just as its successive heads paid insufficient attention to the machinery of government, so too did successive Cabinets – which was particularly surprising in the case of Labour Cabinets, which looked to the state and its officials, rather than to the market, for economic and social advance. There was also the genuine constitutional obstacle of ministerial responsibility, which demoralised officials by discouraging them from taking initiatives whilst adding to the ministerial 'overload' and thus led, inevitably, to hasty and ill-considered decisions. The Fulton Committee was noticeably reticent about the consequences for parliamentary democracy of officials' responsibility for policies which would take more than 'one Parliament or even one Government' to implement fully.

Nevertheless the consequence for welfare policy was that the civil service lacked the expertise and the vision to resolve those critical issues which both political parties failed to confront in opposition – whereas officials in Italy and France during the 1950s made good even more serious failings in national politics.[21] It also lacked the management expertise and drive to establish beyond doubt the efficacy of state intervention even in those areas where the market had demonstrably failed in the 1930s. An attempt was made to correct these failings in the early 1970s. In the wake of the Fulton Report, both business and personnel management within Whitehall were gradually improved. Heath also introduced such reforms as programme analysis review and the Central Policy Review Staff in order to keep the effectiveness of individual policies under continuous review and to fix the Cabinet's attention on broad strategic objectives. Under the pressure of external events, however, the Heath government became, ironically, the postwar government most characterised by 'U-turns' in policy and by ministerial 'overload'.

The period from 1945 to 1975 has also been portrayed as one of decline for local government. In the late 1940s the Attlee government deprived it of many traditional responsibilities (such as for gas and electricity) as well as newer ones (such as national assistance and hospitals). In the 1970s it also lost its residual health services and responsibility for water. Its financial dependence on Whitehall grew as the percentage of its income coming from central government grants rose from 30 per cent to 45 per cent. Its administrative dependence was well illustrated by the need after 1970 to seek approval from the Department of Health and Social Security for all appointments to the post of director of social services.

Conversely, the period has also been described as 'the years of greatest affluence for local government'.[22] Its aggregate expenditure trebled in real terms and consumed an ever greater percentage of GDP (see Appendix 1, Table A1.1). Its formal dependence on Whitehall may have grown but there remained, as argued in Chapter 3.1.3, considerable scope for independent action in the implementation of major spending programmes such as education and housing. Some legislation was even designed to encourage local variation; and in 1958 the major change in central government finance from specific to general grants, whilst placing a ceiling on Treasury commitments, reduced detailed supervision of expenditure. Moreover, as has been seen, Whitehall departments preferred to advise rather than to direct. The 1944 Education Act, for example, gave the Ministry of Education the constitutional power to 'control and direct' local education authorities, and yet there was the well-documented case of the Ministry's acquiescence in the refusal by Cardiff in the 1940s to fulfil its statutory obligation to abolish all-age schools.[23] Finally, during this period local government acquired many new responsibilities, especially in the area of the personal social services. It could therefore be argued that it was only in the mid 1970s, with the greater politicisation of local government and the perceived need to combat inflation through greater control of public expenditure, that the independence of local government came seriously under attack.

Wherever the real power lay, the quality of many welfare services still depended on the administrative capacity of local government; and this, at the time, was widely agreed to be defective. On the one hand there were serious doubts about the quality of administrative staff and councillors, internal management systems and the coordination of policy. There was a series of enquiries in the 1960s which led to later, and by no means wholly successful, experiments in corporate planning. Most significant for welfare policy was the report of the Seebohm Committee on Local Authority and Allied Personal Social Services (1965–8) which dismissed the existing specialist services of local authorities as 'irrelevant to people's problems' because they prevented all the problems facing one individual or family from being tackled collectively.[24] Hence the Report's recommendation, and the achievement in 1970, of a single social services department in each local authority. On the other hand there was the question of local government structure. The historical legacy of some 1500 authorities had resulted in an irrational system in which many authorites were too small for efficient administration. Moreover, the confusion of responsibilities between various highly antagonistic types of authority was demoralising administrators and the public alike.[25] County councils, for instance, were responsible for the personal social services in their areas (including the problem of homelessness), but they had no authority over the building or allocation of housing, which was the responsibility of the smaller district councils.

The nettle of local government reform was finally grasped in 1966 by the Redcliffe-Maud Royal Commission, and it provided as damning an indictment of the existing system as the Fulton Committee. It argued that:

> Each local authority should be responsible for a continuous area that makes, so far as practicable, a coherent social and economic whole, matching the way of life of a mobile society and giving the authority the space it needs to assess and tackle its problems. . . . Whether an authority is resolving people's housing problems, settling the pattern of schools and colleges, or providing personal services for families and individuals in need of care or help, it is

more likely to meet people's requirements and make most effective use of resources if its responsibility extends over the whole area that includes people's homes, the offices and factories they work in, the schools where their children are taught, the shops they buy their goods from and the places they go to for entertainment and recreation.[26]

Consequently it recommended the creation of 58 'unitary' authorities, containing no less than one-quarter of a million people and with sole responsibility for all the services in their area. Only in Manchester, Liverpool and Birmingham were these services, as in London, to be divided between two tiers of government. The Commission, however, fell victim to party politics. It had been commissioned by the Wilson government and had recommended, in essence, the extension throughout the country of the existing county boroughs (where the Labour Party was politically strong). This was rejected by the incoming Heath government because it would have effectively destroyed all the existing county councils (where the Conservative Party was strong). Heath's own Local Government Act, implemented in 1974, duly reduced the number and increased the size of local authorities on the ground of efficiency; but, largely for political reasons, it retained county councils and thus the two-tier system. This perpetuated the old administrative antagonisms and the damaging divisions between inter-related services. In the 47 non-metropolitan counties of England and Wales, for example, responsibility for the personal social services and housing continued to be divided between the county and its districts.

The quality of administration in both central and local government was not entirely without merit. At the centre there remained an exceptional degree of integrity (although locally the granting of planning permission and housing contracts did occasion several well-publicised, and presumably many unpublicised, cases of corruption). There was also much successful improvisation and innumerable individual examples of effective management. The sweeping criticisms of Fulton and Redcliffe-Maud should also be counter-balanced by their own admitted weaknesses.[27] Both ignored commissioned evidence when it contradicted their prior assumptions and, in the drive for technocratic efficiency, disregarded the political dimension of policymaking. Both reports, therefore, not only provided a vivid picture of the administrative weaknesses of both central and local government, which seriously hampered welfare policy at this time, but also reflected the continuing inability to resolve them.

4.5 THE CULTURAL CONTEXT

A final determinant of welfare policy is the prevailing cultural values of society, to which policymakers not only respond but of which they themselves are also an integral part. The formulation of policy is obviously influenced by public opinion (particularly as expressed at elections) and political perceptions of what is publicly acceptable (especially in relation to taxation). Similarly the successful implementation of policy depends in large part on public willingness to accept the necessary consequences of desired objectives. For instance the 1944 *Employment Policy* white paper emphasised that the attainment of a high and stable level of employment depended ultimately not on government but on 'the understanding and support of the country as a whole'.[28] The values of leading vested interests or 'governing institutions' are also important if corporatist assumptions (as summarised in Chapter 2.3.1) are accepted. Finally, a full appreciation of public attitudes to welfare policy depends on their being seen as part of a wider set of values, which are expressed alternatively in changing patterns of consumption, lifestyles and artistic achievement.

The postwar period is the first for which detailed evidence of public opinion exists, following the establishment in the late 1930s of such organisations as the Gallup Poll and Mass Observation. There remain, however, many problems of interpretation. As Addison has warned, 'judgements about the "movement" of public opinion have always to be tempered by the knowledge that many people never change their opinion, while some never have any to change'.[29] In the late 1940s it also became generally accepted that, in relation to welfare policy, one-third of the population was either 'chronically ignorant or apathetic'. Such a conclusion would seem to be confirmed by later polls. In 1956 for instance, 49 per cent of mothers polled neither recognised nor could define the term 'welfare state', and in 1964 there was discovered a 'widespread civic illiteracy' over the cost of the social services.[30] Public opinion is, therefore, an elusive concept and is best divided (for analytical purposes) into three inter-related categories: general and uninformed opinion (such as the 'latent' opinions which in 1943 obliged the Coalition government against its better judgement to adopt the Beveridge Report); special and informed opinion (such as pressure groups and the 'Middle England' on which, according to Donnison, the democratic socialists relied); and public opinion as perceived by politicians.[31]

Public opinion, both expressed and perceived, strongly supported welfare policy between 1945 and 1975 and, as the most authoritative study of electoral behaviour in the 1960s has concluded, 'the rise and endurance of the welfare state was directly related to this fact'.[32] Certainly Conservative Party policy was strongly influenced by it in the 1940s and continued to be so in the 1950s, as the resignation of Thorneycroft testified. However, public opinion was also contradictory and restrictive, and this severely constrained the positive role that the welfare state could play in the resolution of Britain's underlying structural economic and social problems. The contradictions can best be illustrated by the findings of two surveys. In 1963 and 1970, 97 per cent and 92 per cent respectively of those polled by Butler and Stokes wanted expenditure on pensions and the social services either to increase or remain stable. Yet simultaneously 52 per cent and 65 per cent wanted tax cuts as opposed to increased welfare expenditure. Similarly in October 1974 84 per cent of those polled by Sarlvik and Crewe felt that it was 'very' or 'fairly important' that expenditure on the NHS and anti-poverty programmes should increase, whilst 70 per cent wanted expenditure on the social services to be either cut back or stabilised.[33]

Such contradictions might be interpreted as simply reflecting the incompatibility of views held by the respondents. However, as has been persuasively argued, it is more likely that they reflected a support for the welfare state that was both selective and selfish. People were willing to accept higher taxation so long as it financed services (such as the NHS or pensions) which did – or would – directly benefit themselves. They were far less sanguine about expenditure that helped minorities, such as the unemployed and one-parent families (who might be deemed responsible for their own problems) and, more surprisingly, children. There was little evidence here of the community spirit, the altruism or the desire for greater equality which Titmuss and the Labour Party in particular hoped the welfare state could either build upon or foster.

This lack of altruism was matched by a popular reluctance to accept the duties, as opposed to the rights, implied by welfare policy. This reluctance was most pronounced in the field of industrial relations where, in defiance of the hopes expressed in the 1944

Employment Policy white paper, resistance to technological change continued and calls for wage restraint were spurned. In the older industries, where attitudes and institutions had been forged by the permanent threat of unemployment, such behaviour was perhaps understandable in the short term; but it was common also in the newer industries which were even more reliant for their international competitiveness on adaptation to changing demand and production methods.

The reasons for such behaviour, and their consequences for welfare policy, were analysed in a classic study of the 'affluent worker' in the 1960s.[34] Following Labour's third election defeat, it discovered that manual workers were being neither drawn into the middle class nor alienated by increasing affluence but were developing a more private and materialistic lifestyle. Hence increasing membership of trade unions represented not so much workers' greater sense of communal or class solidarity, but rather a calculated desire to belong to a 'service organisation of advantage to them in defending and furthering their personal economic interests'. Just as only 8 per cent of those polled were actively seeking to realise their material ambitions through self-advancement or promotion, so only a minority were concerned with the broader social objectives of the trade unions and the Labour Party. On the other hand 83 per cent participated in the election of shop-stewards because it was at the factory, as opposed to the national, level that the power to secure improvements in pay and working conditions was believed to lie. Accordingly there was an escalation in unofficial strikes led by shop-stewards which came to be widely identified abroad as a major cause of Britain's relative economic decline.[35] It would be wrong to conclude from this evidence, however, that short-term materialism was restricted to the affluent worker. It was endemic throughout society. As one pragmatic justification of Macmillan's 'you've never had it so good' election of 1959 has concluded: 'the generation which came to maturity in the 1950s had been born in the Great War, schooled during the slump, conscripted in the Second World War and rationed for years afterwards. It had no inclination to forego the security and comforts now within its grasp in the hope of long-term economic growth.'[36]

The prime responsibility for changing such attitudes, so that they not only reflected the new reality of full employment and social security but could also ensure their continuance, was the government's. In the interwar period liberal opinion had become increasingly reconciled to state intervention by the concept of 'active citizenship'. By relieving basic need, welfare expenditure was seen not as a rival to philanthropy and self-help, but as a means of freeing charities to concentrate on other challenges and of providing the poor with a basic independence. In the 1940s the Labour government strove to ensure that the cost and availability of the social services demoralised neither the tax-payer nor the recipient. On the Appointed Day in July 1948, for instance, it launched a campaign to remind the recipient that the social services were not 'free', but had to be earned through higher productivity; and to stress to the tax-payer that state welfare was more cost-effective, and therefore represented better value for money, than private insurance.[37] However, the campaign was attacked in Parliament and in the press both as party propaganda and as unnecessarily expensive and, when the Conservatives returned to power, all such attempts at 'public education' were largely abandoned.

Another campaign, prepared by Gaitskell, to nurture those attitudes which the 1944 white paper had identified as essential for the attainment of high and stable employment was also suspended and only bore fruit (too little and too late) with the publication of the 1956 white paper, *The Economic Implications of Full Employment* (Cmd 9725). Thereafter, throughout the corporatist attempts to plan the economy, successive governments increasingly limited their ambition to mere 'mechanical' change: the superficial manipulation of public opinion rather than an active attempt to win people's minds.

The values of the corporatist élite also were – and remained – essentially antipathetic to any sustained, collective attempt to resolve Britain's long-standing weaknesses. Financiers remained more concerned with short-term pressure on sterling than with the underlying health of the economy. Their conversion to Keynesianism, and in particular deficit finance as a remedy for unemployment, has been widely questioned and their acceptance of increased welfare expenditure was largely expedient. As one international banker remarked in response to the chancellor's resignation in 1958: 'I would like to see the Government cutting every penny of expenditure, but if it is a matter of political judgement I would prefer to trust Macmillan rather than Thorneycroft.'[38] The TUC sought to act 'responsibly' with the successful attempt to contain wages between 1948 and 1950, its membership of the NEDC after 1961 and the 'social contract' of 1974. It remained, however, a prisoner of its own history, trying to reconcile the competing interests of its member unions without the necessary central resources or authority. Moreover, to retain authority over their increasingly militant shop-stewards, union leaders had to respond to the short-term materialistic demands of their members – with few tangible concessions from government, which would have enabled them to argue that increases in the 'social wage' justified restraint over the industrial wage. Rather, during the 1950s the TUC regarded Conservative attempts to revive the economy through tax cuts 'not as an industrial dynamic but as class politics, likelier to increase middle-class consumption than general production', and their suspicions were intensified by repeated later attempts to introduce prices and incomes policies.[39] In other words the TUC, unlike the LO in Sweden, was in no position to agree with government on – let alone implement – any long-term commitment concerning the future development of the welfare state.

Finally, there were the employers, to whom both Crosland and Butler looked with confidence for the exercise of greater social responsibility – 'private enterprise in the public interest'. Certainly by 1960 they were so disillusioned with 'stop-go' economic policies that they were willing to enter into tripartite talks on the planning of the economy. As a whole, however, they demonstrated neither the readiness nor the hard-headed competence to take the long-term investment decisions which modern industry required, to break down the class barriers between management and the shop-floor, or to implement the code of good industrial practice that would have minimised the need for state intervention. Even more than the TUC they lacked a sense of unity – the CBI only being formed in 1965 through the merger of three rival national associations of employers. Certainly they lacked the necessary collective will to agree and implement long-term decisions that might have conflicted with their members' short-term interests. The individualism and suspicion of government, validated by Britain's industrial dominance in the nineteenth century, was still all-pervasive. 'The commonsense of nearly 200 years ago', as Marquand has argued, 'was the chief obstacle to successful economic and social adjustment.'[40] What was needed after 1945 to counteract the legacy of the industrial revolution was an equally dramatic cultural revolution.

A cultural revolution did indeed occur after 1945, but it was one which intensified rather than reduced individualism. Pioneered in the USA, driven on by advertising (especially after the inauguration of commercial television in 1955) and increasingly financed by hire-purchase (especially after 1958), there was a consumer boom which transformed the austerity of the rationed 1940s into the affluence of the 'swinging sixties'. In 1950, for instance, there were only 350 000 televisions and 2.3 million cars whilst only 8 per cent of households had fridges. By 1971 91 per cent of households had television, 69 per cent had fridges and there were 11.8 million cars. This was the context of the increasingly private, domestic lifestyle of the affluent worker and the abandonment of the war-time acceptance of 'fair shares'. Accompanying the incipient consumer boom in the mid-1950s there was also a questioning of established values. 'Angry young men' such as Kingsley Amis and John Osborne – the authors, respectively, of *Lucky Jim* (1954) and *Look Back in Anger* (1956) – attacked the superficiality and snobbery of existing society and were accorded a reception more usually associated with French novelists and playwrights. Even the monarchy came under considerable attack. This was the start of the general questioning of established institutions, which culminated in the Fulton and Redcliffe-Maud reports.

It was also the start of the satirical movement, which spawned *Private Eye* and such television programmes as *That Was The Week That Was*. Attempts to plan the economy and to engineer a more equal society 'from the top down' were not aided by such widespread irreverence for politicians and political institutions. They also appeared inconsistent with the remarkable spectacle, after the opening of Mary Quant's first boutique in 1955 and the arrival of rock 'n' roll in 1956, of the old and the rich following the lead of the young and the relatively poor. There were those who argued that such consequences of affluence represented a lowering of class barriers and a popular vitality which provided the opportunity not just for radical anti-establishment movements but also for government, through the welfare state, to achieve a major redistribution of political and economic power. As has been seen, however, this was a challenge to which successive governments were extremely reluctant to rise.

4.6 CONCLUSION

Welfare policy is heavily influenced by, and is itself an influence upon, the broad economic, social and political development of society. Between 1945 and 1975, in the highly favourable climate of economic growth and political consensus, its steady evolution was interrupted and shaped by short-term economic crises, an unstable birthrate, an ageing population, the general inflexibility of the political and administrative system and, above all, by an ingrained cultural resistance – despite the common sacrifices of the Second World War – to collective action. All the major problems posed to the maintenance of full employment and rising living standards by an outdated economic structure and class system were, as later chapters will show, successfully recognised. This did not mean however that each could be successfully resolved.

4.7 FURTHER READING

There are innumerable books on individual aspects of postwar Britain, but few good comprehensive histories. The most recent and the best is K. O. Morgan, *The People's Peace: British History 1945–1989* (Oxford, 1990), to be supplemented on points of detail by C. J. Bartlett, *A History of Postwar Britain* (1977). Two particularly good sets of essays for the periods 1945–51 and 1951–64, respectively, are M. Sissons and P. French (eds), *Age of Austerity* (1963) and V. Bogdanor and R. Skidelsky (eds), *The Age of Affluence* (1970).

On the economy there are three introductory books whose particular strengths are, respectively, clarity of analysis, a comprehensive bibliography and a wealth of detailed information: J. F. Wright, *Britain in the Age of Economic Management* (1979), B. W. E. Alford, *British Economic Performance, 1945–1975* (1988) and S. Pollard, *The Development of the British Economy 1914–1980* (1983). On demography the dominant books are A. H. Halsey (ed.), *British Social Trends since 1900* (1988) and J. F. Ermisch, *The Political Economy of Demographic Change* (1983), although neither concentrates exclusively on the 1945–75 period. Of the many political histories, the most lively is arguably P. Hennessy and A. Seldon (eds), *Ruling Performance* (Oxford, 1987) which has detailed chronologies and bibliographies for each postwar government. The range of oral testimony and academic debate on which its essays are based, and which is ever expanding, can be savoured in the journal of the Institute of Contemporary British History, *Contemporary Record*.

P. Hennessy has also written the most authoritative introduction to the civil service, *Whitehall* (1989). A succinct historical introduction to local government is A. Alexander, *The Politics of Local*

Government in the United Kingdom (1982), whilst M. Loughlin *et al.* (eds), *Half a Century of Municipal Decline* (1985) provides a more analytical and pessimistic view. K. Middlemas has produced the boldest, but not always an accurate and clear, summary of the views of the 'governing institutions' in *Power, Competition and the State* (3 volumes, 1986 and 1990). M. Shanks, *The Stagnant Society* (1961) and C. Booker, *The Neophiliacs* (1969) are stimulating contemporary accounts of the 1950s and 1960s, which can be put into context by P. Lewis, *The Fifties* (1978) and, more generally, by A. Marwick, *British Society since 1945* (Harmondsworth, 1984). A. Sinfield provides a modern overview in *Literature, Politics and Culture in Postwar Britain* (1989).

5 Employment Policy

The maintenance of a high and stable level of employment was one of the fundamental assumptions of the Beveridge Report and an objective to which all governments were positively committed after 1944. Its achievement was seen as a direct way to enhance individual welfare as well as a stimulus to all other areas of welfare policy. If the workforce were fully employed, economic growth was more likely to be achieved and revenue sufficiently buoyant to finance expanding services. Moreover, if Keynesian techniques of demand management were used, there would also be a positive economic reason (the maintenance of aggregate demand) to justify increased social expenditure when it was most needed, in a depression. Economic and social policy would, in theory, be once again in harmony – rather than in direct conflict as they had been in the interwar years, when classical economic theory had required cuts in public expenditure during a depression in order to reduce costs and thereby encourage investment.

As shown in Chapter 4.1, employment was maintained at an historically high level between 1945 and 1975; but whether this achievement was the result of either government intervention in general or Keynesian demand management in particular is a matter of continuing dispute. At the time, but more especially after the renunciation of the commitment to full employment by both the Labour and Conservative Parties in 1976, critics argued that high employment was the consequence not of government action but of buoyant market conditions, arising from a backlog of technological innovation and rising world trade. Demand management, rather than being helpful, actually destabilised the economy in the short term and in the long term increased unemployment by discouraging investment (through its stop-go cycles and by fuelling inflation). Callaghan's denunciation of Keynesian economics in 1976, quoted on the first page of the Introduction to this book, was the first official endorsement of such an historic undercurrent of criticism. Moreover, the advantages of Keynesianism to social policy have also been questioned. If increased public expenditure were the remedy for periods of deficient demand, then in periods of excess demand (which predominated after 1945) the corollary was that expenditure should be cut – regardless of administrative logic or social need. Was it logical to leave a hospital half-built or, once built, unequipped and un-staffed? Further, if Titmuss's argument is accepted that the social costs of economic change fall disproportionately on the poor (see Chapter 2.2.2), would the need for social expenditure automatically fall in an inverse relationship to economic growth? In practice, there-fore, Keynesianism provided no simple elixir for either economic or social policy.

The purpose of this chapter is to examine this dispute. To what extent was government responsible for the achievement of full employment; and what part did social policy play in its economic strategy? To answer such questions, the two halves of that strategy, macroeconomic demand management and microeconomic industrial intervention, must be examined in the light of both the original commitment to a high level of employment and its later renunciation.

5.1 THE COMMITMENT TO FULL EMPLOYMENT

The 1944 *Employment Policy* white paper is conventionally regarded as the genesis of postwar economic consensus, by which all three major parties positively committed themselves to the maintenance of a high level of employment and the Keynesian method of its achievement. Such a view has its justification in the first and third sentences of the paper's foreword:

> The Government accept as one of their primary aims and responsi-bilities the maintenance of a high and stable level of employment after the war. . . . A country will not suffer from mass unemploy-ment so long as the total demand for its goods and services is maintained at a high level.[1]

The rest of the paper was, however, both contradictory and vague.

Chapters 4 and 5, admittedly, did advance a Keynesian analysis of the causes of unemployment and its possible cures. A depression, it was argued, could result from a shortfall in one or more of the five components of demand in the economy (private consumption and investment, the government's current and capital expenditure, and foreign trade), and it was the government's responsibility to counteract immediately such a shortfall. This responsibility, it was acknowledged,

> involves a new approach and a new responsibility for the State.

It was at one time believed that every trade depression would automatically bring its own corrective, since prices and wages would fall, the fall in prices would bring about an increase in demand, and employment would thus be restored. Experience has shown, however, that under modern conditions this process of self-recovery, if effective at all, is likely to be extremely prolonged and to be accompanied by widespread distress, particularly in a complex industrial society like our own.

Monetary policy would not be enough to effect a speedy recovery. A five-year programme of public investment needed to be prepared for immediate implementation should private investment falter. Similarly the government should be prepared to·vary taxation, social security contributions and its own bulk purchases to compensate for shortfalls in private consumption. 'The Government believe', it was concluded, 'that in the past the power of public expenditure, skilfully applied, to check the onset of a depression has been underestimated.'

However, the optimism of these two chapters, which were initially drafted by academic economists within the Economic Section of the War Cabinet, was qualified by the more pessimistic or 'realistic' joint authors of the report on which the white paper was based – experienced administrators within the Treasury. They disagreed with the Economic Section on both the predominant cause of unemployment and the practicability of the proposed remedies. Their concern (in line with classical economic theory) was not with cyclical unemployment, caused by a temporary shortfall in demand but with the structural – and in particular regional – unemployment which had predominated in the interwar years. Its only permanent remedy lay in a revival of world trade and in greater industrial investment to restructure and re-equip industry and thereby restore its international competitiveness; and these remedies were dependent, respectively, on the actions of foreign governments and on the initiative and self-restraint of the two sides of industry (in relation, for example, to long-term capital investment, restrictive practices and wage restraint). There was little the British government itself could do other than provide such microeconomic measures as retraining programmes and the provision of grants or tax concessions to encourage both investment and a 'balanced' geographical distribution of industry. Macroeconomic demand management could at best merely provide the general market conditions under which such structural adjustment might be encouraged.

Treasury officials, furthermore, doubted the ability of government in the real world directly to influence the level of employment. First, how would it know the precise moment at which to intervene? The available statistical information would never be sufficiently up to date or accurate. Secondly, how could unemployment in an export industry be suddenly relieved by an increase in domestic consumption? The transfer of labour between one abstract category of demand and another was in practice impossible. Thirdly, how speedy and effective could remedial action be? Keynes claimed that a planned programme of public works could vary demand by £150 million over two years, but Treasury officials were convinced by their interwar experience that such a figure was wildly optimistic. Finally, there was the question of probity. A balanced budget in the past had automatically imposed a discipline on politicians and civil servants who might attempt to respond to a short-term crisis with financial concessions which, rather than solving the underlying problem, would more likely fuel future demands for concessions and thus inflation. How was public expenditure to be controlled once the precedent had been set that, in order to balance demand within the economy, government expenditure could exceed its revenue?[2]

Given these basic theoretical, administrative and political disagreements, it was hardly surprising that the white paper contained many thinly-disguised contradictions and was, on specific issues, extremely vague. Two of the most blatant contradictions concerned budget deficits and labour mobility. In Paragraph 74, for example, it was clearly stated that 'none of the main proposals contained in this Paper involves deliberate planning for a deficit in the National Budget'. Yet in Paragraph 77 it was argued that government action should not be restricted by 'a rigid policy of balancing the Budget each year. . . . Such a policy is not required by statute nor is it part of our tradition'. Similarly in Paragraph 29 it was stated that 'where a large industrial population is involved, the Government are not prepared either to compel its transfer to another area or to leave it to prolonged unemployment and demoralisation'. Conversely it was argued in Paragraph 56 that 'if an expansion of total expenditure were applied to cure unemployment of a type due . . . to the failure of workers to move to places and occupations where they were needed, the policy of the Government would be frustrated'.[3] Amongst the issues shrouded in uncertainty were the means by which the government should intervene and its precise objective. The white paper contained few detailed proposals to guide future policy – the one major exception being the proposal to vary social insurance contributions, which ironically was never implemented.[4] The commitment to 'full employment' was also modified to a guarantee of a 'high and stable level of employment'. What percentage of unemployment did that actually mean? The appendix hinted at a figure of 8 per cent which – as has been shown in Chapter 4.1 – was a target considerably below the figure which Keynes and Beveridge considered feasible at the time.

Beveridge was, in fact, the reason why the Coalition government permitted such a contradictory and vague white paper to be produced. It was the assumption of the 'maintenance of employment' in his 1942 Report that had started an urgent debate within government on postwar economic policy; and Beveridge himself had mounted a simultaneous enquiry. The government had been seriously embarrassed by the popular acclaim which had greeted the 1942 Report and was determined not to be embarrassed again. All official assistance was denied Beveridge's new enquiry and, when it was learnt in the spring of 1944 that its report was complete, the government was determined to act quickly in order to steal his thunder.[5] It was as well that it did, for Beveridge (despite his early insistence on a minimum of state intervention) produced a radical report which recommended a 20-year programme of industrial planning, under a national investment board, both to modernise the country's economic infrastructure and to ensure the defeat of the five giant evils of Want, Disease, Ignorance, Squalor and Idleness. Only then was the market to be given the freedom to determine the pace and nature of economic change.

As has been argued, the whole thrust of Beveridge's report (which he significantly called *Full Employment in a Free Society*) was that 'while employment policy *per se* does not require the socialisation of industry, it does require the effective subordination of private investment to public policy.'[6] He expressed shock at the relative timidity of the white paper which, he argued, appeared to treat 'British industry as if it were a sovereign independent State, to be persuaded, influenced, appealed to and bargained with by the British State'. Its priorities were misconceived. 'The Government in the White Paper are conscious of the need for giving confidence to businessmen', he concluded, but 'they appear to be unconscious of the still greater need of giving confidence to the men and women of the country that there will be continuing demand for their services.'

Judged by its actual contents, therefore, the 1944 white paper was far from an impressive document. Nevertheless, like the Beveridge

Report before it, it did have an immense political impact because it aroused within the electorate an expectation which politicians subsequently felt unable to disappoint. The Labour Party committed itself in the 1945 election to the maintenance of full employment. The Conservatives, under the combined influence of the Treasury and Hayek's *The Road to Serfdom*, temporarily played down their commitment (to their obvious cost); and there undoubtedly remained an undercurrent of feeling within the party that the threat, or even the reality, of unemployment was necessary to ensure industrial discipline and wage restraint. After 1951, however, their decisions in government (such as the rejection of the Robot proposal to float the pound in 1952, the enforced resignation of Thorneycroft in 1958 and Heath's dramatic U-turn away from the policy of 'disengagement' in 1972) proved beyond doubt that they had by then accepted the maintenance of full employment as an electoral, if not an economic, necessity.[7] *Full* employment moreover by the 1950s was the correct phrase since, in a statement to the United Nations, Gaitskell had committed the British government to a level of 3 per cent unemployment; and thereafter reflationary measures always appeared to be taken when unemployment approached 2.5 per cent. The fundamental objective of economic policy had, therefore, been politically resolved. What remained unresolved was the means by which it could be attained. This was a continuing dilemma which Britain – unlike other European countries – appeared unable to resolve.

5.2 THE MANAGEMENT OF THE ECONOMY

The Attlee government did not immediately seek to clarify and implement the 1944 white paper. More direct interventionist measures, such as nationalisation and economic planning, were its chosen weapons to combat unemployment. However, in the absence of any perceived alternative to moderate inflation, the budget was unbalanced in 1947 to reduce aggregate demand, and thereafter demand management became the principal economic tool of government (supplemented increasingly by monetary policy after 1951 and by economic planning and direct industrial intervention after 1961). Did the continuing low level of unemployment belie the Treasury's conviction that demand management was impractical; and what were the consequences for social expenditure of its use as an economic regulator?

The overwhelming consensus is that Treasury officials had been correct both to challenge the practicability of demand management (at least insofar as very precise and ambitious policy objectives were sought) and to predict its destabilising impact on the economy. The key to demand management was the annual spring budget. The previous autumn statistics were collected for each major indicator (such as employment, the balance of payments and consumer spending) and a forecast made of likely trends over the next twelve to eighteen months. If it was predicted that there would be insufficient demand in the economy fully to employ all the country's productive resources (the 'deflationary gap') or conversely if excessive demand were predicted (the 'inflationary gap'), then remedial action was proposed in the budget and, after lengthy parliamentary debate, implemented. The potential pitfalls in such a procedure were many.

First, as Treasury officials had forewarned, the statistics used were likely to be outdated and inaccurate – especially when the burden and cost of their collection fell on non-government bodies. In the 1960s, for instance, quarterly statistics for the balance of payments took ten weeks to collect and those for employment nine months. These statistics then had to be assimilated into an economic model which (given the imprecision of economics, as suggested in Chapter 3.2.1) was unable to identify all the constantly evolving interrelationships between the various indices. Finally, the appropriate remedial measures had to be decided by a chancellor of the exchequer fully alive to their political as well as their economic consequences. Given such fallible statistics, the imprecision of economic modelling and the political interest of the chancellor, it was unlikely that – in economic terms – the correct remedial action would be agreed. Moreover, even if it were (and it remained uncompromised by sudden crises, such as Suez) it was by no means axiomatic that it would have the desired effect. The time lag between the ratification of policy changes by Parliament and their full impact upon the economy was typically two years. The period between the trough and the peak of postwar economic cycles was approximately two and a half years (see Chapter 4.1). There was, therefore, the very real danger that any 'remedial' action, rather than assisting natural market adjustments within the economy, would actually counteract them.

Examples of incorrect economic statistics, forecasts and policy decisions during this period are legion.[8] Statistics for private consumption were particularly unreliable. It has been calculated, for example, that for only three of the years between 1955 and 1969 was the retrospective revision of the statistics for a particular year less than the consequences (the 'full-year revenue effect') of the tax changes in that year's budget. Export statistics, as the Treasury had predicted, were also notoriously unreliable and directly responsible for major forecasting errors. In 1962, for example, a neutral budget was agreed on the basis of a forecasted 4 per cent growth in exports. Exports did not increase and by the autumn unemployment was rising because of deficient demand. The consequence was the dismissal of Selwyn Lloyd as chancellor in the 'night of the long knives' which so discredited the Macmillan government (see Chapter 4.3). Similarly in 1967 a 4 per cent growth in exports was forecast whereas the actual out-turn (aggravated by a dock strike and a slump in world trade) was a 7 per cent decrease. This seriously affected the timing of devaluation.

Equally serious were the budget errors of 1959 and 1963 which, it is now generally agreed, resulted in the excessive reflation of the economy. These errors were caused only in part by the chancellor's concern about an impending general election. They also arose out of the Treasury's continuing inability to estimate correctly the full effects of tax cuts on demand. Given economists' relative ignorance about changing consumption patterns this is hardly surprising; but it also reflected a genuine technical dilemma – how to devise a budget strategy which would have the required short-term impact without any unwanted long-term effects. This dilemma was all the more difficult to resolve because the immediate impact of tax cuts was *reduced* by unavoidable administrative delays (such as the reworking of tax codes) and the government's clawback of purchasing power (through taxes on expenditure). Conversely the long-term impact was increased by the 'secondary' effects of any such cuts. Immediate purchases would give employment to others, who would spend their increased income ('the multiplier') and thereby encourage manufacturers to expedite investment ('the accelerator'). Indeed in the 1960s it was estimated that only 66 per cent of the *total* impact of income tax cuts (and only 80 per cent of the *direct* impact) would be felt in the first year. The Treasury traditionally overcompensated for the immediate shortfall. In 1961 a major new innovation was designed to alleviate this problem. Changes in indirect taxation were believed to have a less complex and more immediate impact and so the 'regulator' was introduced, whereby purchase tax and excise duty (on such goods as cigarettes and alcohol) might be altered between budgets by up to 10 per cent of their existing rate.[9] 'Fine-tuning' however remained an extremely hazardous art.

Demand management was therefore bedevilled by technical difficulties. It was bedevilled also by confusion over policy instruments, principal amongst which was the frequent incompatibility of fiscal policy (the variation of taxes or public expenditure) and monetary policy (the variation, in particular, of interest rates and the money supply). This confusion reflected in part the differing needs of the domestic economy and of sterling as an international reserve currency. The war had massively increased Britain's international indebtedness ('sterling balances') as a result both of military expenditure abroad and the imbalance in trade resulting from the restriction of exports. In 1939 sterling balances and the country's gold and dollar reserves had virtually been in balance, but by 1945 the former stood at £3567 million and the latter at only £610 million. In the 1950s and 1960s, moreover, the gold and dollar reserves were sufficient to cover only two months' imports, whereas in most other European countries they covered six months'.[10] Both these factors made sterling vulnerable to speculators, and it was frequently deemed necessary after 1950 to have a high bank rate in order to maintain confidence in sterling and attract funds to the City of London. High bank rate, however, increased interest payments on borrowing in general and on the national debt in particular, thus contradicting two of the Treasury's other traditional objectives – industrial investment and low public expenditure.

This conflict was but one of the dilemmas thrown up by the attempt simultaneously to achieve four potentially incompatible objectives through demand management: full employment, balance of payments equilibrium, price stability and economic growth. Full employment (defined as 3 per cent unemployment) in particular conflicted with the other objectives. It conflicted with economic growth because the constant modernisation of industry required a reserve of labour which was both geographically and industrially mobile. It conflicted with price stability (especially in the eyes of monetarists) because, *inter alia*, it strengthened the power of trade unions to demand high wages and the ability of employers to finance them by passing on – in the short term at least – the increased cost to consumers in higher prices. However, as shown in Chapter 4.2, its main conflict was with the balance of payments, the consequences of which were the 'stop-go' cycles of the 1950s and 1960s. When unemployment threatened, demand was expanded. This increased imports and diverted potential exports into the home market, which in turn created a balance of payments deficit. Demand was then decreased and unemployment started again to mount.

The underlying problem, which the incompatibility of the policy objectives of full employment and balance of payments equilibrium revealed, was the uncompetitiveness of British industry. To an extent this was not a new problem. From the time records began until 1939 Britain had had a deficit in visible trade in all but four years, but the net income from investments overseas had been sufficient to cover half the cost of imports in 1914 and a quarter in 1939.[11] The wartime sale of assets reduced the figure to 15 per cent; and simultaneously the price of imports in relation to exports (the 'terms of trade') rose so sharply, owing to world shortages, that by 1950 it required a 75 per cent increase in the 1938 volume of exports to balance imports running at only 70 per cent of their 1938 volume. The immediate challenge was met under the Labour government; and then fortuitously the terms of trade changed dramatically in Britain's favour so that in the 1950s, on average, an extra £100 million worth of imports could be financed each year by the same volume of exports. Oil in particular, which rose from supplying 10 to 50 per cent of Britain's energy needs, became relatively cheap.

In the 1960s however the terms of trade stopped improving and after the quadrupling of oil prices in 1972–4 (combined with a world boom and the consequent rise in the cost of other scarce resources) they deteriorated dramatically. This exposed the true vulnerability of the British economy, no longer shielded by the windfall profits derived from its nineteenth-century world monopoly. Radical measures were duly taken. The withdrawal of troops stationed abroad, especially after 1968, was designed to improve the balance of payments by reducing government expenditure abroad; and also in 1968, sterling ceased to be an international reserve currency. In 1967 the pound was devalued and in 1972 allowed to 'float' so that the market could determine its value. The effectiveness of such measures, however, was lessened by their being, in essence, reactions to immediate crises rather than an integral part of a sustained modernisation programme.

In addition to the technical complexities and the policy-conflicts of demand management, there was also substance in the Treasury's forewarning that the government lacked the political freedom to determine the level of economic activity. The oil price rises which helped to double the total cost of imports between 1972 and 1974 were a prime example of Britain's vulnerability to international pressures. Moreover, as was shown in Chapter 4.5, financiers and employers collectively failed to identify and implement the long-term investment decisions needed to maintain the competitiveness of British industry; the workforce as a whole displayed neither the adaptability nor the self-restraint for which the 1944 white paper had called; and the electorate was perceived to demand from government short-term benefits regardless of their long-term costs. In vain, it would appear, had Treasury officials inserted into the foreword of the 1944 white paper the warning that 'employment cannot be created by Act of Parliament or by Government action alone'.

Despite all this evidence it would nevertheless be wrong to conclude – as have the monetarists – that demand management was wholly deleterious, or that government was in no way responsible for the full employment which lay at the root of the exceptional improvements in economic and social welfare before 1975. Full employment may well have resulted from an increase in world trade and private investment, but such 'spontaneous' developments were unquestionably assisted by international agreements to reduce trade barriers (such as the General Agreement on Tariffs and Trade) and the known commitment of government to increase demand in order to prevent a repetition of the great depression of the 1930s. Stop-go policies may, at the margin, have discouraged long-term investment, but overall there had never been – as Britain's trading rivals recognised – a more rational time at which to undertake such investment. If British industry did not respond, there may well have been a case – as Beveridge had argued – for more, rather than less, government intervention.

The potential conflicts in demand management were nowhere more evident that in the field of social expenditure. As already shown in Chapter 4.2, the level of social expenditure could be affected by cyclical fluctuations in the economy regardless of the amount of social need. Variations in taxation, designed to regulate such fluctuations, could also have a social impact. An increase in indirect taxation, for example, could disproportionately affect the low-paid and (in particular) pensioners, whilst a decrease in income tax could disproportionately favour the rich. Consequently tax changes made for economic reasons could jeopardise the effectiveness of other policies designed to reduce poverty or to achieve a greater equality of income through progressive taxation (see Chapter 11). Even more seriously, however, constant variations in the level of social expenditure could demoralise those responsible for its administration and thereby jeopardise all attempts to achieve maximum cost-effectiveness. This was certainly the conclusion of the Plowden Committee on the Control of Public Expenditure, appointed in 1959 as concern in government and Parliament grew over its escalating cost.

The Plowden Report directly refuted the assertion of the 1944 white paper that 'in the past the power of public expenditure . . . to check the onset of a depression has been underestimated'. Rather it argued that, after a decade of practical experience, the Treasury's earlier pessimism had been duly confirmed. As it concluded:

> The Government are required by public opinion to seek to manage the national economy with only small variations in the level of employment. It is natural, therefore, to explore the possibilities of using variations in public expenditure to help in this task. Experience shows, however, that Government current expenditure cannot be varied effectively for this purpose. Attempts, at moments of inflationary pressure, to impose short-term 'economies' (or to make increases at moments when 'reflation' is called for) are rarely successful and sometimes damaging, and we think that these attempts should be avoided. There has been a tendency in the past to overestimate the possibilities of useful short-term action in public investment, and to under-estimate the indirect losses caused by sudden changes. Experience shows that . . . . the effect of the action taken may well appear at the very moment when the economy is already on the turn. The remedy may, therefore, be worse than the disease.[12]

The Committee's recommendations were, therefore, that the use of current and capital social expenditure to regulate the economy should be minimised, and that its cost-effectiveness should be assessed by the strengthening of both the civil service's technical and administrative expertise and the Cabinet's sense of collective responsibility. In particular a five-year survey of public expenditure should be prepared annually to relate future spending plans to the anticipated rate of economic growth. This was the genesis of the Public Expenditure Survey Committee (PESC) – a committee which since 1961 has collated all departmental spending plans in preparation for the government's autumn public expenditure white paper (first published in 1963 to demonstrate the 'modernity' of the Conservative government, and then published regularly after 1969).

Before 1975 PESC was not a conspicuous success. The government continued to vary social expenditure contracyclically, and neither the civil service nor the Cabinet displayed the committed responsibility for which the Plowden Committee had called. An over-optimistic estimate of economic growth, for example, was adopted which reduced the need to take hard decisions about the priority to be accorded different policies; it was not until the introduction of Programme Analysis and Review in the early 1970s that a sustained critical look was taken at the cost-effectiveness of existing, as opposed to new, proposals.[13] Ultimately therefore the Plowden Committee was more significant for what it failed to, rather than for what it did, achieve. It provided a belated opportunity for the adjustment of both political and administrative attitudes and structures to the demands of the positive new responsibilities which government had assumed since 1945. It also offered a chance to reconcile the competing demands of economic and social policy, which demand management had done much – but clearly not enough – to minimise. Both opportunities were largely missed, to the particular disadvantage of long-term investment in the social services.

Two broader questions arise from the history of postwar demand management. Was there a 'Keynesian revolution' in policymaking and did there ever exist a 'Butskellite' consensus? Keynesian economic assumptions undoubtedly became predominant after the war in the economics profession and in Whitehall – especially after the retirement of the 'interwar' generation of civil servants by the mid 1950s. There were also institutional innovations which favoured the adoption of Keynesianism. The establishment of the Central Statistical Office, for example, in 1940 led to the collection of aggregate statistics needed for national income accounting, and their approach to economic analysis was insinuated into the budgetary process in the late 1940s. In 1941 for the first time the object of the budget was not just to balance the government's books but to secure the optimum allocation of resources within the economy; and, as has been seen, it was deliberately unbalanced in 1947 to counteract inflation. For many, however, the crucial test of a full 'Keynesian revolution' is a government's willingness to use a budget deficit deliberately to combat depression. Until 1975 there was always excess demand in the economy, and so the role of demand management was necessarily limited to the variation of the amount by which the budget was

in surplus. There was no need for a deficit budget until the mass
unemployment of 1975 – and then, as has been seen, the challenge
was declined. Would it have been so declined had a depression
occurred earlier when the wartime commitment to avoid the wastage
of interwar unemployment was still burnt into political and public
consciousness?

Such evidence as exists suggests that the challenge might well have
been refused. In 1954, for example, Butler (as chancellor) was faced
with an anticipated depression in the USA which would have reduced
British exports, but despite the explicit commitment in the *Industrial
Charter* he refused to contemplate a deficit budget. His explanation
was, essentially, that it would undermine foreign confidence.[14] In the
event the depression was not sufficiently severe to affect the British
economy and so Butler's resolution remained untested. The critical
point remains however. Given the postwar weakness of both
Britain's reserves and balance of payments, governments were
dependent on foreign bankers to support sterling and to finance the
national debt. They certainly were not converts to Keynesianism.
Had a serious depression occurred earlier, therefore, would the
needs of the unemployed or the interests of bankers have triumphed?
The question must remain an open one.

Butler's hesitation in 1954 raises doubts over the historical value
of the term 'Butskellism', coined by *The Economist* to describe the
coincidence between Butler's instincts and those of the former
Labour chancellor, Gaitskell. Both sought to moderate the extreme
demands of their backbenchers (respectively for a return to the free
market and an extension of nationalisation) and to use Keynesian
techniques temporarily to manage aggregate demand. *The Economist*
itself, however, cast doubt on whether this coincidence of instincts
could have withstood a harsher economic climate than that prevailing
in the 1950s. Certainly Butler himself, whilst admitting he spoke the
same 'language of Keynesianism', denied he shared any of Gaitskell's
political convictions; and Gaitskell, prior to the Labour government's
defeat in 1951, had been preparing a new employment white paper
to give real teeth to its 'tentative and speculative' predecessor. The
philosophy behind the paper was summarised at the time as:

> Always keep demand just above supply, in order to hold full
> employment, and rely on physical controls – especially of total
> imports, capital exports, building location and essential materials
> – even when no longer 'in short supply' – to hold inflation. . . .

Always have a bit of inflation pressure, but use physical controls to prevent it breaking through.[15]

Such a permanent commitment to physical controls would have been anathema to Butler. Beneath the superficial similarity of their policies there remained, therefore, fundamental ideological differences. Essentially Butler, as a reluctant collectivist, relied upon the rationality of the market whilst Gaitskell, as a democratic socialist, relied upon the rationality of government planning (see Chapter 2.2.1 and 2.2.2). This fundamental ideological difference between the two parties was to become more explicit when it was commonly agreed, in the early 1960s, that macroeconomic management needed to be supplemented by microeconomic industrial intervention.

5.3   DIRECT INDUSTRIAL INTERVENTION

After 1945 four alternatives, or supplements, to demand management were advanced and – with varying degrees of commitment and success – implemented. They were the Treasury's suggestions for microeconomic intervention, put forward in the 1944 white paper; the Labour Party's long-term commitment to nationalisation and economic planning (which many continued to equate with industrial efficiency, especially after Russia's triumph over the USA in 1957 with its launching of the first space satellite); 'indicative' planning, which became the fashionable explanation in the early 1960s for Europe's high growth rate; and direct discriminatory industrial intervention.

Not surprisingly it was the Treasury's proposals, based largely on prewar precedent, which were the most consistently applied. Hence, to remove restrictive practices, the Monopolies Commission was established in 1948, a Restrictive Trade Practices Court in 1956 and the Office of Fair Trading in 1973.[16] An attempt to create a more skilled workforce was made not just through the expansion of the education system but also by such legislation as the 1964 Industrial Training Act, which enabled government to establish supervisory training boards with the novel power to raise a compulsory levy on all firms within their respective industries. Industrial investment was also encouraged by a wide range of tax allowances (by which the initial cost and depreciation of capital equipment could be set against tax) and, between 1966 and 1970, cash grants (to assist those industries which were insufficiently profitable to qualify for the full tax concessions). These allowances and grants were especially generous in areas where unemployment was relatively high. 'Regional' policy, in accordance with Chapter 3 of the 1944 white paper, was more explicitly pursued in the 1940s with the building of new towns, a ban on investment in overcrowded regions and grants to encourage the transfer of key workers and equipment from those areas. In the 1960s, in the absence of – and as a stimulant to – local government reform, regional planning councils were also set up to coordinate local economic and social development; and between 1967 and 1970 a regional employment premium was paid for each employee in areas of high unemployment which amounted effectively to an 8 per cent subsidy on wages. All these measures were additional to the normal range of government activity – from taxation to factory legislation – which had both intended and unintended consequences for industrial development.[17]

Regional policy has frequently been attacked for confusing economic and social policy, to the benefit of neither. Private profitability is not always the best guarantor of the public interest (see Chapter 3.2.1), and before 1939 government had slowly come to recognise that the migration of workers to jobs had economic disadvantages such as the increased congestion of the Midlands and the South East and the need to supply there, at the tax-payer's expense, the social infrastructure (such as housing and schools) abandoned elsewhere. However political influence on regional policy – especially on prestige projects such as the building of a new car plant at Linwood near Glasgow – resulted in many investment decisions which were never able to gain long-term commercial viability.

Regional policy has therefore always promised more than it has actually delivered. Similar problems dogged nationalisation. In the 1940s nationalisation was seen by many within the Labour Party as the means by which the state could control and develop the economy in the public interest; and this belief was vigorously renewed in the early 1970s when the Labour Party became committed, in opposition, to the nationalisation of the leading twenty-five companies. In the 1950s however, the practical experience of those essential but loss-making industries which had been nationalised (such as coal and the railways) was widely considered to show that improvements in industrial relations and efficiency could not be realised – although a symbolic battle was fought over the essential *and* profitable steel industry which was nationalised, denationalised and subsequently renationalised. A major cause of the weakness of the nationalised industries was the continuing uncertainty over whether they should be run on strictly commercial lines or, alternatively, assist 'full employment' policy by providing both abundant jobs and subsidised services for other industries. In 1961 the first serious attempt was made to resolve this dilemma. The white paper *Financial and Economic Obligations of the Nationalised Industries* specified that 'although the industries have obligations of a national and non-economic kind, they are not, and ought not, to be regarded as social services absolved from economic and commercial justification'.[18] Specific commercial criteria were established for determining both investment and pricing. Continuing political pressure meant, however, that these criteria – difficult enough to meet in the industrial world – were inevitably compromised.

When the deficiencies of demand management became increasingly apparent in the early 1960s, therefore, the microeconomic policy of successive governments took the form not of further state ownership but of state intervention in private industry. The first attempts at such intervention had been made by the Labour government after the war, when innumerable controls existed to allocate scarce materials throughout industry. Any attempt in peacetime to institute direct economic planning along Soviet lines (whereby government *replaced* the market by determining the output targets for each industry) was rapidly acknowledged to be undesirable. Although the terminology of 'economic planning' was retained, it was admitted that:

> Economic planning in the United Kingdom is based upon three fundamental facts: the economic fact that the United Kingdom economy must be heavily dependent on international trade; the political fact that it is, and intends to remain, a democratic nation with a high degree of individual liberty; and the administrative fact that no economic planning body can be aware (or indeed could ever be aware) of more than the very general trends of future economic development.[19]

Consequently what the Labour government sought to implement was 'indicative' planning. In its economic surveys it set broad targets for the economy over the following year; and it then strove to ensure that industry acted in accordance with such targets, largely by persuasion.

These experiments in indicative planning provided the initial inspiration for successful French planning in the 1950s to which ironically

Britain turned in the early 1960s for a cure for her relatively low growth rate.[20] Even more ironically, planning was resurrected by a Conservative government (under Macmillan) with the active encouragement of the Federation of British Industry (which had become disillusioned with the impact on investment of stop-go policies) and of Keynesian economists (who, in an open economy committed to free collective bargaining, had become convinced of the need for import and wage controls). There were three major institutional innovations: the National Economic Development Council, at which government discussed particular economic problems and planned growth with the two sides of industry; its secretariat, the National Economic Development Office; and the establishment of individual Economic Development Councils to identify the problems and needs of specific industries.

In opposition, the Labour Party cast doubt over the Conservatives' commitment to planning, suggesting that it was essentially a political stratagem both to reconcile trade unions to wage restraint and to project a failing party in a 'modern' light. In government it sought to prove its own commitment by creating, uniquely for Britain in peacetime, a specialist planning ministry – the Department of Economic Affairs. The Department hastily produced a National Plan to expand the economy annually by 4 per cent over five years. Equally hastily, however, the plan was undermined by the deflationary measures designed to correct the severe balance of payments crisis. Direct intervention in industry nevertheless accelerated. A Ministry of Technology was established in 1964 to take responsibility for the government's sponsorship of research and development, and it expanded thereafter as the active, sponsoring department of a wide range of well-established industries (such as aerospace) and new industries (such as computers). Its path was smoothed by the Industrial Expansion Act of 1968, which gave government the power to finance individual investment decisions without recourse to further legislation; and it was assisted by the newly created Industrial Reorganisation Corporation which (in potential conflict with monopoly policy) was charged with the encouragement of industrial mergers – to particular effect in the electronics and car industries, where GEC and British Leyland were formed. Through the Ministry of Technology and the IRC, British government started slowly to shed its traditional, neutral role and to move towards the European practice whereby, in key strategic decisions, the judgement of officials replaced the judgement of the market.[21]

Such a development naturally concerned the Conservative Party which had in opposition, as Labour had predicted, renounced its support for economic planning. On its return to office in 1970 a policy of 'disengagement' was implemented with, for instance, the abolition of the IRC and many of Labour's regional initiatives. However, the bankruptcy in 1971 of Rolls-Royce (a key defence contractor) and rising unemployment in 1972 changed the government's conception of what was electorally, if perhaps not economically, necessary; and its 1972 Industry Act restored, and even expanded, the interventionist powers which the Ministry of Technology and the IRC had enjoyed. Indeed so great was its interventionist potential that the incoming Labour government of 1974 could with little controversy establish a National Enterprise Board – not to nationalise the leading 25 companies but, with a budget of £1000 million, to stimulate the modernisation of British industry in general and of the nationalised industries in particular.

These successive attempts at direct, discretionary intervention failed to match the success of parallel developments abroad. Why was this? The widely accepted reason is the lack of the necessary administrative, political and cultural support to sustain, over a sufficiently long period, a consistent policy. The British civil service as a whole, as noted in Chapter 4.4, lacked the specialist expertise either to use public investment or to intervene decisively to accelerate industrial modernisation. Its instinct was also to act as a referee not as a participant in such a process. Moreover, even when it painstakingly acquired specialist knowledge and a readiness to act, these virtues were precipitately dissipated by political action – such as the abolition of the IRC in 1970. Both political parties, indeed, conspired to create the worst of all possible worlds. In government, both (with the possible exception of the Conservatives between 1970 and 1972) had a common policy of 'state-supported capitalism'. In practice, however, both frustrated it. This was not just because, in opposition, they reverted to the adversarial policies of 'disengagement' and 'nationalisation' when they should have been planning practical policies. It was also because, in office, they sought to achieve consensus through tripartite bodies such as the NEDC and this prevented them, unlike their French counterparts, from seeking advice from and acting through the most dynamic industrial leaders, who were by definition both atypical and mistrusted by their colleagues. Instead they were tied to the 'canker of the average firm' and the very industrialists and trade unionists who were most sensitive to the fears aroused by ideological rhetoric.[22] Consequently industrial policies were far from exhibiting 'the celebrated realism' which continental observers had come to expect of Britain. Rather, in the words of one permanent secretary to the Ministry of Technology, there was a 'virtually unique (amongst advanced countries) lack of understanding or even hostility between government and industry'. What was desperately lacking was 'the will and creative power to make an effective relationship and community of interest between government and industry'.[23]

The failure of indicative planning and industrial intervention was critical to the long-term future of the welfare state because it undermined government's ability to honour their guarantee of a high and stable level of employment. Experience had shown that demand management was not enough and that Keynes's faith was ill-founded that the market, given an adequate level of aggregate demand, could restructure the economy and ensure both the requisite quantity and quality of investment. Not only did government require an industrial strategy because it was itself directly responsible for approximately two-fifths of capital investment. It required one also because, in an advanced technological society, international competitiveness depended on long-term investment decisions which could conflict with the short-term requirements of private profitability. Government was thus required to anticipate the needs of the community and – where necessary – to override the logic of the market. There might be valid ideological objections to such intervention, but abstention was no longer feasible because, as the first report of the National Enterprise Board argued:

> It is a feature of the western world that governments of almost every major manufacturing country respond to public pressures and try to stimulate the pace and direction of industrial development. If we stand aside in this country and allow market forces alone to operate we shall be overtaken and displaced by those of our competitors who have learned the skills of forcing the pace of development and seizing the market opportunity by reinforcing commercial drive with the impetus of public financial support.[24]

During this period private industry (despite its own declared preferences) required but did not receive consistent government support. Consequently demand management was also denied what it (despite the claims of its original advocates) most required, the underpinning of an effective industrial policy.

5.4 CONCLUSION

The maintenance of full employment was both a direct contribution to individual welfare and an essential support for other welfare services because it simultaneously maximised revenue and minimised demand for them. Informed opinion at the time accorded much of the credit for the maintenance of full employment to government and, despite Treasury forebodings, it would appear that government policy (whatever its technical shortcomings and mystifying complexity) did help to create the conditions in which the spontaneous buoyancy of world markets could be exploited. Government policy, however, had its drawbacks. The stop-go cycles in demand management, which led to sudden cuts in investment being succeeded by equally sudden bursts in demand, could not but be debilitating.[25] Similarly stop-go cycles in industrial policy discouraged the development of the administrative expertise necessary to identify and implement the hard investment decisions which are functionally required of government in an advanced industrial society.

This chronic instability of macro and microeconomic policy was all the more surprising because, in government, both the Labour and Conservative Parties appeared to accept the need for 'state-supported capitalism'. Beneath the surface, however, there lay a fundamental ideological conflict over whether power should lie ultimately in the market or with the state; and herein perhaps lay the initial and continuing attraction of Keynesian demand management. It allowed this conflict to remain unresolved because, although the day-to-day power to determine the speed and nature of economic change was clearly left with the market, democratic socialists (such as Crosland) could believe that ultimate power lay with the state, should it choose to act. The ultimate attraction of Keynesianism, in other words, was essentially a negative and not a positive one.

The direct effect of economic policy on social expenditure was similarly ambivalent. Keynesian policy promised a constructive role for welfare policy in a depression, but Beveridge had warned that 'keeping communal investment on tap to fill gaps in private investment' was not only unacceptable but also impractical.[26] After a decade of practical experience, the Plowden Committee confirmed his judgement by demonstrating that current and, above all, capital welfare expenditure had suffered from its use as an economic regulator. On the other hand continuing economic growth ensured an increase in the absolute (and relative) amount of resources allocated

120

The Classic Welfare State, 1945–75

to welfare expenditure – as the tables in Appendix 1 demonstrate. Also it permitted a consolidation of the changed attitudes to welfare initiated in the 1940s. However tenacious the traditional aims of economic policy (including the defence of sterling and heavy military expenditure overseas) the traditional means of financing them in times of perceived crisis (cuts in social expenditure) were, at least after Thorneycroft's resignation in 1958, no longer accepted.[27] Economically, welfare expenditure had come of age. However, just as the future of demand management was threatened by the continuing absence of an effective industrial policy, so this new-found legitimacy of welfare expenditure was threatened by the continuing rise in unemployment. This was the spectre overshadowing 1975.

5.5 FURTHER READING

Three of the best introductory texts, by Alford, Pollard and Wright, have already been cited in the further reading for Chapter 4. Amongst the other, fuller, political economies of the period the outstanding ones are A. Cairncross, *Years of Recovery: British Economic Policy, 1945–51* (1985); J. C. R. Dow, *The Management of the British Economy, 1945–60* (Cambridge, 1970); and S. Brittan, *Steering the Economy* (Harmondsworth, 1971). Complementary texts include A. Shonfield, *British Economic Policy Since the War* (1959); W. Beckerman (ed.), *The Labour Government's Economic Record, 1964–70* (1972); and F. T. Blackaby (ed.), *British Economic Policy, 1960–74* (Cambridge, 1978). A. Shonfield, *Modern Capitalism* (1969), despite its forbidding title, is extremely illuminating on foreign comparisons.

Two good introductions to economic planning are A. Budd, *The Politics of Economic Planning* (1978) and the more detailed J. Leruez, *Economic Planning and Politics in Britain* (Oxford, 1975). S. Young and A. V. Lowe, *Intervention in the Mixed Economy* (1974) provides an introduction to industrial policy between 1964 and 1972, whilst A. M. Gamble and S. A. Walkland, *The British Party System and Economic Policy, 1945–1984* (Oxford 1984) presents the stimulating, and conflicting, views of two political scientists on demand management and industrial policy. There has been a lengthy debate in the *Economic History Review* on the character and significance of the 1944 *Employment Policy* white paper, details of which are provided in G. C. Peden, *Keynes, the Treasury and British*

Economic Policy (1988). Two more recent contributions are S. Glynn and A. Booth, *The Road to Full Employment* (1987), which provides a good introduction to its origins, and N. Rollings, 'British Budgetary Policy, 1945–54: A "Keynesian revolution"?', *Economic History Review*, vol. 41 (1988) pp. 283–98, which provides a review of its early fate. Nothing is more stimulating, however, than the original texts themselves: *Employment Policy* (Cmd 6527) and Sir W. Beveridge, *Full Employment in a Free Society* (1944).

6 Social Security

Together with the maintenance of full employment, the provision of social security was the principal objective of both the Beveridge Report and the postwar Labour government. The concept of social security was novel to Britain in the 1940s – having been first formally acknowledged in the 1941 Atlantic Charter – and it means, in essence, the guarantee by government to all its citizens of an income sufficient to ensure an agreed minimum standard of living. In the 1940s, the realisation of this guarantee depended largely on the expansion of various interwar insurance schemes; but, as argued in Chapter 2.1, the nature of these schemes was fundamentally changed by their being extended to the whole population, to cover all risks to an individual's income and to provide – in theory at least – subsistence-level benefits.

The adoption of these three principles of universalism, comprehensiveness and adequacy meant that the government's social services were no longer 'reserved for the poor' and therefore, almost inevitably, poor services. Society became, in essence, more egalitarian and humane through the involvement of everyone (including the rich) in a programme of mutual insurance which, for the first time in history, freed everyone from the threat of absolute poverty. Moreover the guarantee of subsistence by government came to be widely accepted not so much as a threat to, but as a precondition of, personal responsibility. It was this revolution in values and in the role of government which led to the coining, and the public acceptance, of the term 'welfare state'.

From the start, the cost of social security dominated postwar welfare expenditure. The size of the social security budget exceeded that of defence by the mid-1960s and remained thereafter the most expensive single item of government policy (see Appendix 1, Tables A1.3 and A1.4). Its share of *public* expenditure rose from 12.1 per cent in 1951 to 17.8 per cent in 1971 before declining slightly. It also accounted for one-third of all *social* expenditure and was conventionally 50 per cent more costly than the next most expensive item, education. These figures, however, can be misleading. On the one hand they exaggerate the importance of social security expenditure because the money involved was only being transferred from one individual to another ('transfer payments'). Except for the cost of administration, it was not being consumed by government – as it was for example in education or defence policy, where government employed trained staff, constructed and maintained buildings, and purchased equipment. Consequently the government's role was limited to the determination of who should spend money rather than how it should be spent and this limited its economic, if not its political, significance (see Appendix 1.2). On the other hand the figures underestimate social security expenditure because they excluded most expenditure in kind – such as the right to free health care – which is as essential to an individual's peace of mind as cash benefits.

The enormous sums of money within the social security budget were, as demonstrated by Table 6.1, dispensed in three ways. The vast bulk, varying over time from 59 to 73 per cent, was paid out in national insurance benefits, for which recipients qualified through the payment of insurance contributions (see lines 1–7 of Table 6.1). Between 10 and 14 per cent was dispensed through means-tested benefits, financed out of general taxation (lines 10–13, 15). A percentage, rapidly declining from 24 to 7 per cent, was paid through tax-financed benefits, such as family allowances/child benefits, to which all qualified people were automatically entitled (lines 8–9, 17). The beneficiaries were overwhelmingly and increasingly the elderly, who never received less than half of the total expenditure (lines 1, 9–10, 14). Expenditure on the unemployed also expanded from 3 to 10 per cent as the economy faltered (lines 6–11). In contrast the relative value of benefits for children declined, whilst that for other groups, such as the sick, remained largely static.

Despite its seminal importance to the concept of a 'welfare state', its initial popularity and its potential electoral significance (arising from both its overall cost and its direct relevance to all voters), social security policy attracted little popular or political enthusiasm after 1945. Initially it aroused little open controversy. Beveridge was somewhat oversanguine when he claimed 'reconstruction of social insurance . . . to ensure security of income from all risks . . . raises no issue of political principle or of party', but even Hayek admitted that 'there is no reason why in a society that has reached the general level of wealth which ours has attained, the first kind of security [the certainty of a given minimum of sustenance] should not be guaranteed to all without endangering general freedom'.[1] All political parties were soon agreed upon a universal, comprehensive scheme, financed in the main through contributory insurance. Moreover, as

Table 6.1 Social security: government expenditure, 1951–77

	1951–2		1956–7		1961–2		1966–7		1971–2		1976–7	
	£m	%	£m	%	£m	%	£m	%	£m	%	£m	%
National Insurance		59.2		63.1		70.3		73.2		68.9		69.6
1. Retirement pensions	281	40.0	455	42.7	800	47.8	1290	48.8	2091	45.7	5573	48.3
2. Widows' benefit and guardians' allowances	25	3.5	40	3.7	83	5.0	146	5.5	203	4.4	439	3.8
3. Sickness benefits	66	9.4	101	9.5	161	9.6	271	10.3	434	9.5	1091	9.5
4. Maternity benefits	9	1.3	15	1.4	25	1.5	38	1.4	44	1.0	72	0.6
5. Death grants	3	0.4	3	0.3	6	0.4	8	0.3	14	0.3	15	0.1
6. Unemployment benefits	16	2.3	24	2.3	41	2.4	85	3.2	250	5.5	578	5.0
7. Industrial injuries benefit	16	2.3	35	3.3	60	3.6	95	3.6	117	2.5	250	2.2
8. War pensions	77	10.9	91	8.5	103	6.1	118	4.5	136	3.0	290	2.5
9. Non-contributory o.a.p.	25	3.5	17	1.6	10	0.6	3	0.1	–	–	–	–
Supplementary Benefits		10.6		10.3		10.0		11.5		14.5		14.0
10. Old	34	4.8	61	5.7	89	5.3	167	6.3	286	6.2	489	4.2
11. Unemployed	6	0.9	9	0.8	22	1.3	32	1.2	155	3.4	601	5.2
12. Sick	18	2.6	23	2.2	32	1.9	54	2.0	84	1.8		
13. Other	16	2.3	17	1.6	25	1.5	52	2.0	140	3.1	518	4.5
14. Old person's pension	–	–	–	–	–	–	–	–	24	0.5	38	0.3
15. Family income supplement	–	–	–	–	–	–	–	–	5	0.1	20	0.2
16. Attendance allowance	–	–	–	–	–	–	–	–	6	0.1	144	1.2
17. Family allowances	66	9.4	119	11.2	140	8.4	156	5.9	359	7.9	564	4.9
18. Administration	45	6.4	56	5.3	78	4.6	116	4.4	230	5.0	845	7.3
Total public expenditure on social security benefit	703	100	1066	100	1675	100	2642	100	4578	100	11527	100

Sources: *Social Trends* (1970, 1977); *Annual Abstract of Statistics* (1964).

shown in Chapter 3.2.1, many economists still regard compulsory state insurance as technically superior to private insurance.

By the mid-1950s, however, doubts were beginning to grow about the long-term cost and viability of existing policy, and in the mid-1960s the 'rediscovery' of poverty raised serious doubts about the government's ability to resolve existing problems. Amidst growing public disillusion, a technical debate was initiated on how to simplify an increasingly bureaucratic and complex system, and thereby target help more cost-effectively on those in need. Simultaneously there was an increasingly bitter political debate on the fundamental purpose of social security policy. Was it essentially to support the capitalist economy (by compensating its victims, whilst reinforcing its values) or to engineer a more equal society (through the modification or even supersession of market criteria for the allocation and distribution of resources)? Disputes over the respective merits of 'universalism' and 'selectivity' and the erosion of the work ethic by guaranteed subsistence benefits, last voiced in the 1930s, were revived.

The purpose of this chapter is to analyse the development of policy, both in general and in relation to the needs of particular social groups, in the context of such controversies. First, however, it is necessary to establish the objectives of – and the objections to – the Beveridge Report, upon which the postwar social security system was largely based, and the nature of the 'rediscovery' of poverty.

6.1 THE BEVERIDGE REPORT AND ITS CRITICS

Despite its somewhat unglamorous title (and author), the Beveridge Report on *Social Insurance and Allied Services* immediately acquired immense popularity, both at home and abroad, as a practical programme for the elimination of poverty, and it has subsequently come to be regarded by many as a 'blueprint' for the welfare state (see Chapter 2.1). The government's intention had not been to produce so popular a report. Indeed Beveridge's assignment to what was originally intended to be a secret and highly technical exercise to minimise the overlapping responsibilities of the existing social services had been an attempt to remove him from a central wartime role. However, through a combination of Beveridge's own skill (both as a propagandist and as a synthesiser of other people's ideas) and luck (the coincidence of the Report's publication in November 1942 with a burst of national optimism following Britain's first major victory at El Alamein), the Report revolutionised perceptions in Whitehall and Westminster of what was politically possible – and necessary. The urgent search for a postwar economic policy, which culminated in the 1944 *Employment Policy* white paper, is a measure of its success.

Beveridge rightly saw social security as something more than the provision of a minimum cash income. He acknowledged, in his own distinctive language, that apart from 'want' four other 'giants on the road to reconstruction' had to be slain: disease, ignorance, squalor and idleness.[2] However, the bulk of the Report's 299 pages was devoted to the eradication of want. What, then, were the Report's major principles? Why did it initially arouse such opposition within government? How appropriate a solution to postwar poverty did it, in retrospect, offer?

The Report itself summarised 'the main feature of the Plan for Social Security' as:

> A scheme of social insurance against interruption and destruction of earning power and for special expenditure arising at birth, marriage or death. The scheme embodies six fundamental principles: flat rate of subsistence benefit; flat rate of contribution; unification of administrative responsibility; adequacy of benefit; comprehensiveness; and classification. . . . Based on them, and in combination with national assistance and voluntary insurance as subsidiary methods, the aim of the Plan for Social Security is to make want under any circumstances unnecessary.[3]

Its whole logic was, therefore, based on the far from revolutionary decision to maintain the prewar system of contributory insurance, based on the weekly payments of employees, employers and the state. No other system (such as one financed solely from taxation – long advocated by the Labour Party) was seriously considered on the ground that it would be a 'departure from existing practice, for which there is neither need nor justification and which conflicts with the wishes and feelings of the British democracy'.[4]

Insurance, Beveridge argued, suited the interests of government, employers and the public alike. Government, faced with increasing demands for public expenditure, required an acceptable form of taxation. Contributory insurance was, moreover, cheap to administer, automatically established a claimant's right to benefit and could moderate demands for greater expenditure by fixing in the electorate's mind the need to match higher benefits with higher contributions. Employers might complain of a tax on employment, but a healthy 'secure' workforce would be a productive one. Thus for business, as well as humanitarian reasons, employers should be directly involved in its administration. Above all, contributory insurance was what the British public – through the increasing popularity before 1939 of statutory and voluntary insurance – had shown that they wanted. As the Report maintained: 'the capacity and the desire of the British people to contribute for security are among the most certain and most impressive social facts of today'. One reason for this was a desire for independence. People wanted 'security not as charity but as a right'. Another, less propitious for the future of the welfare state, was a residual dislike and distrust of government. Insurance implied a contractual obligation on which, it was felt, government could not renege.

Many issues were left unresolved by the decision to retain the principle of insurance. Who, for instance, was to be included in the scheme and what should the premium be? The Report proposed that cover, unlike interwar practice, should be universal and that there should in the main be a common flat-rate contribution. Both recommendations, as will be seen, aroused considerable controversy. An obvious disadvantage of a flat-rate scheme, tied to what the poorest-paid contributor could afford, was the limitation of the scheme's income. This was partly counteracted by the three assumptions upon which the Report was based: the provision by government of universal family allowances and a comprehensive health service (both financed by taxation) and the maintenance of a high level of employment.[5] The first two assumptions relieved the insurance scheme of two of the most expensive prerequisites of social security; the latter maximised the number of active contributors whilst minimising the number of claimants.

An equally obvious problem for a universal scheme, based on insurance contributions made at work, was how to cater for the variety of people's work experience, and indeed for those who had no paid employment. To counteract this problem the Report classified the population into six groups, each with their own different level of contributions. The groups were (1) employees, (2) the self-employed, (3) housewives, (4) others of working age, not gainfully employed, (5) those below working age, and (6) the retired above working age. The most difficult groups to cover were groups (3) and

(4). With regard to the former, it was recommended that all married women should qualify for a wide range of benefits 'by virtue of their husbands' contribution'.[6] If they worked, they might in addition opt to pay a lower contribution to qualify for the full range of benefits, albeit below the standard rate. With regard to the latter, there was no option – for claimants such as non-working single women who were unable to make contributions – but to provide relief through the tax-financed, but means-tested, national assistance scheme. National assistance was, nevertheless, expected to be a subsidiary scheme covering a very small and ever-decreasing number of people.

What benefits were to be secured by these insurance contributions? It was recommended that the three guiding principles should be comprehensiveness, a flat rate of benefit, and adequacy. In the main, all insured persons – whatever the reason for the loss or interruption of their income – should receive an identical cash benefit which was adequate to provide an agreed minimum standard of living and would last as long as required. Inevitably there was some variation in the availability, value and duration of benefits. Those in classes (2) to (4) for example would not qualify for unemployment benefit; for class (3) Beveridge designed an exclusive 'housewives' charter' which included a furnishing grant upon marriage, free domestic help when ill, and a separation allowance on the breakdown of marriage. Several benefits were also paid above the flat-rate subsistence level, either to encourage 'desirable' behaviour or to maintain an individual's customary (as opposed to subsistence) standard of living. The former included a supplement to the standard pension for those who continued to work after the official retirement age; the latter industrial injury benefit which, after thirteen weeks, was related to previous earnings. Finally, the duration of benefit for widows of working age without dependants was limited to thirteen weeks and the continued payment of unemployment benefit could become dependent on retraining.[7]

Despite these anomalies, which were necessary for the adaptation of the scheme to the wide variety of individual circumstances and need, the principle was largely maintained – at least within each class – of flat-rate contributions and benefits. This, as the Report itself acknowledged, set Britain apart from the normal practice in other countries, which was that both contributions and benefits should be earnings-related. Beveridge, however, was determined that Britain should remain different in order to enhance the self-reliance that the popularity of insurance had earlier demonstrated.

'To give by compulsory insurance', he argued, 'more than is needed for subsistence is an unnecessary interference with individual responsibilities.'[8] If people wanted to insure themselves against a fall in their customary standard of living, then they should insure themselves privately. Indeed Beveridge wanted to involve trade unions and other non-profit-making friendly societies (of which there were over 19 000 in 1939) in the administration of state benefits, not just to humanise the state system and to prevent possible abuse but also to make private insurance readily available. Such a hope was to prove forlorn, however, as was demonstrated by the need for government to introduce earnings-related benefits in the 1960s. Equally to be disappointed was Beveridge's final hope that the unification of administrative responsibility (through both the consolidation of payments into one insurance stamp and the establishment of one responsible ministry) would achieve 'co-ordination, simplicity and economy'.[9]

Such, then, were the Report's main proposals. Why did they provoke such criticism, particularly within the Conservative Party and the higher civil service? Objections were based largely on personal, political and logical grounds. Personally, Beveridge was intensely disliked for his awkward, autocratic manner and, no doubt more pertinently, for both the unerring accuracy with which he exposed administrative shortcomings and the success with which he forced the pace of political change against even Churchill's wishes. Politically, the concept of social security was attacked as excessively expensive. The Treasury in 1943 calculated that postwar governments would have at best a surplus revenue of £925 million, of which all but £100 million would be required for defence, the repayment of the national debt and the remission of taxes.[10] It would therefore be impossible to spend, as Beveridge wanted, £86 million on social security, especially as (within the social services) priority should be accorded to housing and education policy. These policies would at least assist the economy by helping to create a mobile and trained workforce, whereas to spend money on social security would, in the Chancellor of the Exchequer's words, be simply to 'throw it down the sink'.[11] Even worse, by guaranteeing workers subsistence benefits and demanding higher payments from employers and taxpayers, the Beveridge proposals might even be counterproductive by discouraging hard work and entrepreneurial risk-taking. The dangers of non-compliance and hostility from the USA were two further objections. The poor, the employers and the rich (who had no need for insurance benefits) might refuse to pay insurance contributions on the grounds that they either could not or should not pay such high premiums. Likewise American loans – on which postwar Britain would inevitably rely – might not be forthcoming if their purpose was seen to subsidise such an unproductive project.

Beveridge had been alerted to these objections during the Treasury's lengthy perusal of his draft proposals and he was thus able either to revise his plans or to answer his critics directly in the final report. In relation to the overall costs, he contemptuously dismissed the Treasury's traditional pessimism. 'There are no easy care-free times in early prospect', he admitted, 'but to suppose the difficulties cannot be overcome . . . is defeatism without reason and against reason.'[12] He did, nevertheless, make some major concessions (and thereby partly jeopardised the Report's principles) in an attempt to cut costs. He proposed, for instance, to delay for twenty years the payment of pensions at the full subsistence rate 'in view of the vital need of conserving resources in the immediate aftermath of war'; and in order to save a further £100 million per annum, he decided that no family allowance should be paid for the first child.[13] This meant that many elderly people and large families on low incomes might not have their subsistence needs met automatically and that, consequently, they would have to resort to national assistance. Such concessions, however, did reduce the overall cost of his proposals to little more than the sum to which government was already committed, given inflation and various wartime promises. 'The Chancellor of the Exchequer', concluded Keynes, 'should thank his stars that he has got off so cheap.'

On the intrinsic value of social security, Beveridge rebutted each of the Treasury's objections with equal vigour. Social security, he argued, would encourage not discourage economic growth because the elimination of poverty would improve workers' physical and mental well-being and thereby increase productivity. Claimants would not be demoralised because, as has been seen, the whole purpose of the Report was to encourage self-sufficiency. Indeed, as one recent commentary noted, 'the crucial consideration' for Beveridge appeared to be 'not the provision of adequate subsistence benefits but the maximising of personal responsibility and the maintenance of the conditions of social independence'.[14] Neither workers nor employers would refuse to pay their contributions because, on average, the former were being asked to contribute less than they were already paying in voluntary and statutory premiums, whilst employers were to pay no more than their European counterparts.[15] Finally, in relation to the American reaction, Beveridge effectively called the politicians' bluff. His proposals, he explained, were merely a practical demonstration of how to 'cover ground which must be covered, in one way or another, in translating the Atlantic Charter into deeds'. Surely Churchill was not intending to renege on his wartime promises?

Far more ominous for the Report's future success were two logical inconsistencies identified by its critics in relation to the principles of universalism and adequacy. If Beveridge's objective really was to eliminate 'want', they argued, why was relief not targeted on those in need? Universalism would involve a 'vast and essentially purposeless' bureaucratic exercise to collect contributions from and distribute benefits to those who did not need state support. It would then (given the ultimate resource constraints on the social security budget) fail effectively to relieve those in genuine need because benefits would have to be distributed too widely. Family allowances were singled out as a particularly expensive universal benefit which, despite their aggregate cost, would lack the necessary finance to attain their foremost objectives of relieving child poverty and encouraging larger families.[16] If the major reason for universalism was a desire to eliminate the means test, then this again was illogical because such a test was to be retained for many pensioners, those with high rents and – above all – in the assessment of the income of taxpayers, who were expected to help finance social security. In the 1960s, as the cost of the welfare state escalated, such arguments in favour of 'selectivity' were to be revived.

The principle of adequacy proved to be the Report's Achilles' heel. Beveridge admitted that 'any estimate of subsistence income' could not be scientific but had to be 'to some extent a matter of judgement'. He justified his basic flat-rate benefit of £2 per week for a couple in terms of Rowntree's 'absolute' poverty, which was based on an estimate of an average household's expenditure on food, rent, clothing and sundries – although the latest research would suggest that (in his determination to maintain the work ethic) he actually calculated the lowest normal manual worker's income and then fixed his subsistence level just below it.[17] Whatever the basis of the calculation, the fundamental anomaly remained that Beveridge was attempting to provide a subsistence-level payment through a flat-rate benefit, when in practice the price of 'necessities' varied considerably between seasons and, above all, between regions. Rowntree himself recognised this in relation to one of the more volatile items in the working-class budget – rent – and he suggested that both the insurance and the assistance schemes should provide a nominal subsistence benefit plus the claimant's actual rent. Beveridge rejected this suggestion, as he also rejected the objection of civil servants that it was illogical to provide a full subsistence benefit when it was known that most claimants had some income either in kind (such as help from relatives) or in cash (such as savings). His objection in both cases was that a means test would be required.

However, given the essential artificiality of the concept of subsistence and the variety of benefit levels which (as has been seen) the Report already envisaged, it was inevitable that cost-conscious governments would ultimately reject the principle of adequacy. Just as the commitment to 'full' employment had been watered down by 1944 to the 'maintenance of a high and stable level of employment', so social security was modified first to 'social' and then to 'national' insurance. Both parties within the Coalition government agreed that the rate of benefit should only be one which provided 'a *reasonable* insurance against want'.[18] The effect of this compromise was to destroy the whole logic of the Report because the payment of insurance contributions would no longer automatically guarantee freedom from poverty. If claimants had no other source of income, they would have to apply for means-tested national assistance in order to supplement their inadequate insurance benefits.

With the passage of time, the Beveridge Report was indeed to be exposed as a flawed blueprint for the eradication of poverty. Both practical and conceptual flaws were revealed. The major practical limitation was the attempt to base an extremely expensive system of relief (universal benefits) on a very restricted source of income (flat-rate contributions tied to what the poorest worker could afford). This meant that there would never be sufficient resources to respond flexibly to inflation or to changes in either social need or social demands. The assumption of full employment inevitably raised the spectre of inflation, but there could be no resources set aside to fund increases in benefit above the level warranted by the original, actuarially-based contributions. Such increases would have to be provided on a 'pay as you go' basis from the current workforce, which undermined the whole principle of insurance.

The Report also assumed that most risks to income were 'insurable', whereas demographic change in particular swelled the ranks of those who were unable to make insurance contributions.

The needs of the increasing number of one-parent families, for instance, had to be met – in the absence of any contingency fund – by means-tested benefit. This in turn meant that the role of national assistance, rather than diminishing as predicted by the Report, became increasingly important. Most seriously of all however, lack of resources jeopardised the acceptance of the principle of 'adequacy' not only in the 1940s, when poverty could still be defined as an 'absolute' concept to be measured in terms of a given set of subsistence needs, but more especially thereafter, when it became increasingly defined as a 'relative' concept (see Chapter 6.2). As the Report itself acknowledged, its proposals were based on a restricted definition of poverty; but it lacked the resources to eradicate it by this definition, let alone the later one.[19]

The Report was also exposed, in time, as having failed to anticipate the merging of the taxation and benefit systems. Given the principle of 'universalism', most people were to be provided with insurance benefits whilst, with increasing affluence, most were also to enjoy the privilege of being taxpayers. Yet two separate administrative bodies, the Inland Revenue and Ministry of Social Security (under its various titles), continued to collect direct taxes in the form of income tax and insurance contributions and to dispense benefit in the form of tax allowances and insurance payments. In the payment of benefit, they were also joined by the National Assistance Board/ Supplementary Benefits Commission and other agencies, such as local authorities responsible for rent and rate rebates. Each essentially worked in isolation, with its own administrative criteria, and thus there was none of the 'co-ordination, simplicity and economy' which the Report had envisaged.

Attempts were accordingly made to replace the whole bureaucratic basis of Beveridge's proposal with a unified tax and benefit system, such as a negative income tax. Such a new system, whilst admittedly blurring the distinction between tax and insurance, would have had the additional advantage of confronting one part of the welfare system which Beveridge had totally overlooked: tax allowances or 'fiscal welfare'. Tax allowances might have been used, after the war, to encourage what Beveridge had particularly wanted – private insurance – but they cost government considerable sums of money (which, it was argued, were not available for the underwriting of the insurance scheme) and, by redistributing resources from the poor to the rich, conflicted with the essential purpose of the report.

With regard to the Report's conceptual flaws, one major attack by feminists has already been noted in Chapter 2.3.3. These critics have sometimes overlooked Beveridge's proposal for a 'housewives' charter', which successive governments failed to implement. They have also tended to discount the genuine efforts made to meet the needs of underprivileged groups, such as non-working single women. No-one else at the time (including the feminist groups to which Beveridge appealed) was able to devise a practical means of relief within an insurance system, which was what the vast majority of the public was then demanding. There was no question, however, that an insurance system based on participation in a labour market, in which women were not equally represented or rewarded, could only disadvantage women in relation to men.

An equally fundamental attack on the Report has been made by those who view poverty as the result not of a temporary loss or interruption of earnings but of the inequality inherent in a capitalist society. In 1943 some within the Labour Party warned that the Report offered no more than the 'co-ordination of the nation's ambulance services': true social security was dependent on full employment and high wages.[20] More radically, it was argued in the 1960s and 70s (with the development of the concepts of 'relative poverty' and 'relative deprivation') that poverty could only be reduced by a major redistribution of economic resources and hence of political power. Beveridge did envisage some redistribution. Family allowances and the health service, for instance, were to be funded by general taxation. In *Full Employment in a Free Society*, he was also insistent (as has been seen in Chapter 5.1) that industrial investment should be directed by the state towards the elimination of the 'five giants'. Redistribution, however, was not to be too radical. Abolition of want, the Report argued, could not be achieved solely by increased production. There would have to be some redistribution of income, but 'correct distribution does not mean what it has been taken to mean in the past – distribution between different agents in production, between land, capital, management and labour. Better distribution of purchasing power is required among wage-earners themselves.'[21] The Report has, therefore, been seen by many as not merely technically unsuited to the relief of 'relative poverty' by the state, but as philosophically inimical to it.

Far, therefore, from being a revolutionary and logical document – as it was popularly portrayed in the 1940s – the Beveridge Report was conservative, illogical and ultimately impractical. Its objectives at the time appeared visionary – the abolition of want through a comprehensive social insurance system in which subsistence-level benefits would be available to everyone as of right and without a means test. It also effectively destroyed the fatalism of the Coalition government and the higher civil service, and thereby transformed perceptions of what was politically possible and necessary. It was, however, inherently conservative in its retention of the insurance principle, its limitation of the state's responsibility to the provision of a subsistence-level benefit and its emphasis on voluntary insurance. Other countries (with no noticeable erosion of individual responsibility) were already providing earnings-related benefits in return for earnings-related contributions. The Report's logic, especially in relation to the principles of universalism and adequacy, was also inherently flawed and it perceived neither the need nor the opportunity for a merger of the taxation and benefit systems. The Report, in short, might have been an excellent blueprint for the relief of poverty in the interwar period, when unemployment had been high and public expectations low. It was not, as will be seen, well-suited to a period of rising affluence.

6.2 THE 'REDISCOVERY' OF POVERTY

Throughout the 1950s there was growing concern within government about the nature of the social security system, but there was no sustained public criticism of it until Christmas Eve 1965. It was then that, for maximum effect, Brian Abel-Smith and Peter Townsend (two of Titmuss's colleagues) published *The Poor and the Poorest*, in which they claimed that the number of people living in poverty, rather than decreasing under the welfare state, had actually increased from a minimum of 600 000 in 1953–4 to two million in 1964. This 'rediscovery' of poverty needs to be qualified in two ways. First, unlike the poor of late Victorian England or the 1930s, the poor of the 1960s were neither a coherent social group who attracted widespread public sympathy nor a perceived political threat. Rather, as has been remarked, poverty in postwar Britain was 'essentially a statistical concept. The poor did not make themselves visible; they were discovered at the bottom of income tables by social scientists.' Secondly, as Deacon and Bradshaw have stressed, 'poverty was rediscovered only after it had been redefined'.[22] By the definition adopted in the Beveridge Report, very little poverty could be said to have existed after the 1950s. Nevertheless, within policy-making circles, the 'rediscovery' had a profound effect. What was the new definition of poverty; and in what ways was it a more 'accurate' measure than previous definitions?

The definition of poverty employed by the Beveridge Report was the one developed in the classic house-to-house surveys of local poverty in the first part of the century, particularly by Rowntree in York. It was in essence an 'absolute' or subsistence-level definition based on the minimum expenditure on food, rent, clothing and 'sundries' required by a family to maintain its 'physical efficiency'. It could be measured on two levels. 'Primary' poverty referred to families which simply lacked the income to meet this minimum expenditure. 'Secondary' poverty referred to a family which had sufficient income but was, in the opinion of the investigator, living in a state of *actual* poverty because part of its income was 'absorbed by other expenditure, either useful or wasteful'. The new definition of poverty was a 'relative' one. As Townsend has argued:

> Individuals, families and groups in the population can be said to be in poverty when they lack the resources to obtain the type of diet, participate in the activities or have the living standards and amenities which are customary, or at least widely encouraged or approved, in the societies to which they belong. Their resources are so seriously below those commanded by the average individual or family that they are, in effect, excluded from ordinary living patterns, customs and activities.[23]

The concept of relative poverty was not as novel as many have assumed. As Townsend himself admitted, it had a pedigree stretching back to Adam Smith in the 1770s. It had also been used, if somewhat mutedly, in the twentieth century in line with rising public expectations. For example, Rowntree himself had consistently allowed increased expenditure on 'sundries' (such as presents and holidays), so that his supposedly 'static' poverty line actually increased by 75 per cent in real terms between his surveys of York in 1899 and 1950.[24] The measurement of secondary poverty in the surveys also depended on his investigators' judgement of whether families, despite their 'adequate' income, were in fact living in conditions below those which were 'customary or at least widely encouraged and approved' at the time. Even the Conservative government itself raised the level of national assistance in 1959 above that justified by inflation, so that claimants could have a 'share in increasing national prosperity'. The approach of Abel-Smith and Townsend was novel only in that it attempted to break totally with a concept of poverty based on a finite set of minimum needs.

It is not just the definition of poverty that provokes controversy but also the means by which *any* definition can be translated into a practical measure of those living in poverty. Critics had condemned calculations of the earlier and simpler concept of absolute poverty as abstract, arbitrary and subjective. They were abstract because measurement was based on 'scientific' need (the amount of food, for example, that could be bought most cheaply to provide the requisite number of calories) rather than 'observable' need (the actual spending patterns of the poor which were based not just on nutritional but also social and psychological need). They were arbitrary in, for example, their ever-changing choice of sundries. Finally, they were subjective because the measurement of secondary poverty was dependent on the personal judgement of each investigator. Can the measurement of relative poverty be any more 'accurate'? One possible solution is simply to classify as being in poverty any household whose income falls below a given percentage of national average income. However the choice of the particular percentage cannot but be arbitrary; and, in the assessment of the national average, there are problems in the standardisation of the difference between earnings and effective take-home pay (given, for example, variations in the incidence of personal taxation and other unavoidable expenditure such as travel expenses to work). Another method, employed by Townsend in his major study of poverty in 1968–9, is to construct an index of 'relative deprivation' which measures not only income but also the ability of people to participate in normal activities (such as holidays) and to control their own lives (especially in the housing market).[25] The trouble with such an index is again its arbitrary nature and the fact that non-participation in 'customary' activities may result from individual choice, not from a lack of resources. Townsend's index, it could be argued, was based upon assumptions about how people *should* behave which were just as subjective and as moralistic as those made by the early poverty surveys about how people *should not* behave.

Largely by default, the standard against which relative poverty has come conventionally to be measured is the current level of national assistance/supplementary benefit. For policy-analysis, this approach has the additional advantage that it measures the number of people falling below the government's 'official operational definition of poverty' and thus the success of the policy at any given time.[26] However, it is by no means uncontroversial because the benefit level is itself a far from objective standard. The exact basis on which the government makes its calculations has never been publicly disclosed. It reflects not so much a standard of living which is 'widely encouraged or approved', but what government at a given time feels it can afford. Moreover it has the peculiar 'scientific' quality that, should government raise the level of benefit, more people will automatically be classified as living in poverty – whereas, should the level be allowed to fall, poverty could (without any change in actual living standards) be eradicated.

There are also major problems in determining the current level of national assistance/supplementary benefit. Benefits consist, as Rowntree recommended to Beveridge in 1942, of a cash payment plus claimants' actual housing costs. Allowances for children also vary according to their age. Any one figure for the current value of benefit has therefore to assume a rather abstract average figure for rent and children's allowances. Moreover, in the official calculation of need, certain existing income (such as small savings) is disregarded and regular additional payments or one-off lump sums can be made at the discretion of officials to meet exceptional need. For these reasons the main standard of poverty used in *The Poor and the Poorest* was 140 per cent of the basic rate of national assistance plus rent, and by this standard the numbers in poverty rose dramatically from 600 000 to four million in 1953–4 and from two to 7.5 million in 1964. The choice of the figure of 140 per cent was, however, somewhat arbitrary and has not been uniformly adopted by other social scientists.

Other technical problems arise when the basis of measurement is changed from house-to-house surveys to the more remote analysis of government statistics, all of which have been compiled for purposes other than the analysis of poverty. The longest running series of any value is that published by the Inland Revenue on the distribution of income, but inevitably it excludes non-taxpayers. The most recent is the General Household Survey, compiled since 1971, but it lacks adequate detail. The series most commonly used, therefore, is the Family Expenditure Survey, which has been compiled since 1957 to determine actual patterns of household expenditure so that the correct weights can be incorporated into revisions of the retail price index. The use of this series tends, for a number of reasons, to underestimate the incidence of poverty. The returns are voluntary and the sample is consequently biased because the response of the elderly and the sick tends to be disproportionately low. Respondents who are temporarily without earned income (for example because of sickness or unemployment) are required to return their 'normal' income. The series also records the circumstances of whole households rather than individual 'tax' or 'benefit' units – so that for example, pensioners, who are not claiming the benefits to which they are legally entitled may not appear to be in poverty because their income is being supplemented by relations with whom they are living. The importance of the last two factors can be vividly illustrated in relation to the 1971 Fiegehen survey. This survey recorded a poverty level of 4.9 per cent, but the figure would have risen to 6.5 per cent had 'actual' been substituted for 'normal' income and to 8.8 per cent had 'benefit units' been used rather than households.[27]

The use of the Family Expenditure Survey raises other statistical problems, the effects of which are less clear-cut. For example information is supplied for only two weeks. For people with irregular earnings, were those weeks typical? The samples are also small, and the numbers in poverty even smaller. In the 1960 survey analysed in *The Poor and the Poorest*, for instance, there were only 3450 respondents from an original sample of 5000 and the number of those living below the national assistance level was 167.[28] The smallness of the samples provides one explanation for the variety of findings derived from the Family Expenditure Survey material. It also raises the question of whether such surveys are any less abstract than those of the earlier house-to-house surveys.

The results of the principal postwar poverty surveys are provided in Table 6.2.[29] There were only two major house-to-house surveys, by Rowntree in 1950 and Townsend in 1968–9. Rowntree's survey was the last of the classic surveys of local poverty and concluded that virtually no-one in York remained in primary poverty, whilst only 1.66 per cent of the total population was in secondary poverty. Complacency about the success of the welfare state was compounded by the calculation that whereas 2.77 per cent of the working-class population were in secondary poverty, the figure would have risen to 22.18 per cent had it not been for recent welfare legislation.

To generalise from such figures would, however, be dangerous. Was York a sufficiently representative town upon which to base estimates of national poverty? The survey was also based upon a very idiosyncratic definition of the working class (which alone was examined) and of course on a measure of absolute poverty. Atkinson has reworked the figures to show that had the current level of

Table 6.2 Estimates of poverty in the UK, 1950–75

Year	Study	Source	Unit	Total population	
				%	Number
1950	Rowntree*	Survey	household	1.7	
	Atkinson*			5.8	
1953–4	Abel-Smith and Townsend	FES	household	1.2	0.6
1954	Gough and Stark	IR	tax unit	12.3	6.3
1959	Gough and Stark	IR	tax unit	8.8	4.6
1960	Abel-Smith and Townsend	FES	household	3.8	2.0
1963	Gough and Stark	IR	tax unit	9.4	5.1
1967	Atkinson	FES	household	3.5	2.0
1969	Atkinson	FES	household	3.4	2.0
1968–9	Townsend	Survey	household	6.4	3.8
1971	Fiegehen et al.	FES	household	4.9	2.6
1975	Beckerman and Clark**	FES	household	2.3	1.3
1975	Layard et al.**	GHS	household	8.7	4.6
1975	Berthoud and Brown	GHS	household	11.3	6.1

* York only.   ** Great Britain only.
Source: Adapted from R. Hemming, *Poverty and Incentives* (Oxford, 1984) p. 53.

national assistance been used 5.8 per cent of the population would have been recorded as living in poverty.[30] Townsend's figures are somewhat higher than corresponding surveys and may provide some corrective for the underestimates of poverty inherent in the use of the Family Expenditure Survey. The estimates based on the Inland Revenue Series and the General Household Survey are also high. This is mainly because the former is based on tax units rather than households and the latter on the higher long-rates of supplementary benefits to which few claimants other than pensioners were actually entitled. The figures for Abel-Smith and Townsend, as explained earlier, represent their minimum rather than their preferred calculations.

Bearing in mind these qualifications, and the statistical anomalies identified earlier, the findings of the surveys detailed in Table 6.2 are surprisingly consistent. They suggest that in the 1960s and early 1970s there were, at minimum, between 1.3 million and 2.6 million people living in poverty representing, respectively, 2.3 per cent or 4.6 per cent of the population. Higher estimates can be justified by the use of different criteria and statistical conventions. No one figure is incontrovertible, however, because – despite all claims to the contrary – neither the concept of relative poverty nor its measurement is or can be scientifically precise.

6.3 THE ABANDONMENT OF BEVERIDGE

The Beveridge Report provided a powerful and popular set of principles upon which to develop a system of social security and they were, in the main, followed by the first postwar governments. Within twenty years, however, poverty had been 'rediscovered' and the system was coming increasingly under attack. Why was this? Was it because successive governments had failed fully to implement Beveridge's recommendations? Was it because these recommendations, as suggested earlier, were impractical? Or was it simply because, with rising affluence, political values and public expectations changed? If it were the latter, what alternative policies were proposed and implemented?

Postwar policy can be divided into four broad stages. In the first – from 1945 to 1956 – there was a general satisfaction that, through the implementation of the Beveridge Report (by such legislation as the 1945 Family Allowances Act, the 1946 National Insurance Act and the 1948 National Assistance Act), poverty had been virtually eliminated. Complacency was encouraged by the findings of Rown-tree's 1950 survey of York, the rising surplus in the National Insurance Fund (resulting from unemployment being far lower than estimated)[31] and continuing economic growth (which, it was assumed, would mean increased living standards). The one cause for concern was the number of claimants on means-tested national assistance which, far from declining, had increased by 1954 to 1.8 million. The obvious reason for this blemish was successive govern-ments' refusal to make flat-rate insurance benefits 'adequate' because, as seen earlier, it was adjudged both illogical and impracti-cable. Consequently their value fell consistently below the 'official poverty line' of national assistance which, in particular, met claim-ants' *actual* housing costs and was regularly increased in line with inflation. The majority of claimants for national assistance were, therefore, those seeking to 'top-up' insurance payments; and in an exceptional attempt to resolve this anomaly, insurance benefits were raised by 22 per cent just before the 1955 election.

The second phase lasted from 1957 to 1965. It opened with the Conservative government, in the aftermath of Suez and confronted by a sterling crisis, seeking to build an 'opportunity' rather than a 'welfare' state. It had also, rather more prosaically, to refashion the national insurance scheme in the light of a decline in its surplus and a rise in public expectations. The core of the problem was the non-implementation of another of Beveridge's proposals – the more regressive suggestion that, because of the need to build a healthy surplus in the Insurance Fund to meet the long-term cost of the population's increased longevity, full subsistence pensions should not be paid for twenty years. The Attlee government, however, had found such a proposal politically unacceptable and had authorised the immediate payment of the full pension, albeit below the subsist-ence level, to all those who qualified. After ten years it was to be made universal – which meant that a 55-year-old man, who had only started to contribute in 1948, would then be entitled to a pension ten times higher than his contributions actuarially warranted.[32]

The chickens thus released came home to roost in 1957, when both the Cabinet and the Treasury were already becoming concerned about the rising level of existing public expenditure. Their solution was two-fold. First, to cut government expenditure the Treasury's contribution to the Insurance Fund was capped; and its relative size declined thereafter from Beveridge's target of 33 per cent of total contributions to a mere 14 per cent by 1973–4.[33] This starved the Fund still further of resources, and explicitly transformed the national insurance system from an actuarial scheme (in which the level of contributions was determined by the anticipated cost of future liabilities) to a pay-as-you-go scheme (in which current contributions directly financed current outgoings). Secondly, to raise revenue, the foreign example of earnings-related contributions was adopted with regard to pensions. This initiative had other advantages. It was electorally popular; and by providing eventually an earnings-related supplement to the flat-rate pension, it could both lift many claimants off supplementary benefit and offer, in an 'opportunity' state, some reward for hard work. However, it had the disadvantage that were it to be administered exclusively by government it would threaten voluntary insurance and private initiative (not to mention the interests of private insurance companies). Despite Treasury protests about lost revenue, therefore, contributors were allowed to 'contract out' of the state scheme, should they so choose, into an approved tax-subsidised occupational pension. The relevant Act was passed just before the 1959 election.

The third phase lasted broadly from the publication of *The Poor and the Poorest* in 1965 to Labour's election defeat in 1970. To raise extra revenue and to 'float' further claimants off means-tested benefit, the earnings-related principle was extended to unemployment, sickness, industrial injury and widows' benefit in 1966 (without any provision for contracting-out or matching state contributions). There was also a major extension in both the range of, and the number of claimants on, means-tested benefit. For example rate rebates (to be administered by local government) were introduced in 1966, and the number dependent on national assistance/supplementary benefit alone rose to 7.7 per cent of the population (see Table 6.3). This growth of means-testing conflicted not only with Beveridge's proposals but also with traditional Labour Party policy. In particular it contradicted the Party's election pledge to introduce an 'income guarantee', whereby no-one would have to apply for subsistence benefit but would receive it automatically through the tax system. The realities of office, however, soon convinced the Wilson government that such a guarantee was administratively and financially impractical. Equally it was convinced by the deteriorating economic situation that no major uprating of universal benefits could be afforded. There was, therefore, no alternative to an extension of means-tested benefit.

Table 6.3 Claimants receiving national assistance/supplementary benefit, 1948–74 (000s)

	National assistance				Supplementary benefit	
	1948	1951	1961	1965	1970	1974
1. Retirement pensioners and national insurance widows 60 years and over	495	767	1075	1239	1745	1712
2. Others over pension age	143	202	220	196	156	96
3. Unemployed with national insurance benefit	19	33	45	34	73	73
4. Unemployed without national insurance benefit	34	33	86	78	166	228
5. Sick and disabled with national insurance benefit	80	121	134	149	164	95
6. Sick and disabled without national insurance benefit	64	98	133	138	159	165
7. Women under 60 with dependent children	32	41	76	108	191	245
8. National insurance widows under 60	81	86	58	55	63	42
9. Others	63	81	17	15	20	24
10. Total persons receiving supplementary benefit	1011	1462	1844	2012	2738	2680
11. Total number of claimants and dependants	1465	2048	2608	2840	4167	4092
12. Claimants and dependants as a percentage of the total population	3.0	4.2	5.1	5.4	7.7	7.5

Figures are for Great Britain only.

... (DHSS ... pamphlet no. 22, 1975) p. 9

A positive attempt was nevertheless made to make such benefits more acceptable and accessible. To minimise stigma, the administration of national insurance and national assistance was united – as Beveridge had wished – in a Ministry of Social Security; national assistance was renamed supplementary benefit; and the claimant's legal right to benefit was made explicit. To combat low take-up, greater publicity was given to the full range of benefits, application procedures were simplified and all the discretionary payments for which pensioners in particular might qualify were consolidated into a single 'long-term additional' benefit. However, the continuing economic crisis and declining popular sympathy for the poor both restricted the resources and discouraged the changes in official attitude which were essential if such reforms were to be fully effective. Disillusion and dissatisfaction amongst the well-informed and the politically committed began to escalate; and there was a consequent proliferation of expert pressure groups (such as the Child Poverty Action Group, founded in 1965 on the publication of *The Poor and The Poorest*) and militant protest groups (such as the local Claimants' Unions which started to form, especially in universities, in 1968).

The final phase extended from 1970 to 1975 and saw both a further, deliberate expansion of means-testing and renewed attempts to rationalise the whole social security system. The objective of means-testing was to target the poor more effectively, and in particular to relieve child poverty and to counteract the ravages of inflation. In 1968 the only serious postwar attempt to increase the value of universal family allowances had been made, with any extra benefit accruing to the better-off being 'clawed back' through the tax system. In 1971 – in defiance of the Conservatives' election pledge – this expedient was not extended. Instead a new means-tested benefit, Family Income Supplement, was introduced, guaranteeing to the low-paid half the difference between their gross pay and the appropriate level of supplementary benefit. To combat inflation mandatory rent rebates and more generous rate rebates were introduced; and national insurance benefits were divided more distinctly into long-term and short-term benefits with the more generous long-term benefits being reserved for those (such as pensioners) unable to participate in the labour market and therefore in rising real wages. The intention behind such reforms was well-meaning, but they greatly added to the complexity of an already confused, and confusing, system. Before 1970, for example, concern had been expressed about the 'unemployment trap' – the disincentive to an increasing number of supplementary benefit claimants to take low-paid work because, with the loss of means-tested benefits and an increase in both their tax liability and travel costs, their real income could actually fall. Family income supplement created a similar 'poverty trap', whereby the take-home pay of low-paid workers could actually fall after the award of a pay increase.[34]

It had been the initial intention of the Heath government to remove all such anomalies by rationalising the tax and benefit systems through the introduction of 'tax credits'; but like the earlier income guarantee this reform was ultimately rejected as administratively and financially impractical. A more modest administrative rationalisation was sought by the returning Labour government in its 1975 Social Security Act. All insurance contributions were made earnings-related. Beveridge's class 4 contributions (made by those of working age, not gainfully employed) were abolished. So too was the working wife's right to opt out of full insurance contributions. The distinction between long-term and short-term insurance benefit was also consolidated, with the former being index-linked to earnings (thereby maintaining its relative value) and the latter to prices (thereby only maintaining its real value). The Act was, however, wholly incapable of resolving the escalating problems arising from mass unemployment and inflation, as was illustrated by the rise in the number of those within the poverty trap from 12 000 in 1975 to 63 730 in 1979.[35]

The outstanding characteristic of these four periods was the fact that all Beveridge's principles were either rejected outright or surreptitiously jettisoned. 'Adequacy', as has been seen, was never accepted despite Beveridge's restricted definition. Consequently a significant, and ever-rising, number of those in need were never – as his Report had promised – automatically freed from the fear of poverty but had to claim means-tested benefit. The principle of flat-rate contributions and benefit, which Beveridge himself had qualified with his special arrangements for different insurance classes, was wholly abandoned with the introduction of earnings-related contributions and benefits and, later, with the differentiation between long-term and short-term insurance benefits. The principle of comprehensiveness was also breached, in the coverage of persons, with the contracting-out clauses in the pensions legislation. Finally, Beveridge's system of classification was eroded by the abolition of class 4 contributions.

The abandonment of these five principles in turn affected the whole nature of the social security system. The 'subsidiary' service of national assistance did not, as predicted, wither away; and with the introduction of earnings-related benefits, voluntary insurance was no longer entrusted exclusively with the task of ensuring relative – as opposed to subsistence – living standards. Voluntary insurance, it is true, did increase with rising affluence, but it was not the type of expansion which Beveridge had sought. The successful insurance companies were not the small, participatory friendly societies (which had so impressed him as an example of working-class self-help) but the large, impersonal profit-making companies which were better able to exploit the artificial market conditions created by tax-exemptions and the contracting-out clauses in pensions legislation.

Even the very essence of the Beveridge Report – the insurance principle – was eroded. No scheme of national insurance could tailor contributions to individual circumstances as could a private policy, but since 1911 contributions had been based on an estimate of the Insurance Fund's future liabilities. Beveridge had adjudged this modified insurance contract to be to everyone's advantage; but when the cost of national insurance began to rise in the late 1950s the government's contribution was capped and any attempt to maintain an actuarial system abandoned. Contributions were continued because they provided a relatively uncontentious form of taxation and discouraged demands for higher benefits. The insurance principle was therefore a convenient political fiction. By the late 1970s, however, it was becoming an increasingly costly fiction. Not only were some 100 000 civil servants required to collect the contributions at an annual cost of £100 million, but it also obstructed the much-needed rationalisation of the tax and benefit systems.[36]

The unnecessarily high administrative costs of social insurance underline the failure of Beveridge's sixth principle: the unification of administrative responsibility. Superficially unification had been achieved in 1966 with the creation of the Ministry of Social Security. 'Want', however, continued to be relieved by a wide range of means-tested benefits, administered by local government and the NHS, such as rent rebates, school meals and free prescriptions. In 1975 there were, indeed, forty-five major means-tested benefits, each with its own assessment criteria. Moreover, not even the unification of national insurance and national assistance under the Ministry of Social Security achieved Beveridge's objectives of 'coordination, simplicity and economy'. Social insurance may have been unnecessarily expensive, but its administrative costs were, on average, only 3 pence

in every pound. The cost of the expanding and more labour-intensive
supplementary benefit system was over 10 pence in the pound.[37]

Far more seriously, supplementary benefit was so uncoordinated
and complex that it not only discouraged personal initiative (through
the creation, for example, of the unemployment and poverty traps),
but it actually denied the poor their legal rights through either a
lack of information or the deliberate action of officials. Despite
the extensive publicity campaigns of both the Wilson and Heath
governments; under 50 per cent of those entitled to claim were
applying for supplementary benefit and under 40 per cent of those
entitled to rate rebates and family income supplements. The single
major reason for this was lack of knowledge.[38]

The growing complexity of the system also demoralised officials.
'The book of rules', lamented the chairman of the Supplementary
Benefits Commission between 1975 and 1980, 'which in 1945 every
National Assistance Board officer had been able to carry around in
his pocket had grown to several massive volumes, so often amended
and so complicated that even the staff could not understand them.'
10 000 pages of new or amended rules were added in 1975 alone. The
only way in which staff could reduce their work-load to manageable
proportions (as suggested in Chapter 3.1.3) was actively to discourage people from making claims.[39] The social security system was,
therefore, not – as Beveridge had planned – making 'want under
any circumstances unnecessary'. Rather, it was making it inevitable.

Why was a more satisfactory system not devised? Both parties, as
has been seen, did try unsuccessfully to merge the tax and benefits
systems. The Labour Party's income guarantee was a modified form
of negative income tax (ironically championed by the right-wing
Institute of Economic Affairs) which would provide, through the tax
system, an automatic payment to anyone whose income fell below
a given limit. Such a universal payment would have been costly, but
the main objections were administrative. At a time when it was being
asked to prepare a wealth tax, the Inland Revenue would have had
to locate all non-tax-payers (no easy task, as the introduction of the
poll tax in 1990 demonstrated), redesign all its assessment forms and
institute weekly, as opposed to annual, assessments (as those in
need could scarcely wait for retrospective annual payments). The
Conservative Party's tax credits were a more modest attempt to
replace personal tax allowances, family allowances and family
income supplement. Their value would have been equivalent to these
benefits and, should anyone's level of taxation have fallen below that

value, the balance would have automatically been paid to them. The draw-backs were again cost and administrative duplication. If the value of the credits had been sufficiently high to 'float' most claimants off supplementary benefit (which was after all the reform's main justification), the basic tax rate would have had to be raised to approximately 45 per cent. This conflicted with the Conservatives' commitment to reduce taxation in order to restore incentives. Moreover, all but one of the 45 means-tested benefits would have survived.

Both schemes consequently suffered from the typical weaknesses of all such attempts to merge the tax and benefits systems.[40] They were superficially attractive in that, through automatic payments, they would resolve the problem of the non-take-up of means-tested benefits. They would also remove the absurdity, and the administrative expense, of government taxing the poor with one hand and paying out benefit to them with the other. However were such schemes to be universal, they would have typically required basic tax rates higher than 45 per cent, which successive governments adjudged politically unacceptable. Were benefits to be withdrawn pound-for-pound as income increased, personal incentives would also have been undermined (as with the poverty trap). No simplified system, could, moreover, be sufficiently flexible to deal with the wide variety of human need. A residual relief agency would have had to be retained. Finally, and most importantly, all such schemes begged major questions about the fundamental purpose of social security: was it to redistribute income simply to relieve basic need, or significantly to reduce inequality?

This was the critical issue in the academic debate which broke out over the future of social security in the 1960s, of which the 'rediscovery of poverty' was a part. The protagonists were the 'universalists', led by Titmuss, and the 'selectivists', of whom the IEA was the most effective representative. The universalists favoured not a merger of the tax and benefit systems but a 'back to Beveridge' approach. Insurance benefits should be made 'adequate' so that the majority of claimants could be 'floated' off supplementary benefit. In addition non-means-tested benefit should be introduced for groups, such as one-parent families, for whom Beveridge had failed to cater. The cost was to be borne by such redistributive measures as the withdrawal from the better-off of tax allowances, the removal of the ceiling on national insurance contributions and greater state contributions to the insurance fund (financed in part by a wealth tax). Universal state provision by such means was justified not only as administratively efficient but also, as seen in Chapter 2.2.2, on moral and ethical grounds.

This was of course anathema to the IEA. It saw the rediscovery of poverty as proof that Beveridge's war-time opponents within the Treasury and the Conservative Party had been right to condemn universalism as impractical. With rising affluence, it argued, state provision of welfare should wither away. Everyone should buy services (including pensions, education and health) in the open market – supported if necessary by state subsidies, to ensure either a necessary minimum personal income, or sufficient demand for such public goods as education. Personal responsibility and initiative would thereby be strengthened and competitive efficiency amongst the producers increased (see Chapter 2.2.3). The role of state bureaucrats should be reduced to helping directly only those in absolute poverty.

This battle of ideas was conducted at a rarefied level and had little direct impact on policy, although the increasing provision of means-tested benefits after 1966 did reflect the influence of the selectivists' arguments. Essentially neither political party could accept the full logic of either side. Within the Labour Party, Crossman (secretary of state for social services) clashed bitterly with the universalists, and especially Townsend, on the grounds that the electorate simply would not tolerate the degree of redistribution they were advocating.[41] Similarly the Heath government became disillusioned with means-testing as a result of the low take-up (despite extensive publicity) of family income supplement. It also shied away from the electoral repercussions of withdrawing tax allowances from the better-off and of the increased inequality that any return to the market in areas such as health care would entail. Social scientists, both as technocrats and as polemicists, were therefore, unable to provide practical answers to the dilemmas facing politicians and, more importantly, the poor themselves. The consensus which sanctioned the extension of means-testing, and thus of the growing confusion of supplementary benefits, was essentially a negative one based on the lack of any perceived practical alternative.

6.4 THE TARGETING OF NEED

How well in effect did this increasingly complex system cater for those in actual need? Unquestionably one of the major postwar achievements was the virtual elimination of absolute poverty – and, equally importantly, the fear of absolute poverty, which as late as the 1930s had been a reality for many working-class families. This achievement, however, has to be qualified in four ways. First, it was an achievement not just of the social security system but also of full employment. Secondly, the 'absolute' level of poverty, as has been seen, was not the sole concern of the poor. Relative living standards were of equal importance. Thus although the real value of benefits approximately doubled between 1945 and 1975 (with the noticeable exception of child support), the poor felt hardly any 'better-off' since the relative value of benefits remained remarkably stable at about 20 per cent of the average wage for single people, 30 per cent for couples and 40 per cent for couples with two children (see Tables 6.4 and 6.5). Thirdly, the means test was becoming more, rather than less, prevalent. Finally there were, as shown in Chapter 6.2, a significant and growing number of people living below the official poverty line. Supplementary benefit was failing as a safety net not just because of non-take-up but for two other reasons: it was unavailable to those in work and claimants could not receive in benefit more than they had been paid in their previous job, even if their wages had been below the poverty line. This latter restriction, the 'wage-stop', was not abolished until 1976.

Those who had to resort to means-tested benefits, and those who remained below the official poverty line, were largely drawn from the same groups of people: separated, divorced and widowed women; the sick and disabled; the unemployed; and the elderly (see Tables 6.3 and 6.6). The one major difference, which was the exceptional finding of *The Poor and the Poorest*, was the large number of families with children living below the poverty line because of low wages – who were, by definition, unable to claim national assistance/supplementary benefit.

The first two groups were ones for which Beveridge had been unable to find any satisfactory solution within an insurance scheme. His instinct to treat the breakdown of marriage as an 'insurance risk' foundered on the technical problem of moral hazard (see Chapter 3.2.1): a wife might either be responsible for or collude in the breakdown. Moreover any special treatment might inadvertently favour the unmarried over the married (as had unemployment insurance in the 1930s) and contravene fathers' legal responsibility for maintenance. These problems remained unsolved; and, in particular one-parent families (who numbered some 276 000 by 1975) had to resort to supplementary benefit, where special payments were

Table 6.4 Benefits as a percentage of average male manual earnings, 1948–74

	Retirement pension		Unemployment benefit (flat-rate)		Supplementary benefit (ordinary)		Supplementary benefit (long-term)	
	single	couple	couple	couple + 2 children	couple	couple + 2 children	single	couple
1948	18.9	30.5	30.4	38.1	29.0	39.9	–	–
1950	17.3	27.9	27.9	35.1	28.9	39.6	–	–
1955	17.9	29.2	29.1	38.1	28.3	39.0	–	–
1960	17.2	27.5	27.5	36.8	29.2	40.3	–	–
1965	20.4	33.2	33.2	43.8	32.0	43.5	–	–
1970	17.8	28.9	28.9	38.7	28.0	38.0	20.3	32.1
1974	20.6	32.9	28.6	38.9	28.1	37.9	21.4	33.6

Supplementary benefit figures exclude rent and assume the children to be under 5 years of age.
Source: R. Lister, Social Security (1975) pp. 34–7.

Table 6.5 The real value of social security benefits, 1948–75 (pound sterling, 1981 prices)

	July 1948	April 1961	September 1971	November 1975
1. Unemployment benefit	19.64	26.88	34.96	36.47
2. Retirement pension	19.64	26.88	34.96	42.96
3. Supplementary benefit	17.93	25.31	33.39	35.10
4. Child support:				
one child	4.87	4.36	4.27	3.67
three children	17.60	16.62	15.36	13.81

Lines 1–3 are standard benefits for couples; line 3 excludes payment for rent; lines 4–5 include tax allowances.
Source: R. Hemming, *Poverty and Incentives* (Oxford, 1984) p. 29.

154

Table 6.6 The immediate causes of poverty, 1936–60

| | Rowntree | | Abel-Smith and Townsend* | |
	1936 %	1950 %	1960 %	approx. number (millions)
1. Old age	14.7	68.1	33	2.50
2. Death of chief wage earner	7.8	6.4	10	0.75
3. Sickness	4.1	21.3	10	0.75
4. Unemployment	28.6	–	7	0.50
5. Inadequate wage/large family	44.8	4.3	40	3.00

* At their preferred poverty line of 140 per cent national assistance plus rent.

not forthcoming until 1976. Beveridge's suggestion that the state should pay maintenance directly to deserted mothers and then pursue defaulting fathers through the courts was not adopted.[42] In contrast the treatment of widows by successive governments was more generous than Beveridge had recommended. They were not deprived of their pension after 13 weeks, the expectation that they would return to work was relaxed in 1956, and the higher initial rate of payment (to permit adjustment to changed circumstances) was extended to six months in 1966.

Beveridge had also failed to cater adequately for those disabled other than in war or at work.[43] These 'civilian' disabled were either unable to build up an adequate insurance record or found that the level of insurance benefit was inadequate for their special needs. By the late 1960s there were about 1.1 million 'civilian' disabled, of whom 140 000 were receiving no benefit. One of the objectives of targeted legislation after 1970 was to meet their needs and those of their carers; and the resulting measures were sufficiently comprehensive to have met fully those needs, had they only been adequately funded.

Remarkably less generous was the treatment of the unemployed. Their insurance benefit was not limitless, as Beveridge had recommended, and there were strict disqualification rules in relation to strikes. Moreover, the interwar practice of refusing payment for the first three days of unemployment ('the waiting period') was reintroduced in 1971. Once on supplementary benefit the unemployed were treated with suspicion. Disqualification could start after four weeks if (in another throw-back to the 1930s) claimants could not prove that they were 'genuinely seeking work' and the long-term unemployed were denied the enhanced benefits that were accorded to other long-term claimants after 1966. Government action reflected the popular prejudice that – despite the deteriorating economic situation in the 1960s – unemployment was the fault of the individual and should under no circumstances be condoned.[44] This permanent emphasis on the danger of scrounging (which surveys repeatedly showed to be grossly exaggerated) and the 'four week' rule were taken by critics of the social security system as proof that its priority was not the welfare of individual claimants but the maintenance of the work ethic and of the capitalist economy.

The largest groups of people living on or below the poverty line were, however, the young, the low-paid and the elderly. By 1975 approximately 20 per cent of those dependent on supplementary benefit were children (see Table 6.3, line 11); and the actual number of children living below the poverty line because of their parents' low wages was even higher. The related problem of low wages and child-poverty had long been identified as a cause of poverty. In 1936, for example, Rowntree had identified inadequate wages (that is, wages inadequate to provide for a family with three children or less) as the cause of 9.2 per cent of poverty, and 'large families' (with four or more children) of 8 per cent. By 1950 the respective percentages had fallen to 1.1 and 3.2 per cent; but, by the relative standard of Townsend and Abel-Smith, the combined figure had risen by 1960 to 40 per cent of individuals living in poverty – a figure which included 2.25 million children (see Table 6.6, line 5).[45]

Three practical remedies for these interrelated problems were readily available. A national minimum wage, by increasing labour costs, might have made certain industries uncompetitive and thereby priced workers out of a job, but trade boards, or wages councils, had existed since 1908 to determine realistic minimum wage levels in individual industries. Latent political opposition to such price-fixing by government had, however, been made explicit by Conservative back-bench opposition to Bevin's Catering Wages Act in 1943 – a breach of the 'party truce' to which Labour back-bench reaction to the government's handling of the Beveridge Report had been an immediate riposte. A second obvious solution was to reverse the increasing tax burden on the low-paid. By 1971, for example, it has been calculated that income tax alone – regardless of expenditure taxes, national insurance contributions and rates – was pushing the income of many of the low-paid below the official poverty line.[46]

Above all, however, the remedy lay in the raising of the real value of family allowances. The withdrawal of family allowance from the first child had been one of the economies conceded by Beveridge in his unsuccessful attempt to placate the Treasury in 1942; and, in addition he had breached the principle of adequacy by making them only an aid to subsistence. To make matters worse they were never paid at the level Beveridge had suggested, on the ground that children would be receiving benefit in kind – which either never materialised (such as universal free school meals) or were withdrawn (such as universal free welfare foods). They were also rarely adjusted to inflation – there being no cash increase for the second child between 1952 and 1968 or for any other children after 1956. Consequently the value of child support, in total contrast to every other major benefit and to practice abroad, especially in France, consistently fell throughout the period (see Table 6.5, lines 4–5).[47] Easy remedies existed, therefore, to eradicate the problem of low wages and child poverty. What did not exist, as illustrated by Thorneycroft's desire to remove family allowances from the second child in 1957 and the consistent hostility to family allowances identified in opinion polls, was the political and popular will to employ them.[48]

It was, however, not the young but the elderly who from the start dominated the social security system and created the greater political problems. Pensions and other benefits for the elderly consistently accounted for over half of social expenditure, and over half of supplementary benefit claimants were retired people (see Tables 6.1 and 6.3). Despite this, old age remained a major cause of poverty. Rowntree in 1950 found it accounted for 68 per cent of those living below his poverty line and although the figure in 1960, as recorded in *The Poor and The Poorest*, had fallen to 33 per cent, this was because of the relative increase in other causes. It still represented, at minimum, 2.5 million people (see Table 6.6). The potential cost of any pensions system that could 'float' so many off national assistance/ supplementary benefit created something approaching panic in government circles.

Beveridge had been alert to the problems which could arise from increased longevity, in particular the ultimate cost of pensions. 'It is dangerous', he warned, 'to be in any way lavish to old age.'[49] He consequently recommended, despite his commitment to 'adequacy' and an end to means-testing, that full subsistence pensions should not be paid for twenty years. Both to maximise production and to minimise government expenditure, he also proposed that both men and women should be encouraged to stay at work after their respective 'official' retirement ages of 65 and 60, with insurance contributions after those ages being matched (in defiance of his principle of flat-rate benefits) by additions to pensions when they were finally drawn. Successive governments, however, in direct contrast to their attitudes towards child support, rejected such harsh measures. Full pensions were paid immediately – with a delay of only ten years for those who had not contributed before 1948. Why was this? Such action made little economic sense because it would have been far more logical to invest in the future, rather than to reward the past, workforce. It could not have been solely the result of compassion because those who benefited from the ten-year rule were, by definition, not the poorest but those whose income had exceeded the maximum for the prewar scheme. In essence it was a crude political decision, reflecting the voting power of the elderly and the greater popularity of pensions over family allowances, as consistently revealed by opinion polls. In deference to the TUC and employers, successive governments also failed to match their words about late retirement with action; and even those workers who expressed a preference to stay at work soon bowed, as in other countries, to peer pressure.[50]

The relative 'lavishness' of successive governments towards the elderly did not eliminate distress, as the figures for those living below the poverty line demonstrate. 'Full' pensions were kept below the subsistence level. Their 'limited objective' was, in the words of one official report, to 'provide a reasonable basis of provision for old age involving supplementation in only a modest percentage of cases'.[51] By 1965, however, the 'modest' percentage of those who were entitled to national assistance/supplementary benefit had reached 47 per cent and many others remained above the poverty line only because their state pension was supplemented by private income (most noticeably occupational pensions). Inevitably many of those entitled to supplementary benefit (numbered at some 855 000) did not claim, largely because of pride or lack of information.[52]

By the late 1950s the question of pensions was beginning to dominate social security policy; but because of fundamental political differences between the Conservative and Labour Parties little was achieved for twenty years. To contain cost, both parties were agreed upon the need for earnings-related contributions and pensions. They remained implacably opposed, however, on the extent to which any reform should be redistributive and, alternatively, on the extent to which market forces and personal initiative should be encouraged by the right of contributors to 'contract out' of the state scheme.

The original proposal, designed by Titmuss and adopted by the Labour Party in 1957, was highly redistributive. It would have guaranteed all those on average pay or below a state pension worth 50 per cent of their final salary. The Conservatives' riposte, the 1959 National Insurance Act, was wholly inadequate in terms of policy. In return for extra contributions, it offered a very low return which was not inflation-proofed. It was, however, a major political triumph. As 'reluctant collectivists', the Conservatives wanted to minimise the role of the state and the possibility of social engineering. As the then Minister of Pensions and National Insurance explained:

The modest nature of these proposals derives from the dilemma

> which faces a Conservative government in extending well above
> subsistence level a State administered scheme of National
> Insurance. We all of us desire to keep any graduated scheme as
> small an animal as possible, both because we dislike intruding
> further than we must into the sphere of private enterprise and
> because we fear the extension of state liability, and consequently
> the field of political pressure, any higher up the pensions scale
> than is necessary.[53]

This is exactly what the Act achieved because, through its contracting-
out clauses, it won time for private insurance companies to extend
the coverage of occupational pensions to over half the work force
(12.2 million people). No Labour government, already under pressure from white-collar unions to permit contracting out, could in
future afford to ignore so powerful a vested interest. Thereafter both
parties produced major new bills reflecting their different principles.
Crossman's 1969 plan for Labour was substantially redistributive in
that it guaranteed an inflation-proofed state pension, worth at least
half the national average wage, and permitted contracting-out only
on terms which were far from favourable to private insurance companies. The 1973 Joseph Bill for the Conservatives proposed a far
less generous state scheme, which was not inflation-proofed and was
designed to encourage the majority of contributors to opt for private
occupational pensions. Both shared the same fate of being annulled
by electoral defeat.

Whilst the parties bickered, the elderly suffered. They typically
received a pension worth only 35 per cent of their final salary, whilst
their counterparts in Germany and the USA received pensions worth
60 and 56 per cent respectively. Pensions policy, therefore, provides
the prime example of that lack of constructive consensus in Britain
which was responsible for the gradual development of a relatively
expensive but poorly-targeted social security system.

6.5   CONCLUSION

The history of postwar social security was riddled with contradictions. The promise of the Beveridge Report to realise the new ideal
of social security, through a simplified system of state relief without
resort to the hated means test, aroused immense popular enthusiasm
and lay at the heart of the new values and perspectives upon which

the welfare state was initially built. Yet within ten years the social security system was no longer popular. 'Most services', concluded one poll of public attitudes towards the welfare state in 1956, 'are felt to be helpful by those who use them. This is least likely to be the case where national insurance and national assistance are concerned.'[54] The means test did not wither away and the system started to become so complex that it became self-defeating.

The contradictions, superficially at least, went even further. In the formulation of policy, the Beveridge Report was soon revealed to be far from revolutionary and logical. The Labour Party, despite its commitment to greater egalitarianism, advocated earnings-related pensions and thus the continuation into retirement of the inequality experienced at work. The Conservative Party, in its emphasis on means-tested benefits, attacked the principle of 'universalism' from which its own supporters, in relation to pensions especially, had so benefited. More generally, it was the lower-paid who were the most vehement opponents of more generous relief, particularly to the involuntary unemployed. The concepts of 'absolute' and 'relative' poverty were portrayed as being radically different, although (with the constant additions to the list of sundries in the former and the measurement of the latter in the 1950s in relation to the 'subsistence' national assistance level) each contained common elements. Moreover, scientific accuracy was often claimed for the new 'relative' definition, although it was in fact as abstract, arbitrary and subjective as the old 'absolute' measure. Finally, plans to simplify the payment of relief through a merger of the tax and benefits systems threatened not to reduce but to increase confusion.

These contradictions can in part be resolved. The Beveridge Report was revolutionary in its vision of a society freed from the historic fear of absolute poverty. Labour Party policy reflected trade unions' traditional adherence to pay differentials, whilst the Conservative Party was careful not to attack those universal services which most benefited its supporters and, above all, tax exemptions. The reaction of the poor may be taken as an example of the third face of power (see Chapter 3.1.1). The adoption of the relative standard of poverty, however measured, was also the inevitable consequence of rising living standards – achieved by postwar economic growth – and accurately reflected both long-standing popular instinct and international practice. The one set of contradictions that could not be resolved was that inherent in the proposed merger of the tax and benefit systems. Any cost-effective policy targeted upon the poor could not but undermine incentive as benefit was withdrawn in line with rising income. Equally, any automatic system of payment – designed to overcome the problem of low-take-up – could not but lack the necessary flexibility to deal with the full range of human need.

Such difficulties underline the fact that no ideal system of social security is ever attainable; and all criticisms of the Beveridge Report and the subsequent development of policy should acknowledge this fact. This does not mean, however, that the transparent lack of constructive consensus between 1945–75 should be condoned. Hard decisions were not taken when necessary, at either a political, administrative or popular level, about the amount of resources that should be devoted to social security and how, in the national interest (however defined), those resources should be apportioned. Had such decisions been taken it would have been possible for government to encourage individuals to provide for themselves all the other services they wanted. A residual state welfare service could then have reverted to the task it had performed well during the war and which it had initially been expected to continue in peace: the humane care of those who genuinely could not care for themselves.

6.6 FURTHER READING

There are no good, comprehensive studies of postwar social security. The best introductions are the historical chapters in general texts, in contemporary poverty surveys and in later attempts to reform the system. Amongst the first, the best is perhaps P. Alcock, *Poverty and State Support* (1987). The two outstanding contemporary surveys, from the full list provided in Note 30 of this chapter, are the forbiddingly entitled A. B. Atkinson, *Poverty in Britain and the Reform of Social Security* (Cambridge 1970) and G. C. Fiegehen *et al.*, *Poverty and Progress in Britain, 1953–73* (Cambridge, 1977). The contemporary mood is also well evoked by D. Bull (ed.), *Family Poverty* (1971) and K. G. Banting, *Poverty, Politics and Policy* (1979). Of the latter books, the most rewarding are R. Berthoud *et al.*, *Poverty and the Development of Anti-Poverty Policy in the United Kingdom* (1981) and A. W. Dilnot *et al.*, *The Reform of Social Security* (Oxford, 1984).

On particular topics, the Beveridge Report is well served by a magisterial biography, J. Harris, *William Beveridge* (Oxford, 1977) and by K. and J. Williams *A Beveridge Reader* (1987). There is also a shrewd review of the report's long-term impact in J. Harris, 'Enterprise and Welfare States: a comparative perspective', in *Transactions of the Royal Historical Society*, 40 (1990) 175–95. Legislative changes to social insurance are covered exhaustively, in an international context and with a few telling insights, in P. A. Kohler and H. F. Zacher, *The Evolution of Social Insurance, 1881–1981* (1982). Means-tested benefit is particularly well covered by A. Deacon and J. Bradshaw, *Reserved for the Poor* (1983) and the reflections of an erstwhile chairman of the Supplementary Benefits Commission, D. Donnison, *The Politics of Poverty* (1982). A comprehensive, if partial, history of postwar pensions is provided by E. Shragge, *Pensions Policy in Britain: a socialist analysis* (1984), whilst L. Hannah, *Inventing Retirement: the development of occupational benefits in Britain* (Cambridge, 1986) is one of those few academic books which one wishes were longer.

Contemporary poverty surveys are of course valuable in their own right. Particularly stimulating are the very short B. S. Rowntree and G. R. Lavers, *Poverty and the Welfare State* (1951); the more technical B. Abel-Smith and P. Townsend, *The Poor and the Poorest* (1965); the more impressionistic study of Nottingham in 1966–7, K. Coates and R. Silbourn, *Poverty: the Forgotten Englishmen* (1970); and the exhaustive 1968–9 survey, P. Townsend, *Poverty in the United Kingdom* (Harmondsworth, 1979). Predominant amongst contemporary texts, however, is the Beveridge Report itself (Cmd 6404, 1942). Its length and its close, if sometimes inconsistent, reasoning can be forbidding, but it provides effective summaries of its main proposals (paras 1–40), the insurance principle (272–99), its main principles (303–9) and its three assumptions (410–43). Particular problems are also summarised in relation to women (107–17, 339–48) and both rent and old age (193–264). There is a preemptive strike against its critics (444–61) and there is also an extremely helpful summary of international practice (appendix F).

7 Health Care

As the initial enthusiasm for social security waned, the NHS quickly became, as it was to remain thereafter, the most popular welfare service. Within three months of its establishment it was being hailed in a Gallup poll as the greatest achievement of the Labour government; and later opinion polls rarely recorded levels of support below 80 per cent. Indeed, so dominant a position did the NHS come to command in popular perceptions of the welfare state that the two terms were commonly regarded as synonymous.[1]

The reasons for the popularity of the NHS are not hard to identify. Poor health and the inability to pay for adequate medical treatment have traditionally been amongst people's greatest fears. In the 1940s, therefore, the promise of comprehensive medical care, free to all equally in time of need, represented as revolutionary a social advance as the guarantee of social security – and one of more direct value because, whilst poverty had been alleviated by full employment since 1940, the legacy and incidence of poor health remained. The interwar system of health care had also been unpopular.[2] The National Health Insurance scheme (under which most manual workers received free treatment from a panel of GPs) was widely criticised for its incomplete coverage of both treatment and people. Hospital care, for example, was excluded, as were the most vulnerable members of society – 'non-working' mothers and pre-school children. It was also actively disliked because of the unequal treatment GPs were perceived to give private and 'panel' patients, and the clear restriction by the 'approved' insurance companies of doctors' clinical freedom in order to safeguard their profits. At the same time private patients (who included most non-manual workers) were becoming increasingly concerned at the escalating cost of private insurance premiums, or of health care itself, at a time when their income was being more heavily taxed. Consequently there was never any serious danger of opposition, as there was in the field of social security, to the principle of universalism.

A further reason for the popularity of the NHS was the coincidence of its establishment with major medical advances. The war pioneered major advances in surgery and ancillary services, such as blood transfusions. It also greatly increased the supply of drugs, such as sulphonamides and antibiotics, which were able to effect dramatic reductions in the incidence and virulence of infectious disease. For example the four traditional killer diseases of children (scarlet fever, diphtheria, whooping cough and measles) were quickly brought under control after the war with the result that infant mortality, which had been cut in England and Wales by two-thirds between 1900 and 1940, was cut by a further two-thirds between 1940 and 1975 (from 56 deaths per 1000 live births to 16). Doctors, for one of the few times in history, appeared to have effective cures for disease and the NHS offered the means by which their expertise could be shared equally by all.

During the 1950s and 1960s, however, doubts began to grow about whether the popularity of the NHS was justified. Improvements in postwar health standards provided no real proof of its efficiency because such improvements were common to all industrial nations, whatever their system of health care. Moreover, they were largely dependent on medical advances attained before 1948 and on factors outside the health service, such as improvements in real income and housing. The NHS was certainly directing much-needed money into health care, consuming two-fifths of social expenditure (see Appendix 1, Table A1.4); but was this money well-targeted and efficiently spent? In particular an increasingly disproportionate percentage of the health budget, amounting to some 70 per cent by 1975–6, was being allocated to hospitals (see Table 7.1). Did this mean that the NHS was providing a national *sickness* rather than a national *health* service, devoting too many resources to the curing of individuals rather than to the prevention of ill-health? There were also persistent complaints from both within and without the NHS about the nature and quality of its administration. GPs had bitterly opposed its establishment in 1948 and threatened to withdraw their labour in 1965. Junior doctors and hospital consultants resorted to similar threats in 1975. Simultaneously, in the late 1960s the Labour government planned, and in 1974 the Conservative government effected, a radical administrative overhaul. Clearly all was not well.

The history of the NHS between 1943 and 1975, therefore, provides an intriguing contrast between the popularity of the service as a political ideal and its increasingly criticised record as a practical deliverer of health care. In this respect at least its close identification with the welfare state may be justified because it represented, in microcosm, the problems inherent in any collective attempt to provide a 'just' and cost-effective service in a society characterised by inherited inequalities, self-interest and scarce resources. The NHS

Table 7.1 The National Health Service: selected current and capital expenditure, 1951–76

	1951-2 £(m)	1951-2 %	1956-7 £(m)	1956-7 %	1961-2 £(m)	1961-2 %	1966-7 £(m)	1966-7 %	1971-2 £(m)	1971-2 %	1975-6 £(m)	1975-6 %
Current expenditure:												
1. Hospital services	268	52.7	377	57.0	538	57.4	797	54.5	1462	59.1	3943	70.0
less receipts from patients	-4		-5		-6		-9		-13		-23	
2. General services	165	31.9	202	27.3	274	25.1	387	25.3	609	22.2	1134	18.8
less receipts from patients	-5		-24		-41		-22		-65		-85	
of which (net cost)												
3. Pharmaceutical	53	10.6	-	-	78	8.4	163	11.3	224	9.1	456	8.1
4. Dental	36	7.2	-	-	52	5.6	67	4.6	96	3.9	200	3.6
5. Ophthalmic	10	2.0	-	-	10	1.1	14	1.0	14	0.6	55	1.0
6. General services	48	9.6	-	-	88	9.5	112	7.8	196	8.0	338	6.0
7. Local authority health services	39	7.8	55	8.4	81	8.7	132	9.1	151	6.1	-	-
8. Departmental administration etc.	13	2.6	23	3.5	31	3.3	47	3.3	59	2.4	169	3.0
9. Total current expenditure	477	95.2	628	96.1	875	94.4	1332	92.2	2203	89.8	5138	91.8
Capital expenditure:												
10. Hospitals	15	3.0	20	3.1	42	4.5	98	6.7	191	7.8	355	6.4
11. Local authority	3	0.6	2	0.3	8	0.9	14	1.0	54	2.2	91	1.6
12. Other	6	1.2	3	0.5	2	0.2	2	0.1	5	0.2	12	0.2
13. Total capital expenditure	24	4.8	25	3.9	52	5.6	113	7.8	250	11.2	458	8.2
14. Total NHS expenditure	501	100.0	653	100.0	927	100.0	1445	100.0	2453	100.0	5596	100.0

The statistics in lines 1, 7 and 11 were assimilated in a slightly different fashion after 1971–2, and are therefore not strictly comparable.
Sources: Social Trends (1970, 1976); Annual Abstract of Statistics (1984).

sought to use the 'rationality' of central planning to secure the better coordination and fairer distribution of services as well as to safeguard the interests of the less articulate (which the market had traditionally overlooked). However, it thereby placed in jeopardy two vital prerequisites of effective policy – local knowledge and professional expertise – and introduced major new administrative problems. Could local initiative be encouraged without endangering the integrity of central planning and the 'responsible' expenditure of central finance? Could professional expertise be trusted without upsetting the delicate balance between clinical freedom and the pursuit of professional self-interest? As the size of the NHS grew (so that by 1975 it was employing just under one million people, or one-thirtieth of the population of working age), could the traditional bureaucratic failings of inefficiency and insensitivity to changing public needs be avoided? Finally, given rising public expectations and the boundless possibilities of medical science, could the technical expertise be developed to ensure the optimum allocation of scarce resources? These were the fundamental challenges facing the NHS during its stormy inception and during the years of pragmatic adjustment before its radical overhaul in 1974.

7.1 THE ESTABLISHMENT OF THE NHS, 1943–51

Both the planning and the early years of the NHS were overshadowed by a permanent sense of crisis. This arose initially from the complex and bitter negotiations between government and the medical profession over the nature of the service, which began in earnest once the Beveridge Report had recommended the establishment of a 'comprehensive health and rehabilitation' service. The negotiations were complex because they had not only to seek the rationalisation of existing services (each with its own jealously-held traditions) but also to surmount two changes of government and the mutual suspicion of the two main professional negotiating bodies, the British Medical Association (which represented mainly, but not exclusively, general practitioners) and the Royal College of Surgeons (whose president, Lord Moran – Churchill's personal doctor – was considered, not least by himself, to represent hospital consultants). The resulting bitterness was epitomised by the rejection in March 1948, just three months before the Appointed Day, of the Labour government's detailed proposals for the NHS by 90 per cent of doctors voting in a BMA membership ballot.

After 1948 the sense of crisis was perpetuated by the inability of the NHS to keep within its budget. The Labour government, already beset by economic difficulties, was accordingly obliged to resort to a series of expedients, the last of which was the introduction in May 1951 of charges for dental and ophthalmic care. This breached the principle of a free health service and provoked Aneurin Bevan (who, as minister of health between 1945 and January 1951, had had prime responsibility for planning the service) to resign from the Cabinet. It was thus the financial difficulties of the NHS which occasioned the split within the Labour Party which was so to damage its chances of reelection in the 1950s and consequently its ability directly to shape the development of the welfare state. Might not these successive crises have been handled better to the mutual advantage of the Labour Party and the NHS?

In retrospect the complexity and bitterness of the negotiations preceding the establishment of the NHS would appear to have been wholly unnecessary. Agreement was virtually universal on the basic principles of reform – the provision of a comprehensive, free and equal service which would provide the 'best possible' care for patients whilst simultaneously safeguarding doctors' clinical freedom.[3] As early as 1920 an authoritative advisory body to the Ministry of Health had established, in the famous Dawson Report, the principle of 'best possible' care. In 1926 the Royal Commission on National Health Insurance had suggested that health care should be financed out of general taxation. The public had long been demanding, and the government pressurising the 'approved' societies to provide, a more comprehensive coverage of both specialist treatment and the insured's dependants. Finally, GPs and consultants alike had become increasingly frustrated by the restrictions placed upon their clinical freedom by, respectively, the commercial interests of the approved societies and the impending bankruptcy of voluntary hospitals. Indeed, with the creation of the Nuffield Provincial Hospital Trust in 1939, there had even been an autonomous move within the voluntary hospital system to confront traditional antagonisms and to pool resources. The one major breach in this consensus concerned the future financing of a national health service. Instead of a tax-financed system, the BMA wanted to retain contributory insurance and to restrict its coverage to 90 per cent of the population so that some income could be ensured from private practice.

Small though it might appear, this reservation went to the heart of the conflict between government and the medical profession and explains much of its bitterness, because it raised the fundamental question of where power was ultimately to lie within the new service. The doctors feared that, should they become wholly dependent on the state for their income, both their independent status and their clinical freedom would ultimately be jeopardised. This was the explicit fear that had been exposed during the battle over the organisation (as opposed to the principles) of the NHS, as it evolved from a utopian ideal in the 1920s through to the Coalition's reconstruction white paper in 1944; and it dominated the negotiations thereafter. The critical organisational challenge facing the NHS was the need to provide an administrative framework which could effectively coordinate the three separate services, provided respectively by individual practitioners (GPs, dentists and opticians), hospitals and the local authorities. There was, as will be seen from a review of the interwar health services, a clear and logical solution; but this was the very one which the medical profession feared most.

During the 1930s the individual practitioner service was dominated by some 30 000 registered GPs. Their morale was low on account of both overwork and their perceived inability to keep abreast of rapid medical advance.[4] This was partly their own fault. In contrast to prevailing experience abroad, they mostly worked on their own rather than in group practice, where costs could be shared, rational working hours arranged and medical views exchanged. Consequently, after a lengthy and costly training, they had typically to take out a loan to purchase the goodwill of a practice for about £2000–3000, which in turn had to be financed from an annual salary that rarely rose above £1600. Capitation fees – the fixed annual fees for panel patients – were kept low by local Insurance Committees among which the 'approved' societies had a dominant voice; and so GPs had, out of financial necessity, to move from poor areas (where need was greatest) to richer areas (where they could generate more income from private practice). GPs, as in other countries, also feared that their generalist skills were becoming less appreciated and relevant as they were increasingly excluded from both advanced surgery in hospitals and the specialist clinics run by local authorities.

Dentists and opticians were equally demoralised. By international comparison there were few well-qualified dentists in Britain; and in any one year, only 7 per cent of those insured received any dental treatment.[5] In ophthalmology 75 per cent of the population had no access to free care, and there were bitter professional disputes between the dispensing opticians in the high street and those providing specialist treatment in hospitals and local authority clinics.

The hospital service was similarly divided. There were approximately 2000 local authority hospitals, providing 40 000 beds. Most of these had been inherited from the Poor Law, following the 1929 Local Government Act, and had yet to be fully integrated with the other hospitals run by the local authorities. Almost half the beds were accounted for by 300 large mental hospitals. In contrast there were a thousand voluntary hospitals, most of which were very small, providing some 100 000 beds. A quarter had fewer than 30 beds and only 75 had more than 200. These larger hospitals included the prestigious teaching hospitals where most medical advance was pioneered and where consultants offered their services free – their income coming from private practice elsewhere. In the smaller 'cottage' hospitals GPs undertook minor surgery, often to a very low standard.

The majority of voluntary hospitals were facing severe financial problems in the 1930s. The London teaching hospitals, for example, derived only 34 per cent of their income from their major traditional source of finance, voluntary donations, despite the increasing number of 'flag days' on which medical staff openly solicited money from the public. Government provided only 8 per cent of income, and so the vast bulk had to be raised from the patients themselves either directly (23 per cent) or through subscription schemes (16 per cent).[6] This meant that voluntary hospitals had to turn from their original purpose, the free treatment of the poor, to the care of those who could afford to pay for their treatment. As a consequence the poor, and especially the chronically ill, were obliged to apply for admission to local authority hospitals – which were themselves bedevilled by financial difficulties and acrimonious disputes (especially over financial liability when, for example, a patient's last place of residence fell outside the receiving hospital's catchment area). So complex had the system become by 1939 that a 62 page booklet had to be issued to cover all the eventualities that might arise should wartime evacuees require hospital treatment.

The logical solution to this chaotic and highly inefficient situation, and one favoured at the time by both officials within the Ministry of Health and the Labour Party, was a concentration of responsibility on the third provider of health care – the local authorities. In the nineteenth century local government had pioneered advances in public health (such as the provision of drainage and supplies of pure water); and after 1900 it had taken the initiative in health education and the curing of disease through the School Medical Service (1906), TB sanatoria (1911), welfare clinics for mothers and children (especially after 1918) and cancer clinics (1939), in addition to the inherited Poor Law hospitals (1929). The gradual concentration of responsibility on local government, therefore, appeared the most natural way to construct a coordinated national health service, which would both be under democratic control and – as with the education service – have an assured source of finance through a combination of local rates and national taxation. This development was indeed being actively promoted before 1939 by certain progressive Labour local councils, such as the LCC. Their ideal was that each neighbourhood should have a 'health centre' to coordinate the 'primary care' provided by individual practitioners, clinics and the public health service; and that from these centres patients requiring more specialist treatment should be referred to the 'secondary' level of district hospitals.

This was the objective also broadly endorsed by the Coalition government in its 1944 white paper. It proposed that, under the supervision of the Ministry of Health, there should be some 30–35 joint regional boards (consisting of councillors coopted from local authorities in the relevant area) to plan both primary and secondary care.[7] They would themselves directly administer the hospitals, whilst individual local authorities would employ under contract the majority of GPs (who would increasingly work in health centres) and discharge their traditional public health functions. Overall coordination of policy would be ensured by the relevant councillors' membership of the joint board. The importance of professional autonomy was also not overlooked. Each tier of government was to have a professional advisory committee, and a central medical board, consisting mainly of doctors, would act as the ultimate 'employer' of GPs, overseeing their contracts with local authorities, their geographical distribution and, above all, professional discipline.

The fatal flaw in this otherwise logical plan was that it was perceived, in the short term at least, to be administratively and politically impractical. Medical officers of health (the senior doctors employed by local authorities) had, despite their pioneering role in the nineteenth century, become increasingly conservative and there were serious doubts about their ability to provide the requisite local leadership.[8] There were also serious objections to the proposed regional boards. The ideal local authorities, it was agreed, were the county councils, provided they were able to incorporate the independent county boroughs within their boundaries. However, this was impossible because the two types of authority, the one traditionally Conservative and the other increasingly Labour, had a long history of territorial rivalry (see Chapter 4.4). Joint boards were no effective substitute because they lacked the authority of a directly elected body and would have deprived existing local authorities of control over their existing hospitals – which they were determined to keep. Even more importantly, doctors were appalled at the prospect of becoming the employees of local government. Consultants had traditionally shunned local authority hospitals with their lack of 'glamorous' responsibilities. GPs throughout the interwar period had been fighting a guerrilla war with local authority clinics over the specialist treatment of patients. Both despised the medical officers of health and were fearful of bureaucratic and political encroachment upon their clinical freedom.[9] The Coalition government was, therefore, forced to retreat hastily from its 1944 proposals.

After Labour's election victory in 1945 it was the prejudices of the medical profession (rather than those of local government) which dominated the negotiations that led eventually to the National Health Service Act of May 1946 and the inauguration of the service in July 1948. To the surprise and dismay of many (including the leaders of the progressive interwar Labour councils) the conclusion of these negotiations was that interwar trends were reversed and local government deprived of all responsibility for hospitals.[10] In its place, fourteen regional hospital boards (RHBs), consisting solely of persons appointed by the minister of health, were charged with the planning of the service and the supervision of 380 hospital management committees (HMCs, likewise appointed by the minister of health), which were to be responsible for the day-to-day running of each hospital or group of hospitals. Moreover the ideal of administrative unity was not attained. RHBs could not fully coordinate hospital policy because, although each region was designed to include at least one major teaching hospital, these hospitals were to remain independent under a separate board of governors. Nor could they coordinate health care as a whole. GPs, dentists and opticians remained independent under their executive councils, whilst local authorities retained control over a miscellaneous 'rump' of responsibilities, including vaccination, ambulances and the public health services.

This administrative settlement was therefore far from ideal. As later events were to prove, the tripartite division between hospitals, executive committees and local authorities discouraged rather than encouraged coordination; and in the first two services there was the danger that professional self-interest might predominate over democratic accountability. 'Effective decisions in policy', the 1944 white paper had insisted, 'must lie entirely with elected representatives answerable to the people for the decisions they take', but the initial constitution of the NHS was anything but democratic – with the one exception that ultimate power lay with an elected minister.[11] Undue power was also conceded to doctors, especially hospital consultants, and this unbalanced structure had major policy implications. Not only might scarce resources be allocated to those who had power (in particular, hospitals) at the expense of others (such as the preventive health services administered by local government), but other inequalities also became entrenched. Within publicly funded hospitals for instance, private practice or 'pay beds' was permitted (to increase consultants' salaries) and provided a continuing source of political dispute. Despite financial constraints, consultants were also allowed to award themselves permanent merit awards, which in many cases doubled their effective salary. In relation to general practice, the power of the Central Medical Board to direct GPs to under-doctored areas, as recommended in the 1944 white paper, was modified and health centres, rather than becoming the common focus of all primary care in a given region, were reduced to an infrequent experiment.[12] The fate of health centres might, indeed, be taken to exemplify the balance of power enshrined in the new organisational structure. Patients were expected to seek out professional care – doctors were not expected to make themselves readily available to patients.

It was, therefore, in its original administrative structure that the genesis of the conflicting reputations of the NHS as a political ideal and as a practical deliverer of health care lay; and yet it is this structure for which the Labour government in general and Bevan in particular were accorded at the time – and have been accorded since – considerable praise. Was, and is, such praise justified?

Neither the challenges facing Bevan nor his undoubted achievement should be minimised. The interwar health services were inefficient and inequitable; and interwar politicians had abjectly failed to reform the structure of local government which otherwise would have provided a natural administrative framework for a democratically controlled national health service. The prestige of the medical profession worldwide was such that it was not only in Britain that there was an undue concentration of power in the hands of hospital consultants. Public opinion in Britain also tended to support the doctors in their battle for 'independence' against the government and, perhaps as a consequence of imperfect knowledge, little resentment was expressed at the inconvenience resulting from the tripartite division of health care.[13] Despite such pressures, however, Bevan succeeded in removing two of the commercial intrusions into health care which had been most resented in the interwar period: the approved societies and the sale of GPs' practices.[14] Uniquely he also abolished the system of contributory health insurance which (despite the acknowledged fact that it was less cost-effective than state provision, see Chapter 3.2.1) was retained by every other Western country. Thereby the *political* ideal of a free and equal service for all was secured. These undoubted achievements should not, however, obscure the fact that Bevan was not the most skilled of negotiators and that he actively promoted some of the key decisions which lay at the root of the NHS's later problems.

The negotiations with the medical profession required a considerable degree of tact and self-control. Tact, however, was not one of Bevan's greatest strengths. When he finally dropped his initial insistence on a salaried medical profession, for instance, he confided publicly that 'there is all the difference in the world between plucking fruit when it is ripe and plucking it when it is green'.[15] This did little to reassure GPs about the future intentions of Labour governments. Similarly, as part of the embattled middle class, doctors were somewhat less than enthusiastic about his description of the Conservative Party, two days before the Appointed Day, as 'lower than vermin'. Having thus raised suspicions, Bevan then, however, often appeared to make over-ready concessions. For instance hospital consultants (the élite within the profession whom the Labour Party might have been expected to favour least) completed the negotiations not only with considerable advances in their income (through assured salaries, merit awards and pay beds) but also greatly increased power (through their appointment to RHBs and HMCs, as well as the independent status of teaching hospitals). Even a militant conservative member of the BMA was amazed, recalling of the early days:

> We assembled at the first meeting expecting that our beautiful profession was to be hung, drawn and quartered. Instead we were reprieved . . . . On one point after another . . . the Minister had

accepted what we were demanding before we had the opportunity
to ask him for it. We were jubilant and stunned.[16]

Given the well-known divisions within the profession (which might
have been better exploited), its interwar financial difficulties and its
wartime flirtation with the idea of salaries and health centres (both
of which were to become perfectly acceptable in the 1960s), might
not a harder bargain have been struck? After all, in the 1940s the
medical profession was as much in need of state finance as the NHS
was in need of its expertise.

In the determination of the NHS's administrative structure,
Bevan's lack of previous ministerial and administrative experience
would also appear to have been a handicap. His strong personal
convictions had been forged in South Wales, where the relative
absence of well-equipped modern hospitals had denied ordinary
people the benefits of rapid medical advance and where commercial
intrusions into health care had been particularly resented. His natural
instinct was, therefore, to give priority to the better national distribution of hospitals and the appointment of doctors to positions of
administrative importance. 'Doctors', he declared on one notable
occasion, 'deserved to participate fully in the administration of their
own profession.'[17] As has been seen, however, such objectives carried with them the dangers that curative might predominate over
preventive medicine, and professional self-interest over democratic
accountability. Were such dangers to be avoided, a greater specialist
expertise and a ready willingness to intervene had to be instilled into
officials in the Ministry of Health, who were the ultimate guarantors
of democratic control. There is no evidence, however, that Bevan
recognised the need for, let alone encouraged, such an initiative.
Indeed, in his handling of administrative matters, he appeared to be
'radical in everybody else's ministry except his own'.[18]

Bevan's raw instincts, therefore, may have been invaluable in
sustaining the political ideals behind the NHS where more worldly
ministers might have compromised, but his lack of administrative –
and ultimately political – insight prevented the establishment of an
administrative structure through which those ideals could be realised.
In a long-term perspective – embracing the growing interwar consensus for a national health service, the spur to greater regionalisation
and rationalisation provided by the wartime Emergency Medical
Service, and the need for a radical administrative overhaul as early

as 1974 – it would appear that the 1940s represent an opportunity missed, not seized.[19]

The NHS's reputation for efficiency – and with it Bevan's reputation as an administrator – was further tarnished by the battles within Cabinet between 1948 and 1951 over the escalating cost of health care. In its first two years the NHS exceeded its budget by almost 40 per cent (see Table 7.2); and thereafter, although expenditure was kept within the estimates, its net overall cost was three times higher than that forecast in the 1946 National Health Service Act. It was, moreover, only contained at this high level by two extreme expedients: the appointment of a senior Cabinet committee in May 1950 to monitor the monthly expenditure of the NHS (a humiliating experience for Bevan as the 'responsible' minister) and the introduction of charges a year later.[20]

The initial high cost of the NHS was to an extent justified. It was caused principally by the need to relieve the backlog of interwar ill-health and to make good the chronic underfunding of the health services. Thus by 1953 26.1 million pairs of glasses and six million sets of false teeth had had to be provided. In addition a series of independent review boards had awarded pay rises well above the rate of inflation.[21] Such expenditure was exceptional and unlikely to recur. A steep rise in the cost of medicine posed a more permanent problem but, given the increased efficacy of drugs, this too could be justified. What could not be justified was the Ministry of Health's inability to predict (despite much outside advice) the cost of exceptional short-term need and to devise a sound financial and administrative structure for future expenditure decisions. The declared policy of 'universalising the best' provided no effective criteria for the allocation of scarce resources (given that the possibilities of medical science and public expectations were boundless). Similarly the effective devolution of power over expenditure to doctors (either in GPs' surgeries, through the prescription of drugs and referral to hospitals, or on RHBs) was inherently dangerous since it defied the first principle of public finance, that those who benefit from spending taxpayers' money should also share the unpopularity of raising it.

Various solutions to these problems were considered by the Cabinet committee on the NHS. In order to restore fiscal responsibility, for example, it was suggested that RHBs should be abolished (with the Ministry of Health assuming their planning and supervisory role) and that those responsible for maintaining financial discipline on the HMCs should be given 'protected' status so that they could be

Table 7.2 Parliamentary estimates for the NHS, 1948–52 (£m)

| | 1948/9 (9 months) | | | 1949–50 | | | 1950–1 | | 1951–2 | |
	Original	Final	Excess	Original	Final	Excess	Original	Final	Original	Final
Gross total	198.4	275.9	77.5	352.3	449.2	96.9	464.5	465.0	469.1	470.6
Appropriation in aid	48.7	67.6	–	92.6	90.7	–	71.6	72.1	71.0	71.0
Net total	149.7	208.3	58.6	259.7	358.5	98.8	392.9	392.9	398.1	399.5

Figures for Great Britain
Source: C. Webster, *The Health Services Since The War*, vol. 1 (1988) p. 136.

dismissed only with the express approval of the minister. More direct economies were also suggested, such as the compilation of a list of proscribed drugs, the moderation of consultants' merit awards and, above all, the introduction of charges. To each of these suggestions Bevan at times appeared to give his support. He admitted for instance that the RHBs (which he had just established) were an administrative anomaly in that 'it was inherently impossible to ensure a proper implementation of national policy at the periphery when that policy is mediated by fourteen separate regional bodies, all naturally watchful of their prestige and their independence'. Most surprisingly he accepted in 1949 the need for prescription charges, not so much to raise revenue but to prevent abuse – to moderate, in his words, the 'ceaseless cascades of medicine pouring down people's throats'.[22]

Such apparent concessions, however, he later dismissed as tactical manoeuvres to offset more immediate threats to health expenditure; and once these threats had diminished, he reverted to a robust defence both of the principle of a free service and professional autonomy. Indeed he even went further, actively justifying high spending as a sign of the success and popularity of the NHS. 'The cost of the health service', he argued in 1950, 'not only will, but ought to increase'; and rather than welcoming the eventual containment of expenditure within its cash limit, he demanded that any surplus should be spent immediately.[23] Such bravura might have won him the admiration of his civil servants, who were impressed by the resources he acquired for the NHS, but it only served to exasperate his Cabinet colleagues who, in deference to the principle of collective responsibility, continued to contain their own expenditure within agreed budgets.

The final break between Bevan and the Cabinet occurred over the decision in the April 1951 budget to introduce charges for dental and ophthalmic care. As has been seen, tensions had been building up within Cabinet since the foundation of the NHS almost three years earlier; and they were exacerbated by the wider battle Bevan was fighting over the speed at which the government should move towards 'socialism' (see Chapter 4.3) and his personal anger at being overlooked for higher office (and especially the chancellorship of the exchequer, which went in October 1950 to Gaitskell, some nine years his junior with sixteen years' less experience in the House of Commons).

The specific dispute between Bevan and Gaitskell over NHS

charges was nevertheless clearcut. Gaitskell had been frustrated by a series of defeats at the Cabinet committee on the NHS for proposals to limit health expenditure and thereby release money for other areas of welfare policy, such as retirement pensions, which he regarded as of equal importance. Charges for ophthalmic and dental care, he argued, were politically acceptable because they would reduce demand only in 'non-essential' areas of health care and would not lay the government open to the accusation (as would prescription charges) of removing a free service which had been available to the poor since 1911. They would also raise some revenue for the NHS. Above all they would symbolise the ability of Cabinet to take hard decisions on the allocation of scarce resources and to determine priorities within the social services. In reply Bevan denied the time was right for the betrayal of so important a principle as a free health service. The immediate need to control social expenditure, he claimed, arose from the need to finance the rearmament programme for the Korean War and he was confident that from the overall cost of that programme (£1250 million) savings could be made of some £13 million, the estimated revenue to be raised from charges in their first year. Charges were therefore financially unnecessary, whilst the political damage to the Labour Government would be immense. To abandon the principle of a free health service would be 'a shock to their supporters in the country and a grave disappointment to socialist opinion throughout the world'.[24] The Conservative Party would also take the Labour government's action as a precedent to justify the further erosion of the NHS by the introduction of prescription charges.

There was considerable justice in both Bevan's and Gaitskell's case. Bevan was correct, in the short term, to predict that the rearmament budget would not be fully spent and that the Conservatives would introduce further charges. Gaitskell was equally correct, for the longer term, to insist that the resources available to the social services in general and the NHS in particular were limited and that priorities had to be determined. The resolution of the confrontation was, however, eventually to be determined not by principle but by circumstance and personality. Attlee was ill during the budget discussions and in the absence of his skilled chairmanship the longstanding exasperation of Bevan's colleagues began to boil over, especially when he indulged both publicly and privately in displays of personal pique against Gaitskell.[25] He became virtually isolated and was able to secure only the resignation of one Cabinet colleague and three votes in the House of Commons for what he portrayed as an attack not only on the NHS but on the welfare state as a whole. In contrast Gaitskell remained relatively calm and conciliatory and, by his increase in retirement pensions, demonstrated that there was to be no fundamental attack on welfare expenditure.[26] The tragedy was, however, that there was also to be no constructive attempt by the Treasury to determine the criteria on which resources should be allocated to and within the NHS. All that Gaitskell's victory ultimately signified was the end of the special treatment that the NHS had enjoyed since 1948.

The establishment of the NHS was, for so idealistic an institution, remarkably unaltruistic.[27] Its planning was taken by the medical profession as the opportunity to advance its own self-interest, whilst its early development was the occasion for bitter infighting within the Labour Cabinet. Its first years were dominated by the charismatic personality of Bevan, and to him must go the credit for both the actual establishment of the service and the winning for it of the lion's share of available resources. His legacy, however was not wholly benevolent. His eventual choice of administrative structure impeded the development of a more cost-effective and equitably distributed service; its tripartite division, the devolution of power to the medical profession and, above all, the failure to develop specialist managerial skills at the centre discouraged rather than encouraged the greater coordination and efficiency that was the principal justification for nationalisation. The policy of 'universalising the best' encouraged high hopes which could only lead to demoralisation when, inevitably, they were not met. Finally, the initial overspending of the budget permanently labelled the NHS – whatever the contradictory finding of the Guillebaud Report in 1956 – with the reputation for extravagance. Bevan's ultimate legacy was, therefore, an administratively flawed service which, despite its close public identification with the welfare state, was to be denied direct representation in Cabinet for the next eleven years.

7.2 CONSOLIDATION AND RECONSTRUCTION, 1951–74

After the traumas of its establishment, the NHS experienced a decade of consolidation before its structure, if not its ideal, came under increasing attack. The period of consolidation was epitomised by the content of, and the reaction to, the report of the Guillebaud

Committee which had been appointed in 1953 to examine 'the present and prospective cost of the NHS'. To the exasperation of those who had commissioned it, it concluded that there was – and had been – no 'widespread extravagance' in the NHS and that accordingly there was no need for any major reorganisation. 'No fundamental changes recommended', proclaimed the Ministry of Health press release, 'Service needs time to settle down'.[28] By 1962 that time had evidently passed. The Conservative government drafted an ambitious ten year plan to modernise the hospital service; and the medical profession itself, in the Porritt Report, recommended the full integration of the three separate services within the NHS. The former was a major attempt from the centre to determine priorities and to allocate resources within the service, whilst the latter was the first stage in a lengthy campaign which was to culminate (amidst escalating pressure from both within and outside the NHS) in its wholesale reorganisation.

The Guillebaud Report has been accorded a strangely mixed reception. To some it has appeared an 'impressive document', to others a 'bluebook full of whitewash'.[29] These different judgements arise from the competing criteria used. The first is based on the Report's pioneering achievement in relating health expenditure to inflation and economic growth, so that its real and relative cost could be properly established – an achievement that depended on the work of two rather incongruous research officers for an intended Conservative cost-cutting exercise, Titmuss and Abel-Smith. As a result of their research, the Report could authoritatively dispel the myth that the real cost of health care had escalated since 1948 and would escalate further owing to the 'ageing' of the population. Rather, it concluded, NHS expenditure per head had been virtually static between 1948 and 1954, and in relative terms had actually fallen from 3.75 per cent to 3.5 per cent of GNP; capital expenditure on hospitals, far from being extravagant, had fallen dangerously to only 33 per cent of pre-war levels; and the additional health costs incurred by an ageing population could easily be accommodated by the expected rise in economic growth. Consequently the Report dismissed demands for radical reorganisation. There was, it admitted, some administrative inefficiency, arising in particular from the tripartite division of the NHS, but such inefficiency had been even greater before 1948 and was inherent in any large organisation. What was required was not another administrative upheaval, but time for attitudes to change. More, rather than less, expenditure was needed.

Such conclusions naturally appalled the Treasury (which had been anticipating major savings) and in retrospect they have been criticised as overcomplacent. After the imposition of a ceiling on NHS expenditure and the introduction of charges, it is argued, financial control might at last have become 'sufficient'. Was it, however, 'efficient'? Did it, in other words, ensure full value for the very large sums of money devoted to health care? In this respect the Report has been attacked on three main grounds. First, on the critical issue of how demand should be regulated in a 'free' service, the Report dismissed Bevan's implicit assumption that there was an objective standard of 'adequacy', but it offered little guidance on how governments should determine the percentage of GNP to be allocated to health care. Secondly, although the Report encouraged the building of homes for the elderly (as an alternative to hospital care) and conservation in dentistry (including fluoridisation), it largely accepted the medical profession's bias towards hospitals and curative medicine. Indeed it maintained that 'those who have criticised the Health Service for spending far too much on disease and far too little on prevention have tended to overstate their case'.[30] Finally, it rejected most of the expedients for raising additional income (which were to remain remarkably constant between the 1940s and the 1980s): the raising of existing charges, the introduction of a hospital boarding charge, the extension of pay beds and the exclusion from the NHS of the 'non-central' ophthalmic and dental services. In fact it recommended the abolition of the Labour government charges on ophthalmic and dental care on the grounds that they were seriously discouraging treatment – although it conversely argued that the prescription charge, introduced by the Conservatives, had no such deterrent effect. Given such negative advice it is hardly surprising that the committee's critics have concluded that it was mesmerised by the *status quo*.

Any reforms which Conservative governments might have introduced in the 1950s were first delayed by the deliberations of the Guillebaud Committee and then discouraged by its recommendations. Two measures were, nevertheless, given serious consideration: the redeployment of resources from curative to preventive medicine, and the financing of the NHS wholly through contributory insurance. The former foundered not just on the vested interests of hospital consultants but also, more surprisingly, on those of Treasury officials. They recognised that preventive medicine represented the best value for money within health care, but their principal concern was not the cost-effectiveness but the control of public expenditure. This required that new expenditure must be balanced by cuts elsewhere in the health budget (which, owing to Bevan's reforms, consultants had the power to resist) and that increased grants should not be made to local authorities (which the Treasury could not directly control). The latter was a centrepiece of the Conservatives' drive for an 'opportunity' as opposed to a 'welfare' state and was strongly supported by Macmillan as prime minister. Beveridge had anticipated that insurance contributions would provide one-third of the costs of the NHS and it was a popular misconception that they covered the full cost. By 1956, however, they in fact contributed only 6.4 per cent; and it was felt that a move to total funding by insurance would not only enable income tax to be reduced (thereby increasing work incentive) but also instil into both doctors and patients a new sense of responsibility. If, as in social security, a direct link could be established between contributions and benefit, doctors would be more restrained in their prescriptions and patients in their demands. Thus an effective antidote would have been established to the policy of 'universalising the best'.[31]

There were, however, major practical drawbacks to such a policy. As Beveridge himself had recognised, the cost of a comprehensive health service was so great that it could not be financed by a flat-rate insurance scheme based on what the poorest contributor could afford. Moreover, in the late 1950s insurance contributions were already being raised to offset the cost of old age pensions (which were seen as an ever greater threat to government solvency) and so there was a very real problem of non-compliance. Finally, if some individuals failed to pay their premiums, could they really be denied medical care? The proposal was therefore reluctantly dropped although (as Table 7.3 illustrates) the relative contribution of the Insurance Fund to the NHS in the 1960s did significantly increase.

The 1960s, in the wake of the Plowden Report, were themselves characterised by a greater confidence in economic planning (see Chapter 5.2); and this led to a more intense scrutiny by government of both the delivery and organisational structure of health care, best illustrated by the 1962 Hospital Plan and the 1974 administrative reorganisation of the NHS. Neither of these reforms was a marked success. As has been seen, the NHS inherited (largely from the Poor Law and the bankrupt voluntary sector) an ill-assorted, ill-equipped and ill-distributed collection of hospitals, and capital expenditure upon them during the 1950s had been well below the minimum

Table 7.3   NHS sources of finance, 1950/1–1974/5 (percentages)

Financial Year	Taxation	Insurance	Charges
1950–1	87.6	9.4	0.7
1952–3	87.6	8.0	4.0
1954–5	86.9	7.9	5.0
1956–7	88.7	6.4	4.7
1958–9	80.3	14.4	5.0
1960–1	81.9	13.3	4.5
1962–3	77.1	17.2	5.5
1964–5	79.6	15.0	5.1
1966–7	84.8	12.4	2.4
1968–9	84.8	11.8	3.1
1970–1	85.8	10.8	3.2
1972–3	87.0	9.0	3.6
1974–5	91.3	5.7	2.6

Figures exclude local authority health expenditure.
Source: A. Leathard, *Health Care Provision* (1990) p. 38.

recommended by the Guillebaud Committee. The hospital service therefore presented the ideal challenge for both the planned expansion of welfare expenditure (as advocated by Plowden) and a Ministry of Health, revitalised by the simultaneous appointment in 1960 of a new minister (Powell), a new permanent secretary (Sir Bruce Fraser) and a new chief medical officer (Sir George Godber).[32] The last, as a doctor committed to the more equal distribution of health care, brought to the Ministry the expert drive that had characterised Whitehall's wartime success. The planning credentials of Powell (who had resigned in 1958 with Thorneycroft over excessive welfare expenditure) and Fraser (the Treasury official formerly responsible for containing health expenditure) were, however, less apparent.

Both were nevertheless to play a highly constructive part in the development of the Hospital Plan. The plan's overriding object was to guarantee access for both the medical profession and the public to the most modern and comprehensive facilities. Accordingly 1250 hospitals were to be closed and, at the cost of £500 million, 360 extended and 90 new ones built to provide a national network of 6–800 bed district general hospitals, each serving a catchment area of between 100 000 and 150 000 people. It was the role of Powell to persuade each RHB to draft an appropriate plan for its area and to determine the principles on which it should be integrated into a national plan. Fraser's role was to persuade the Treasury that, through a more concentrated and capital-intensive service, better medical care could be provided at a relatively low cost.

Despite the rise in capital expenditure on hospitals from 3.1 to 7.8 per cent of the health budget (see Table 7.1), neither the promised savings, nor indeed the full complement of district general hospitals, had been achieved by the time of the Plan's abandonment in the early 1970s. The reasons for failure were many. As Plowden's critics had predicted, the 'rationality' of long-term building programmes was disrupted by short-term expenditure cuts (necessitated by balance of payments crises) and by rising inflation. As Plowden himself had feared, there was also an absence of the requisite sense of political and public responsibility. Politicians favoured short-term rather than long-term measures (for which others might gain credit), whilst the medical profession favoured the expenditure of scarce resources on salaries and not facilities.

Even more seriously, failure exposed the limitations of centralised, technocratic planning. Not only was there public protest at the closure of local hospitals, thereby refuting Bevan's belief that it was better to be 'kept alive in the efficient if cold altruism of a large hospital than expire in a gush of warm sympathy in a small one'[33]; but planning also failed because, as Hayek had predicted (see Chapter 2.2.3), it was dependent on imperfect knowledge, and uniform decisions had to be imposed on a wide variety of local circumstances for which, as both central planners and local implementers discovered to their mutual frustration, they were only partially suited. Foremost amongst the technocratic failures was the hospital construction programme itself. Here experiments with standardised designs did not repeat the success of the 1950s school-building programme but resulted instead in the bankruptcy of many contractors and both a slowness of completion and a poor quality of finish that had few international parallels.

The success of the Hospital Plan had also been dependent on the implementation of a complementary programme, outlined in the 1963 and 1966 white papers *Health and Welfare: the Development of Community Care*, which was designed to reduce pressure on district general hospitals by providing alternative accommodation for the elderly, the mentally handicapped and the convalescent. By 1972 it was intended that £200 million would have been spent on the building of 1000 new residential homes and 1000 new training centres for the mentally and physically handicapped, and that there would have been an increase of 45 per cent in local authority staff (such as health visitors) to provide care for people in their own homes. As with the Hospital Plan, however, achievement fell far short of these objectives, and consequently many patients had to remain in the district general hospitals, where their treatment was not only more expensive but also less effective. The conclusion drawn by government from the failure of the community care programme, however, was not that centralised planning was defective but that greater unification and centralisation were needed. The programme had been the responsibility of local government and, with its independent financial and electoral base, it could not be easily brought into line. Accordingly one of the principal objectives of the 1974 reorganisation of the NHS was the integration of the remaining local government health services into the NHS.

The 1974 reorganisation has also been deemed a failure. Indeed, it can hardly be judged otherwise because it had to be severely modified as early as 1982 and so survived unscathed for an even shorter period than Bevan's own reforms, which it was designed to replace. The pressure for reform came from two main sources – the medical profession and the Ministry of Health. The former was dissatisfied with a tripartite division of health care that not only filled highly-capitalised hospitals with inappropriate, long-stay patients but also discouraged the joint development of preventive and aftercare services which GPs (on the retirement of their interwar cadre) and local authorities were now increasingly ready to provide. The Ministry of Health desired, above all, clearer lines of management communication. Accordingly, in the initial restructuring plan, it was proposed that under the Ministry there should be some 40–45 area health authorities (AHAs) each responsible for the *full* range of health care within a given locality. They should also be coterminous with the major local authorities, which the Royal Commission on Local Government was expected to recommend (see Chapter 4.4), because it was recognised that closer coordination with social workers was necessary if many of the underlying problems giving rise to ill-health and disrupting convalescence were to be resolved.

By 1974, however, this simple structure had been changed beyond recognition. The AHAs had been adjudged too small for planning purposes and too large for the detailed implementation of policy. The Royal Commission on Local Government had also recommended smaller local government units than anticipated. Consequently the final plan proposed 90 AHAs which were to be coterminous with the new local government units responsible for social work. Above them, responsible for planning, were to be 14 regional health authorities (coterminous with the old RHBs), and beneath them, responsible for the actual implementation of policy, a further 200 district management teams, each shadowed by a community health council to give expression to public opinion. Medical care was no longer to be unified because the executive committees for GPs, dentists and opticians (renamed family practitioner committees) were excluded from the remit of the AHAs, and managerial lines of communication were no longer to be clear because membership of the various authorities was based not purely on managerial but also on representative criteria. Members of the AHAs for example were to be drawn in equal proportion from the nominees of local government, the medical profession and the state. The overriding objective of this restructuring was identified as the 'maximum delegation downwards, matched by accountability upwards', but in fact what was created was a Byzantine structure in which there were too many tiers of administration and in which senior executive officials were responsible to authorities which might include among their members one of their subordinates.[34] 'An attempt to please everyone', as Klein has concluded, 'satisfied no-one.' It was a disaster.

7.3 THE DELIVERY OF HEALTH CARE

Neither the pragmatism of the 1950s nor the centralised planning of the 1960s could rapidly make good the defects in either individual services or the overall structure of the NHS, inherited respectively from the interwar years and the 1940s. To what extend did this failure affect adversely those working within the service and those who received treatment from it?

In a profession notorious for understaffing and low pay, all those within the service unquestionably benefited from state control. Between 1948 and 1973 staff costs rose from 60 to 70 per cent of an expanding budget, and the number of staff rose to almost one million. The improvement in morale that should have resulted from these advances was, however, dissipated by the unevenness of pay awards, the disappointment of expectations (built in part upon the unrealistic hopes of the 1940s) and bad management. The formidable number of enquiries into the pay, training and conditions of work of not only consultants, GPs, dentists, doctors and nurses but also administrators and ancillary staff reflected both the size and the historical complexity of the problems facing each branch of the profession – and the continuing inability of the NHS managers to resolve them.[35] As a result militancy grew. In the mid-1960s GPs threatened to withdraw from the service (only to be appeased by the granting of a 'GPs' charter'); in 1966 junior hospital doctors formed their own association; and in 1973 ancillary workers (whose trade unions had only started to organise seriously in the late 1960s) held their first national strike. The junior hospital doctors and then the consultants threatened similar action two years later. There was thus little of the altruism which Titmuss had presumed would be fostered by the welfare state in general and the NHS in particular.

The experience of GPs, whom Bevan rather belatedly recognised as 'the most important' people within the service, provides the best illustration of the mixed impact of the NHS upon its workforce.[36] British GPs retained their unique status after 1948, neither developing particular specialisms nor undertaking more hospital work as did their European and American counterparts. Exclusion from specialist work was in part a result of the social prejudice of hospital consultants and the increasing sophistication of surgery; but it also reflected the fact that after 1911 the capitation fee paid by the state enabled doctors in Britain, in contrast to those abroad, to earn a living from general practice. However, the GPs' insistence in 1948 on the continuation of capitation fees – to the exclusion of salaries – had some major disadvantages: a flat fee for each patient on their list provided no reward for the good care of patients, the responsible prescription of drugs or the purchase of modern equipment.

Accordingly GPs found themselves in an increasingly disadvantageous position. Denied their former right to sell the goodwill of their practices upon retirement, and with little private practice, they enjoyed few market incentives. On the other hand, without a clear salary structure they were denied the incentives of promotion and merit awards which hospital doctors enjoyed after 1948. Cut off from the glamorous world of hospitals (upon which the media concentrated) and with inflation gradually eroding the value of the generous Danckwerts award of 1950 (which, at the cost of £40 million, far exceeded the value of any economy achieved by the Conservative government), GPs felt increasingly isolated and demoralised in the 1950s.

This demoralisation was countered by the 1960 Pilkington pay award, the institution of an annual pay review and, above all, by the 1965 GPs' charter which, through the provision of cheap loans and a basic salary to underpin capitation fees, encouraged the modernisation of surgeries and offered some reward for initiative. As GPs gradually abandoned their initial hostility towards health centres, there also opened up for them the possibility of a constructive new role, not as junior hospital consultants (which they had been in danger of becoming in the 1930s) but as senior social workers (at the head of a team of district nurses, health visitors and midwives) promoting 'community' or 'positive' medicine.[37] Thus from a base in 1948, when they had at least secured their historical objectives of minimum financial security and clinical freedom, they had the chance to rebridge the gulf between curative and preventive medicine and to establish, as the unique hallmark of the British NHS, the provision of health care by doctors alive not only to their patients' medical but also to their social needs. That GPs were unable fully to rise to this challenge was another of the missed opportunities of the 1960s.

Like the conditions of those working within the service, the general standard of health also improved between the 1940s and the 1970s.[38] In England and Wales the death rate, for example, declined by 16 per cent (if the changing age structure of the population is taken into account); life expectancy at birth increased from 66.4 to 69.6 years for men and 71.5 to 76 years for women; and infant mortality between 1940 and 1975 fell from 56 to 16 per 1000 live births. Illness (morbidity), as measured by absence from work, increased rather than decreased (as Beveridge had assumed), although this might simply have reflected changing attitudes to health and to work once full employment had been achieved. Most of the major killer diseases also declined, although they were then replaced by others, such as lung cancer and heart disease, which arose either from an unhealthy life style or old age.[39]

Amidst the general improvement, however, there were two significant grounds for concern. First, by international standards Britain's progress was slow. For example infant mortality (although decreasing) was relatively high and becoming even higher in relation to countries such as Holland, which did not have a national health service. Secondly, despite the more equitable geographical distribution of consultants and GPs at least until the 1960s, there was little advance towards the greater equality of health standards between regions or between social classes. This had been one of the principal objectives of the NHS. It has been estimated, for example, that in 1970 the chances of a child of an unskilled worker (Registrar General's class 5) dying within one month and one year of birth were, respectively, twice and over three times as high as a child of a professional worker (Registrar General's class 1). Moreover people in class 5 were in general two and a half times more likely than people in class 1 to die before retirement age – reflecting not a decline but a growing disparity in mortality rates between the classes.

Not all the blame for these disappointing trends should be placed on the NHS. The poor international comparisons can be explained in part by Britain's relatively low economic growth rate whilst increasing inequality reflected also conservative attitudes towards diet and exercise. Even in relation to diet and exercise, however, the NHS must shoulder some blame because of its failure to promote a more effective health education policy. Indeed, historically the most effective health education programmes had been provided by local authorities (especially through their mother and baby clinics); and this was, of course, the very area of health which became demoralised and suffered most from the postwar diversion of resources into hospitals.

The decline of maternity clinics was one of the ways in which women's interests were not best served by the NHS. Having been largely excluded from national health insurance in the 1930s, women were clearly among the major beneficiaries of the NHS but (as argued in Chapter 2.3.3) there were surreptitious ways in which, both as workers within the service and as patients, they were disadvantaged.[40] Childbirth in hospital, for instance, increased from approximately 50 to 96 per cent of all births between the mid 1940s and the 1970s. This was not the intention of government but a consequence of the determination of hospital consultants to wrest responsibility from GPs whom (with some justice) they regarded as ill-trained. Initially mothers themselves also appeared to favour hospital deliveries. However, when housing conditions improved and mothers' attitudes changed, a policy designed to help women physically became one which could damage them psychologically; and its retention smacked of an insensitive paternalism which also discouraged open parental access to children in hospitals and husbands' attendance at births. The lack of resources assigned to family planning and abortion, after state provision of both was legalised in 1968, also reflected the low priority accorded to health services required exclusively by women.

One of the most disadvantaged groups, however, was the mentally ill. Again it was the intention of successive governments to capitalise on new drugs (such as phenothiazine) to control mental illness and consequently to release patients from the large Victorian asylums, where at best care rather than a cure was provided. This was the explicit purpose behind the 1959 Mental Health Act and one of Powell's principal objectives in the 1962 Hospital Plan.[41] However, owing to the slow provision of residential and training centres under the community care programme, the release of patients was delayed. Then, after the 1967 Ely Hospital (Cardiff) scandal over the maltreatment of patients, a series of abuses was exposed in other mental hospitals. The mentally ill represented exactly the type of (largely) inarticulate patient for whom the NHS should have been able to cater far better than the market, and it is to the credit of successive governments that a problem long hidden from public view and carrying no obvious electoral advantage should have been brought into the open. Their best efforts were, however, frustrated by a general lack of interest within the medical profession and the conservatism of public opinion. The medical profession was attracted towards more glamorous responsibilities whilst, to stimulate greater public concern, governments had to subsidise pressure groups such as MIND to expose the shortcomings of their own hospitals. This strategy well represents the irrationality into which professional vested interests, Bevan's paternalistic administrative structure and poorly-informed public opinion had plunged the NHS by 1974.

7.4 CONCLUSION

'A free health service', Bevan proclaimed after his resignation, 'is a triumphant example of the superiority of collective action and public initiative applied to a segment of society where commercial principles are seen at their worst.'[42] In interwar Britain commercial principles had indeed intruded into health care and the results had left much to be desired. Many present-day economists would also agree that, in theory at least, state provision of health care is more efficient than either private or social insurance (see Chapter 3.2.1). The establishment of the NHS in 1948, therefore, certainly provided an opportunity to demonstrate the superiority of collective action and public initiative.

This opportunity was not fully seized. The NHS did succeed in retaining the affection of the public, but it failed to resolve the two fundamental administrative and political challenges with which it was faced. In the absence of a suitable system of local government, hospitals had to be nationalised; and nationalisation required the development of both an organisational structure to integrate hospitals with the other health services and new administrative skills within Whitehall. In the inevitable absence of sufficient resources to satisfy all medical demands, clear criteria had also to be developed to determine priorities and to ensure the efficient allocation of scarce resources. The NHS, as originally designed by Bevan, was unable to rise to these challenges. As the medical profession had itself come to recognise in 1962, the tripartite system discouraged rather than encouraged cooperation and only in the 1960s did the Ministry of Health start seriously to develop the skills by which the relative merits of centralised planning (as opposed to those of the market and local initiative) could be truly tested. The policy of 'universalising the best' was also retained in order to maintain consensus, long after it had been exposed as essentially meaningless. Sufficient resources only existed to provide either the best in a given area (be that geographical or medical) or to 'universalise the adequate'.

Given its benighted legacy (in terms of backlog of ill-health, entrenched professional prejudice and dilapidated facilities) it is perhaps unsurprising that the NHS was not immediately successful. However, its difficulties were increased rather than decreased by certain early developments. For example the altruism latent in certain sections of the medical profession, which might have provided the bridgehead for a more enlightened service, was dissipated by the bitter negotiations between the Labour government and the medical profession. The genuine political will that existed in the 1950s to improve preventive medicine and the care of the mentally ill was frustrated by the institutional power earlier conceded to hospital consultants. 'A vested interest in denigration' had also developed amongst those working within the service (despite their unquestionably improved conditions) as a result of the exaggerated hopes excited in the 1940s. In the absence of any market criteria, the disappointment of these hopes was blamed not on a genuine lack of resources but on the perfidy of politicians and the incompetence of senior administrators.[43] By the time a concerted effort was made to revitalise the service in the 1960s, not only were the techniques of centralised planning still seriously underdeveloped but the economic and the cultural climates had become far less favourable (see Chapter 4.4 and 4.5).

Many theoretical reasons have been advanced for the relative failure of the NHS (see Chapter 2.2 and 2.3). From a pluralist perspective however, what is outstanding is the close identification of the NHS with the welfare state as a whole. To contemporaries the two institutions often appeared synonymous. To the historian the inability of the NHS to develop the requisite administrative structures, to forge a firmer professional commitment and to nurture informed public support equally mirrors the larger failure of the welfare state effectively to respond to the new positive responsibilities placed upon government after the Second World War. As a consequence, confidence in both the NHS and the welfare state was not reinforced by a series of proven successes but undermined by a series of perceived failures.

7.5 FURTHER READING

The NHS is well served by introductory texts. Among the best are R. Klein, *The Politics of the National Health Service* (1983) and B. Watkin, *The National Health Service: the first phase, 1948–74 and after* (1978). Both contain good bibliographies and can be supplemented by the well-documented official history, C. Webster, *The Health Services Since the War*, the first volume of which was published in 1988. D.M. Fox provides useful comparisons in *Health Policies, Health Politics: the British and American Experience, 1911–1965* (Princeton, 1986). Two brief insights into the history of GPs and health centres can be found in F. Honigsbaum, *The Division of British Medicine* (1979) and P. Hall, 'The development of health centres' in P. Hall *et al.*, *Change, Choice and Conflict in Social Policy* (1975). C. Ham, *Health Policy in Britain* (1982) identifies the main theoretical approaches to the history of the NHS.

The origins of the NHS have attracted much attention. In addition to the texts cited above, H. Eckstein, *The English Health Service* (Cambridge, Massachusetts, 1958) presents an American perspective, whilst insider accounts are J. E. Pater, *The Making of the National Health Service* (1981) and more briefly, but with equal illumination, P. Benner, 'The early years of the National Health Service', in T. Gorst *et al.*, *Postwar Britain* (1989). The various interpretations are dissected in C. Webster, 'Conflict and consensus: explaining the British Health Service', *Twentieth Century British History 1* (1990) 115–51. The political battle over the early financing of the NHS is recorded in M. Foot, *Aneurin Bevan*, vol. 2 (1973) and, rather more reliably, in P. M. Williams, *Hugh Gaitskell* (1979).

8 Education

Education initially attracted as much popular enthusiasm as the NHS and, until the 1970s at least, it was more successful in attracting public finance. Its exceptional degree of political support was demonstrated by the fact that the 1944 Education Bill was the only major piece of reconstruction legislation to be enacted during the war and, in its wake, public opinion was recorded as providing 'overwhelming support for extra expenditure on education'.[1] The war thus reversed, if only temporarily, the widespread popular indifference – and even hostility – to education which had followed the introduction of compulsory schooling in 1880. Because of full employment, children's earnings were no longer so vital to family income and consequently many parents were able for the first time to regard education not as a short-term financial loss but as an opportunity for their children to secure a good job and hence long-term financial security.

Partly because of this increased popularity, expenditure on the formal education system grew faster in the 1950s and 1960s than on any other social service.[2] Between 1951 and 1975 it rose from 6.8 per cent to 12.5 per cent of public expenditure and from 19.5 per cent to 23.1 per cent of social expenditure; and, as a result, education permanently supplanted the NHS as the second most expensive social service after social security (see Appendix, Tables A1.3, A1.4, A1.5). There were two other explanations for the increased size and the changing structure of the education budget (see Table 8.1). The first was demographic. The baby boom of the mid 1940s required the expansion of primary education in the early 1950s, secondary education in the late 1950s and higher education in the early 1960s. This cycle was repeated after the unexpected baby boom of the late 1950s (see Chapter 4.2). The other was increased educational attainment. In the 1960s especially, Britain was fully part of an 'educational explosion, probably . . . unique in the western world'.[3]

Despite this explosion, however, the education service soon became the subject of informed criticism, mounting disillusion and political disagreement. As early as 1956 the very system of secondary education, through which the 1944 Act had been expected to secure greater 'equality of opportunity', was attacked by Crosland as 'divisive, unjust and wasteful'; and in the same year the paucity of technical education was identified by the Prime Minister as a major

Table 8.1 Education: selected current and capital expenditure, 1951–77

	1951–2		1961–2		1966–7		1971–2		1976–7	
	£m	%	£m	%	£m	%	£m	%	£m	%
Current expenditure:*										
1. Schools	220	53.9	531	50.1	883	48.3	1401	44.4	4148	54.3
of which:										
2. Nursery	–	–	2	0.1	–	–	8	0.3	153	2.0
3. Primary	122	29.9	246	23.2	366	20.0	639	20.3	1542	20.2
4. Secondary	91	22.3	269	25.4	413	22.6	699	22.2	2012	26.4
5. Further and adult education	23	5.6	87	8.2	186	10.2	351	11.1	940	12.3
6. Teacher training	8	2.0	25	2.4	69	3.8	129	4.1		
7. Universities	31	7.6	87	8.2	187	10.2	336	10.7	627	8.2
8. Total current expenditure	338	82.8	877	82.7	1521	83.3	2661	84.4	6960	91.2
Capital expenditure:										
9. Schools	52	12.7	114	10.7	160	8.8	327	10.4	483	6.3
10. Further and adult education	9	2.2	31	2.9	37	2.0	64	2.0	88	1.2
11. Teacher training	1	0.2	12	1.1	11	0.6	12	0.4		
12. Universities	6	1.5	26	2.5	80	4.4	81	2.6	102	1.3
13. Total capital expenditure	70	17.2	183	17.3	306	16.7	493	15.6	673	8.8
14. Total public expenditure	408	100.0	1060	100.0	1827	100.0	3154	100.0	7633	100.0

* Excludes grants to students.
For 1951–2 and 1966–7, lines 1–7 and 9–12 exclude Northern Ireland.
Source: Social Trends (1970, 1979).

reason for Britain's declining international competitiveness. 'The prizes', Eden warned,

> will not go to the countries with the largest population. Those with the best systems of education will win. . . . Our scientists are doing brilliant work. But if we are to make full use of what we are learning, we shall need many more scientists, engineers and technicians.[4]

The launching by the Soviet Union of the first space satellite (Sputnik) in 1957 came as a profound shock and was taken as confirmation that, because of the backwardness of its education system, Britain was in no position to 'win'.

There was a brief return to wartime optimism and political consensus in the early 1960s, but disillusion and party disagreement returned. This was principally because of the perceived incompatibility of the three continuing objectives of policy: equality of opportunity, improved technical education and the maintenance of educational standards. There was in theory no reason why these objectives should have been – or should have been seen to be – incompatible. Education had long been recognised as a public good (see Chapter 3.2.1). Hence any increase in equality of opportunity, by enabling more children to reach their full potential, was acknowledged to be in the national interest. Technical education had in the past been popularly regarded as a subtle device to divert children from humbler backgrounds away from prestigious and well-paid administrative jobs; but, given the shortage of skilled manpower and consequently the high wages it could command, this suspicion was no longer valid. Finally, any lowering of standards to obtain a spurious equality would not just have denied children a genuine opportunity to develop their talents fully, but would have undermined Britain's industrial competitiveness, the creation of wealth and thus the buoyancy of government revenue upon which all welfare services ultimately depended.

Such interdependence was recognised by the advocates of educational reform within both the major political parties. Crosland, for example, steadily maintained that greater equality of opportunity was the key to increased educational attainment and faster rates of growth. Eccles, Eden's minister of education, likewise identified educational expenditure as the 'wisest investment' not just because it would satisfy industry's technical needs and enable everyone to respond to market opportunities but because it would also instil that sense of personal responsibility for which the 1944 *Employment Policy* white paper had called. 'Problems such as forestalling inflation, preventing and settling strikes and abandoning restrictive practices', he insisted, 'will, in the end, only be solved by better education.'[5]

Beneath such apparent consensus, however, there lay a deep political divide. Crosland (as a democratic socialist) ultimately sought to employ educational reform as a means of creating a 'classless society'. In contrast Eccles (as a reluctant collectivist) sought to maintain as much as possible of the *status quo* and accordingly advised his colleagues that any 'political party, aiming to poll more than half the votes at future general elections, must be clearly identified with one sector of the sprouting Welfare State, and . . . education is a service marked out as peculiarly Conservative in purpose'. Such conflicting objectives raise fundamental questions about the ultimate purpose for which the two parties were seeking greater equality of opportunity and improved technical education and, above all, about the contemporary criteria by which 'educational standards' were judged. Any assessment of the achievements of the postwar education system must, therefore, be prefaced by an examination of the precise political nature of the Act which provided its statutory basis.

8.1   THE 1944 EDUCATION ACT AND ITS CRITICS

The 1944 Education Act, as has been seen, enjoyed exceptional popular and political support during the war. It was also to provide the statutory basis for the education system over the following forty years. It is little wonder, therefore, that it was once described as the 'greatest measure of educational advance since 1870, and probably the greatest ever known'. However, as defects have come to be perceived in postwar education provision, so criticism has mounted and one educational historian has gone so far as to attack the act as a 'clever exercise in manipulative politics by a past master of the art (of the possible) with the aid of a state bureaucracy devoted to highly conservative objectives'.[6] Which of these assessments is the more accurate? To answer this question three basic issues have to be resolved. What precisely did the Act propose? What did it deliberately, or accidentally, omit? Finally, were the perceived deficiencies in postwar education directly attributable to the Act itself or to those who implemented it?

The interwar system of state education, which the Act sought to reform, was as confused and confusing as the interwar health services. There were two particular sources of confusion. The first was the uneasy distinction between 'elementary' and secondary or 'higher' education. The latter did not (as today) cover all children over the age of eleven, but only those who attended grammar schools – be they the old, privately endowed foundations or the schools established by local government after 1902. Fees were chargeable at these schools (although by 1938 48 per cent of places were free) and they were attended by only 20 per cent of children between twelve and the minimum leaving age of fourteen. All other children remained within the free 'elementary' education system – and often within the same 'all-age' school which they had attended since the age of five. The different status and the lack of cooperation between these two levels of education was emphasised by their different administrative status. Secondary education was solely the responsibility of county councils and county boroughs, but within the counties 'elementary' education was often the direct responsibility of the much smaller and potentially less efficient non-county boroughs and urban districts.

The second major source of confusion, within both elementary and secondary education, was the 'dual' nature of the schools. Until local government was itself permitted to provide elementary and 'higher' education (in 1870 and 1902 respectively) voluntary organisations, and in particular the churches, had been responsible for its provision – with the government's role limited to the payment of subsidies. Throughout the interwar period the voluntary sector (despite increasing financial difficulties) survived; and so in many schools the appointment of staff, the overall organisation of the school and all new buildings were the responsibility of independent boards of governors and not the local education authorities (LEAs). In 1938, for example, one half of schools in the elementary sector, catering for just under one-third of children, were voluntary.[7]

The principal purpose of the Act was to end this confusion and accordingly there were four major administrative changes. First, responsibility for the implementation of policy was placed solely on county councils and county boroughs, thereby more than halving the number of LEAs from 315 to 146. Secondly, voluntary schools were not nationalised (as was to be the case with voluntary hospitals), but their independence was reduced and their financial problems alleviated by two new types of subsidy. 'Aided' status was to be offered to those schools whose governors were still prepared to pay half the cost of alterations, improvements and external repairs (with the LEA meeting all other costs).[8] In return the governors would be permitted to retain control over the appointment and dismissal of teachers and the nature of religious instruction. 'Controlled' status was to be applied to all other voluntary schools (for which LEAs would assume full financial responsibility) with the rights of the governors limited to consultation over the appointment of the head master and those teachers responsible for religious instruction. Finally, in order to ensure standardisation of educational provision, the Board of Education was elevated into a ministry with the authority not just to 'superintend' but to 'control and direct' LEAs; and all teachers were to be paid uniformly according to the nationally negotiated Burnham pay scales.[9]

These administrative reforms were a necessary precondition for major advances in both the nature and quality of state education. It was for the first time made entirely free.[10] The school leaving age was raised to 15, with the proviso that it should be raised to 16 as soon as was 'practical'. A clear break was also introduced at the age of eleven between 'primary' and 'secondary' education, so that all children had the same potential 'ladder' to university. In addition, for those who left school at the minimum age there was to be compulsory attendance at county colleges and local authorities were required to provide further education courses in technical, commercial and art education. Finally, as practical measures to increase equality of opportunity, there were to be increased provision of nursery education; free school meals, milk and medical inspection (to ensure that all children were physically able to benefit from their education); and a major upgrading of facilities in primary schools.

The Act therefore represented – as was clearly recognised at the time – a major step towards the creation of an efficient, cost-effective and 'just' education system. The concentration of responsibility on county councils and county boroughs created within each locality a single authority for primary, secondary and further education with a sufficiently large population and financial base to ensure a fully comprehensive service.[11] Should any authority prove recalcitrant, then the ministry had the ultimate power to 'control and direct' it. The new deal for voluntary schools, whilst retaining within the state system a much-needed source of non-government finance, removed the major impediment to the upgrading of primary schools and the provision of specialist secondary education. The poor facilities for children aged between seven and eleven in voluntary schools had been highlighted by *Educational Reconstruction*, the white paper which preceded the 1944 Act; and lack of finance had also led to the inequitable position that only 16 per cent of their pupils received specialist 'post-primary' education, whereas the comparable figure in the state sector was 62 per cent.[12]

Equality of opportunity was advanced even more explicitly through the abolition of fees and the raising of the school leaving age. The former made the criterion for educational advance children's ability, rather than their parents' financial or social status, whilst the latter, by ensuring four years of specialist secondary education, significantly reduced the disparity between the amount and quality of education received by children from different classes. Increased support for voluntary schools also reduced another source of inequity which war-time evacuation had exposed: the considerable difference in the quality of education provided in the countryside (where church schools predominated) and the towns.

Despite such achievements, however, the 'progressive' nature of the Act has been seriously questioned. There have been three main criticisms. The first is that it attempted little that was new. The raising of the school leaving age to fifteen (with a clear distinction between primary and secondary education at the age of eleven) was first recommended, so it is argued, by the Hadow Report of 1926. In the implementation of this report, not only was the school leaving age scheduled to be raised in September 1939, but local government had grudgingly started to replace 'all-age' schools with specialist junior technical and central 'modern' schools. Moreover, through the increasing provision of free places in grammar schools, the whole of 'post-primary' education had in certain areas effectively become free. The weakness of such an argument, however, is that interwar progress was gradual and geographically uneven – not least because it was constrained by the financial weakness of the voluntary sector and by the latent antagonism both between voluntary and state schools and between the two responsible levels of local government. A major achievement of the Act was that it removed these historic impediments to progress and thereby enabled interwar ideals to become postwar reality.

The second criticism is that the Act halted the momentum towards a long overdue expansion of technical education, which had been vigorously advocated in 1938 by the Spens Report. The *Educational Reconstruction* white paper fully acknowledged the justice of Spens' case, admitting that:

> Too many of the nation's abler children are attracted into a type of education which prepares primarily for the University and for the administrative and clerical professions; too few find their way into schools from which the design and craftsmanship sides of industry are recruited. If education is to serve the interests both of the child and of the nation, some means must be found of correcting this bias.[13]

By encouraging the development of technical schools, making continuing education compulsory and placing a requirement on local government to provide further technical education, the Act might also appear well designed to have redressed the balance. There is nevertheless some validity in the charge that – as in other proposals for industrial reconstruction – 'the wartime coalition and its civil servants came, they saw, and they shirked' this particular challenge.[14] In contrast to the zeal with which he tackled the problem of church schools, for example, Butler (the Conservative minister principally responsible for the Act) quickly passed the question of technical education to his officials. The one initiative he took was to appoint the Norwood Committee on the secondary school curriculum and when, as expected, its report provided a strong defence of the traditional qualities of public and grammar school education, he expressed his satisfaction. 'This well written report', he noted, 'will serve our book very well – particularly the layout of the secondary world. Spens will be furious.'[15] The political drive to galvanise Whitehall into a radical reappraisal of technical education was therefore clearly lacking.

In practical terms, however, what more could the Act have done to instil into the education system, and into society at large, a new industrial culture? Within the Labour Party Bevin had proposed that all school-leavers should be sent at fourteen to boarding schools and then, at sixteen, into industry for four years of compulsory training. Within the Conservative Party a powerful advisory committee had simultaneously recommended *inter alia* compulsory technical and vocational training for all fourteen to eighteen year olds and the replacement of classics by a national curriculum of science and technology. With some justice such proposals were dismissed at the time – and have been dismissed since – as 'semi-fascist'.[16] They were clearly impractical. Whilst the traditionalism of Butler and his civil servants should be acknowledged, it is unclear what more they could have done. Corelli Barnett, one of the Act's foremost critics, may thus be justified in arguing that:

> The vaunted 1944 Education Act offered not so much an executive operational framework as an open gate to an empty construction site on which local authorities might or might not (depending on their zeal and the effectiveness of the Ministry's nagging) build the technical and further education system that Britain so desperately needed.[17]

However, at least the gate had been fully opened. The critical question is not why the Act's proposals were so insubstantial but why, given the nagging of Conservative governments throughout the 1950s, the opportunities they did offer were not fully seized.

The third and most substantial criticism of the Act, to which allusion has already been made, is its innate conservatism. The war, so it is argued, provided an unparalleled opportunity for four radical reforms: the abolition of public schools, the secularisation of state education, the raising of the school leaving age to sixteen and the unification of secondary education within multilateral or comprehensive schools.[18] None of these reforms was achieved. Public schools, which had been in serious financial and political trouble in 1940, survived to gain in strength after the war. The place of religion was consolidated, as part of the deal with voluntary schools, with the obligation on all schools to hold daily, corporate acts of worship. The raising of the school leaving age to sixteen was deferred until 1972. Finally, the Act's endorsement of diversity within secondary education ensured the survival of the grammar school and thus, within the state sector, a sense of educational privilege and hierarchy – in place of the 'popular culture' and democratic values which, it was believed, multilateral or comprehensive schools would disseminate. The multilateral school had quickly been recognised within the wartime Board of Education as 'the only full solution to the problem of a truly democratic education', whilst the grammar schools had not fully thrown off their nineteenth-century legacy as schools for middle-class children. Moreover they were imbued with the Platonic ideal of 'education for leadership': they, together with the public schools, would train the country's chosen élite, whilst it was the duty of all other schools to provide the willing followers.[19]

There is again some justice in these criticisms. Senior civil servants initiated reconstruction planning with the explicit intention of forestalling more radical change and later many assumed 'the mantle of spokesmen within the government' for the independent and grammar schools.[20] One of the main reasons, for example, why eleven was chosen as the age at which to divide primary and secondary schooling – despite the doubts of educational psychologists and Butler himself – was the defence of the traditional structure and curriculum of grammar schools. Butler (a governor of Felstead, with two sons at Eton) also advised the representatives of public schools on how to deflect public hostility and later admitted that he had appointed the Fleming Committee – which reported on the future of public schools in June 1944, just after the third reading of the Act – to minimise public discussion. Indeed it was his commissioning of this, and of the Norwood Committee, which has led directly to the charge that the Act was a 'clever exercise in manipulative politics'.

What such a charge overlooks however is that manipulation was needed not just to thwart radical reform but to achieve any reform at all. It was not preordained that the only piece of reconstruction legislation to be passed during the war should be the Education Bill. That it was enacted was a triumph for, and a tribute to, Butler's political skills. His predecessor at the Board of Education had after all been dismissed for being too radical and his own initial proposals had been rejected by Churchill because they raised party controversy 'in the most acute and dangerous form'.[21] Without the prime minister's backing (usually a prerequisite for any major reform), Butler had also to reconcile the conflicting interests of Conservative and Labour backbenchers. The potential hostility of the former was demonstrated by their successful defence of direct grant schools (which Butler wished to abolish), whilst the radicalism of the latter was reflected by their imposition on Churchill, during the passage of the Act, of his only wartime parliamentary defeat (over equal pay).[22] In such circumstances the achievement of so substantial an Act cannot be dismissed simply as a triumph for conservatism. It was a genuine triumph for reform.

Although its radicalism may have at times been exaggerated, therefore, the Act did represent a major advance in education policy. It swept aside the historic impediments to change and, by guaranteeing to all children four years of specialist secondary education, it ensured a significant increase in educational opportunity. Certain controversial issues, such as public schools, were deliberately evaded. Others, such as technical education, were not incisively handled. Moreover, in relation to multilateral education (which was favoured by an articulate but unrepresentative minority), the Norwood Report was deliberately commissioned and published to signal the government's hope that, whatever its possible educational and social disadvantages, the postwar education system would be a tripartite one.

However, even if Butler and his officials thereby revealed an innate conservatism, it is of equal significance that – as with technical education – they left all options open. They were never as dogmatic as were, for example, Beveridge and Bevan in their respective spheres. Indeed the perfect riposte to those who criticise the conservatism of the Act is the later complaint from the New Right that, 'as a giant umbrella under which all sorts of experiments could flourish', the Act 'hardly suggested a coherent Conservative policy for education'.[23] The essence of the Act, therefore, was its pragmatism and, in consequence, its ultimate impact on policy was determined not by its authors but by those who implemented it.

8.2   EDUCATION AND EQUALITY

The overriding objective in the implementation of postwar education was greater equality, but its attainment was complicated by a perceived conflict with the maintenance of educational standards and, above all, by a fundamental redefinition of equality. In 1944 equality had essentially meant 'equality of opportunity' (the assurance that no accident of parental circumstance, place of residence or sex would prevent children from developing their talent to the full) and 'parity of esteem' (the equitable distribution of resources between children of different aptitudes). To these definitions had been added by 1975 'equality of outcome' (the reduction of differences in educational achievement between children of different social groups, so that the educational system did not simply reflect and reinforce existing class differences). The means of attainment also changed, most dramatically within secondary education where the tripartite system was progressively supplanted by comprehensive schools. What were the major phases in the implementation of educational policy? And why did the tripartite system collapse so quickly?

Postwar policy may be broadly divided into three phases. During the first, between 1945 and 1954, the simple priorities were to maintain prewar standards and to lay the foundations for the achievement of 'equality of opportunity'. To maintain standards one-third of school buildings had, as a result of war damage, to be either rebuilt or repaired; and, as a result of the baby boom, extra resources had to be assigned to primary education to meet the needs by 1954 of almost one million extra children (see Table 8.2).[24] To achieve greater equality the school leaving age was raised to 15 in 1947, grammar school fees were removed and grants to university students made mandatory in 1953 (albeit under varying local conditions) and the provision of school milk and meals was expanded.[25]

These reforms were extremely expensive in terms of manpower and money and, in the given economic circumstances, major achievements. Within the Cabinet indeed the raising of the school leaving age provoked considerable heart-searching because, at a time of acute manpower shortage and restrictions on public expenditure, it both deprived the labour market of 400 000 school leavers and required the emergency training of an extra 35 000 teachers, together with the diversion of scarce building labour and materials to the extension of schools (in the famous HORSA operation).[26] As the Minister of Education admitted at the time, it was an 'act of faith rather than an act of wisdom'; but, by honouring the 1944 commitment, the Labour government revealed its ultimate determination not to sacrifice long-term social need to short-term economic demands – as had happened after the First World War.

In 1951 however the incoming Conservative government – despite Butler's authorship of the 1944 Act – apparently felt no such commitment. To reduce public expenditure the Chancellor of the Exchequer advised his colleagues that they should 'plan changes in policy as well as constant pruning'; and amongst the economies considered, but ultimately rejected, by Cabinet were the raising of the school entry age from five to six (as on the continent), the reversion of the school leaving age to fourteen, and the charging of fees not only in secondary but also in primary schools.[27] Remarkably the Chancellor was none other than Butler himself.

By late 1954 the economic situation had eased, building labour and materials had become more plentiful (with the peaking of Macmillan's housing drive) and a new minister, Eccles, was appointed who was committed to 'bringing the Butler Act to life'.[28] This was to be the priority for the next decade. Under the stimulus of the 1958 white paper, *Secondary Education for All: a new drive* (which committed the government to planned capital expenditure of £300 million over five years), a major attempt was made to modernise

Table 8.2 Maintained nursery and primary schools, 1946–75

	Nursery schools				Primary schools			
	Number	Pupils (000)	Teachers	Pupil teacher ratio	Number	Full-time pupils (millions)	Teachers	Pupil teacher ratio
1946	75	6	229	–	23 991	3.7	116 820	32.0
1950	416	21	905	–	23 133	4.0	130 046	30.4
1955	464	23	1168	–	23 664	4.6	148 739	30.9
1960	454	24	1082	–	23 488	4.2	144 693	29.0
1965	461	28	1085	22.0	22 882	4.3	151 084	28.3
1970	482	34	1307	19.4	23 075	4.9	180 008	27.4
1975	612	48	1481	21.4	23 280	5.1	213 055	24.2

The statistics for nursery schools exclude direct grant schools. Figures for pupils include part-time pupils in nursery schools but exclude them for primary schools. Figures for teachers are full-time equivalents.
Source: Department of Education and Science, Statistics of Education (1978) vol. 1, Historical Tables.

secondary education. There was a belated reduction of all-age schools between 1954 and 1963 from 3528 to 411 (catering for 93 000 as opposed to 636 000 pupils) and the building of over 2000 new schools, mainly secondary moderns. Primary education obviously benefited from such rationalisation, as it did also from the ebbing of the birth rate, but by the late 1950s the effect of the postwar baby boom was starting to be felt in higher education. Accordingly it too began to expand with the upgrading of certain university colleges (including Exeter, Sheffield and Southampton) and the sanctioning of seven new universities (Sussex, East Anglia, York, Essex, Lancaster, Kent and Warwick) even before the commissioning in 1961 of the Robbins Committee on Higher Education.[29] This committee recommended an increase in student numbers from 8 per cent to 17 per cent of the relevant age group and so enthusiastic was its reception that within 24 hours the government had accepted its interim recommendation that numbers should be virtually doubled within ten years.

The decade from 1954 to 1963 was therefore one of unprecedented educational expansion. It also marked 'the high point for popular belief in the state system of education'.[30] It was, however, also the time at which serious misgivings began to be widely expressed about not only the lack of technical education (which will be examined in Chapter 8.4) but also the structure of secondary education. These doubts were fuelled by the conclusions of a succession of official enquiries – the 1954 report, *Early Leaving*; the 1959 Crowther Report on the education of young people between fifteen and eighteen; and the 1963 Newsom Report, *Half Our Future*, on the education of children of average or below average ability between the ages of thirteen and sixteen. These reports did not directly attack tripartism. They did demonstrate, however, that the accident of parental circumstance still greatly influenced children's chances of entering grammar school and their subsequent academic performance; and that (given the failure to implement two of the 1944 Act's proposals, county colleges and the raising of the school leaving age to sixteen) many children were still not realising their full potential.

These academic findings had two major political consequences. First, they confirmed the practical misgivings and complaints about the eleven-plus examination (by which children were allocated to different types of secondary school) expressed by LEAs and many parents – not least those whose children had 'failed' the examination. Because of these objections well over half of LEAs were actually planning to introduce comprehensive schools by 1963.[31] The findings also helped to validate a switch in Labour Party policy after 1953 from the nominal support of multilateral schools to a commitment to comprehensive education in which (for both educational and social reasons) academic 'streaming' would be kept to a minimum.

The third phase of policy between 1964 and 1976 saw a sustained attempt, at all levels of education, to engineer greater educational and social equality. Most notoriously, Crosland (as secretary of state for education) requested all LEAs in 1965 to submit 'plans for reorganising secondary education in their areas on a comprehensive basis' in order to realise the Labour government's 'declared objective to end selection at eleven plus and to eliminate separatism'. In the same year a Public Schools Commission was also established to reexamine the proposals of the wartime Fleming Committee on private schools with particular emphasis on the need to reduce 'the divisive influence they now exert'.[32] Within the primary and nursery sector there was a further official enquiry which resulted in the 1967 Plowden Report on *Children and their Primary Schools*. It was generally complimentary, but expressed serious concern about the continuing disadvantages suffered by children from 'deprived' backgrounds. Heavily influenced by the contemporary War on Want programme in the USA, it recommended the establishment of educational priority areas in which positive discrimination could be exercised in favour of such children by means of extra money and staff – this policy was duly implemented by the Labour government.

Finally, within higher education the Robbins's targets were not only met but exceeded, with the number of students expanding between 1962–3 and 1970–1 not by 59 but by 104 per cent.[33] However, instead of the proposed unitary system (by which the majority of students would have been taught in some sixty universities) a 'binary' system was established with the creation between 1969 and 1973 of thirty polytechnics under local government control. As Robbins himself remarked, it appeared to be a 'supreme paradox' that a government 'pledged to abolish artificial hierarchy and invidious distinctions in the schools' should create them in higher education. The divide was nevertheless defended by Crosland on egalitarian grounds: the polytechnics, he argued, would ensure a less élitist and a more socially responsible and responsive form of further education. Only one new university was indeed to be sanctioned after 1965, and it was a far from traditional one – the Open University, founded in 1969 and enrolling its first students in 1971.

These deliberately egalitarian measures, initiated by the 1964–1970 Labour governments, were – somewhat surprisingly – sustained by the incoming Heath administration. Admittedly the attack on private education was halted and LEAs were no longer requested – or, as had been the intention of Labour's draft 1970 Education Bill, compelled – to introduce comprehensive education.[34] Rather ministers encouraged and then used parental opposition to reject LEA proposals for the closure of individual grammar schools, thereby undermining the social and educational logic of many reorganisation plans. Nevertheless out of 3612 proposals for reorganisation, only 326 were ultimately rejected; and more grammar schools were closed between 1970 and 1974 than in any comparable period, with the result that the proportion of secondary school children within comprehensive schools rose from 32 per cent to 62 per cent (see Table 8.3). More deliberately, in 1972 the school leaving age was finally raised to sixteen (as had initially been requested by the 1944 Act) and the government simultaneously announced its intention in the white paper, *Education: A Framework for Expansion* (Cmnd 5174), to maintain the momentum of the 1960s by increasing education expenditure by 50 per cent over the next ten years. The main beneficiaries, in accordance with the recommendations of the Plowden Committee, were to be nursery and primary education, but within higher education – where the Open University had been saved, almost literally, over the dead body of the Chancellor of the Exchequer – the number of full-time students was also to rise from 15 per cent to 22 per cent of the relevant age group. Each of these measures was justified in egalitarian terms. The Secretary of State for Education, for example, defended the Open University because it provided 'educational opportunity for those prepared to work for it' and increased expenditure on nursery education on the ground that it could 'help redress the balance of those born unlucky'.[35] No less remarkably than in the early 1950s, when Butler (as Chancellor) had seemed intent on destroying his own Act, the secretary of state for education between 1970 and 1974 was none other than Margaret Thatcher.

The seeds of the 'Thatcherite revolution', however, had been sown. During the surreptitious expansion of comprehensive schooling in the late 1950s there had developed a local populist movement (which increasingly found expression at Conservative Party conferences) to defend grammar schools.[36] As a result of student unrest in the late 1960s a series of 'Black Papers' was published attacking 'progressive' changes' initially in universities but then in primary

	1946	1950	1955	1960	1965	1970	1975
Secondary modern:							
Schools	2843	3227	3550	3837	3727	2691	1216
Pupils (000)	719	1095	1234	1638	1555	1227	697
Teachers	–	47759	56770	74281	78567	65259	38702
Pupil/teacher ratio	–	22.9	21.7	22.1	19.8	18.8	18.0
Grammar:							
Schools	1199	1192	1180	1268	1285	1038	566
Pupils (000)	488	503	528	672	719	605	344
Teachers	–	27155	29195	36365	41879	36940	21367
Pupil/teacher ratio	–	18.5	18.1	18.5	17.2	16.4	16.1
Technical:							
Schools	324	301	302	251	172	82	29
Pupils (000)	60	72	87	102	85	44	18
Teachers	–	4362	5083	5517	4965	2719	1102
Pupil/teacher ratio	–	16.6	17.6	18.5	17.0	16.1	16.4
Comprehensive:							
Schools	–	10	16	130	262	1145	2596
Pupils (000)	–	8	16	129	240	937	2460
Teachers	–	386	807	6709	13403	53732	145506
Pupil/teacher ratio	–	20.7	19.7	19.2	17.9	17.4	16.9
Total:							
Schools	4366	4765	5144	5801	5863	5385	5035
Pupils (000)	1269	1696	1915	2723	2819	3046	3827
Teachers	58455	80545	94390	131591	150736	171343	222591
Pupil/teacher ratio	21.7	21.1	20.3	20.7	18.7	17.8	17.2

The 'total' figures include a small number of hybrid schools and, after 1968, middle schools 'deemed secondary'.
Source: Department of Education and Science, *Statistics of Education* (1978) vol. 1, Historical Tables.

and secondary schools. Finally, after the Conservative government's encouragement of parental opposition to comprehensive reorganisation and its electoral defeat in 1974, there was a media attack on declining educational standards which culminated in the exposure of two 'scandals' in London: at the William Tyndale primary school and the Polytechnic of North London, where progressive teaching methods and student participation respectively were seen to have resulted in anarchy. This attack finally drove the Labour prime minister, Callaghan, to launch a 'great debate' on education in a speech at Ruskin College, Oxford in October 1976 which called for a more disciplined structure of learning at all levels of education, within which the educational benefits of modern teaching methods could be more effectively realised. Just as the 1973 oil crisis (by halting the planned increase in expenditure) had foreshadowed a new era of educational 'cuts', so this speech (with its references to a 'core curriculum' and the need for greater vocational training) was a portent of the future.

There were beneath the ideological rhetoric of this educational backlash, two issues of substance. The first concerned standards. Superficially there would appear few grounds for doubting the dramatic improvement in educational standards after 1944. Between 1948 and 1964 for example, the average reading age for eleven year olds improved by seventeen months and for fifteen year olds by twenty to thirty months.[37] The number of children voluntarily staying on at school for a fifth year had risen to 60 per cent by 1972 (thus making the raising of the school leaving age a far less traumatic event than in 1947). The number of children gaining academic qualifications had also soared – not least between 1970 and 1976, when those leaving school with no graded results fell from 44 to 19 per cent. Complaints about falling standards would therefore appear to reflect sheer prejudice against the greater equalisation of educational opportunity and the slow erosion of traditional values for which wartime reformers had called.

Such prejudice did exist, and was expressed most vividly by novelists such as Kingsley Amis, who repeated in the first Black Paper of March 1969 his earlier charge that 'more means worse', and Evelyn Waugh, who had ironically written in relation to Amis and his peers in the 1950s:

Have you heard of the Butler Education Act? In it he provided for the free distribution of university degrees for the deserving poor. I could make your flesh creep by telling you of the new wave of Philistinism with which we are threatened by these sour young people who are coming off the assembly line in their hundreds every year and finding employment as critics, even as poets and novelists.[38]

A similar prejudice was also expressed more sinisterly by educational psychologists such as Burt and Eysenck, who continued to insist in the Black Papers that there was a 'fixed pool of ability' and that consequently any attempt significantly to increase educational opportunity would merely lower standards. Nevertheless, there was a modicum of evidence to support the critics' case. For example, a marginal drop in reading standards after 1960 amongst seven year olds was identified by the 1975 Bullock Report (which had been commissioned by the Conservatives in 1972). It is also questionable whether, either in absolute terms or in relation to Britain's industrial competitors, educational standards were rising as fast as increases in expenditure and decreases in staff/pupil ratios warranted (see Tables 8.2 and 8.3).

The second issue of substance arose from the conflicting definitions of equality. To the traditional supporters of the 1944 Act, 'the essential point', as expressed by Sir Edward Boyle (the most undogmatic of Conservative education ministers, whose political career was broken in the 1960s by the populist backlash), was that 'all children should have an equal opportunity of acquiring intelligence and of developing their talents and abilities to the full'.[39] Such an objective required the equal allocation of resources to children of different educational aptitudes. It could also justify a measure of positive discrimination in favour of children from deprived backgrounds. What it specifically did not condone was the standardisation of educational methods and, above all, results for children of different aptitudes and abilities. Just such a standardisation, however, was perceived to be inherent in certain 'progressive' postwar educational developments and especially in unstreamed comprehensives, where particular emphasis was placed on the social integration of gifted children and the stimulus that their presence in the same class could provide for the less able.[40]

Any such attempt to engineer 'equality of outcome', so its critics argued, was both pernicious and self-defeating. Rather than advancing justice and increasing educational standards, it would deny gifted children both freedom of expression and the opportunity to develop their talent fully. It would also – at a time of increasing international competitiveness and decreasing social cohesion – deprive the country of the economic and political leadership of a well-trained élite. The creation of such an élite was not in itself unjust because – in accordance with Rawls' theory of social justice – the 'inequality of educational outcome' it represented was morally defensible so long as it was to the benefit of the least advantaged in society (see chapter 3.2).

What would have been unjust was the creation of an irresponsible, closed élite. However, it was the particular mission of public and – later – grammar schools to instil into their 'privileged' pupils a sense of civic responsibility; and, once grammar school fees had been abolished, entry into the educational élite was assumed to be genuinely open. To the traditional supporters of the 1944 Act, therefore, 'progressive' educational reform after 1964 was pernicious because, for no clear social or educational gain, one form of inequality and injustice (which the Act had done much to curb) was merely being replaced by another. In place of the unequal treatment of equally talented children on purely social and financial grounds (which had been prevalent before the war) there was now to be imposed the equal treatment of unequally talented children on purely ideological grounds.[41]

The dominant political battle over educational equality thus concerned inequality between social classes. There were, however, other forms of inequality. There were (as will be noted in the following section) major geographical disparities in the quality and type of secondary schools. Even more seriously there was widespread sexual inequality. The eleven-plus examination, for example, was weighted heavily against girls on the ground that they matured earlier. Within secondary schools girls were directed by both the formal and a 'hidden' curriculum into different subjects from boys, which prepared them not for paid work outside but for unpaid work inside the home. Moreover, the percentage of female students fell the more advanced education became. As late as 1964, for example, only a quarter of university undergraduates were women and, at Oxford and Cambridge, the percentage was as low as 10 per cent and 13 per cent respectively. A combination of all relevant factors meant, at the most extreme, that in the early 1960s a middle-class boy in Cardiganshire was 160 times more likely to enter full-time education than a working-class girl from West Ham.[42] It was the realisation that inequality on this scale continued to exist some twenty years after

the 1944 Act which led to the major discontinuity in postwar education policy – the replacement of the tripartite structure of grammar, technical and secondary schools with comprehensive education.

8.3   THE COLLAPSE OF TRIPARTISM

Because of Butler's pragmatism, tripartism had not been the explicit
objective of the 1944 Act. It was, however, the clear recommendation of the 1943 Norwood Report. It was also the clear objective of
the civil servants responsible for the Act's immediate implementation
– if only because of the pressing economic need physically to base
the expansion of secondary education on existing 'post-primary' and
secondary school buildings.[43] Moreover, to the public the specialised
training of children in accordance with the three broad types of
educational aptitude identified by Norwood – stemming from a
child's interest in the 'abstract', the 'mechanical' or the 'practical' –
appeared both rational and in line with European experience. Once
established, therefore, tripartism attracted little criticism and the
plans to consolidate it further in 1958 were largely uncontroversial.[44]
Yet within 15 years it had been virtually abandoned and two-thirds
of secondary school children were attending comprehensive schools.
Why was there so dramatic a change?

The principal reasons were practical, not ideological, and centred
on two issues: the continuing failure of technical and secondary
modern schools to achieve the promised 'parity of esteem' with
grammar schools, and the fallibility of the eleven-plus examination
by which children were allocated to a particular type of secondary
school. As the only true prewar 'secondary' school, grammar schools
had inherited better facilities and higher public esteem than had their
rivals and, until 1958 at least, these advantages were accentuated
rather than reduced by the actions of both central and local government.[45] Such continuing disparity so confounded one of the main
objectives of the 1944 Act – that children of different aptitudes
should have an equal opportunity to develop their talents fully – that
serious doubts were cast on whether it could ever be attained within
a tripartite system. Of even greater concern was the perceived fallibility of the eleven-plus examination. The results of this examination
were not necessarily conclusive. They could be modified by teachers'
reports and interviews. Moreover, the examination itself was not
uniform throughout the whole country, although it did have a

common core of written tests in English, mathematics and 'intelligence'. What did become uniform, however, was the increasing conviction of LEAs and parents (supported, as has been seen, by academic research) that the examination was neither fair nor objective.

There were, as Michael Sanderson has noted, three particular criticisms of the eleven-plus: 'there was too much misallocation of talent, too many extraneous factors impeding the flow of ability and too close a relationship of selection and success with social class background.'[46] By 1958, for example, it was well established that some 10 per cent of children were misallocated at the age of eleven. The clearest proof of this lay in the number and distribution of candidates for the examination specifically introduced in 1951 to maintain academic standards, the GCE 'O' level. By the end of the decade many grammar school children were failing to stay at school until sixteen to take this examination, while some 22 000 secondary modern pupils – classified by the eleven-plus as non-academic – were sitting it with considerable success.[47]

Foremost amongst the 'extraneous factors' was the continuing inequality of geographical provision. In 1959, for example, there were grammar school places for 35 per cent of children sitting the eleven-plus in the south-west of England, whereas the comparable figure for the north-east was 22.4 per cent and in other areas (such as Nottingham) the figure could fall as low as 10 per cent. Other 'extraneous factors' included the accident of children's birthdays and their home circumstances. In the February examination, for example, ages could range from 10.6 to 11.5 years (depending on the exact relationship of birthdays to the start of the school year) to the obvious benefit of the older children. Moreover, a close correlation was identified between pass rates and children from small families with supportive parents, who had the opportunity to study in relative peace and comfort.[48]

The importance of such 'environmental' factors also played its part in the consolidation of the relationship between examination success and class background and the advantage of middle-class children was further increased by an unconscious bias in the examination towards concepts and language with which they would be more familiar, and the realisation by teachers that (contrary to educational psychologists' initial beliefs) coaching could enhance examination performance. The latter was perhaps the more pernicious because it led to widespread streaming in primary and even nursery schools (where 'squirrels' were separated from 'rabbits'). Teachers tended to place disciplined, articulate middle-class children in the higher streams, and the expectations implicit in such streaming tended to become self-fulfilling. Consequently, schooling started from an early stage to reinforce class divisions.

By the early 1960s, therefore, the process – and thereby the principle – of selection had come under sustained attack. The geographical disparity of grammar school places exposed the underlying national purpose of the eleven-plus to be the allocation of children within a given mix of schools (which had been determined largely by historical accident) rather than their selection for a particular kind of education according to proven aptitude. The correlation between social class and success in the eleven-plus also demonstrated that abolition of grammar school fees alone could not guarantee genuine equality of opportunity. Consequently, it was on traditional educational grounds that the concept of comprehensive (or at least multilateral) schools gained ground in the 1950s – regardless of any social, or broader educational, advantages the greater mixing of children of different classes and ability ranges might bring. Comprehensives had already been built in new housing estates and in rural areas, where there were insufficient children to justify three separate schools. By providing educational facilities on one site for children of all aptitudes and abilities, they could now be seen also to offer a practical solution to the problems associated with 'parity of esteem' and misallocation. In addition, by removing the need to examine children prior to entry into secondary school, they could enable decisions about the nature of the child's education to be delayed until thirteen – an age which many experienced teachers and educational psychologists considered to be more appropriate.[49]

That the eleven-plus, and thereby tripartism, was so quickly discredited can be explained by two main factors: the critical importance it assumed was largely fortuitous and the validity of its results – insofar as they were based on intelligence testing – came under increasing scientific attack. To the authors of the 1944 Act the eleven-plus was both unwanted and unwarranted. As the 1943 white paper *Educational Reconstruction* insisted, for example:

There is nothing to be said in favour of a system which subjects children at the age of 11 to the strain of a competitive examination on which, not only their future schooling, but their future careers may depend. Apart from the effect on the children, there is the effect on the curriculum in the schools themselves.[50]

Norwood himself – despite, or perhaps because of, being chairman of the Secondary Schools Examination Council – agreed and, like the National Union of Teachers, favoured selection based solely on teachers' reports. Educational psychologists (who dominated educational thinking in the 1940s) were also scornful of an examination which used an *intelligence* test to identify a child's *aptitude*; and the irrationality of the process was duly exposed by the selection of children for technical schools on the basis not of a test of mechanical aptitude but of an IQ which just failed to secure entry into grammar school.[51]

However, some practical means of allocating children between existing schools was required by those responsible for the implementation of policy at both central and local level; and the eleven-plus, with its emphasis on intelligence testing, appeared to provide the best solution. Ironically, the basis of this presumption was the increased use of intelligence tests in the 1930s by progressive LEAs, which wished to counteract social bias in the award of grammar school scholarships. As a perceived measure of a child's 'innate, unalterable and asocial ability', they were believed to neutralise not only the impact on examination results of poor teaching and disadvantaged home backgrounds but also the bias towards middle-class children inherent in teachers' reports (a bias confirmed by postwar research).[52] In addition, because the tests could be conducted on a standardised national basis, they were less idiosyncratic and less expensive than any practical alternative.

This faith was, however, ill-founded. This was not just because intelligence testing was used incorrectly to diagnose educational aptitude, but because the very assumption that intelligence was 'innate, unalterable and asocial' was scientifically unsound. Postwar research by educational psychologists and sociologists (who came to rival the formers' influence on policy-making) increasingly suggested that, whereas the limits of an individual's intelligence might be biologically determined, varying social or 'environmental' factors would determine how quickly a child's potential had been realised by any given time. This new orthodoxy was summarised by Jean Floud when, in her submission to the Robbins Report, she wrote that an individual's IQ was the 'result of a cumulative process of development which is not unilinear throughout childhood, which proceeds at an irregular pace, does not stop at any particular age, and is susceptible to a startling degree to environmental influences'.[53] If this were true, it was hardly surprising that the eleven-plus tended to favour middle-class children (or at least children with supportive parents) and that it failed to identify 'late-developers' who were accordingly branded as 'failures'. In consequence the eleven-plus was being condemned by the early 1960s as not only scientifically inappropriate but also scientifically invalid.

This condemnation was based largely on practical and theoretical considerations, but there was also an ideological dimension – as became apparent with the contribution of Burt and Eysenck to the Black Papers.[54] The concept of general intelligence, and the confidence that it could be measured, had first developed within the eugenicist movement at the end of the nineteenth century and had been concerned initially with the measurement of racial differences and mental subnormality. After the First World War it had been applied to vocational training and eventually to education, where it had had a considerable influence on the Hadow and Spens Reports. If innate intelligence could be accurately measured, it was rational to test children so that they could be provided with the most appropriate education and guided into the most suitable occupations. The trouble was that the assumptions underlying this 'scientific' process were highly circular. Members of each vocational category, and hence social class, were assumed to have a similar IQ. Most non-manual workers, for example, would have an IQ over 115 and most manual workers an IQ under 115. 115, however, was the minimum score to ensure a place at grammar school and so, if intelligence were genetically determined, it was inevitable that most grammar school places would be awarded to children of non-manual workers – who would then qualify for middle-class occupations. Only the exceptional working-class child would be recruited into grammar school and hence into the educational élite. Even more perniciously, this reasoning could justify higher expenditure on middle-class children because they had the innate intelligence which could – and in the interest both of the individual and the nation should – be developed the furthest. It was on such grounds that IQ testing, and thereby tripartism, was condemned for being highly conservative. Instead of providing genuine equality of opportunity they both reflected and reinforced social inequality.

Tripartism was, therefore, the principal victim of the postwar commitment to equality. Initially such a commitment appeared to pose little threat either to existing educational practice or to the existing social order. Through a scientific examination all children would be allocated to the secondary school most suited to their educational aptitude. Consequently, no talent would be wasted. Because intelligence was believed to be genetically determined, it was assumed that there would not automatically be an even social mix in every type of school, or at each level of education. The opportunity would be available, however, for exceptional children from the lower classes to rise up through the educational system to join, and thereby reinforce, the economic and political élite. By the 1960s, however, such conservative assumptions had been undermined by both practical experience and sociological research. The concept of 'equality of opportunity' had also been challenged by that of 'equality of outcome' and there was a growing political move to engineer a more equal society through the educational, as well as through the social security system. This combination of practical, theoretical and political challenges made irresistible the momentum towards the replacement of tripartism by comprehensive, or at least multilateral, schools.

8.4　THE MAINTENANCE OF EDUCATIONAL STANDARDS

Some indication of the overall advance in postwar standards has already been given in Chapter 8.2. The record was impressive, although by 1975 there was some evidence of a slowing down (or even decline) in the attainment of young children, especially from poorer homes and there were grounds for questioning the cost effectiveness of educational investment. What, however, was the specific record of achievement at each level of education in both the public and private sector, from nursery education to universities?

　　Nursery education represented a 'black hole' in postwar policy. It could have developed in one of three forms: day nurseries (open throughout the hours parents were at work), specialist nursery schools (open during conventional school hours) or nursery classes attached to primary schools. Before the war the first – as in many other countries – had been discredited as a receptacle for 'problem children'. Nursery classes were opposed by the educational establishment. It was therefore to nursery schools that the Churchill coalition turned, both to release women for war work and to counteract, after the war, the social deprivation of inner-city children that had been highlighted during evacuation.[55] After the war, however, nursery schools fell victim not only to economic retrenchment but also to an underlying political and medical prejudice that young children were best cared for by their mothers. Consequently their numbers contracted rather than expanded.

This experience was repeated in the 1960s. Then nursery schools came to be recognised as an 'outstandingly economic and efficient way' to counteract deprivation and, in 1972, the Conservative government committed itself to the fulfilment of the Plowden recommendation that nursery school places should be made available for 50 per cent of three year olds and 90 per cent of four year olds.[56] Economic retrenchment after the 1973 oil crisis, however, thwarted their expansion. Thus nursery schools in Britain never successfully took off and, although the number of children they catered for doubled between 1960 and 1975 (see Table 8.2), the most sustained expansion in pre-school care occurred within the private sector under the aegis of such self-help initiatives as the Pre-School Playgroups' Association.

Primary education enjoyed both a mixed reputation and mixed fortunes after 1944. Britain was widely recognised as a pioneer in child-centred learning, based on individual activity and experience rather than the desk-bound accumulation of facts. 'Progressive' educational theory had become predominant in the 1930s and its practice had been unexpectedly accelerated during the war as a result of the lack of conventional facilities in many evacuated schools. Consequently the Plowden Committee could report in 1967 that, in sharp contrast to prewar elementary schools, only 5 per cent of primary schools were 'markedly out of touch with current practice and knowledge'.[57] However, the actual quality of education provided varied greatly. To be fully effective, child-centred teaching required adaptable premises, classes of under 30 pupils, well-trained teachers and freedom from a set curriculum. In very few areas were all these conditions fulfilled. Despite a steady programme of school building (peaking in 1952 and 1968 with 439 and 736 completions respectively) many premises remained outdated. As late as 1976, for instance, 20 per cent of pupils were being taught in schools built before 1900. Despite falling staff/pupil ratios, a high turnover of teachers conspired to keep the size of most classes above 30. Above all, as a consequence of the eleven-plus most pupils were streamed.

The objective of the Plowden Committee, which made primary

education a political priority for the first time since the war, was to resolve these difficulties by minimising inequality and extending good practice. The expansion of primary education in educational priority areas, however, largely failed because of lack of support from parents (whose indifference lay at the root of their children's disadvantage), from teachers (who generally opposed the appointment of parent-teacher associations and of untrained aides) and from the government (which restricted public expenditure after the 1976 devaluation crisis).[58] Retrenchment after 1973 similarly aborted the Conservative commitment to replace all Victorian buildings. On the other hand 'progressive' teaching methods were able to advance rapidly as the eleven-plus was withdrawn. Whereas only 4 per cent of schools had been unstreamed in 1964, by 1978 only 4 per cent of eight year olds were being streamed. So dramatic a change inevitably made primary education a principal target for the Black Papers.

Within the secondary sector two types of school lay outside local authority control: independent (public) schools and some 150 direct grant schools, such as Manchester Grammar School, which received direct subsidies from central government but were permitted to enrol fee-paying students. Both came under severe attack during the war. The latter appeared anomalous even to Butler (see Chapter 8.1, Note 10). The former had been in considerable financial trouble before 1939, with falling rolls obliging headmasters to spend 'half their time in commercial travelling . . . touting on preparatory school doorsteps'.[59] In 1940 they also became the target for much political venom because the qualities of leadership, which they were supposed to instil in their pupils, had been found wanting by the failure of appeasement and the retreat to Dunkirk. 'They had been trained to lead', railed their foremost critic (himself inevitably an ex-public schoolboy), 'and they had led us up the garden.'[60] A further vehement attack was launched in the 1950s, when Crosland (another ex-public schoolboy) identified them as the 'strongest remaining bastion of class privilege', and again in the early 1960s, when the institutional impediments to growth came under scrutiny and Eccles (yet another) was moved to reflect that 'a small minority of children coming from more or less the same kind of homes and receiving an exceptional kind of education is bad for our society'. The corollary was the appointment of the Public Schools Commission in 1965.

In the wake of this Commission's reports, direct grant schools were abolished in 1975 but, despite the loss of some tax privileges, public schools survived.[61] This was because of covert official support, the schools' adaptability and public demand. Official support did not include the widespread payment of state bursaries as proposed by the wartime Fleming Committee and by the Public Schools Commission. These were rejected – by the schools themselves as a threat to their independence, by local authorities because of the expense, and by working-class parents on account of the social pressures to which their children would be subjected. Rather, abolition was dismissed because it would have infringed individual freedom and because the official conviction was that the schools were centres of educational excellence and experiment which provided a rounded education particularly for their boarding pupils. They also proved to be adaptable to changing need, not least because of a £2 million subsidy from industry (channelled to them through the civil service) to improve their science facilities. Indeed by the 1960s more school leavers were joining industry and business than the professions.[62] Finally there was public demand. Increasing affluence enabled those middle-class parents who so desired to buy the social privilege for which public schools were condemned. The most powerful parental motivation, however, was the desire to secure the 'best possible' education for their children, and this motivation increased as standards in state schools were perceived to fall. Between 1947 and 1976 the percentage of children attending private schools almost halved from 10.2 per cent to 5.7 per cent, but as the number of comprehensive schools expanded so too did the demand for private education.[63]

Secondary education was provided under local government control by an evolving mixture of grammar, technical, secondary modern and comprehensive schools (see Table 8.3). At their peak in 1960 technical schools catered for only 2 per cent of pupils and their establishment was actively discouraged after 1958. The technocratic élite, which they had been intended to train, were to be trained instead by grammar schools which – as the traditional guarantor of both academic excellence and working-class upward mobility – continued in the 1950s to retain the fierce loyalty of teachers, parents and many Labour councillors. With the onset of comprehensive education after 1965, however, their number also began to fall, although (as has been seen) they provided in many areas the focus for popular resistance.

Essentially their decline reflected their inability to match the adaptability of public schools. The eleven-plus was designed to supply them with children from all classes 'interested in learning for its own sake'; and the GCE 'O' and 'A' levels had been introduced in 1951 specifically to ensure the maintenance of high academic standards until the age of 18 when (it was assumed) the majority of their pupils would progress either to university or into the professions. As research soon demonstrated, however, the eleven-plus was flawed and, of those working-class children who did gain admittance a disproportionately high percentage either left at fifteen or performed poorly in the sixth form. Various expedients were tried. Fines were even proposed for parents whose children left early and scientific subjects were expanded as much to maintain the interest of the academic 'misfit' as to train a technocratic élite.[64] Many working-class children and parents, however, continued to be alienated by the traditions, discipline and social values permeating grammar schools. In short, despite many individual successes, grammar schools as a whole failed to bridge the two critical gaps between the arts and the sciences and between middle and working-class culture.

Secondary modern schools, which catered for three-quarters of pupils in the 1950s, represented one of the saddest failures of postwar policy. The intention behind them had been liberal. Teachers, in conjunction with parents and local industrialists, were to design courses free from a centrally imposed curriculum which would best suit their particular pupils. Secondary moderns, in other words, were to enjoy the essential qualities which, in the German tripartite system after the war, were to make the vocationally oriented Hauptschule so great a success. In Britain, however, the experiment failed.[65] This was in part because secondary moderns were identified with prewar elementary schools and were denied adequate resources. As late as 1960, for instance, only 10 per cent of schools were purpose-built and one-fifth of teachers graduates. The commitment made in 1958 to honour the wartime pledge of 'parity of esteem' came a decade too late.

More pertinently, secondary moderns came to be judged by wholly inappropriate criteria. Very reluctantly central government had been persuaded in 1953 that, rather than being transferred to grammar schools, 'academic' pupils should be permitted to sit GCE 'O' levels within secondary moderns; and thereafter – to the detriment of the majority of pupils – the interest of teachers, the ambition of parents and the reputation of .the school became focused on these results (which could on the whole only be inferior to those of grammar schools). Equally reluctantly central government consented to the introduction of a new national examination in 1965 for the majority of secondary modern pupils, the CSE. As had been warned, such an examination

> on a national basis would induce uniformity of syllabuses, curriculum and methods at stages and ages where uniformity would be most undesirable. Schools would feel unable to resist pressure to enter pupils for it . . . it would prejudice the more widespread development of the varied and lively courses already to be found in the best modern schools. There is also a risk that it would be regarded as an index to the efficiency of schools, a conception which would be unrealistic and even oppressive in view of the wide differences in circumstances and in the range of ability of their pupils.[66]

A large amount of local variety and teacher assessment was built into the examination, but this merely became one of the reasons why it came to be regarded as inferior to GCE. Secondary modern schools, in short, fell victim to a lack of imagination and conviction on the part of educationalists and parents. Neither group was willing to accept that equality could best be achieved through the development and rigorous testing of different, but equally valuable, aptitudes and skills.

Comprehensive schools, as has been seen, rapidly replaced grammar and secondary modern schools after 1965 (see also Table 8.3). For all the speed of their advance, however, their positive educational purpose was never clear. Comprehensive education had long been advocated within the Labour Party on educational, social and economic grounds. Through the education of children of all abilities and classes within one school, it was believed, genuine equality of opportunity could be provided and class barriers eroded with the result that individual fulfilment, social cohesion and economic efficiency could be maximised. However, given the nature of existing school buildings and of vested interests both inside and outside the teaching profession (which it was the ultimate purpose of comprehensivisation to change), the implementation of policy posed many practical problems. Thus the postwar Labour governments, despite the opportunities offered by the 1944 Act, actually rejected plans for comprehensivisation drafted by exceptional LEAs such as Middlesex. Their basic reasons were that at a time of economic stringency other educational policies should take precedence and that it would be imprudent to replace wholesale a proven avenue of working-class upward mobility (the grammar school) with an untried experiment.

To ensure an adequate sixth form, it was calculated, a comprehensive school would need to have at least 750 pupils – whereas the average size of grammar and secondary modern schools as late as 1964 was only 560 and 420 respectively.[67] In so large a school, would there be adequate pastoral care for the disadvantaged and would head-teachers be able to 'control and inspire' the educational development of all pupils, including the academic minority?

Similar problems attended the implementation of Crosland's Circular 10/65, which has been condemned as a 'toothless tiger' because it provided neither a positive educational lead nor any new injection of finance.[68] The momentum for reform, as has been seen, gathered pace for largely negative reasons – such as the prevention of misallocation and the removal from children (and their parents) of the stigma of having 'failed' the eleven-plus; and until 1975 no government was willing to intervene directly in 'professional' matters such as the nature of the curriculum or the age of selection for specialist training. Even the most progressive LEAs, moreover, became increasingly concerned at the damage to teachers' morale caused by overspeedy and underfunded reform which might result in split-site schools with a small sixth form, presided over by an unenthusiastic head-teacher.[69]

Consequently the positive social and educational purpose behind the ideal of comprehensivation tended to be obscured. Given the continued existence of grammar (let alone public) schools, under half of comprehensives in the early 1970s could claim to be teaching children of all abilities within their locality; and, given the continuing demand on educational grounds for streaming from parents, teachers and even ministers (such as Crosland himself), under a quarter provided mixed ability teaching even in their first year. There was, indeed, even a danger that social inequality might be increased. For example, the introduction of the CSE examination (which was designed to cater for the middle band of pupils, whilst the top 20 per cent sat GCE and the bottom 40 per cent nothing) encouraged streaming; and such streaming by teacher assessment, together with the movement of middle-class parents to the catchment area of schools with good results, militated against the very principle of greater equality of opportunity which comprehensives were supposed to foster. Comprehensivisation may thus have provided the structure in which certain failings of the tripartite system could be remedied, but it is an open question whether all the emotional, financial and political capital expended might not have been put to a better educational purpose.

Beyond schools, there was higher and further education. Until the first polytechnics were opened in 1969 higher education was dominated by universities and, as has been seen, they expanded dramatically after the war, first with the opening of Keele in 1951, then with the upgrading of five university colleges and the commissioning of seven new universities, even before the publication of the Robbins Report; and finally with the raising to university status of the nine colleges of advanced technology (CATs).[70] Aided by the mandatory provision of grants, which established the 'tradition' of English students studying away from home, the number of students tripled between 1951 and 1975 (see Table 8.4). Such an expansion was not openly sought by the universities, but was forced upon them by international trends, the needs of industry and, above all, by popular demand. By 1961, for example, 6.9 per cent of eighteen year olds were qualified for university entrance but – in comparison with the USA where the comparable figure was 18 per cent – there were places for only 4 per cent. The number of eleven-plus failures alone, who were qualified, was sufficient to fill Leicester University (though, contrary to some suggestions, this never actually happened).

This imbalance between supply and demand reflected universities' innate conservatism. Ministers and civil servants in the Department of Education and Science (to which universities became responsible in 1962) had a particular vested interest in exaggerating this conservatism; and indeed they used it to justify the concentration of post-Robbins expansion in the more 'socially responsive and responsible' polytechnics. They resented the fact that universities, whilst becoming increasingly dependent on government finance after 1945, had succeeded through the University Grants Committee (UGC) ·in maintaining their autonomy.[71] Nevertheless there was some justice in the charge. Despite the international reputation of certain research centres, undergraduate curricula and teaching methods were frequently outdated, the number of female undergraduates (as has been seen) was indefensibly low and the development, at government's request, of teacher training and applied (as opposed to pure) science was less than enthusiastic. Consequently, when expansion was forced upon them, universities did not handle it particularly well – although the UGC, pressurised by the government's insistence on precipitate change and by uneven funding, did remain a more effective planning

Table 8.4 Students in further and higher education, 1951–75 (thousands)

	1951	1955	1960	1965	1970	1975
Further education:						
Full-time/sandwich	46	58	117	186	271	387
Part-time, day	298	391	488	680	749	743
Evening	550	634	713	796	736	802
Teacher training	25	25	34	73	111	99
Universities:						
Students	82	85	108	169	228	261

Figures for further education are for England and Wales only; for universities, the whole of the UK.
Sources: Department of Education and Science, *Statistics of Education* (1977), vol. 3; B. Simon, *Education and the Social Order, 1940–1990* (1991).

agency than any devised by the Department of Education and Science. The result was the student unrest of the late 1960s and the drop in public esteem which led to the backlash of the mid 1970s.

Further education embraced a bewildering array of institutions, run largely by local government, which catered for an equally bewildering array of students studying for pleasure, for individual self-improvement or, more rarely, within structured day-release or 'sandwich' courses. Institutional restructuring and upgrading were a constant feature of this sector. For example, there was the merger in 1956 of technical colleges into CATs (which duly became universities in 1965) and the amalgamation of a further 94 colleges into 30 polytechnics between 1969 and 1973. Absent from all this restructuring, however, was any sustained attempt to reduce what the 1959 Crowther Report had termed the 'no man's land' between formal education and employment – to create, in other words, the county colleges envisaged in the 1944 Act (and duly developed in postwar Germany) to which school leavers, whilst being trained by employers in particular skills, might be systematically released to acquire a more rounded understanding of theoretical, business and social issues. The money spent on raising the compulsory age of formal schooling could well have been better spent on developing this area of further education. Moreover, stronger central support should have been given to polytechnics – and to a lesser extent CATs – to prevent them, under popular demand, from repeating the mistake of the CSE examination in relation to GCE: the increasing imitation of academic university courses.

Therefore, whilst there was an unquestionable improvement on prewar standards at each level of education, the record was by no means unblemished. The most successful initiatives were in the private sector, be it in pre-school playgroups or public schools. Within the public sector the full benefit of equally valuable initiatives such as secondary modern, technical and comprehensive schools was denied by a lack of sustained support and resources; and élite institutions, such as grammar schools and universities, were insufficiently flexible to adapt adequately to changing economic and social needs.

Within the schools sector, however, what principally restricted progress was the quality of teaching. The period between 1944 and 1975 has been identified as the 'golden age of teacher control'.[72] The 1944 Act had laid down no specific requirements for the curriculum outside religion and, when a measure of greater central control was mooted in the early 1960s, a Schools Council for the Curriculum and

Examinations was established instead which further consolidated teachers' authority. In the development of comprehensive education, Crosland duly confirmed that government influence over the content of education would be limited to inspection and sponsored research, and consequently the 'key to the secret garden of the curriculum' was not actively sought until Callaghan's Ruskin College speech in 1976.[73]

Given such autonomy it was essential for sustained educational progress that teachers should be well-trained, well-paid and well-regarded. However none of these criteria was fully met. The most serious failure was training. During the war (and again in the Robbins Report) an attempt was made to enhance the quality of training by associating it more closely with universities. Preoccupied by other issues, however, they were largely unenthusiastic. Instead, in the 1950s training was overshadowed by the interwar legacy of small, isolated and single-sex voluntary institutions; and when it was expanded under greater central control in the 1960s, it was subject to a 'deliberate policy of overcrowding' and absurd fluctuations which led to a trebling of student numbers between 1960 and 1969 and a subsequent halving between 1975 and 1978. Indeed, in the late 1960s the Department of Education and Science had no reliable statistics on the number of trainees, let alone on the quality of their training.[74]

8.5   TECHNICAL EDUCATION

Within the varied record of educational achievement, the most notable failure was that of technical education – defined in the broadest sense as vocational training within schools for non-academic children, a balanced programme of industrial training and day-release courses for school-leavers and an emphasis on applied (as opposed to pure) science in higher education. What was the cause of this failure?

Before the war the need to reshape secondary education to meet the needs of a more technocratic society had been recognised by the 1938 Spens Committee, and its concern was shared by the 1943 white paper *Educational Reconstruction* (see Chapter 8.2). The war itself also highlighted the need both to forge closer links between industry and universities and to expand the supply of skilled managers and technicians. Consequently two major reconstruction plans were drafted. The 1945 Percy Committee on Higher Technological Education anticipated the binary principle of the 1960s by proposing a national network of technical colleges, to run parallel to universities, which would offer diplomas and degrees validated by a National Council of Technology. Somewhat contradictorily the 1946 Barlow Report on Scientific Manpower (Cmd 6824) recommended a rapid doubling of scientific graduates within the existing university structure – albeit one strengthened by the establishment of a new technological university and three institutes of technology with the authority to supervise postgraduate research.

By the mid-1950s the 'critical mass' for technical education – by which, it was hoped, Britain's culture and thereby its international competitiveness would be transformed – had failed to materialise and the Conservative government (as has been seen) was expressing increasing concern. Few technical schools had been built by LEAs and the experiment was abandoned. Instead, the teaching of science was strengthened in all other schools in both the public and private sector. In higher education exactly the opposite happened. Initially an attempt had been made to expand the existing system. Imperial College (London), for example, was given increased resources and status, although no new technological university or institute was founded (to the anger of Churchill's scientific adviser, Lord Cherwell, who resigned from the Cabinet in 1953). In 1956, however, the Conservatives announced an ambitious five year programme to create, in line with the Percy Report, a hierarchy of technical colleges outside the university system. Local and area colleges would provide teaching up to the level of Ordinary National Certificate; some 25 to 30 regional colleges would concentrate on preparing full-time students for the Higher National Diploma; and, at the apex, there would be 10 CATs preparing students for a new National Diploma of Technology overseen by a National Council of Technical Awards (the Hives Committee).[75]

In the 1960s there was a temporary reversion to the Barlow principle with the transformation of CATs into technological universities by the 1964–70 Labour government. This government, in its desire to generate the 'white heat' of a scientific revolution, also despaired of voluntaryism within industry and passed the 1965 Industrial Training Act which established within each industry an Industrial Training Board with the power, for the first time, to impose a levy on all employers from which companies with a structured training programme could be subsidised. The Act had in fact been drafted under the Conservatives and, on their return to power, they tightened its provisions. Their 1973 Employment Training Act gave significant new powers to the semi-independent Manpower Services Commission, and thus initiated a shift in responsibility for training from the educational establishment to industry, which was to be dramatically accelerated after 1976.

These structural changes had their beneficial effects. The number of arts and science undergraduates, for example, rose roughly in parity and so, with the explosion of the total student population, the absolute number of scientists and technologists significantly increased. In relation to Britain's competitors however, neither the rate nor the rigour of the advance either in schools or in further education was adequate. As has been seen, contrary to the intention of wartime planners academic examinations were introduced first into secondary modern schools and then for the less able pupils in comprehensive schools. As a consequence the vocational needs of non-academic pupils were neither clearly defined nor satisfied. Moreover, even after the establishment of Industrial Training Boards, the nature of training on the shop floor remained highly conservative and unleavened by the broader perspectives that the 1944 Act had intended to, and German practice did, introduce through day-release courses.

The corollary of these defects was a relatively unqualified workforce and low productivity. Whereas in the mid 1970s the number of university graduates within British and German industry was broadly similar, two-thirds of German workers had 'intermediate' qualifications, compared with only one-third of British workers; and these proportions were reversed for those with no qualifications. 'The Germans', as Sanderson had noted, were 'much better at educating the lowest half of the ability range and they have successfully developed from within that half much of the technically skilled labour force on which their industrial strength rests'.[76] Even at the higher level, the swing towards science, for which the planners in the 1940s and 1960s had hoped, failed to materialise. The Robbins Report, despite the presence of only one scientist on the committee, recommended that two-thirds of the increase in university students should be in science and technology. By the late 1960s further committees were being appointed to discover why this objective remained unrealised.

The composition of the Robbins Committee was symbolic of a latent bias amongst policymakers which consistently impeded the development of technical education. Although the need to redress the balance of the British educational system was well recognised, the principal danger (reinforced by the experience of Nazism) was still identified as 'unbridled scientism' rather than the absence amongst political and industrial leaders of scientific understanding and business skills. Hence the first postwar university was not the technological university planned by Barlow but a centre of liberal studies, Keele; and, when the new universities were commissioned before the Robbins Report, their sites were in historic rather than industrial centres. Proposals for a University of Scunthorpe excited little enthusiasm.

In addition to this residual bias, policymakers also simply lacked the competence to plan and direct the necessary transformation. Butler, as has been seen, quickly passed the issue to his officials and it is to their lack of expertise and drive that the failure successfully to develop technical and secondary modern schools has conventionally been attributed. To dispense, for example, with a fixed national curriculum and to proclaim of secondary moderns (as did the 1943 white paper *Educational Reconstruction*) that 'their future' was 'their own to make' may have displayed commendable liberalism. Less charitably however, it could be argued that it also revealed a culpable lack of positive purpose. In the place of a centralised curriculum, what these schools needed for their success was a central source of expert advice, committed support and, above all, an unequivocal guarantee of equal resources.[77]

Policymakers alone, however, were not responsible for the failure of technical education. Local government remained extremely reluctant either to build technical schools or to relax its historic control over technical colleges and so the colleges could not readily aspire to national (let alone international) standards of excellence. The teaching profession as a whole also proved extremely conservative not only in universities but also in further education (where it remained wedded to a mass of arcane qualifications) and in schools (where any variation in professional practice to achieve a greater exchange of ideas and personnel between education and industry was resisted). On the demand side parents in the 1950s showed as little enthusiasm for technical and secondary modern schools as did students in the 1960s for the post-Robbins expansion in science and technology. Social, rather than applied, science was the preferred area of study. Most damaging of all, however, was the negativism of industry. Even during the war employers had displayed a preference for poaching skilled workers from other firms rather than for developing their own training programmes; and when a modicum of compulsion was imposed on them in the 1960s, their response lacked the positive endorsement of national standards and the virtues of day-release courses which characterised their German counterparts. Moreover, by accepting the academic GCE and CSE as the recognised certificate for school leavers, they – as much as universities – discouraged the development within schools of vocational skills. In the 1956 white paper, *Technical Education*, the Conservative government had stressed that the support of parents and industry was vital for the success of their policy.[78] Short of the 'semi-fascist' methods which had been rejected during the war, it remained far from clear how this support could be generated.

8.6   CONCLUSION

Education has historically been regarded as one of the most important areas of state intervention. Classical economists, even in the nineteenth century, excluded it from their general demand for laissez-faire and communist regimes have traditionally accorded it high priority. The Second World War in Britain proved no exception. Education was regarded as being of central importance to the achievement of the dual reconstruction aims of building a more meritocratic and technocratic society; and after 1945 it rapidly became the second most expensive welfare service. As a result, and in common with the experience abroad, formal educational achievements by 1975 had exceeded all possible prewar expectations – and such an achievement did not reflect, as some Conservatives insinuated, any general decline in standards.

The consensus which supported this educational expansion was, for so political an issue, remarkable. It did, however, conceal considerable disagreement. Pedagogically, was an individual's independence best secured by a training in 'liberal' values or in marketable skills? Politically, was the ultimate objective of education to reinforce traditional social values and structures or to engineer social change? Such questions, which went to the heart of the conflict over whether the fundamental purpose of the welfare state should be to improve the functional efficiency or the equality of society, had been left unresolved by the 1944 Education Act. Innately conservative, it had nevertheless prescribed no rigid structure for schools nor – uniquely in Western Europe – a centralised curriculum. It had merely removed the historical impediments to reform.

The opportunity thus offered was not seized as effectively as it was in other countries. Policymakers clearly identified the key issues and the full range of relevant policy options. New initiatives, however, were either abandoned before they had had the opportunity to achieve their objectives (such as technical and secondary modern schools) or compromised by overhasty implementation and underfunding (such as the expansion of comprehensive and higher education). Other policies such as tripartism and intelligence testing (as one amongst many tools for determining children's schooling), were also abandoned for no good educational reason. Tripartism after all remains the organisational principle behind the highly effective German education system and intelligence testing (under the guise of 'verbal reasoning') is still employed within British schools to measure children's progress. Each fell victim, however, to an ill-conceived attempt to resolve by structural means the fundamental educational and social dilemma of how to meet children's individual needs without reinforcing social divisions. Such an attempt evaded rather than resolved the issue, and, by reinforcing the bias against vocational training, further discouraged the development of an 'industrial' culture upon which international competitiveness and ultimately individual welfare depended.

Policymakers within central government were not solely responsible for these failures, although they did fail to ensure one of the preconditions of success: the proper payment and training of teachers. Their chosen policy was not to employ their residual power to 'control and direct' but to allow the implementation of policy to be determined, under the aegis of LEAs and the UGC, by public demand, the vested interest of the teaching profession and the apathy of industry. When such decentralisation failed, especially in relation to technical education, the demand for greater centralisation became inexorable.

8.7 FURTHER READING

The history of education has spawned a large and varied literature. It is best summarised in Roy Lowe, *Education in the Postwar Years* (1988), which covers the period to 1964, and B. Simon, *Education and the Social Order 1940–1990* (1991). Additional information, particularly on unglamorous but essential issues such as curricula and examinations, is provided in P. Gosden, *The Education System since 1944* (1983). The journal, *History of Education*, contains the latest research.

The war period is definitively covered by P. Gosden, *Education in the Second World War* (1976) and the same author, together with P. R. Sharp, has provided a good case-study of policy implementation in *The Development of an Education Service: the West Riding, 1889–1974* (1978). The issue of equality is covered incisively in M. Sanderson, *Educational Opportunity and Social Change in England* (1987) and further education authoritatively in W. A. C. Stewart, *Higher Education in Postwar Britain* (1989).

The latter covers technical education, which has otherwise been as neglected by historians as by policymakers. C. Barnett in *The Audit of War* (1986) has led the offensive and two more balanced but brief introductions are P. E. J. Landymore, 'Education and industry since the war', in D. Morris (ed.), *The Economic system in the UK* (Oxford, 3rd ed., 1985) and J. Sheldrake and S. Vickerstaff, *The History of Industrial Training in Britain* (Aldershot, 1987). The initial findings of more detailed historical research have been published in P. Summerfield and E. J. Evans, *Technical Education and the State since 1950* (Manchester, 1990).

There is also a rich supply of contemporary literature. An insight into the earlier period is provided by O. Banks, *Parity and Prestige in English Secondary Education* (1955), while the optimism of the 1960s is well captured in J. Vaizey, *Education for Tomorrow* (1962) and R. Pedley, *The Comprehensive School* (1962). The ambitions and frustrations of two reforming ministers of education, Sir Edward Boyle and Anthony Crosland, are recorded in M. Kogan (ed.), *The Politics of Education* (1971). Finally, two excellent collections of primary sources, for official reports and educational research respectively, are J. S. Maclure, *Educational Documents* (5th ed., 1986) and H. Silver, *Equal Opportunity in Education* (1973).

9 Housing

In contrast to education, housing policy enjoyed little wartime consensus and remained throughout the postwar years at the heart of party conflict. During the war, admittedly, a white paper had been published on the related issue of land use; and after the mid-1950s the Labour Party endorsed the Conservatives' earlier call for a 'property-owning democracy'. However, the wartime coalition was unable eventually to agree upon the white paper's proposals and the ownership of land, as Michael Foot has remarked, became 'the rock' upon which it was broken.[1] Thereafter it was to remain a key election issue. So too were the management and finance, if not the principles, of the housing programme. In the 1951 and 1964 elections, for example, the Conservative and Labour Parties respectively used the promise to build 300 000 houses a year and the Rachman scandal over the terrorising of private tenants to discredit the 'socialist' and 'free-market' approaches to housing and thereby their opponents' overall attitude towards the welfare state.

The interest of the electorate itself was initially intense, with 41 per cent of those polled in 1946 identifying it as their principal concern (whilst only 15 per cent chose full employment).[2] Despite a steady improvement in housing standards, however, disillusion soon became endemic. A survey of public attitudes towards the welfare state in 1956 revealed that it was 'the only service about which there were widespread complaints'; and dissatisfaction mounted with the rapid increase in high-rise estates (which were the mirror image of people's stated preferences) and the reports of corruption which affected this area of the welfare state alone. The distribution of subsidies also provoked dissatisfaction. In middle-class demonology, scroungers on the dole queue were quickly replaced by tenants in subsidised council housing with 'private cars outside and television aerials which festooned the roofs'. On the left, a similar hatred was reserved for private landlords and property developers.

Such widespread antagonism and resentment were a reflection of the extent and complexity of government intervention in the housing market. Within the constraints set by private landlords, financial institutions, the construction industry and local authorities, central government was expected to implement a wide range of controls (covering, for example, land use, housing standards and rent) and to provide extensive subsidies for both the public and private sectors. State intervention on this scale was not unique to Britain. Subsidisation of housing, for example, was – and is – common to all Western countries, in part because the costs of construction are high in relation to average wages and in part because housing is recognised to be a public good (see Chapter 3.2.1). As the One Nation group of Conservative backbenchers acknowledged in 1950, for instance, good housing can both assist labour mobility (and hence economic growth) and also reduce expenditure on other social services (by improving health and enhancing the quality of life – thereby reducing the number of broken marriages and, arguably, crime).[3] Where Britain is unique, however, is that subsidies are not spread evenly – as elsewhere – through a wide network of agencies, and government itself owns much of the housing stock (the comparable figures for Britain and France in the early 1970s, for example, being 31 and 0.5 per cent). Consequently the opportunity for political antagonism in Britain is far greater. Moreover, in Britain there is the anomaly that only two of the three major types of housing tenure – council housing and owner-occupancy – are subsidised. The third – private rented accommodation – is not, although ironically it is the one to which the poorest have traditionally had most recourse.

The extent and complexity of government intervention makes the accurate assessment of housing costs over time extremely difficult. As demonstrated in Table 9.1, current expenditure consists largely of loan repayments to private financial institutions and is offset by both subsidies (from taxpayers and ratepayers) and by rent paid by tenants. More particularly, tax relief on mortgage interest payments – as a prime example of 'tax expenditure' – is not recorded in conventional government accounts (see Appendix 1.4) and its full cost was only made public in the 1970s as a result of public pressure following the dramatic increase in house prices, and thus in the government's liability. Aggregate figures do, however, clearly demonstrate two underlying trends. First, as conventionally defined, housing expenditure declined between 1951 and 1971 from approximately 20 per cent to 10 per cent of social expenditure, before rising again to 16 per cent in 1976. Secondly, it was extremely volatile as a result of its sensitivity to both political fashion and the needs of the managed economy. In the 1950s, and again after 1974, its growth was less than any other welfare service, whereas in the early 1970s it expanded at almost double the average rate (see Appendix 1, Tables A1.4 and A1.5).

Table 9.1   Housing: selected current and capital expenditure, 1951–76

	1951–2 £m	1956–7 £m	1961–2 £m	1966–7 £m	1971–2 £m	1975–6 £m
Current expenditure:						
Local Authority housing (net)	15	30	45	75	72	189
Repairs, maintenance, etc.	47	65	97	114	284	764
Loan charges	81	167	258	420	701	1524
Less: rent received	−84	−154	−232	−396	−681	−1236
government subsidies	−38	− 67	− 78	−101	−232	− 863
Total current expenditure	78	108	137	187	348	1534
Tax relief on mortgages	–	–	–	–	328	770
Capital expenditure:						
Local Authority	298	293	279	679	673	2041
Public Corporation	21	32	25	54	73	298
Total capital expenditure	340	382	431	825	917	2966
Total public expenditure on housing	417	490	568	1012	1265	4500

Sources: Social Trends (1970, 1977), *Annual Abstract of Statistics* (1964).

In comparison with other welfare services, therefore, postwar housing policy was not only more politically contentious and publicly disliked but also more administratively complex and economically volatile. Its principal objectives nevertheless remained relatively consistent: the provision, within a well-planned environment, of a sufficient number of houses of an adequate quality at a fair price. It is against these criteria that its record will be assessed.

9.1   PLANNING

The one area in which the war did achieve a continuing measure of consensus was, ironically, the most contentious: land ownership. Before the war, only 3 per cent of land had been effectively subject to planning permission. After the war, no land could be developed without prior consent from local or central government. This was a revolutionary restriction on the traditional rights of private property and, together with the Beveridge Report and the Keynesian input into the 1944 *Employment Policy* white paper, may be seen as a classic example of the confidence of 'disinterested' experts that they could use the dislocation of war to realise reforms long championed by informed opinion. How was this modicum of consensus achieved? Why was consensus not more extensive? Finally, how effectively was planning policy implemented?

The acceptance of planning permission was a consequence of both long-term trends and short-term need. Since the turn of the century there had been growing concern about uncontrolled urban development; and such pressure groups had been formed as the Town and Country Planning Association and the Campaign for the Preservation of Rural England, respectively to encourage better urban planning and to discourage urban sprawl. They had met with partial success. Locally, for instance, the London County Council had adopted in the 1930s the principle of green belts and satellite towns and nationally the 1940 Barlow Report had advocated the creation of a 'central authority' to oversee the dispersal of industry and people from congested areas.[4] The war reinforced such trends. Detailed legislative change was considered by two reconstruction committees, the Scott Committee on Land Utilisation and the Uthwatt Committee on Compensation and Betterment.[5] Even more importantly, extensive bomb damage created an urgent need for redevelopment. In a last flowering of Victorian optimism and utopianism, planners such as Patrick Abercrombie (who was responsible for the 1945 Greater London Plan) exuded the confidence that they could mastermind such redevelopment and the minimum power they needed, it was agreed, was the power to forestall the worst excesses of unrestricted 'market' forces.

More extensive powers to permit an active government role in urban redevelopment, however, aroused greater controversy, not least because they went to the heart of the ideological differences between the Conservative and Labour Parties over whether power should lie ultimately in the market or with the state. Three particular issues were to dog policymakers. First, should betterment (the large increase in the value of land once it had been granted planning permission) be enjoyed by the private landowner or by the community? Secondly, how could a steady supply of land for development be ensured, especially if the owner were to be denied betterment? Thirdly, how successfully could central and local government adjust to, and discharge, their new positive responsibilities? Both would acquire considerably more power as the rights of private property declined. Officials would also have rapidly to develop new skills if local government were to draft development plans (and consequently to anticipate the future economic and social needs of each locality) and central government were (in the absence of clear market criteria) to value land in order to implement a tax on betterment.[6]

In order to maintain political unity, the coalition's 1944 white paper, *Control of Land Use*, sought to resolve these problems by steering a middle course between the traditional Labour and Conservative preferences for the nationalisation of, and a free-market in, land. It rejected the outright nationalisation of land or of development rights (as recommended by Uthwatt) but, whilst thus defending private ownership, it agreed that no land should be developed without planning permission. Owners should be compensated for the loss of any anticipated profit from the unrestricted development of their land. Should they thereafter be granted planning permission, however, they should be subject to a betterment tax equivalent to 80 per cent of the increased value of their land. Finally, the white paper proposed a land commission to oversee both the levying of this tax and the payment of compensation.

The authors of the white paper were fully alive to the political sensitivity of these proposals. As the introduction stated: 'proposals for controlling the use of land are bound to raise again issues which for many years have been the subject of keen political controversy. . . . No proposals on this subject – on which widely divergent views are held with conviction – can be wholly satisfactory to all shades of opinion.' At the same time, however, they were aware that agreement was urgently needed were a repetition of interwar failures to be avoided and the proposed compromise, they felt, successfully reconciled the 'rights of land tenure . . . with the best use of land in the national interest'.[7] Landowners were to be denied windfall profits from decisions by local government to zone certain areas, but not others, for development. The supply of land would be maintained because nationalisation (with its attendant political and financial problems) was to be avoided and owners were to retain 20 per cent of the enhanced value of their land. Finally, the land commission would not develop into a bureaucratic monster, as it would not itself own or develop land (again as Uthwatt had proposed) or acquire a large independent income (as revenue from betterment tax would be matched by outgoings on compensation).

After the war, however, neither Labour nor Conservative governments endorsed this compromise and, to the detriment of their respective housing programmes, followed sharply divergent policies. Labour government policy was dominated by two main principles. First, the community rather than the private landowner should enjoy the major benefits of betterment. Consequently in its major legislation – the 1947 Town and Country Planning Act, the 1967 Land Commission Act and finally the 1975 Community Land Act – a betterment tax was introduced at the respective rates of 100 per cent, 40 per cent and 60 per cent. Secondly, government should have the ultimate right to buy and develop land, so that a ready supply could be guaranteed for house-building. Hence in 1947 and 1967 the Land Commission was established, and in 1975 local authorities were empowered to buy land below its full 'developmental' value.[8] This land could then either be used for public building, thereby reducing *inter alia* the cost of council housing, or it could be sold to private developers at its full market price, thereby generating a profit from which 'unprofitable' but socially desirable developments, such as recreational facilities, could be financed.

The need for Labour governments to introduce three separate acts reflected the antipathy of intervening Conservative governments towards any interference in land development beyond planning permission. They maintained that, once the worst war damage and the absolute shortage of housing had been made good, the supply and price of land could best be determined by the free market. Thus, on their return to office, the two Land Commissions were abolished (in 1953 and 1971 respectively) and after 1959 local government was required to purchase land for development at its full market price, with all betterment accruing to the landowner. In the 1970s the justification for such a policy was that any private profit would be subject to capital gains, or to the later development gains, tax.

The policies of both parties were a failure.[9] Labour's imposition of a 100 per cent betterment tax in the 1940s removed all incentive from landowners to sell and consequently there was a 'development strike'. Moreover, the Land Commission was unable to guarantee the supply of land since the money at its disposal (£100 000 in the first year) was derisory and its powers of compulsory purchase were ill-defined. In the 1960s the new Land Commission traded constantly at a loss and, by the time of its abolition, it had sold only 913 acres of land. Similarly, under the Community Land Act only 6000 acres were purchased by local authorities and by 1979 they had accumulated debts of £33 million. Labour's practical achievements were therefore minimal.

It might be argued, especially of the 1967 and 1975 Acts, that this failure was due not to any inherent defect but to the ideological bias of incoming Conservative governments which repealed them just as they were about to bear fruit. Such an argument would, however, be fallacious because within each Labour government there were major obstacles to, and serious reservations about, the full implementation of policy. Economically, each piece of legislation coincided with a sterling crisis which strictly limited the money available for land purchase. Politically, grave concern was expressed about any policy which – whatever its long-term gains – might in the short term delay the release of land and thus disrupt the housing programme. It was also significant that in the 1940s and 1960s the ministers responsible for so radical a new policy (Silkin and Willey) were denied seats in the Cabinet and that in 1976 the Office of Planning and Local Government was abolished as soon as the requisite legislation had been passed. Administratively, the instinct and advice of officials (even in the Land Commissions) were to defend the private market; and the Treasury was vehemently opposed to the creation of any new body which had the right to raise, and to dispense the proceeds of, taxation.[10] Constitutionally, there were also serious reservations about an unelected body such as the Land Commission usurping the power of local government to buy and to plan the development of land. Consequently Labour policy ultimately failed because, whilst paying lip-service to manifesto commitments, ministers and their officials remained resolutely opposed to their practical implementation.

The policies of successive Conservative governments were even more disastrous. The need was acknowledged for planning permission and even for compulsory purchase in exceptional circumstances. Their major objective was, however, to ensure that landowners received the full market price of their land; and this led first to the anomalous 'dual' market between 1954 and 1959 (when the full price of land could be charged to private developers but not to local authorities) and then in the early 1960s and the 1970s (when local authorities were obliged to pay the full cost) to an unprecedented explosion in land and ultimately in house prices.

The Conservatives' faith in the market was confounded by the excessive demand in the 1960s for industrial and residential land and in the 1970s for commercial land. In a rising market landowners and land speculators delayed the sale of land to reap higher profits and thereby increased still further both the shortage and the price. In the 1970s such speculation reached exceptional heights because, in its attempt to stimulate industrial growth, the Heath government deliberately made money for investment more readily available. Investors rapidly discovered, however, that easier – and less heavily taxed – profits could be made from property; and consequently not only individual speculators but also all major institutional investors became heavily involved in the property market. Ministers quickly recognised their mistakes. Thus in the 1960s the reintroduction of a betterment tax was seriously debated within Cabinet, and in the 1970s a freeze on office rent was imposed (until it threatened the whole credit structure of the City of London) and then a new tax on development gains. Such remedies were, however, either too little or too late. Whilst betterment accrued solely to the landowner or speculator, the cost of land escalated so sharply that whereas in the 1950s it had accounted for only 3 per cent of the capital cost of a house, by 1975 it accounted for 19 per cent.[11]

The major attempts by both Labour and Conservative governments to regulate land use were therefore singularly ineffective. There were, nevertheless, two relatively minor but successful planning initiatives: the New Towns Act of 1946 and the National Parks Act of 1949. The concept of new towns as well-planned, self-contained and communally owned settlements had been privately pioneered before the war at Letchworth and Welwyn Garden City and it was identified by postwar governments as a means of both relieving congestion in major conurbations and stimulating economic growth in relatively depressed areas. As with other interwar ideals, its implementation was initially over-paternalistic (with the appointed – rather than elected – new town corporations for example encouraging art galleries and museums but actively discouraging cinemas). It was also neglected in the 1950s. Between 1946 and 1951, however, fourteen new towns were designated. The majority were near London (such as Stevenage, Crawley and Hatfield) but others were built near Newcastle (Newton Aycliffe and Peterlee), near Glasgow (East Kilbride) and in South Wales (Cwmbran). Only Cumbernauld, near Glasgow, was commissioned in the 1950s, but in the 1960s a further sixteen were approved either on green field sites (most notoriously, Milton Keynes) or at the centre of depressed or relatively slow-growing regions (such as Warrington, Peterborough, Northampton and Londonderry). These initiatives have been described as 'the single, most ambitious planning experiment in postwar Britain', but their significance should not be exaggerated. They accounted for only 3.5 per cent of the houses built between 1945 and 1970.[12]

The other interwar ideal to be realised was the creation in 1949 or ten national parks and the designation of 'areas of outstanding natural beauty'. This initiative was the consequence of increased popular leisure and, to a lesser extent, of the latent hostility to propertied privilege which had been demonstrated by the 'mass trespass' in the Peak District in 1932. It also represented an early concern for conservation which, in an urban setting, was to be reflected in the foundation of the Civic Trust in 1957 and the creation of conservation areas a decade later.

All these legislative changes consumed much political and administrative energy in Westminster and Whitehall, but the actual implementation of policy fell largely to local government. The 1947 Town and Country Planning Act (like the earlier Education Act) concentrated responsibility on county councils and county boroughs and thereby reduced the number of planning authorities from 1441 to 145; and this remained the situation, although in the 1960s county councils were given responsibility solely for the strategic 'structure plan' whilst their constituent districts were charged with its detailed development. How successfully did local government discharge its responsibilities?

One of the major aims of interwar reforms was realised. Urban sprawl was contained as the annual conversion of land from agricultural use was reduced from 25 000 to 16 000 hectares, or to 0.1 per cent of Britain's land surface.[13] However, two major weaknesses soon became apparent. First, neither the faith of interwar planners nor the 'scientific' techniques of their postwar successors was sufficient, in the drafting of local development plans, to anticipate changing economic and social needs. Planning disasters consequently ensued. In the short term 'planning blight' descended on many areas awaiting redevelopment, whilst in the long term serious damage was inflicted by the destruction of historic city centres. This weakness was compounded by planners' innate paternalism and secretiveness. The second major weakness was the negativism of public planning. Constrained after 1959 by the high cost of land and denied the proceeds of betterment, local government lacked both the opportunity to develop ambitious public projects and the power to enter into a more constructive partnership with private developers. Given the weakness of local government (as described in Chapter 4.4) and the succession of postwar planning disasters, such restrictions might be regarded as highly fortunate; but private development was itself, both before and after the war, far from perfect. A better-planned environment could well have been achieved had a more even balance been maintained between public opinion as expressed imperfectly through the ballot box and through the market.

9.2   HOUSING CONSTRUCTION

The construction of housing generated far less political controversy than planning, although it equally defied the logic of wartime planners.[14] During the war it had been assumed that, once bomb damage had been repaired, the stabilisation of – or even decline in – the number of households would restrict building largely to the replacement of slums and that, given the known size of slum areas, even this task could eventually be completed. Instead, the number of households increased rapidly as a result of changing demographic trends and greater affluence (see Chapter 4.2); and greater affluence also raised public expectations about the size and quality of housing. As a consequence not only did the demand for new housing rise, but so too did the standards by which property was adjudged fit for human habitation – at the very time that more of the old housing stock was falling into serious disrepair as a result of the low quality of much speculative building in the late Victorian and Edwardian periods. Slum clearance, it was gradually realised, was not a finite but a continuing problem.

Government policy to meet these evolving challenges fell into three broad phases: 1945–56, 1956–68 and 1968–75. Each covered both Labour and Conservative governments and so reflected a measure of underlying, bipartisan agreement. Within each phase, however, a change of government could – and did – result in a change of tactics and emphasis. Their combined impact was nevertheless a revolution in the nature of both housing and housing tenure.

The consistent objective of the first phase, despite its punctuation by a severe – and effective – attack on the record of the Attlee government by the Conservatives in the 1951 election, was the eradication of the housing shortage inherited from the war. The Labour government, and in particular Bevan (who was the minister responsible for housing between 1945 and January 1951), did not wholly deserve the criticism to which they were subjected. Almost half a million houses had been destroyed or rendered uninhabitable during the war and a further three million had been damaged. In addition few new houses had been built and few slums cleared (other than by courtesy of the Luftwaffe). There was, therefore, a severe housing shortage. Moreover, in a straitened economy any housing drive had to compete for scarce resources with the building requirements of industry and the other social services: the 1947 convertible crisis, for example, greatly reduced the import of timber (for which dollars had to be paid) and the public expenditure cuts associated with devaluation in 1949 hit capital expenditure particularly hard.[15] Finally, there was an irreconcilable conflict of interest within the housing programme itself. Should priority be given to industrial workers in order to increase labour mobility and thereby economic growth? Should it be given to the returning soldiers, as Churchill had wished, in order to avoid the obloquy that was heaped upon Lloyd George after the First World War for his failure to provide 'homes fit for heroes'?[16] Or should it be given, in accordance with traditional Labour Party policy, to the most needy? Since all three demands could not be met, some public disillusion was inevitable.

Bevan eventually decided upon the last option and consequently the vast majority of building licences (ranging from 90 per cent in 1946 to 80 per cent in 1950) were reserved for the construction of high-quality council houses. He justified his decision not just by need but on the ground that local government, rather than private builders, could be trusted to honour planning agreements. On the quality of housing, he also argued with prescience that while the Labour government 'would be judged for a year or two by the number of houses we build, we shall be judged in ten years' time by the type of houses we build'.[17] The annual number of council houses completed was, in any case, also historically high. At their prewar peak in 1938, 122 000 had been built. In 1948 the total was 217 000 and, despite public expenditure cuts, the figure never fell below 175 000 (see Table 9.2).

Table 9.2   Houses constructed and demolished in the UK, 1938–76 (thousands)

| | Houses built | | | Houses demolished |
	Local Authority	*Private*	*Total*	*(GB only)*
1938	122	237	359	–
1948	217	34	251	–
1951	176	25	202	–
1956	181	126	308	39
1961	122	181	303	67
1966	187	209	396	79
1971	168	196	364	87
1976	170	155	325	51

Sources: D. and G. Butler, *British Political Facts 1900–1985* (1986) pp. 332–3; S. Merrett, *State Housing in Britain* (1979) p. 120.

There were, however, two major flaws in Bevan's policy, which fostered public disillusion and gave substance to the Conservatives' later attack. First, the rehousing programme started slowly; and out of frustration there was an unprecedented outburst of squatting both in the West End of London in 1946 and more permanently in disused army camps.[18] Whatever Labour's later achievements, it was to these acts of defiance that popular memory constantly returned. Secondly, private building was restricted by 1951 to a mere tenth of its annual output in the 1930s; and consequently the total number of houses built was only just over half the prewar average. This shortfall, so the Conservatives argued, was essentially the result not of economic constraints but of mismanagement. Distracted by his battles over the NHS, Bevan had failed to coordinate policy in Whitehall (where responsibility was divided between five ministries), to provide clear targets (a strange oversight for someone supposedly committed to planning) and, as in the NHS, to utilise private sources of initiative (such as the non-profit-making housing associations). It was, so Con-

servatives were later to claim, because of their greater pragmatic
willingness to harness any agency that could contribute to their
housing drive that they were able to exceed Labour's achievements
and thereby all but end the housing shortage.

When the Conservatives returned to power in 1951, one of their
principal welfare commitments was to build 300 000 houses a year
and this target they duly achieved.[19] Despite recurring balance of
payments crises, Harold Macmillan (as housing minister) was able
to win a disproportionate share of scarce resources by capitalising
upon the Prime Minister's support and the fear that any shortfall
in production targets might lead to a questioning of the party's
commitment to the welfare state, and thereby jeopardise its future
electoral success. This angered other social service ministers and
particularly Butler who, as chancellor, was seeking greater economies. Macmillan's permanent secretary and the head of the civil
service were also antagonised by the unconventional means he
employed to coordinate policy within Whitehall, to define targets and
to ensure the local implementation of policy. 'This', he proclaimed in
an all too rare insight into the administrative changes required to
discharge the government's new positive welfare role, 'is a war job.
It must be tackled in the spirit of 1940.'[20]

The key to Macmillan's success, however, was the flexibility of his
approach. Rather than restraining the construction of council housing, he encouraged it so that – just as the largest number of comprehensive schools was opened while Margaret Thatcher was education
secretary – the greatest number of council houses ever to be built
within a four year period was achieved under the Conservatives
between 1952 and 1956. Simultaneously private initiative was encouraged by the lifting of restrictions on land use and the abolition of
building licences by 1954. As a result the 300 000 target was achieved
as early as 1953 and the annual completion figure was never again
to fall below this level until 1978, with the brief exception of 1958
and 1959. The only major blemish in Macmillan's record was a drop
in the quality and size of housing. In the public sector, for instance,
terraces replaced semi-detached housing and average house size fell
from just over 1000 to 900 square feet. Even here, however, it should
be remembered that the average size of council housing in the 1930s
had only been 750 square feet and that the cuts had initially been
planned by Bevan's successor as housing minister, Hugh Dalton.

By 1956 the housing shortage was considered to have been all but
resolved and, as priority in welfare expenditure was transferred to

education, housing policy reverted to the principles of the 1930s: the maintenance of a 'mixed economy' housing market in which the private sector satisfied any 'natural' increase in demand whilst the public sector concentrated on slum clearance. To achieve the desired balance the role of the public sector was reduced in two ways. First, subsidies for construction were reduced after 1954 and restricted in 1956 solely to meeting the 'special needs' of the elderly, slum clearance and new towns. Secondly, local government was fully exposed to market forces by the ending of both cheap loans in 1955 and, as has been seen, preferential land prices in 1959. In contrast demand in the private sector was boosted with a series of tax concessions (which will be discussed in the next section) and, after 1959, increased pressure upon local government to sell council houses, to provide mortgages and to distribute mandatory grants for house improvements.

The major increase in construction was, however, expected in private rented accommodation which, as illustrated in Table 9.3, had declined between 1945 and 1956 from 54 per cent to 36 per cent of the housing market. The principal reason for the decline was believed to be the continuation of wartime rent controls which, in a period of increasing inflation, had restricted the level of rent chargeable to that applicable in 1939 and, in many cases, 1915. A Rent Act was duly passed in 1957 which immediately decontrolled half a million houses and permitted controls on many more to be lifted on a change of tenancy. Rents on all remaining controlled property were also permitted, within certain limits, to be increased to enable landlords to make both essential repairs and a reasonable profit. The private rented market, however, did not revive and under Labour taunts the Conservatives grew increasingly concerned about an increasing housing shortage, especially in the rented sector. To accelerate construction they partially reversed earlier policy by permitting local government in 1962 to build again for 'general purposes' and by encouraging more ambitious programmes of redevelopment, in particular through the use of prefabricated building units. The Housing Corporation was also established in 1964 to channel funds to non-profit-making housing associations which provided rented accommodation.[21]

This construction strategy was not overturned but rather reinforced when the Wilson government took office in 1964. Its vitriol was reserved for the Conservatives' Rent Act which had led, so it believed, to the exploitation of private tenants. However, it no longer sought – as it had before the war – to take the private rented sector into public ownership. Nor did it seek, as it had in the 1940s, to concentrate construction in the public sector. On the contrary its first major policy statement, *The Housing Programme, 1965–1970*, explicitly confirmed the concept of a 'mixed economy' housing market. 'The expansion of the public programme now proposed', it reaffirmed, 'is to meet exceptional needs. The expansion of buildings for owner occupancy on the other hand is normal; it reflects a long-term social advance which should gradually pervade every region.'[22] The only major change made by Labour was quantitative. The annual output of houses was to be raised to 500 000; and, when this target came closest to being met at 426 000 in 1968, construction was duly found to be shared almost equally between the public and the private sectors.

This second phase of postwar policy ended abruptly in 1968 to be replaced by a third, in which the twin priorities were renovation and (within the public sector at least) a concentration of resources on the most needy. This change of policy was announced in the Labour government's white paper, significantly entitled *Old Houses into New Homes*, which stated boldly that 'within a total public investment in housing at about the level it has now reached the greatest share should go to the improvement of old homes'.[23] Such a pronouncement revealed three things. First, in the aftermath of the devaluation crisis, the new policy was designed to save money. Constant expenditure in cash terms during a period of inflation could only mean a fall in the real level of housing investment. Secondly, and again in direct contradiction to earlier Labour policy, construction targets – especially in the public sector – were to be cut. This was effected especially after 1972 when the Conservatives again withdrew 'general purpose' subsidies. Finally, large-scale slum clearance (which had been so strongly encouraged in the 1960s) was abandoned although ironically, because of existing contracts, the number of houses demolished did not peak until 1971 (see Table 9.2).

There were many good reasons for this new emphasis on renovation rather than redevelopment. The largest area of poor quality housing had already been cleared by 1968 and so, logically, a new strategy was required. Public concern was at last being expressed about the demolition of historic and structurally sound, if poorly maintained, buildings; and the conservation of the environment (as well as of grammar schools) had helped the Conservatives to sweeping victories at the local elections of 1967. There were also growing doubts about the social costs of large-scale redevelopment, especially the construction of the new 'high-rise' estates. The new technique of cost-benefit analysis could provide some measure of these costs (see Chapter 3.2.2) and, when combined with the additional cost of rebuilding over renovation, they made redevelopment appear far from cost effective.[24] Finally, there were even serious doubts about the very safety of high-rise flats after the partial collapse of the Ronan Point tower block in East London in 1968. Political expediency, environmental concern, economic logic and even public safety, therefore, all combined to encourage a change of policy.

The major new policy instruments were improvement grants and the creation of 'general improvement areas'. Investment grants had been introduced by Bevan as early as 1949 and had been made mandatory in 1959. General improvement areas, introduced in 1969, were discrete localities of between 200 and 300 houses in which private renovation could be matched by small public improvements to the environment (such as tree planting). Once such areas had been created the number of grants awarded to private owners trebled; peaking at 260 000 in 1973, and within the 964 areas sanctioned by 1975, one-quarter of the 280 000 houses had received grants.[25]

There was, however, one serious drawback to a policy so heavily dependent on private initiative for the disbursement of public funds. Those people, and indeed those properties, most in need of aid tended to benefit least. This flaw was duly identified and remedial action taken. In 1973 the Conservative government imposed stricter conditions on grants, with the result that their number quickly fell back to pre–1968 levels. In addition, and in accordance with its greater emphasis on selectivity in social security (see Chapter 6.3), the government drafted legislation to create 'housing action areas' in which resources would be directed to the most needy areas. The parliamentary passage of this legislation was interrupted by the 1974 election, but it was completed by the incoming Labour government, thereby maintaining the essentially bipartisan approach to postwar construction policy.[26]

These three phases in bipartisan policy transformed the nature of housing in Britain. First, as demonstrated by Table 9.3, the *absolute* shortage of housing was eradicated in the 1960s. This did not mean that there was no *actual* shortage. Some houses were second homes. Some lay empty. Others were simply in the 'wrong' place. More separate households might also have been formed, had additional accommodation been available. The recorded number of homeless people, at 1 per cent of the population, was nevertheless extremely low – although, as was discovered in 1977 when care for the homeless was for the first time made a statutory responsibility of local government, such statistics are also sensitive to changing public perception and definition.[27]

Table 9.3   Households and dwellings in England & Wales, 1951–76 (thousands)

	1951	1961	1971	1976
Total dwellings	12 530	14 646	17 024	18 100
Total households	13 259	14 724	16 779	17 600
Surplus (+) or deficiency (−)	−729	−78	+245	+500

Source: P. Malpass and A. Murie, *Housing Policy and Practice* (1987) p. 75.

The second major change, as demonstrated by Table 9.4, was in housing tenure. Despite the efforts of successive Conservative governments, the private rented market collapsed and was replaced first by council housing (as a result of construction in the public sector outstripping that in the private sector until 1959) and then by owner-occupancy. One reason for this collapse was the continuation of wartime controls and the fear that they might be intensified by Labour governments. A more important reason, however, was that – unlike in Europe – private rented accommodation enjoyed few of the subsidies or tax concessions accorded to other tenures. In contrast owner-occupancy received increasingly generous subsidies and

Table 9.4   Housing tenure in Britain, 1945–76 (per cent)

	Owner-occupied	Public rented	Private rented	Other
1945	26	12	54	8
1951	30	18	45	8
1956	34	23	36	7
1961	42	27	26	6
1966	47	29	19	5
1971	51	31	19	
1976	53	32	15	

'House' is defined as a building or part of a building which provides structurally separate living quarters.
Source: Royal Commission on the Distribution of Income and Wealth, *Seventh Report* (Cmnd 7595, 1979) p. 133.

by 1970 accounted for over half of the housing stock. This was a level far in excess of contemporary European experience where, as late as 1978, the comparable figures for France and Germany respectively were only 47 per cent and 37 per cent.

The final area of major change was the quality of housing. The extent of improvement is perhaps surprising in the light of the deliberate reduction in standards during the Macmillan housing drive and its subsequent condemnation by the official Parker Morris report, *Homes for Today and Tomorrow*, in 1961. 'Homes are being built at the present time', it complained, 'which not only are too small to provide adequately for family life but also are too small to hold the possessions in which so much of the new affluence is expressed'.[28] It advanced new minimum standards of space and heating which, it stressed, should not be regarded as maxima. This, however, is inevitably what happened when they were eventually given statutory force by the Labour government in 1968. Nevertheless, in both absolute and relative terms, the quality of housing rose sharply. Reliable statistics on the number of houses unfit for human habitation were – perhaps significantly – not collected until 1967, but thereafter the number so recorded fell sharply from 1.8 million to 0.9 million in 1975 or from 12 per cent to 5 per cent of the total housing stock.

The authors of the Parker Morris report would no doubt have been unimpressed by these figures. Just as the contemporary poverty lobby had argued for a relative standard of poverty, so they had maintained that the quality of housing should be judged not by low prewar standards but by rising expectations. 'There was a time', they asserted, 'when for a great majority of the population, the major significance of the structure in which they made their home was to provide shelter and a roof over their heads. This is no longer so. An increasing proportion of people are coming to expect their home to do more than fulfil the basic requirements.' A revised list of five 'basic amenities' was accordingly drafted in 1970 to include a fixed bath or shower, a lavatory with an inside entrance, a wash-hand basin, hot and cold water at three points and a kitchen sink. By this new list, the number of substandard housing units had declined by 1975 from 3.9 million to 1.6 million. Considerable problems still remained, therefore, but the pace of rehabilitation had been fast. As Donnison and Ungerson have concluded, 'the biggest slum clearance and grant-aided improvement programmes to be attempted anywhere in the world [had] gone far to eliminate the worst conditions'.[29]

There was, however, one way in which slum clearance rather than enhancing housing standards had actually threatened to reduce them: the building, by experimental prefabricated methods, of large impersonal estates of high-rise buildings, lacking many of the amenities common in similar developments on the continent. The irony was that no-one actively sought these estates. The One Nation group of Conservatives in 1950, for instance, had condemned 'the building of such family nightmares as blocks of flats without balconies or gardens'; and their instincts were confirmed by a Greater London Council survey in 1967 which revealed that 75 per cent of council house applicants wanted a house with a garden, whereas only 9 per cent of the GLC's housing stock fell into this category.[30] Their construction was, therefore, largely fortuitous and the consequence of the convergence of a wide variety of independent factors: architectural fashion and perceptions of 'modernity'; conservationists' determination to halt urban sprawl; the desire of inner-city Labour councils and Conservative councils respectively to keep or rebuff traditional Labour voters; the high cost of land, especially after 1959; and finally the insistence by central government (especially in the early 1960s) on quick results.

In the light of this potent combination of factors, the large construction companies identified their own interests as being to persuade local authorities to undertake large-scale redevelopment and to sanction new construction techniques which were beyond the capacity of local contractors. In addition, through high-pressure salesmanship and (in certain cases) corruption, they persuaded the larger authorities to set a trend which the smaller ones felt bound to follow. They were even assisted by the structure of government subsidies. Official policy was to encourage the construction of 'mixed' estates and, in order to persuade conservative councils to build a certain minimum of high-rise flats, subsidies progressively favoured taller buildings. Hence fifteen and six storey blocks of flats attracted subsidies which were, respectively, three times and twice as generous as those provided for houses. These subsidies proved to be so attractive that, in conjunction with the construction companies' powers of persuasion, they not only eroded councils' conservatism but led to a wholly unexpected concentration on high-rise building.

The replacement of slums by high-rise prefabricated flats was largely confined to a relatively brief but intense period of construction in the 1960s. As soon as the unintended consequences of the subsidy structure were fully appreciated, remedial action was taken in the 1967 Housing Subsidies Act. Consequently the decline of high-rise buildings had started even before the partial collapse of Ronan Point in 1968.[31] Brief though this episode was, however, it graphically illustrated two broader features of construction policy. First, it was a prime example of incrementalism. Subsidies and grants designed to achieve a given end frequently resulted in the achievement of another. Secondly, a vigorous housing policy did not automatically – as the Conservatives had hoped – resolve social problems. It could, and often did, actually intensify them.

9.3   HOUSING COSTS

As may be inferred from the preceding sections, government is able to influence the cost of housing in three ways: through the manipulation of construction costs; through concessions to owner-occupiers; and through rent controls. Between 1945 and 1975 the first two methods proved to be relatively uncontroversial but the latter excited much political controversy.

The direct way in which government has traditionally influenced construction costs is through the payment of subsidies. Subsidies may be used for a wide variety of purposes: to vary the range of building (as with the switch from 'general' to 'special' purposes in 1956), the types of building (as with the progressive storey-height subsidy in 1956) or the type of investor (as with the granting of subsidies to housing associations after 1962).[32] Their principal purpose after 1945, however, was to regulate the pace of construction. Thus, at the start of Macmillan's housing drive in 1952, the subsidy on new houses was virtually doubled to £26.70. Then, when the housing shortage appeared to have been resolved, it was halved in 1955. Construction was encouraged in this way because subsidies were payable annually over sixty years and so the future cost to local government was greatly reduced.

Such long-term subsidies, however, have one serious flaw. In periods of inflation, such as the 1960s, their real value falls and so local authorities are faced with the need dramatically to increase either council-house rents or the rates. To forestall just such an eventuality, the Conservative government in their 1972 Housing Finance Act cancelled all existing subsidies and replaced them with a new grant which was to be adjusted annually to meet the difference between the 'reckonable' (that is, approved) housing expenditure and rent income. The original purpose behind this reform was to reduce the subsidies from central government but, as can be seen from Table 9.5, it was singularly unsuccessful in this respect. As land prices and interest rates soared, so too did 'reckonable' expenditure, and both council tenants and rate payers received unprecedented assistance from the general taxpayer. This unintended consequence of the 1972 legislation was a prime example of incrementalism, with the planned objectives of direct subsidisation being distorted by the unplanned and indirect effects of planning and monetary policy.

Table 9.5   Cost of building subsidies in the UK, 1952–1977 (£ millions)

	Central government subsidies to:		Local authority subsidies	Total
	Local authorities	*Housing associations*		
1949–50	34	2	14	50
1964–5	89	9	53	150
1973–4	299	44	89	432
1976–7	987	171	185	1343

Source: A. H. Halsey (ed.), *British Social Trends since 1900* (2nd ed, 1988), Table 10.27.

The cost of housing for owner-occupiers was reduced, particularly in the 1960s, by both Conservative and Labour governments. The first major concession to owner-occupiers – tax relief on mortgage interest payments – had been made in 1921, but until the 1950s its impact had been slight. Because of relatively high tax thresholds and low house prices, both the number of beneficiaries and the value of benefits had been low. Tax was also levied on the 'imputed' rent which home-owners could theoretically earn from their property and, in any case, interest payments on all loans were treated similarly. All this changed in the 1960s. With tax thresholds dropping and house prices rising, the number of beneficiaries and the value of their hidden subsidy began to escalate.[33] A series of tax reforms also saw the withdrawal of tax liability from 'imputed' rent in 1963; the exemption from capital gains tax in 1965 of profits from the sale of a person's 'principal' home; and the withdrawal in 1968 of tax relief on interest for loans other than mortgages. In addition improvement grants were provided so that home-owners could increase the value of their properties at the tax-payers' expense; and, finally, building societies were provided with subsidies in 1959 and 1974 respectively to encourage loan-advances on pre–1919 property and to insulate mortgages from rises in interest rates.

All these concessions were extremely expensive. In 1975–6, as can be seen from Table 9.1, the cost of tax relief on mortgages was estimated to be £770 million. Simultaneously the estimated cost of exemption of house sales from capital gains tax was £550 million and the estimated amount of tax-free 'imputed' rent was well over £2000 million. The Treasury not surprisingly objected to so great a loss of revenue. It had also initially opposed increased owner-occupancy on the grounds that it could *inter alia* distort investment, encourage personal indebtedness and increase wage claims. Why then were such costly concessions made?

The reason was purely political. After the war, with the perceived advance of socialism, Conservative politicians became convinced that the creation of a 'property-owning democracy' was essential to foster individual initiative and thus economic efficiency and political stability. In the 1950s, when they developed the concept of the 'opportunity state', tax concessions on mortgage interest (as on occupational pensions) were also deemed a justified means of achieving their ends – even if they did distort both the housing market and industrial investment. Likewise, in the 1950s the Labour Party (partly as a result of the ambitions of 'affluent workers' as recorded by opinion polls) came to accept home-ownership as a natural instinct. It was also fully aware that, given so many articulate interests were involved, it would be politically inexpedient to withdraw any concessions even after they had become unexpectedly expensive.

In view of the predominance of rented accommodation even for middle-class households in the nineteenth century, some doubt has recently been cast on whether home-ownership is indeed a response to 'natural' instinct and not merely the 'creation' of preferential treatment.[34] What cannot be denied however is that the financial incentives provided by successive governments reduced the cost of home-ownership to well below its 'market' cost. These incentives were also highly regressive and expanded fastest in the 1960s at the very time when other policies were being constricted because of a perceived lack of resources. Owner-occupiers thus quickly became some of the most privileged recipients of state welfare.

Such favourable treatment was certainly not accorded to tenants in either the private or the public rented sector. Under Conservative governments, the preeminent objective of policy was to ensure that both sets of tenants paid a full market rent. This would encourage those council tenants who could afford it to opt for home-ownership and their places could then be taken by poor families 'shaken out' of the private market. Such a rationalisation of the private sector might cause short-term hardship. In the long term, however, it was deemed necessary in order to achieve greater equality between tenants (with the ending of fortuitous differences between the various controlled tenures), to ensure the most economical use of housing and, above all, to provide landlords with sufficient profits to halt the accelerating degeneration of their property. By 1956, for example, it was estimated that for the 1.9 million and 3.3 million properties which fell respectively under the 1915 and 1939 Rent Control Acts, rents were on average 150 per cent and 80 per cent below their 'true' level; and such a loss of income, it was believed, had to be staunched were conditions in the private sector ever to improve.[35] The 1957 Rent Act and the 1972 Housing Finance Act were the principal means by which the Conservatives planned to attain their objectives. The former, as has been seen, decontrolled 500 000 houses and prepared the way for either decontrol or rent increases in all the others. The latter sought to target subsidies more effectively by obliging local authorities, for the first time, to charge all their tenants a full market rent and then to distribute rent rebates to those in genuine need.

Both pieces of legislation infuriated the Labour Party. It had traditionally equated private landlords with exploitation, and the 1957 Rent Act appeared fully to confirm its suspicions. Several unscrupulous landlords, most notoriously Perec Rachman in London, either bribed or terrorised sitting tenants to leave their homes, which could then be decontrolled and either sold or re-let at a considerable profit. Such exploitation, as an official report later confirmed, was actually rare; but nevertheless, because Rachman had links with certain spy and sex scandals which went to the heart of the Conservative Party, Labour politicians were able effectively to capitalise upon it in the 1964 election.[36] In victory they intensified restrictions on private landlords in three ways. They extended the authority of rent tribunals, which had been set up in 1946 to monitor rents, from unfurnished to furnished property; they granted tenants security of tenure; and they appointed rent officers who might review contracts every three years to ensure that tenants were only being charged a 'fair' rent.[37]

The Labour Party's reaction to the 1972 Housing Finance Act was more tortuous, if no less passionate. On the one hand the Party was concerned that council tenants should be as well subsidised as owner-occupiers. It was also suspicious of any further infringement by central on local government. On the other hand leading ministers had largely come to agree with the Conservatives that local authorities should be obliged to concentrate subsidies on the most needy. 'Help for those who most need it', declared *The Housing Programme, 1965–1970*, 'can only be given out if the subsidies are in large part used to provide rebates for tenants whose means are poor.'[38] Their dilemma was, moreover, intensified by the fact that rent rebates – which had been urged on local government since 1930 – were unpopular with both local authorities and their more prosperous tenants. The former preferred subsidies to the needy to be disbursed by centrally-funded agencies such as the Supplementary Benefits Commission, whilst the latter resented any redirection of resources to their less prudent neighbours.

Violent protests had traditionally greeted attempts to introduce rebates, be it in Leeds and Birmingham in the late 1930s or in St Pancras in the 1960s. The early 1970s proved no exception. The Labour councillors at Clay Cross in Derbyshire refused to implement their mandatory responsibilities under the 1972 Act and they were duly suspended.[39] After much heart-searching the Labour Party supported their stand and, when Labour was returned to office, the increase of council rents to market levels – without which the funds could not be found to finance rebates – was halted. Over the next five years rents, which had risen strongly under the Conservatives (albeit never to a level above 10 per cent of average family income), fell in real terms by 25 per cent.

The influence of central government over the ultimate cost of housing for both owner-occupiers and council tenants was therefore extensive and extremely complex. Indeed, with characteristic elegance, Anthony Crosland described it as a 'dog's breakfast'.[40] What was incontrovertible, however, was that there was no longer any 'free market' in housing and that any attempt, or pretence, to revive one was either misguided or pernicious. Britain was not unique in having such extensive subsidies. What was unique to Britain was that one group of tenants – those in private rented accommodation – were largely assisted by paternalistic controls, whilst in all other tenures the range of subsidies was unduly complex.

9.4 CONCLUSION

Housing has been described as the 'extreme instance of irrationality among all the social services'.[41] It has also aroused extreme political passions and caused deep public disillusion. This is perhaps not surprising. On the one hand central government has had to share power with an exceptionally wide range of independent or semi-independent agencies so that, especially in the long term, opportunities were rife for the initial intentions behind legislation to become distorted during the implementation of policy. This was clearly the case with the unsuccessful attempts in the 1950s to revive the private rented sector, in the 1960s to build 'mixed' council estates and in the 1970s to rationalise subsidies. On the other hand policy has had to address an equally wide range of issues which, like the rights of private property and the need for shelter, went to the heart of political power and individual security. Planning and rent control policy were clearly affected by these pressures.

Despite these complexities and latent conflicts, a 'mixed economy' housing market did successfully evolve between 1945 and 1975. The worst excesses of unplanned development between the wars were avoided. The absolute housing shortage was resolved. General standards of housing also improved remarkably, albeit from a very low base. For all its weaknesses, in other words, housing policy well reflected the pragmatic strength of the classic welfare state. For the more idealistic supporters of collectivism, however, there were two ominous developments. The striking growth of owner-occupancy signified a retreat from the communal values which policymakers had initially tried to foster. In the 1970s there was also in housing legislation – as within the original NHS and the shift in education policy towards a core curriculum – a distinct move by central government to erode local democracy. Both those developments were to gather even greater momentum after 1975.

9.5 FURTHER READING

Two good general introductory books are J. R. Short, *Housing in Britain: the postwar experience* (1982) and D. Donnison and C. Ungerson, *Housing Policy* (Harmondsworth, 1982). The latter is strong on international comparisons, as is M. Daunton, *A Property-Owning Democracy?* (1987) which also places postwar developments in historical perspective. Another excellent introduction, within an explicit Marxist framework, is S. Merrett, *State Housing in Britain* (1979). Although concerned mainly with the period after 1979, P. Malpass and A. Murie, *Housing Policy and Practice* (2nd ed., 1987) has a useful historical introduction and an even more useful bibliography.

The definitive political history of planning is A. Cox, *Adversary Politics and Land: the conflict over land and property in postwar Britain* (Cambridge, 1984). This may be supplemented by G. Cherry, *The Politics of Town Planning* (1982) and M. Aldridge, *The British New Towns: a programme without a policy* (1979). Three other classic works are: P. Dunleavy, *The Politics of Mass Housing in Britain, 1945–75* (Oxford, 1981); M. Boddy, *The Building Societies* (1980); and on Rachman and rents in the 1960s, K. G. Banting, *Poverty, Politics and Policy* (1979).

The complexities of policy can be enlivened by the exploits of three particularly charismatic housing ministers recorded, respectively, in M. Foot, *Aneurin Bevan* (vol. 2, 1975), H. Macmillan, *Tides of Fortune, 1945–1955* (1966) and R. H. S. Crossman, *Diaries of a Cabinet Minister* (vol. 1, 1975).

10 The Personal Social Services

The personal social services are one of the most ill-defined, neglected and yet vital parts of the welfare state. The term covers essentially the residual services provided by, or through, local government for groups such as the elderly, the physically and mentally handicapped, children and 'problem families'. Since the war – and in sharp contrast to earlier Poor Law practice – the ordinary needs of individuals within such groups have been catered for, as for everyone else, by the main welfare services. Moreover, many of these main services (and most notably general practice within the NHS) provide a sympathetic 'personal' service. What is distinctive about the personal social services is that they provide for extraordinary individual need; and that they are concerned not with one specialised area of care but with their clients' overall welfare so that, as far as is possible, these clients can adapt to – or at least come to terms with – society at large.

The personal social services have been unduly neglected for three main reasons. First, they initially lacked a clear professional identity. Those working within them were recruited from a diverse range of sources (including private charities, voluntary hospitals, local public assistance committees and the Assistance Board) and represented an equally diverse range of specialisms (each seemingly in constant dispute with the others). Unlike medicine or teaching, therefore, social work lacked an agreed body of theoretical knowledge and thus clear criteria by which to measure success. Secondly, they were poorly funded, consuming only 1.7 per cent of public expenditure as late as 1966. Finally, they carried little political weight. As a responsibility of local government they were divided and decentralised; and their clientele, by definition, could exert little political influence. Each of these weaknesses, it is true, was steadily corrected after the publication of the Seebohm Report on Local Authority and Allied Personal Social Services in 1968.[1] Thereafter greater coordination was achieved both in administration and training and the personal social services became the fastest growing area of welfare (see Appendix Tables A1.3, A1.5). Even by 1976, however, they still consumed only 3.9 per cent of social expenditure and they tended to attract political attention (to their discredit) only after the exposure of a scandal.

That the personal social services should have enjoyed so little public esteem was the more unfortunate because their role was in many ways central to the evolution of the welfare state. Not only were they caring directly for the most vulnerable members of society (by whose treatment the humanity of any country's social services should ultimately be judged) but they also raised fundamental questions about the proper role of the state and the individual and, in particular, about the respective 'rights' and 'duties' of the citizen. In the past those in need had conventionally been blamed for their misfortunes, discouraged from seeking help from the state and punished if they did so. After the war such attitudes were – in theory at least – totally reversed. All claimants were to be regarded as full citizens, encouraged to identify both their problems and their needs, and helped by the state as much as possible.

Even had such principles been immediately implemented, however, many practical questions would have remained unresolved.[2] To what extent should behaviour deemed 'aberrant' be controlled (as was clearly necessary, for example, in relation to convicted offenders on probation or parents found guilty of child neglect)? To what extent should social workers, as employees of the taxpayer, encourage their clients to conform to conventional norms? Conversely, to what extent should social workers, in serving the interests of their clients, campaign for legislative change or even challenge – and encourage their clients to challenge – society's norms? Finally, what should be the relationship between the state and those families and voluntary organisations which provided so much care for those in need? Such 'community action' was clearly desirable, not just to save the taxpayer money but to maintain an active and caring society. However, one of the principal objectives of the welfare state was to ensure a standard level of care throughout the country. Whilst satisfying the needs of certain groups in certain areas, dependence on non-state agencies might also lead to the neglect of others. If state provision were to be targeted only on areas of neglect, might it not therefore lead to charges of inequity or even to the erosion of voluntary provision elsewhere?

The purpose of this chapter is to look first at the evolution of the statutory social services in the light of such dilemmas and then at the development of voluntary provision. Voluntary action was, after social insurance and full employment, the subject of the third – and least satisfacory – Beveridge Report in 1948[3] and for a time it was widely assumed that organised charity, if not informal care within families or neighbourhoods, would be negligible. However, as will be seen, the size of the problems facing the statutory services were such that voluntary provision, on both a formal and an informal basis, was soon recognised to be a vital supplement and complement to state welfare.

10.1 THE STATUTORY SERVICES

The period from 1945 to 1976 was, far more than for any other service, one of pioneering experiment for the personal social services with a watershed, equal in significance to the Beveridge Report in social insurance, being provided by the publication of the Seebohm Report in 1968. What was the nature of the service before 1968? Why was the Report commissioned and what did it recommend? How fully was it implemented? Finally, and most importantly, what effect did it have on the care of those in need?

The 1940s and 1950s were (with the exception of the actions of a few local authorities) a far from heroic period, in which the formulation and implementation of policy were impaired both by administrative and professional divisions and by the persistence of prewar attitudes and institutions. Responsibility for policy in Whitehall was divided between the Home Office (which oversaw the probation and the children's service), the Ministry of Health (which was concerned with the care of the elderly and the handicapped) and several other ministries such as Education. These divisions were replicated at a local level. After 1948 each local authority had to have a separate children's committee, but political responsibility for other welfare functions was divided between health and welfare committees (which might be separate or combined) and between the housing and education committees. These committees were served by separate departments and they in turn were staffed by different groups of professional workers, each with their own distinct traditions, assumptions and training. Such disunity inevitably impaired the coordination of policy in both central and local government. It also led, in the implementation of policy, to a multiplicity of visits to those in need by a succession of officials, each concerned with only one specialist aspect of care. This was not only extremely confusing and irritating for their clients, but also highly inefficient. There was much duplicated effort and effective care could even be impeded by professional rivalries and jealousies.[4]

The implementation of policy was further impaired by the widespread survival of prewar attitudes. In many areas the belief persisted that individual care for the needy should, and could, be provided only by families and charities.[5] Training was also disparaged by those who still considered success to depend solely upon a good rapport with people and an ability to 'take a firm line and to stand no nonsense'. Moralistic judgements and an overriding concern for social discipline also persisted – with, for example, some senior officials in the mid-1950s defining their principal role as being to 'ensure that people do as they are told and to make them realise they will be punished if they don't'.[6] Such attitudes inhibited the allocation of scarce resources to the personal social services: when held at a political level they left councillors unconvinced about the value of statutory provision; and, when held at an administrative level, they prevented the services from achieving any incontrovertible successes, without which political suspicions could not be allayed. As a result case-loads mounted and the opportunity for 'success' receded still further.

Before 1960 there were two further restrictions on the development of the personal social services, which were not self-inflicted. The first was a genuine lack of resources and, in particular, of building material and labour (which, as has been seen, were monopolised by the housing and school-building programmes). A rare area of agreement throughout the services was that prevention was better than cure and that 'community' was preferable to institutional care. However, the resources simply did not exist to provide the necessary facilities. One of the principal objectives behind the 1948 Children Act, for instance, had been to ensure that all children taken into care should be individually assessed in 'reception centres' before being transferred either to foster care or to a small, substitute 'family home'. However, few reception centres or family homes were built and so – in the absence of a sufficient number of foster parents – children had still to be confined to large residential institutions. The situation was similar with the elderly. Even where there was the political will, sufficient nursing homes and sheltered accommodation could not be built, with the result that over 37 000 elderly people were still living in former Poor Law buildings as late as 1960.[7]

The second external constraint was legislative. The Children Act was in many ways extremely progressive. By insisting on separate children's departments in each local authority it ensured the coordination of policy. It also revolutionised attitudes towards child care. As late as the 1930s the major objective of policy had been defined as 'to set to work and put out as apprentices all children whose parents are not . . . able to keep and maintain' them, but after 1948 it became the furtherance of each child's best interests and the proper development of their 'character and abilities'.[8] The Act failed, however, to make any provision for the *prevention* of neglect or abuse. Parental rights were scrupulously respected and material help, such as cash payments or rehousing, was explicitly forbidden until after the report of the Ingleby Committee in 1960 (Cmnd 1191) and the subsequent Children and Young Persons Act of 1963.

In sharp contrast the National Assistance Act (which dealt with most other people in need) was a 'feeble instrument', but its consequences were the same. It left local authorities with 'limited power and limited guidance to develop their services as they felt inclined or able';[9] and, given the long-standing weakness of local government which was noted in Chapter 4, most local authorities felt 'inclined or able' to do very little. Even where they were so motivated, however, they were prevented from providing the elderly with anything other than residential accommodation or home help. Other forms of domiciliary care, such as meals on wheels, were still implicitly regarded as the responsibility of voluntary care.

Consequently it was only in the 1960s that – in the words of Younghusband – 'curiosity broke free from static and moralistic assumptions'.[10] Such a breakthrough was much needed by government because it was becoming increasingly concerned about juvenile delinquency and the rising number of elderly people who (in the absence of any alternative to institutional care) threatened to impose an ever-heavier burden on the NHS and local rates. Somewhat conversely, it was also made possible by continuing economic growth and the satisfaction of the initial objectives of each of the other major welfare services. A limited amount of money was in consequence available for new initiatives.

Most importantly of all, however, the breakthrough was due to a fundamental change in the attitudes of both social workers and the general public. Moves towards greater professional unity were accelerated by the establishment in 1963 of a Standing Conference of Organisations of Social Workers and the wider acceptance of the 'generic' training course, launched by the London School of Economics in 1954, which provided a core of common knowledge to which individual specialisms might be related.[11] With a change of generation there was also a decline in moralistic assumptions and greater popular support for 'active citizenship' and community care. Scientific advance underpinned these changes in attitudes. The development of new drugs, for example, enabled the mentally ill to be treated safely within the community; and better care for Down's Syndrome children and victims of cerebral palsy was made possible by the realisation that they were, respectively, educable and not mentally handicapped. As a result of all these factors, real expenditure on the personal social services (which had remained largely static in the 1950s) doubled between 1960 and 1968, with the most notable initiatives being taken in the two services for which the Home Office was responsible – the probation and the children's services.

It was, indeed, pressure for reform within the probation service that led to the establishment of the Seebohm Committee in 1965 (although ironically the service was never to be formally incorporated within the personal social services). To minimise juvenile delinquency, the growing conviction was that each local authority should have a 'family service' which could identify aberrant behaviour at an early stage and treat it within the family. Hence the terms of reference for the committee were not only 'to review the organisation and responsibilities of the local authority personal social services in England and Wales' but also 'to consider what changes are desirable to secure an effective family service'.[12] However, many leading academics – including Titmuss – opposed such a development on the ground that it would create further artificial divisions within social work; and the Committee proved itself as adept as Beveridge himself in exceeding its terms of reference. As its report later admitted: 'We decided very early in our discussions that it would be impossible to restrict our work solely to the needs of two or even three generation families. We could only make sense of our task by considering also childless couples and individuals without any close relatives: in other words, everybody'.[13]

The Committee's eventual recommendations were relatively straightforward and this permitted their speedy translation into law – in the 1970 Local Authority Social Services Act – whilst the Labour government's more complex proposals for the reform of pensions, local government and the NHS foundered. There were three main proposals. The principal one was organisational. Each local authority should have not a family service but an enlarged social service department which could unite the various social work professions, coordinate field work (so that both the 'total requirements' of clients could be identified and the service made more 'accessible and comprehensible') and pack sufficient political weight to attract adequate resources.[14] These departments should be headed by directors whose appointments had initially to be approved by the secretary of state for health and social security. Their most challenging task (even above that of uniting their staff) would be to ensure that they did not become 'a self-contained unit but . . . part of a network of services within the community' coordinating, in particular, the work of volunteers. Finally, 'generic' training and further sustained research should also be encouraged. The former was required to further professional cooperation and eventually to ensure that 'as a general rule, and as far as possible, a family or individual in need of special care should be served by a single social worker'. The latter was urgently needed to guide policy at both central and local level. 'Social planning', as the Report admitted, 'is an illusion without adequate facts; and the adequacy of services mere speculation without evaluation.'

Despite their early implementation, these proposals nevertheless aroused at the time – and have aroused since – much controversy. The most substantial criticisms were that the Report provided no explicit justification of social work, identified no criteria by which priorities could be determined and gave no clear indication of where power should ultimately lie. It was unduly self-deprecatory, typically admitting at one stage:

> although we often do not know how to prevent social distress or where our efforts can best be concentrated it is right to strive towards prevention. . . . We must act on the best information and regard what is done as an experiment, in the broadest sense, from which to learn.[15]

Such modesty initially antagonised the Labour Cabinet, which had been looking for a strong lead. It also listed a large number of desirable objectives and clients' rights but neither estimated their cost nor considered the means, and the consequences, of raising potentially large sums of money. Consequently, as one critic has noted, 'expectations raced ahead of available resources and the Babel of universalist aspirations overwhelmed the language of priorities'.[16] Finally, its brief for the social service departments in their key role of 'community development' – to plan from the centre and simultaneously 'to ensure genuine consumer participation' – was dangerously reminiscent of the unresolved dilemmas in the 1940s concerning the implementation of 'democratic' economic planning (see Chapter 5.3). Given that the wishes of the planners and consumers must at times conflict, how were they to be reconciled?[17]

More detailed reservations were voiced by social workers. Administrative duplication was not eradicated because their responsibilities continued, perhaps inevitably, to overlap with other services – especially housing. Generalist skills also appeared to be favoured over specialist ones.[18] Moreover, in the sanctioning of social service directors, greater centralisation appeared to be favoured over local initiative, which was concurrently being promoted by the Royal Commission on Local Government. Most damning of all, however, was the means by which the Committee reached its conclusions. Like Beveridge in the 1940s, it determined the basis of its report (the creation of a unified social service department in each local authority) before it took any evidence. When evidence, however powerful, contradicted this assumption (as it did, for instance, over specialisation) it was rejected. Finally, no independent research or survey of clients' opinions was commissioned. Whatever the premium on the production of an early report, such behaviour was – to say the least – peculiar for a committee which placed such weight on the dispassionate analysis of scientific research and active popular participation.

Such shortcomings within the Report would have confounded the implementation of policy, but the initial work of the social service departments was further complicated by two administrative upheavals (in 1971 and again in 1974, following the reorganisation of local government). These upheavals did result in a greatly increased number of social workers but they were nevertheless damaging because, in the scramble for position and increased salaries, professional self-interest was seen to swamp clients' needs. The public reputation of the departments was also tarnished in two other ways. First, as a deliberate act of policy, resources were diverted to previously neglected areas from well-respected and proven services, such as child care. In consequence an increasing number of specialists resigned – some actually transferring to the voluntary sector where they felt there was greater scope for personal initiative. Secondly, amongst those who remained, an articulate minority (most notably in the Community Development Programme) were committed to the need 'to change society' and so brought social work into still greater political disrepute. Rather than heralding a new dawn, therefore, the implementation of the Seebohm Report appeared to confirm the worst fears of its critics – the social service departments were 'an expensive waste of time, which left much human misery unalleviated'.[19]

Were such fears justified by any deterioration in the standard of care for those in need? The most emotive groups of clients for the social service department were children of whom, by 1974, 91 300 were in care and a further quarter of a million under supervision.[20] Just as the classic welfare state had opened with a tragedy (the death in 1945 of Denis O'Neill at the hands of his foster parents) so it drew to a close with another (the murder in 1973 of Maria Colwell by her stepfather). There was, however, a significant difference. Whereas the first tragedy had preceded – and even accelerated – the passage of the pioneering Children Act, the latter succeeded the establishment of, and thereby discredited, the new social service departments. The quality of child care was therefore seen at the time to decline and this remains the verdict, although the 1969 Children and Young Persons Act (with its controversial attempt to minimise the conviction and maximise the care of 'delinquent' children) did to an extent maintain the momentum of postwar reform.[21]

In contrast the standard of care for the largest group of clients – the elderly – is generally agreed to have improved. Their needs had been traditionally neglected by government, other than through the payment of pensions. They had also tended to be neglected by social workers, in part because – with the near-certainty of constant deterioration and the absolute certainty of only one 'cure' – the work was regarded as thankless. After 1971, however, greater attention was turned to the 2.5 million people aged over 75 and a wider range of domiciliary care became mandatory for local authorities. Consequently, by 1975, the service had so improved that for every thousand people over 75, there were 17 home helps and 15 520 meals distributed annually.[22] Moreover, those polled in one of the few surveys of the elderly living outside residential care expressed considerable satisfaction with both their accommodation and the services provided.[23] Such satisfaction may have reflected low expectations. In addition the service unquestionably remained crisis-orientated and geared to the provision of physical help rather than to the combating of mental deterioration. Nevertheless the standard of care throughout the country as a whole undoubtedly rose.

The final significant group of clients for the social service

departments was the handicapped. They, like the elderly, had previously been neglected by government and the Seebohm Report had
commented in particular on the 'urgent need' for greater care of the
physically handicapped.[24] A start was made with the 1970 Chronically
Sick and Disabled Persons Act, which required all local authorities
to register the disabled and to publicise the services available to
them. A full range of benefits for the handicapped and their carers,
as noted in Chapter 6.4, was also introduced. However, neither the
Act itself nor the cash payments were properly funded and this led
to intense anger. Indeed money was so tight that in certain localities
sample surveys were substituted for registers. Consequently, there
are not even accurate national figures for the number of disabled at
this time. The mentally handicapped fared little better. The targets
in the 1971 programme, *Better Services for the Mentally Handicapped*, had not been realised by 1975 and the parallel document,
Better Services for the Mentally Ill, concluded in 1975 that 'by and
large the non-hospital resources are still minimal'.[25] Such a conclusion was particularly dispiriting because, as was seen in Chapter
7.3, community care for the mentally-ill had – with the support of
powerful ministers such as Enoch Powell – been one of the government's supposed priorities.

After the relative stagnation of the 1950s, therefore, the Seebohm
Report failed fully to capitalise upon the explosion of concern in the
1960s and thereby effect an immediate revolution in the personal
social services similar to that achieved in social insurance by the
Beveridge Report. This was perhaps inevitable because – despite its
traditions stretching back to the nineteenth century – social work
lacked the basic infrastructure, the tried methods and, above all,
the universal appeal of social security. The report did provide an
organisational framework within which the profession could unite
and it did try to encourage further research and the better evaluation
of policy. As in so many areas of welfare policy, however, organisation alone could not resolve conflict over fundamental values and
the allocation of scarce resources; and the basic research – by which
the better identification and treatment of given problems could alone
be translated permanently into effective prevention and cure – still
remained undone. The Report's own silence on resource allocation
also left the service highly vulnerable to the expenditure cuts which
followed devaluation in 1967 and, in particular, the oil crises of the
early 1970s. Disappointed expectations bred further disillusion and
this obscured the real, if rather mundane, achievement of the early

1970s: a general levelling up of standards in previously neglected areas of care.

10.2 VOLUNTARY PROVISION

The statutory services supported, and were in turn supported by, a range of non-statutory services which was so diverse as to defy adequate description, let alone accurate quantification.[26] There were three broad categories: 'informal' care provided by family or friends; voluntary care, provided either by unpaid workers within the statutory services or by formal non-profit-distributing organisations; and commercial services run for profit.

Commercial services had been widespread before 1945, especially in the fields of medical care and burial insurance; and, as has been seen, they were attacked in particular by Bevan and Beveridge on account of their potentially exploitative nature and their administrative inefficiency.[27] One of the initial objectives of the NHS and national insurance (with its statutory death grants) had consequently been their elimination but, as demonstrated by the retention of paybeds in NHS hospitals and the growth of occupational pensions, they continued after 1948 and were even subsidised through tax concessions (see Chapter 6.2). However, they were now concentrated on the welfare of the better-off; and before 1975 there were no serious attempts to privatise services targeted on those in real need. Until 1975, therefore, non-statutory care was not of a commercial but essentially of an informal or voluntary nature.

Informal care was the traditional source of 'care and tending' and after 1945 it continued to dwarf all other forms of provision. In the 1950s, for example, a PEP poll recorded that 'in times of trouble' one-half of mothers received help from relatives and a further one third from friends; and, in the 1980s, whilst the annual expenditure by charities and on the statutory personal social services was respectively £400 million and £3800 million, the value of services provided by informal care was an estimated £24 000 million.[28] Six million people, or 14 per cent of the adult population, were deemed to be 'carers'.

The continuation of informal care on such a scale confounded early postwar predictions that it would wither away as a result either of increased state welfare or of a range of social trends (such as the break-up of families, the increasing number of working women and the destruction of tightly-knit communities by housing redevelopment).[29] That it survived, and even expanded, was in part the consequence of greater need (the increasing number and longevity, for example, of the elderly). It was, however, also the consequence of improved statutory services, such as the NHS and the social security system, which enabled those in need – both physically and financially – to remain longer in their own or their relatives' homes. Amongst the most supportive services were those provided by local authorities, such as home helps; and this revealed the true role of the personal social services to be the support, and not the supplanting, of informal care.[30]

The continuation of voluntary care on a formal rather than an informal basis was initially more controversial, for both political and functional reasons. Politically, the belief of many (which the welfare state was considered to enshrine) was that social security, in its broadest sense, was an inalienable right which could be guaranteed only by a universal, democratically controlled service. 'How', enquired Bevan, 'can the state enter into a contract with a citizen to render a service through an autonomous body?'[31] Many Labour supporters and sympathisers were also hostile to working with organised volunteers because of their past record of social exclusivity and condescension towards manual workers. Functionally, as was well-illustrated by voluntary hospitals in the 1930s, private charity lacked the sufficient, regular income to deploy an adequate number of trained staff or to provide the comprehensive care (in terms of both need and geographical coverage) which the electorate was coming increasingly to expect. Moreover, the experience of evacuation had made the provision of standardised national services a wartime prerogative and this clearly could not be achieved by a patchwork of competing – and often excessively competitive – agencies.

In the 1960s, however, attitudes towards formal voluntary care began to change. Politically, the fundamental assumption of both 'reluctant collectivists' and the New Right had always been that voluntary care was an essential characteristic of a free and dynamic society. This now came to be expressed with increasing confidence. A similar view had been held by some on the right of the Labour Party even in the 1940s, when one minister (in a debate on Beveridge's *Voluntary Action*) had fully accepted that the 'voluntary spirit is the life-blood of democracy'.[32] Rather more surprisingly it also came to be endorsed by the traditional opponents of private charity on the left of the Party, who saw in the increasing number of self-

help and pressure groups an embodiment of participatory democracy
– or even a means of effective protest against the 'capitalist' state.[33]
From, therefore, two very different ideological perspectives a political consensus developed which was more favourable to formal voluntary care.

A similar uneasy consensus also formed over the practical virtues
of formal voluntary organisations, which were later summarised by
the independent Wolfenden Report as the ability to 'complement,
supplement, extend and influence' informal and statutory care.[34]
Since the war voluntary organisations had consistently comp-
lemented the other services in areas where there was either little
political sympathy or opportunity for self-help (such as the care of
vagrants and drug addicts) or where government action was considered to be inappropriate. Impartial information on individual
rights had, for example, been dispensed by Citizens' Advice Bureaux
(founded in 1938) and personal counselling provided by the Marriage
Guidance Council (founded in 1947) and the Samaritans (founded
in 1953).[35] They had also supplemented informal and statutory care
by making available additional money, manpower and facilities (such
as residential homes for children and the elderly).

What really excited reformers in the 1960s however was the way
in which voluntary care could 'extend and influence' state welfare.
Self-help groups, for example, by increasing public participation –
and above all increased participation by the 'consumers' of welfare
and their carers – identified 'real' needs, to which the state had
then to respond. Voluntary agencies were also able to pioneer new
techniques and methods of care because, unlike their official counterparts, they had not always to ensure equity or to consider possible
political objections. Finally, all those involved in the delivery of care
formed a body of informed opinion which could both champion
services (which might otherwise be overlooked politically) and
directly improve their quality. As the Wolfenden Committee noted,
for example, within each service 'the very presence of outsiders can
prevent possible abuses of power and stimulate higher standards of
provision'.[36] Equally powerfully, the Seebohm Report argued that 'a
certain level of mutual criticism between local authority and voluntary organisations may be essential if the needs of consumers are to
be met more effectively and they are to be protected from the
misuse of bureaucratic and professional power in either kind of
organisation'.

During this evolving consensus on its political acceptability and functional desirability, the least contentious type of formal care was the work of unpaid volunteers within the statutory services, such as that undertaken by the 'friends' of hospitals.[37] At the time the major advantage of this type of voluntary work was that it did not seem to challenge the legitimacy of the state services. Rather it strengthened those services by relieving professional staff of the more routine tasks, which they either lacked the time to perform or could perform only at the expense of more specialist work. The major disadvantage was that volunteers could, at times, be unduly moralistic or inefficient (or even both). Some attempt was made to remedy these weaknesses after 1969, once the independent Aves Report had suggested ways in which the recruitment, training and deployment of volunteers could be made more professional. Indeed the Seebohm Report recommended that the new social service departments should become the 'focal point' for their recruitment and by 1975, 140 volunteer bureaux had been established.[38]

The next least contentious form of voluntary care was that represented by self-help groups. Mutual aid had been the form of voluntary action favoured by Beveridge, but in the field of insurance the old nineteenth-century friendly society was already in terminal decline by the 1940s and any expansion of voluntary insurance thereafter was strictly on commercial lines. In the 1960s, however there emerged a different kind of self-help group, which provided practical care and support for its members. They ranged from highly localised and transient groups to the local branches of national organisations, serviced by highly professional coordinating committees. Foremost amongst the latter by 1975 were Age Concern, with its 11 000 local groups, and the Pre-School Playgroups' Association, with its 9400 groups catering for 360 000 children and actively involving three-quarters of their parents under the guidance of leaders, nine-tenths of whom were trained.[39]

The advantage of such self-help groups was that they displayed individual initiative which could act as a therapy for their members and provide cheap and adaptable services in addition to those funded by the state. Their disadvantages were the traditional ones that both the standard of their service and their geographical coverage could be extremely uneven. Even the Pre-School Playgroups' Association, for instance, was strongest in middle-class areas where the need for extra child support was least. They could also arouse political controversy. To some they represented a welcome rejection of dependency upon the state; to others they provided an equally welcome vehicle for protest through which greater resources could be extracted from government.

The most contentious form of voluntary care was that provided by long-established charities (such as Dr Barnardo's and the National Society for the Prevention of Cruelty to Children) or by organisations fully funded by government (such as the Women's Voluntary Service which had been founded in 1938 to meet civil defence needs and had been retained after 1945 as part of the contingency planning for future wars). The major charities had long realised that they lacked the resources to compete with, or to dominate, state welfare as they had done in the nineteenth century. Indeed they largely welcomed the lifting from them of the impossible task of relieving primary poverty. Their main concern now was that state welfare should not sink into a mechanical transfer of resources from the taxpayer to the beneficiary. Rather they hoped that, by giving the poor financial independence and by providing the taxpayer – and themselves – with the opportunity to pioneer new forms of care within the community, state welfare could promote 'active citizenship'. Nevertheless their continued presence was still resented by many, who saw them as a potential obstacle to the provision of universal and comprehensive services by the state and as a vehicle for the imposition of class, as opposed to democratic, values.

There was some justification for these fears in the 1950s because within organised charities, as within the local authority services themselves, old assumptions and habits died hard. Their services were, nevertheless, needed to make good the gaps left by the financial and legislative restrictions upon the statutory services. Hence the specialist needs of certain minority groups (most notably the blind and the deaf) continued to be largely catered for by private charities. The NSPCC undertook most of the preventive work in relation to the neglect and abuse of children. Moreover the WVS – in conjunction, and often in open rivalry, with other organisations such as the National Old People's Welfare Council (later Age Concern) and the Red Cross – provided domiciliary care for the elderly. Indeed, in the rapidly expanding area of care for the elderly, the vast majority of new initiatives (such as meals on wheels and day centres) were pioneered by voluntary organisations[40]

The 1950s, therefore, were not wholly bereft of new initiatives but, as the Wolfenden Committee admitted, it was essentially a period of 'marking time' for organised charity. In the 1960s, however, voluntary organisations played their full part in the explosion of 'creativity, ingenuity and energy'.[41] The traditional agencies were joined by new pressure groups, such as the Child Poverty Action Group and the Disabled Income Group (both founded in 1965) and Shelter (founded in 1966). New service-providing organisations were also established, most notably the National Association for the Care and Resettlement of Offenders which was established in 1966.[42] Equally significantly the assumptions and practices of the traditional agencies themselves were transformed. In 1969, for example, Dr Barnardo's changed its emphasis from residential homes to care within the family and increasingly concentrated upon the needs of problem children and the most deprived areas. Similarly the NSPCC, whose inspectorate had previously been predominantly male and recruited from the police force, was employing by the early 1970s an equal number of men and women as inspectors, who – in addition – were no longer expected to wear uniform.

Such a transformation in attitudes made the provision of care by voluntary agencies more widely acceptable; but what really accelerated their acceptance was a growing awareness of shortfalls within, and the shortcomings of, state provision. As with private charity in the nineteenth century, so with state welfare in the twentieth, it was finally recognised by experts and politicians alike that there were insufficient resources to meet all needs and that formal care could be both insensitive and inflexible. Hence the Seebohm Committee's enthusiasm for a 'mixed economy' of welfare, in which a constructive rivalry between voluntary and statutory care could offset the weakness inherent in both. Hence also the more open acceptance by both political parties of voluntary care both as a means of counteracting the relentless rise in public expenditure and as an antidote to the vested interests of professional social workers.

By the mid-1970s, therefore, formal voluntary care was almost wholly rehabilitated. A Voluntary Services Unit was established in the Home Office by the Conservative government in 1972 to coordinate policy and an increasing number of local authorities started to employ voluntary bodies on an agency basis to discharge their statutory responsibilities. The major national charities had also expanded so fast that by 1976 they were employing a permanent staff which was equivalent in size to one-fifth of that working for the social service departments and which was equally well-trained. Well recognised dangers, of course, attended this increasingly close identification of statutory and voluntary care. With income from private donations (despite tax concessions) falling by 1976 to under half of their revenue and with fee-income rising to 37 per cent, could the major charities maintain their independence and their ability to experiment?[43] Moreover, might not local government lose the first-hand experience it needed to monitor effectively the discharge of statutory duties by outside agencies on their behalf? That such questions were being asked, however, represented a remarkable transformation in the position of voluntary organisations, whose very future had seemed in the 1950s to be under serious threat.

10.3 CONCLUSION

During the 1960s and 1970s, as Younghusband has remarked, the statutory personal social services 'leapt from the margins to the centre' of welfare policy; and in the aftermath of the Seebohm Report, a more comprehensive and professionalised service was provided for all those in need.[44] However, the Seebohm Report was by no means above criticism. It might itself be taken as one of the leading examples of the besetting sin of the classic welfare state – professional self-interest. It also failed to dispel long-standing misgivings about the ability of social workers to discharge all the responsibilities which they sought to reserve for themselves. Indeed, many still remained to be convinced in the 1970s that social work was entitled to call itself a profession. Hard decisions over its key priorities continued to be evaded. No broad theoretical approach to training had been agreed. Moreover, the effectiveness of individual policies was being neither systematically monitored nor evaluated. For instance, it was not until 1976 that the first public statement of 'rational and systematic priorities throughout the health and personal social services' was published and even then it was exposed by the concurrent economic crisis to be unrealistically optimistic.[45] Even in the mid-1970s, therefore, the role and future of the social service departments were far from secure.

The statutory social services were dwarfed by the care provided for those in need by family and friends, but they in turn dwarfed their historical adversary: organised voluntary care. The latter, after a period of stagnation, was revitalised in the 1960s and its expansion was encouraged with increasing enthusiasm by successive governments who saw it to be both cost-effective and an antidote to bureaucratic self-interest. Beneath this apparent political consensus, however, there was a deep ideological divide which went to the heart of the unresolved dilemma concerning the proper role of government and the individual within the welfare state. Was increased voluntary provision to be welcomed as an expression of greater individual initiative which would reduce state intervention? Or was it to be seen as a vehicle of collective action which would ultimately expand, or even transform, the role of the state? Before 1975 this fundamental conflict was not openly addressed and voluntary care mainly expanded only at times when, and in places where, the statutory services themselves were strong. The critical battle, over what the state should not as well as could not do, was not to be fully joined until the 1980s.

10.4   FURTHER READING

The history of the personal social services is exhaustively covered in the encyclopaedic E. Younghusband, *Social Work in Britain, 1950 – 1975* (2 vols, 1978) and at the time of writing it is hoped that an equally informative survey of voluntary provision will be provided by G. Finlayson, *Citizens, State and Social Welfare in Britain, 1830 – 1989* (Oxford, 1992). The funding of both sectors is succinctly summarised in H. Glennerster, *Paying for Welfare* (1985) and his chapter, with M. Evandrou and J. Falkingham, in J. Hills (ed.), *The State of Welfare: the Welfare State in Britain since 1974* (Oxford, 1990) provides an equally authoritative summary of the state of the personal social services in 1975.

A full analysis of the Seebohm Report is provided in P. Hall, *Reforming the Welfare: the politics of change in the personal social services* (1976) whilst other primary material can be found in B. Watkin, *Documents on Health and Social Services: 1834 to the present day* (1975). Particular services are well covered by the draftsman of the Seebohm Report, R. A. Parker, in 'The gestation of reform: the Children Act 1948' which is included in P. Bean and S. MacPherson (eds.), *Approaches to Welfare* (1983); J. Packman, *The Child's Generation: child care policy from Curtis to Houghton* (1975); and by R. Means and R. Smith, *The Development of Welfare Services for Elderly People* (1985). A contemporary classic is P. Townsend, *The Family Life of Old People* (1957).

Three books which put the current role of voluntary provision in historical perspective are M. Brenton, *The Voluntary Sector in British Social Services* (1985), A. Ware (ed.), *Charities and Government*

(1989) and F. Prochaska, *The Voluntary Impulse: philanthropy in modern Britain* (1989). Changes in provision and attitudes may be observed by comparing M. Rooff, *Voluntary Societies and Social Policy* (1957), M. Morris, *Voluntary Work in the Welfare State* (1969) and S. Hatch, *Outside the State: voluntary organisations in three English towns* (1980).

11 The Achievement

The classic welfare state evolved in the 1940s for a variety of reasons. As has been seen, the least contentious of its initial objectives were functional: to make good 'the failure of the market to control avoidable ills' (which had become all too apparent in economic and social policy between the wars) and to standardise the quality of public services (which evacuation had exposed as unacceptably uneven).[1] Even so pragmatic an expansion in the role of government, however, had revolutionary consequences. All citizens were effectively guaranteed, for the first time in British history, an equal right to social security; and it was on the basis of such a guarantee – reflecting, so it was believed, a heightened sense of community during the war – that many came later to argue, more contentiously, that the essential objective of the welfare state was the creation of a more equal and altruistic society. Consequently the record of the classic welfare state has come conventionally to be judged by the twin criteria of efficiency and equality.

By such criteria, no definitive conclusion can be reached about the relative success or failure of the welfare state. This is in part because they are potentially in conflict. Universal welfare policies (designed to achieve equality) have, for example, been widely condemned as an extremely inefficient way of targeting help on those in genuine need. It is also in part because the very terms 'efficiency' and 'equality' are themselves highly contentious. Between 1945 and 1975, for instance, the concept of equality went – as it still does – to the heart of party conflict. This was recognised by Gaitskell, as leader of the Labour Party in 1956, when he wrote: 'If you don't feel strongly about equality, then I think it is very hard to be a genuine Socialist, and if we were to abandon this, then I think there would be very little left to distinguish us from the Tories.' By equality he meant the general levelling out not just of income and wealth but also of social status and power and to the contemporary Conservative Party this was indeed anathema. 'We are frankly opposed', admitted the One Nation group of backbenchers, 'to policies which make everybody more or more nearly equal.'[2] The Conservative Party, nevertheless, did openly champion another type of equality – equality of opportunity. There were and are, therefore, many conflicting definitions by which the record of the classic welfare state may be judged.

The actual measurement of efficiency and equality is equally contentious. Conventional microeconomic analysis can provide some measure for the efficiency of both individual policies and aggregate welfare expenditure (see Chapter 3.2). Within individual policies, however, certain 'inputs' and 'outputs', such as the cost of carers in the community or the benefit of humane care for a dying person, have no objective market price. They have to be assigned a value based on a purely subjective judgement. Similarly any measure of the efficiency of aggregate expenditure has ultimately to depend on its underlying political purpose. To maximise the economic return on investment in the NHS, for example, care would have to be concentrated on 'relievable need' amongst the existing and future workforce to the exclusion of the elderly, the disabled and the dying. Could any government openly espouse so callous a policy? If not, what alternative measures of efficiency are available? The irony is that, in the absence of any agreed alternative, the NHS will inevitably be judged on market criteria – although the very justification for its existence (like that of the welfare state as a whole) is the proven inability of the market, in given areas of welfare, to allocate scarce resources efficiently.

A further obstacle to a definitive assessment of the relative success or failure of the classic welfare state is the one posed by the counterfactual question: what would have happened had it not existed? Given the buoyancy of world markets and the breakthroughs in medical science, for example, would not 'full' employment and improved standards of health have been achieved anyway? Can their attainment, therefore, be legitimately accredited to the welfare state? Conversely, as the white papers *Employment Policy* and *Technical Education* respectively warned in 1944 and 1956, a prerequisite for a sustained improvement in the rate of economic growth or the reform of the education system was the positive support of employers, trade unions and the general public. Given the innate conservatism of postwar Britain, could any form of government have achieved more? The answer to such conceptual, technical and historical questions must ultimately depend on personal judgement; and it is the purpose of this chapter to provide the material upon which such judgements can be based.

11.1   EQUALITY

Equality is a highly controversial concept. It can mean equality of treatment by the state (as implicit in the Beveridge Report), equality of opportunity (as promoted by the 1944 Education Act and later by the Conservative Party) or equality of outcome (as increasingly desired in the 1960s by those seeking to reform the social security and education systems). Similarly it may refer to equality of social status, of power, or of income and wealth. It is by the third definition in each of these categories that equality can be most easily quantified, and consequently it is by the recorded figures for the distribution of income and wealth that the record of the welfare state has most frequently been judged. This has resulted in an effective challenge to the common postwar assumption that the welfare state progressively transferred resources from the rich to the poor.[3] As will be seen, however, this challenge is itself open to attack on both technical and conceptual, as well as political, grounds.

The most authoritative estimates of the distribution of personal income and wealth are summarised in Tables 11.1 and 11.2. They confirm the persistence of inequality throughout the period. Between 1949 and 1975–6, for example, the percentage of post-tax income enjoyed by the bottom 50 per cent of income earners only rose marginally from 26.5 per cent to 27.4 per cent; and, so far as can be judged, the proportion of personal wealth held by the bottom 80 per cent of wealth holders remained static until 1970, after which it increased to a mere 23 per cent. By contrast, in 1976 the top 1 per cent enjoyed respectively 5.5 times and 25 times the means for personal income and wealth.[4] The pace of recorded change was, therefore, remarkably slow and the Gini coefficient (a measure which denotes greater equality as it declines towards zero) actually increased for postwar income before 1964.

The conventional explanation for this lack of recorded redistribution is the decreasing progressiveness of both the taxation and the benefit systems. Soon after the war the Inland Revenue had acknowledged that the way in which government *raised* money could have as significant an influence on individual welfare as the way in which it was spent. As it advised the 1951–5 Royal Commission on the Taxation of Profits and Income:

Tax is no longer simply a matter of raising the revenue required with the minimum disturbance to private and public interests. The

Table 11.1 Distribution of personal income in Britain, 1949–1975/6

Per cent	1949	1954	1964	1970/1	1975/6
Before tax:					
Top 1	11.2	9.3	8.2	6.6	5.6
Top 10	33.2	30.1	29.1	27.5	25.8
Next 40	43.1	46.9	48.2	49.0	49.9
Bottom 50	23.7	22.0	22.7	23.5	24.3
Gini coefficient	41.1	40.3	39.9	38.5	36.6
After tax:					
Top 1	6.4	5.3	5.3	4.5	3.6
Top 10	27.1	25.3	25.9	23.9	22.3
Next 40	46.4	48.4	48.9	49.9	50.3
Bottom 50	26.5	26.3	25.2	26.1	27.4
Gini coefficient	35.5	35.8	36.6	33.9	31.5

Source: Cmnd 7595, Royal Commission on the Distribution of Income and Wealth, *Report* no. 7 (1979), table A.4.

Table 11.2 Distribution of personal wealth in England and Wales, 1950–76

Per cent	1950	1954	1964	1970	1976
Top 1	47.2	45.3	34.5	29.7	25.0
Top 5	74.3	71.8	58.6	53.6	46.0
Top 10	–	–	71.4	68.7	60.0
Top 20	–	–	84.3	84.5	77.0
Bottom 80	–	–	15.7	15.5	23.0

Source: Cmnd 7595, Royal Commission on the Distribution of Income and Wealth, *Report* no. 7 (1979), table 4.5.

social and economic effects of tax are so great and the possibility of the deliberate use of taxation to achieve social and economic ends so important that it is no longer possible to deal with tax purely, or in some instances even primarily, in a fiscal sense.[5]

However, under strict Treasury control, the Inland Revenue thereafter lacked both the resources and the will to monitor the redistributive effect of tax changes. Consequently there are no authoritative contemporary estimates, but undoubtedly they did become decreasingly progressive. The reasons were threefold: modifications to the overall tax structure, the changing incidence of individual taxes and the expansion of tax allowances.

Structurally there was a change in emphasis from the taxation of companies and personal wealth to the taxation of those on average, or below average, income. Between 1955 and 1964, for example, and again between 1965 and 1974 the percentage of total tax revenue raised from companies was halved;[6] and the effectiveness of death duties (which had initially been so swingeing that the heirs of a £2 million estate could expect to receive only £400 000) was steadily eroded by legal avoidance. To overcome such problems most other Western countries had an annual wealth tax, but although one was mooted in Britain in the 1960s it was never introduced. Admittedly, certain other reforms were achieved. For instance, a corporation and a capital gains tax were introduced in 1965 and 1969 respectively. Nevertheless, an increasingly large share of an increasingly large tax burden was borne by the ordinary taxpayer as government revenue became ever more heavily dependent on the proceeds of income tax (despite the Conservative Party's concern for the maintenance of incentive), employee's national insurance contributions (as the Treasury's own contribution plummeted) and indirect taxes (such as excise duty on beer and tobacco, and other sales taxes). The latter were particularly regressive and by the 1970s were responsible for the immediate return to the Treasury of approximately one-fifth of a subsistence pension.

The changing incidence of individual taxes is also well illustrated by the evolution of sales tax from the introduction of purchase tax in 1940 to its replacement by VAT in 1974. Initially the graduated purchase tax was extremely progressive, with the highest rates being levied on luxury items. As Britain grew more affluent, however, the tax was not adapted to changing consumption patterns and it became decreasingly progressive until, on Britain's entry into the EEC, it was eventually superseded by the flat rate VAT.[7] Of even greater significance, however, was the decreasing progressiveness of income tax. This occurred for two reasons: changes in the effective rate of tax and a lowering of the tax threshold (the level of income at which tax becomes payable). Between 1945 and 1975 the standard rate of tax fell from 50 per cent to 35 per cent and, owing to various exemptions, there was a similar fall in the effective rate of surtax levied on high incomes. By contrast the 'reduced' rates of tax were successively withdrawn in 1962, 1968 and 1969, with the result that after 1970 people with sufficient income only just to cross the tax threshold had to pay the full standard rate.[8]

These changes clearly disadvantaged the poor, and this trend was reinforced by inflation which, by increasing money wages and decreasing the value of tax allowances, drew an increasing number of people into the tax system (fiscal drag). The number of income tax payers accordingly rose between 1945 and 1975 from 13.5 million to 20.5 million. Far more serious, however, was the greater weight of taxation on the lower paid. In 1949, for example, the earnings of a married man with two children would have had to reach 103 per cent and 187 per cent of average earnings before he became liable to pay, respectively, tax and tax at the standard rate. In 1975 he became liable to tax at the full standard rate when his earnings reached only 44.6 per cent of the national average.[9]

This lowering of the tax threshold created two indefensible anomalies. First, people living below the poverty line became liable not just to indirect taxation but also to income tax. In 1976, for instance, the poverty line for a married man with two children was £43.50 when in work (the family income supplement level) or £35.05 when out of work (the supplementary benefit level). However, he crossed the tax threshold when his earned income reached £31.40. Money received from family income supplement had, therefore, to be passed back immediately to the Inland Revenue. Secondly, the low-paid were subject to the highest marginal rates of taxation (the percentage of income lost when increased earnings either take the low-paid across the tax threshold or make an existing taxpayer liable to a higher rate of tax). These anomalies lay at the root of the unemployment and poverty traps in the 1970s and led to the unavailing calls for a merger of the tax and benefits systems (see Chapter 6.3).

The final reason for the decreasing progressiveness of taxation was the expansion of tax allowances. They had been overlooked by Beveridge as a source of welfare, but their importance was highlighted in 1955 by Titmuss in his famous lecture on the 'social division of welfare'.[10] He distinguished between three kinds of welfare. State welfare involved the overt and audited transfer of resources to individuals either in kind (such as health care) or in cash (such as supplementary benefit). Fiscal and occupational welfare, by contrast, involved the covert and unrecorded transfer of resources to individuals and companies through the exemption from taxation of that proportion of income spent in an approved manner. Most notorious amongst the former was tax relief on mortgage interest payments (which, as was shown in Chapter 9.3, was costing government an estimated £770 million by 1975). Amongst the latter was the exemption of company contributions to occupational pensions (enjoyed by

11.4 million employees by the mid 1970s) and subsidies on company cars and meals (enjoyed by an estimated two-thirds of senior management).[11]

Fiscal and occupational welfare clearly favoured the rich over the poor and they were, in addition, socially divisive. On the one hand the rich could take maximum advantage of the allowances and simultaneously minimise the proportion of their income liable to higher rates of tax. This reduced the traditional tax-base and obliged government to raise money from those on below-average wages.[12] On the other hand salaried workers were favoured over wage earners and differences in social status were consolidated by subsidised cars and entertainment. Those able to afford a mortgage were also assisted in the purchase of a capital-appreciating asset which would have significant consequences for the later distribution of wealth. The irony was that as state-financed benefits for the well-off were increasingly sought (and financed), state-financed benefits to those in genuine need were increasingly stigmatised (and restricted).

If, as was generally recognised by the 1970s, taxation had become increasingly regressive, the assumption still persisted that the welfare state as a whole was progressive because resources were being transferred from the rich to the poor by the social services. This was certainly the conviction of certain Conservative ministers in 1955 when, following Titmuss's lecture, they asserted: 'substantial social service benefits were being enjoyed by a large number of people who, because of full employment, were not now in real need of them. The burden of providing these benefits fell most heavily on the middle classes.'[13] Twenty years later this remained the conviction of one of the members of the Royal Commission on the Distribution of Income and Wealth, Sir Henry Phelps Brown, who reflected that:

> Taxes as a whole fall on households almost proportionately throughout the top 70 per cent; only the bottom 30 per cent are in some measure spared, but even the poorest tenth contribute a fifth of their receipts. . . . Evidently, if the business of redistribution is to be done effectively, it is the provision of benefits that must do it.

This responsibility, he felt confident, was being discharged by welfare policy. In 1977, for example, he estimated that 'with remarkable consistency', the top 60 per cent of income earners received benefits from government worth £1000 per household, whereas the bottom 40 per cent received benefits worth up to twice that amount. As a result, 'the top 60 per cent gave up nearly 17 per cent of their original income to be transferred to their poorer neighbours'. This was 'markedly progressive'.

Such confidence in the redistributive effects of welfare policy, however, is by no means universal. Cash benefits, it is agreed, do benefit the lower-paid disproportionately although, with the introduction of universalism in 1948, the better-off did enjoy some remarkable windfalls. For example, a man aged 55 in 1948, whose income had previously been sufficiently high to exempt him from compulsory insurance, became entitled in 1958 to a pension worth ten times the actuarial value of his contributions (see Chapter 6.3). The redistributive effects of benefits in kind are, however less certain; and many have argued that they disproportionately favour the better-off. In health care, for example, the middle class in general have easier access to better facilities (owing in part to the historical location of hospitals and the preference of GPs for middle-class areas), enjoy longer periods of consultation with doctors (owing to greater articulacy and perhaps social affinity) and receive more advanced and expensive treatment. Similarly in education a disproportionate number of middle-class children stay on after the end of compulsory schooling to enjoy high-cost further education. In 1958, for example, Abel-Smith calculated that the cost of three years' university education was equivalent to that of ten years' primary and secondary schooling; and he used this as one of his justifications for the charge that 'the major beneficiaries of postwar changes in the social services have been the middle classes'.[14] Twenty-five years later this verdict was endorsed by Le Grand who calculated that, in the late 1970s, the top 20 per cent of income earners were receiving educational and health services worth respectively three times and two-fifths as much as those received by the bottom 20 per cent. 'Almost all public expenditure on the social services in Britain', he concluded, 'benefits the better-off to a greater extent than the poor'.[15]

Such irreconcilable differences, it had been hoped in the 1960s, could be resolved by a new measure of redistribution. First a household's original income was to be calculated; then its disposable income (original income, plus direct cash benefits, minus direct taxes); and then its final income (disposable income, plus benefits in kind, minus indirect taxes). The initial findings of such calculations confirmed that a redistribution of income did occur over an individual's lifetime (enforced thrift) and within economic classes from, say, small to large families and from the healthy to the sick ('contingency' redistribution). It also greatly qualified contemporary assumptions about the extent of vertical redistribution from rich to poor (class redistribution).[16] These calculations were, however, open to many technical reservations. For example, they were based on the Family Expenditure Survey, whose potential unrepresentativeness has already been noted in relation to the 'rediscovery' of poverty (see Chapter 6.2). The Survey also provided no evidence for the redistributive effects of many taxes (such as employer's national insurance contributions) and much public expenditure (especially that on public goods). The take-up of benefits in kind was also based on hypothetical assumptions. In short, such calculations cannot as yet provide conclusive evidence about the redistributive effects of the social services.

It is not, however, just the calculations concerning particular welfare services that are bedevilled by such technical problems. Problems of a similar magnitude – especially when allied to serious conceptual and political reservations – bring into question the very validity of the assumption that the recorded figures for the distribution of income and wealth are an accurate measure of the degree of equality achieved by the classic welfare state. These problems were authoritatively summarised by the 1975–9 Royal Commission on the Distribution of Income and Wealth.

Estimates of wealth, for example, in the absence of an annual wealth tax have conventionally come to be calculated by the so-called 'estate multiplier method'.[17] In any one given year the number of people dying and leaving an estate liable to taxation is taken to be a representative sample of all wealth holders in the country, and through the application to each group of a special multiplier (sensitive to differences of gender, age, wealth and locality) an aggregate figure is finally determined. The potential weaknesses are many. Half the number of people dying in any one year, for instance, do not have any taxable wealth. They do nevertheless own some wealth. Indeed the Royal Commission calculated that the average personal wealth of the 20 million who would otherwise have been excluded from the calculations in 1972 was some £700. How is this wealth to be incorporated? Even more seriously the calculations ignore altogether certain types of wealth, such as the right to social security – which must be regarded as a form of wealth because, before the welfare state, such security was enjoyed only by the wealthy. Had pension rights alone been included in the conventional calculations for 1972, so the Royal Commission estimated, the share of the bottom 80 per cent of wealth holders would have jumped from 19.2 per cent to 40.7 per cent. Finally, the figures are based on individuals and are not age-specific, and therefore ignore the wealth which many enjoy but do not actually own (such as the spouse or dependants of a rich individual) and the wealth which a young person may eventually acquire. Significantly each of these weaknesses greatly exaggerates the degree of inequality that is recorded.

The calculations for the distribution of income are dogged by similar problems. They exclude, for example, non-monetary income (such as perks); they too are based on individuals rather than households (and therefore record a large number of 'non-earning' housewives); and, being on an annual basis, they overlook the irregularity of many people's income (such as the royalties for impoverished authors of books on the welfare state which have taken too long to write).[18] All such conventions again tend to exaggerate the degree of inequality. Furthermore, because other countries work to different assumptions, they also make accurate international comparisons extremely difficult.

There are in addition further technical problems when either national or international data come to be expressed. One of the most effective forms of presentation is the Lorenz curve, which plots the proportion of personal income held by any given percentage of the population (see Figure 11.1). Total parity is represented by the diagonal line and the Gini coefficient is the measure of the area between the curve and the diagonal. As income equality increases, so the curve will shift to the left towards the diagonal and the Gini coefficient will move nearer to zero. One of the weaknesses of this measure, however, is revealed by the graph. In 1964 the distribution of income as measured by the Gini coefficient was more equal in Britain than in West Germany, but this result was only achieved because of a more equal spread of income amongst the top 50 per cent and despite the income of the bottom 50 per cent being further from the average than in Germany. In other words the Gini coefficient (as used in Table 11.1) is an aggregate measure and may obscure the actual experience of different income groups.

Such technical problems reduce the confidence with which the recorded figures of income and wealth can be used to analyse the degree of equality achieved by the classic welfare state. So should their conceptual limitations. Are income and wealth after all an appropriate proxy for welfare? An individual's income may fall for

Source: A.B. Atkinson (ed.), *Wealth, Income and Inequality* (1980) p. 41.

Figure 11.1   Lorenz curve for UK and West Germany, 1964

any number of reasons. A woman may give up work to have, and look after, a child. Students may consciously forego higher earnings in order to gain qualifications which may maximise their future earnings – or even their personal fulfilment. In a distinctly different case (of course) an individual's preference might be for leisure over work. In each of these cases a reduction in income is more likely to represent not a decrease but a real increase in individual welfare. How accurately, therefore, can figures for the mere distribution of income and wealth reflect the distribution of individual welfare?

The recorded figures for income and wealth can, moreover, reveal little about the equally important (albeit less easily quantifiable) issue of the distribution of power and social status; and it is here that the achievements of the classic welfare state may have been most seriously underestimated. The very acceptance by the wartime Coalition of the bulk of the Beveridge Report represented, after all, a marked shift in effective power from Conservative ministers and Treasury officials. The subsequent attainment of full employment has also been described as a 'transfer of power . . . on a momentous scale' not just on the shop-floor (where scarcity of labour gave trade unions greater bargaining power) but also in political decision-making (as corporatist negotiations and bodies, such as the National

Economic Development Council, began to proliferate).[19] Moreover, it has even been argued that industrial management underwent a 'psychological revolution' as a result of the increased power of both the state and the consumer and, in consequence, became increasingly sensitive to public, as opposed to short-term private, welfare. Likewise, in relation to social status, the Beveridge Report – by guaranteeing social security to all – effectively recognised, in T. H. Marshall's words, everyone's 'equal social worth'.[20] The establishment of universal services such as the NHS reinforced this breakthrough, as did other less-publicised reforms such as legal aid (which after 1949 gave to those previously unable to pay lawyers' fees a real – as opposed to a merely theoretical – equality before the law). Finally, full employment and consequent affluence reduced the visible differences between the members of each social class and, as has been seen in Chapter 4.5, led to the creation of a largely classless culture. For many, therefore, the classic welfare state represented a significant redistribution of power and status.

So optimistic a summary of egalitarian trends between 1945 and 1975 might with some justice be challenged. Given the gradual reimposition of Treasury control after 1947, was there really a permanent redistribution of administrative power? In corporatist bodies was there any constructive sharing of power or did the three sides merely talk past, rather than to, each other? For instance, the TUC may have succeeded in securing a third reduced rate of income tax in 1952; but five years later it was rebuffed when the suggestion was made that taxation should be deliberately used to equalise income and thereby forestall demands for wage increases arising from full employment. This was ultimately adjudged by the Conservative government, as its proponents had feared, to be a 'weak-kneed concession to sectional pressure' not a statesman-like attempt to revive wartime social solidarity in the face of an equally serious national threat – inflation.[21] Welfare policy itself could, moreover, even accentuate inequalities of power. As a result of fiscal concessions and the contracting-out clauses of successive insurance acts, for example, powerful pension trusts were created which gave the old financial élite an even stronger control over investment and thus the future structure of the economy. This was far removed from the purpose behind Beveridge's advocacy of voluntary insurance, which had been to encourage 'socially desirable forms of thrift' and diffuse power through small, democratically controlled friendly societies.[22]

Likewise, as has been seen, fiscal and occupational welfare could underpin and even exaggerate status differences.

The redistribution by the classic welfare state of both social status and power is nevertheless undeniable. Freedom from fear of absolute poverty and universal access to services such as the NHS and secondary education dramatically improved the quality of the lives of many. So too did the comparative job security and, above all, the sustained rise in average living standards that emanated from full employment. Tables for the distribution of income can say nothing about *actual* living standards; nor do they reveal how apparently insignificant sums amongst the lowest paid can have – in terms of genuine social and political independence – a significance far beyond their monetary value.[23] As for the distribution of power, the record of the classic welfare state has only to be set beside that of the 1930s and the years after 1975 for its relative achievement to be apparent.

The most powerful objections to an over-mechanistic use of the figures for the redistribution of income and wealth are, however, political. First, it should be remembered, greater equality of outcome was not an initial objective of the welfare state. Secondly, it was never an objective of the Conservative Party. Indeed reluctant collectivists would have regarded it as a disincentive to initiative and thus a threat not only to efficiency but also to the maximisation of individual welfare. Finally, even amongst the supporters of the Labour Party – as Gaitskell had to admit – equality of outcome had 'no great popular appeal'.[24] Skilled workers, with their defence of wage differentials, were amongst its leading opponents and, in order partly to assuage them, Crossman had sharply to remind those campaigning for greater equality in the 1960s: 'in wartime, it is just possible to persuade democratic communities to accept the fair shares of a national siege economy and even to welcome the drastic restrictions and heavy sacrifices involved. But this readiness to share is only "for the duration".' Unskilled workers also stubbornly remained interested more 'in the inequality of horses than the equality of men'. On what grounds, therefore, is equality of outcome the predominant criterion by which the record of the classic welfare state should be judged?

The conclusion to be drawn from all these complex technical, conceptual and political issues is comparatively straight-forward. Clearly it is right that evidence about the tax system and the recorded distribution of income and wealth should be used to correct contemporary assumptions about the progressive nature of the classic welfare state. Equally it is wrong to judge its record too precipitately on that evidence alone.

11.2 EFFICIENCY

The efficiency with which the classic welfare state promoted individual welfare is similarly the subject of technical and ideological dispute. Technically, a standard framework for the measurement of efficiency has been developed whereby the input into a given service (such as the NHS) can be measured against intermediate outputs (such as the number of doctors or hospital beds) and final outputs or 'outcomes' (such as improvements to health standards). Such a framework cannot, however, resolve the problem of pricing which has already been identified. It also raises problems of its own. In the measurement of intermediate outputs, for example, does a decrease in the relative number of hospital beds (as happened after 1945) necessarily represent a decline in health care if the amount of infectious disease requiring hospital treatment declines or if there is a faster 'throughput' of hospital patients as a result of better management? Similarly, in the measurement of final output, does increased morbidity, as measured by absence from work through sickness (which again occurred after 1945), signify a real fall in health standards or merely a change in the 'perceived level of acceptable well-being'?[25] More fundamentally, are final outcomes a fair test of efficiency? Given the general antipathy to any infringement of personal liberty, for example, do they not depend more on individual decisions (in relation, for instance, to personal fitness and diet) than on government policy?

Ideological differences over the efficiency of the classic welfare state are also irreconcilable. As demonstrated in Chapter 2.2, the basic belief of democratic socialists is that the state is better able to promote welfare than the market because the latter inherently undersupplies public goods, is unable sufficiently to measure externalities and, in the real world, is handicapped by both imperfect knowledge and imperfect competition. In contrast the fundamental assumption of the New Right is that state provision – as opposed to state financing – of welfare services is inherently inefficient. Centralised bureaucracies cannot be as efficient as the market in the collection of information, the synchronising of demand with supply, or in their response to changing consumer demand. Despite the assumptions of Beveridge and Keynes, bureaucrats are not disinterested. Nor, despite the theories of Weber, are they rational and expert. Following the mass unemployment and poverty of the 1930s, the former set of beliefs was widespread and underpinned the rapid expansion of state welfare in the 1940s. In the 1960s and 1970s, however, the latter attracted increasing support. Was the misallocation of resources by the classic welfare state really so bad as to justify this dramatic reversal of political and public opinion?

As earlier chapters have shown, there are abundant examples of inefficiency within each sector of postwar welfare policy. Technical deficiencies frequently caused demand management to be destabilising. The initial administrative and power structure of the NHS discouraged the cost-effective allocation of resources and later attempts at reorganisation, most notably in 1974, were little short of disastrous. Education expansion in the 1960s failed to remedy Britain's traditional weakness in technical education and was so precipitate as to provoke a serious backlash. In the slum-clearance programme, the encouragement of prefabricated high-rise buildings solved short-term problems only at incalculable long-term cost. In the personal social services, the Maria Colwell tragedy became a focus for justified fears about the efficiency of the reforms following the Seebohm Report. Finally, and perhaps most seriously of all, there developed – as a result of the increasingly regressive tax system and the expansion of means-tested benefits – so complex a system of social security that by the mid 1970s officials were deliberately discouraging take-up in order to make their workloads tolerable. In a symbolic expression of growing public disillusion with the welfare state as a whole, the Department of Health and Social Security became popularly known as the Department of Stealth and Total Obscurity.

Does such a catalogue of inefficiency, however, accurately reflect the true record of the classic welfare state? There were, after all, specific examples of the efficient exercise of state power, such as the Macmillan housing drive and the Ministry of Education's school-building programme in the early 1950s. There was also, by any historic standard, a dramatic and sustained improvement in the rate of economic growth, the absolute living standards of the poor, the standards of health, the attainment of educational qualifications, the quality of housing and the care of traditionally neglected groups, such as the disabled. These achievements are far superior to those of the 1930s (when, for instance, the reality of poverty and mass unemployment was accentuated by the absence of a comprehensive

health and social security system) and in the period after 1975 (when
there was a return to mass unemployment and escalating inequality).
Above all, however, the very structure of the classic welfare state
was conducive to greater efficiency. As has been seen, in specific
areas of policy state welfare is inherently more efficient than the
market. In relation to the NHS for example, it has been argued that:

> on the demand side, decisions are made by doctors, thus alleviating
> the effects of consumer ignorance; the problems of private
> insurance are resolved by abandoning the insurance principle even
> as a fiction; and treatment is largely free at the point of use, which
> reduces the externality problem and goes a long way towards
> eliminating the influence of income distribution on consumption.
> On the supply side, doctors are not as a rule paid a fee for service,
> thus removing the financial incentive to oversupply.[26]

Thus the comparatively low cost of the NHS (in which administration
typically consumed only 5 per cent of the total expenditure compared
to 8–9 per cent in the insurance-based system of France and Germany
and 15–20 per cent in the market-led system of the USA) was something of which to be proud rather than ashamed. It represented a
more efficient use of resources and in particular a tighter control
over the expenditure of health professionals by the state than could
have been exercised by the market. Moreover, these advantages
were not confined to the NHS, for as another commentator has
retrospectively concluded:

> With a public service presence in education and housing high by
> international standards, the postwar British welfare state was able
> from the start to pursue its objectives and force political control.[27]

Despite particular instances of inefficiency, therefore, the classic
welfare state represented a general gain in efficiency in relation to
both expenditure and the distribution of resources.

Such relative achievements, it might be argued, were largely the
consequence of a fortuitous combination of uniquely favourable factors. The reverse, however, is equally true because the classic welfare
state was in many respects the victim of historical circumstance.
Between 1945 and 1975, for example, neither political party provided
a sufficiently bold or principled lead. The civil service was tardy in
developing the requisite administrative structures and management
techniques. Moreover professionals within the social services,

especially after the mid 1960s, failed sufficiently to curb their self-interest.

Such real-world failings, of course, cannot be used to excuse the relative failures of the welfare state. It was, after all, the essential logic behind the increase in state welfare that resources could be allocated more efficiently by the joint decisions of politicians, civil servants and professionals rather than by the decisions of individual consumers and producers freely expressed through the market. Nevertheless those responsible for both the formulation and implementation of policy were responsive to, and thereby seriously constrained by, a conservative public opinion which – as affluence increased – grew ever more interested in short-term rights as opposed to long-term duties. Indeed if there was one area in which the classic welfare state did incontrovertibly perform inefficiently – especially in relation to the period after 1975 – it was in the way in which its energy (and taxpayers' money) was used to nurture a supportive welfare, as opposed to an entrepreneurial, culture.

11.3 CONCLUSION

By definition, any conclusion about the achievement of the classic welfare state must be a personal one. A balanced review of the evidence, however, can explode certain myths. Just as for prewar, so for postwar Britain the empirical evidence simply does not exist, for example, to support the frequent assertion that state welfare, by undermining the will to work, undermined economic efficiency.[28] It can also prevent the isolation of a single aspect of welfare policy and its subsequent unfavourable comparison to foreign practice without due reference to the overall structure of welfare policy and Britain's distinct cultural heritage. Most important of all, however, it can ensure that judgements are made not against some abstract ideal but against a balanced assessment of what, at any given time in the past, was realistically possible. In the 1960s, as Enoch Powell recognised, professionals within the welfare services compared their situation to an unattainable ideal and as a result, despite historically high standards of salaries and resources, developed a vested interest in the denigration of the classic welfare state.[29] There is no reason why historians should fall into the same trap.

11.4 FURTHER READING

The concern for equity was particularly acute in the 1970s and the Royal Commission on the Distribution of Income and Wealth (1974–9) pioneered much valuable theoretical and empirical research. The reports which are of most relevance to the classic welfare state are no. 1 (Cmnd 6171, 1975), no. 5 (Cmnd 6999, 1977) and no. 7 (Cmnd 7595, 1979). One of its members, Sir Henry Phelps Brown, has subsequently written the wide-ranging *Egalitarianism and the Generation of Inequality* (Oxford, 1988), whilst an extremely valuable collection of readings is A. B. Atkinson (ed.), *Wealth, Income and Equality* (Oxford, 1980). Three more popular works are A. B. Atkinson, *Unequal Shares: wealth in Britain* (Harmondsworth, 1974), F. Field *et al.*, *To Him Who Hath: a study of poverty and taxation* (Harmondsworth, 1977) and W. D. Rubinstein, *Wealth and Inequality in Britain* (1986). A stimulating new approach to the measurement of equality, albeit applied to Britain in the late 1970s, is presented in J. Le Grand, *The Strategy of Equality: redistribution and the social services* (1982).

Books on individual welfare policies provide the best evidence of the relative efficiency of the welfare state. A good theoretical introduction is contained within N. Barr, *The Economics of the Welfare State* (1987), whereas the short classic work is A. M. Okun, *Equality and Efficiency: the big tradeoff* (Washington, USA, 1975). A useful empirical overview is R. Parry, 'UK', in P. Flora (ed.), *Growth to Limits: the Western European Welfare States since World War II* (de Gruyter, Berlin, 1986).

Part III

The Welfare State since 1976

12 The Welfare State under Threat

Despite its historic achievements, the welfare state in Britain – as elsewhere – was widely perceived to be in crisis in the mid 1970s. The immediate causes were economic. The quadrupling of oil prices after the Arab-Israeli war of October 1973 so accelerated the underlying annual rate of inflation that it reached the unprecedented level of 27 per cent in 1975. Simultaneously, a slowing down in the rate of economic growth and an actual fall in GDP in both 1974 and 1975 pushed the number of people out of work, for the first time since the war, to above one million and to a peak in 1976 of 1.5 million. This denied the government the rising revenue it required to meet increasing demands for welfare – not least from the unemployed themselves – and, in the ensuing 'fiscal crisis', forced it to borrow more heavily. This in turn undermined foreign confidence in sterling so that the value of the pound fell, for the first time ever, below $2 and then plunged rapidly to $1.55. The response of successive governments to these disasters was to implement a series of public expenditure cuts; to impose, after November 1975, cash limits on all expenditure programmes in order to ensure the effectiveness of the cuts; and finally, in the battle against inflation, to abandon reflationary demand management and thus the postwar commitment to 'full' employment. The 'party', as Anthony Crosland warned local government in 1975, was truly over.[1]

The perceived crisis within the welfare state, however, went far deeper than the need to respond to these short-term economic shocks. First, there was mounting criticism of the postwar record of government in relation to the identification and resolution of Britain's underlying economic and social weaknesses. Serious doubts had initially been voiced about its effectiveness in the early 1960s, when Britain's relatively low rate of economic growth had belatedly been recognised; and the subsequent management of the economy (culminating in 1975 with an unprecedented combination of high unemployment and inflation) together with the varied record of welfare reform (as described in Part II) had done little to assuage them. Consequently each area of policy came under critical scrutiny – as, for example, in education when Callaghan as Labour prime

301

minister voiced concern about falling standards in his speech at
Ruskin College, Oxford in 1976. Indeed, in 1981 one of his senior
ministers was to go so far as to dismiss the whole of the previous 25
years as a total failure.[2]

More seriously there was a growing conviction that the welfare
state was not only failing to resolve, but institutionally could not
resolve, Britain's problems. Since the establishment of the NEDC
in 1962 the management of the economy had become increasingly
corporatist, but neither side of industry appeared capable of resolving the structural problems of the economy (as predicted by Beveridge in *Full Employment in a Free Society*) or of instilling into their
members the 'responsible' attitudes for which the 1944 *Employment
Policy* white paper had called. The failure of successive prices and
incomes policies, and the imposition of a three-day working week
during the winter of 1973/4, were taken as proof of the ultimate
sterility of all corporatist deals. Likewise in social policy civil servants
appeared – for the first time since the early nineteenth century – to
be more interested in their own welfare than that of the public whom
they were supposed to be serving. Between 1966 and 1976 their
numbers exploded from 2.1 million to 3.3 million (so that they
accounted for 13.2 per cent as opposed to 8.3 per cent of the total
workforce); and the reorganisation of the NHS in 1974 and the
implementation of the Seebohm Report became notorious for the
unseemly scramble for positions and pay which they inspired.[3]

Most seriously of all, however, there was a mounting popular and
intellectual challenge to the very legitimacy of the welfare state. The
popular challenge came first from some of its supposed beneficiaries:
students who, as in the rest of the Western world, responded to
increased educational opportunities in the late 1960s by challenging
not only the educational system but also government itself; workers
in the nationalised industries and particularly the miners, who helped
to bring down the Heath government in 1974; and other public sector
employees whose increasing resort to strike 'action' culminated in
the 1978/9 'winter of discontent' which brought down the Labour
government. Once government had failed decisively to suppress such
militancy, disaffection then began to become more general. A growing conviction about Britain's 'ungovernability' reinforced existing
popular fears about escalating crime, terrorism in Northern Ireland
and even the future of such key institutions as the family (threatened
by a rising incidence of divorce and illegitimacy) and the nation
(following Britain's entry into the EEC and the 1979 referenda on

NEDC : National Economic Developmen
      Centre.

TUC + CBI

devolution for Scotland and Wales). To many, in brief, the welfare state was beginning to appear not only politically but also morally bankrupt.

Such disaffection encouraged the reopening of many questions which had lain dormant since the war about the proper role of the state in society. In other words an increasing number of people – in the jargon of the time – began to 'think the unthinkable'. In the 1960s, admittedly, the 'universalists' within the Labour Party had questioned the egalitarian and even the democratic nature of the welfare state, but in the 1970s the questions asked were far more fundamental. The Marxist critique of the welfare state as a vehicle for capital accumulation and the legitimisation of capitalist society was vigorously refined (see Chapter 2.3.2). It underpinned much of the contemporary shop-floor militancy and especially the demand for workers' control, which was later espoused within the Labour Party by Tony Benn. Of even greater significance was the growing assertiveness of the New Right, especially after the establishment of the Centre for Policy Studies by Keith Joseph in June 1974 and the succession of Margaret Thatcher to the leadership of the Conservative Party in the following February. Its particular targets were Keynesian demand management, the 'collusive conspiracy' of corporatism and bureaucracy; and its proffered remedies were a greater control of money supply (monetarism), the 'discipline' of the market and the 'rolling back of the frontiers of the state' (see Chapter 2.2.3).

The New Right was also inherently hostile to state welfare. Just as in economic policy governments should act like housewives and balance their budgets so, it was argued, in social policy they should behave like responsible parents and strive for the ultimate independence of those temporarily dependent upon them. If those in need were encouraged to look passively to the state for help, they would be denied the invigorating experience of self-help and of family or community care. Moreover, in the country at large, enterprise would be discouraged by higher taxation. As Keith Joseph concluded during his conversion to 'true' Conservatism:

> The only lasting help we can give to the poor is helping them to help themselves; to do the opposite, to create more dependence, is to destroy them morally, whilst throwing an unfair burden on society.[4]

In other words the New Right was committed – just like the Poor

old Liberal Values

Law reformers of the 1830s – to a 'remoralising' of society. Herein lay the basis of the calls for a return to 'Victorian values'.

In the 1970s, therefore, the welfare state came under political, popular and philosophical attack. Were the perceived weaknesses merely superficial? Could they have been remedied by better management? Alternatively were they deep-seated and did they require, for their solution, a radical reordering of political objectives, institutional arrangements and popular attitudes? If the latter, was there a viable alternative to the 'classic' welfare state other than a 'forced march' back to the policies of the 1930s – from which the welfare state had been deliberately designed as an escape?[5] The purpose of this chapter is to examine, in the light of these questions, the development both of welfare policy as a whole and of individual policies.

12.1   THE POLITICAL AND ECONOMIC CONTEXT

After 1976 welfare policy was subject first to an 'economic hurricane' and then to an 'ideological blizzard'.[6] As has been seen, the newly-elected Labour government in 1974 inherited (like its predecessors in 1945 and 1964) a severe economic crisis; and its response was a series of economic cuts culminating, after negotiations with the International Monetary Fund, in the reduction of public expenditure by £2 billion in 1976. This action temporarily restored the economy but not its own political fortunes and it was defeated in the election of May 1979. The incoming Conservative government inherited and then, through its monetarist policies, intensified a new economic crisis; but by 1982 a revival was under way and between 1984 and 1989 Britain enjoyed a faster rate of growth than any other European country. This was a remarkable reversal of fortune which not only transformed the reputation of the country abroad but also established that of the Prime Minister.[7] It did not lead to any abatement in the attack on the underlying assumptions and broader objectives of the classic welfare state. To what extent, however, were the social services (for which the term 'welfare state' had surreptitiously been reduced to a synonym) adversely affected?

The initial priority of the Labour government had been not to resolve the immediate economic crisis but *inter alia* to give substance to its 'social contract' with the unions and thereby increase public expenditure. It was consequently a time when, in the words of one despairing Treasury minister, the government seemed to spend money 'we did not have'.[8] Only in June 1975 were the economic problems finally addressed with the introduction of a voluntary prices and incomes policy and the imposition of both cuts in and cash limits on public expenditure.

After Harold Wilson's surprise resignation in March 1976 the same policies were maintained by the new prime minister, Callaghan; but he soon came under attack not only from foreign bankers but also from activists within his own party (who wished to see the realisation of the 'fundamental and irreversible' shift in wealth promised by the 1973 *Labour's Programme for Britain* and implicit in the social contract). The bankers were quickly assuaged by the terms of the IMF loan and the revival of the economy. Balance of payments problems were relieved by the coming on stream of North Sea oil; unemployment began to decline; and by early 1978 inflation had fallen below 10 per cent, whilst the value of the pound had risen above $2. Callaghan began to exude confidence and to taunt the Conservatives – who had after all been out of power for all but four of the previous fourteen years – that Labour were the 'natural party of government'. The welfare state, it seemed, might not be exposed after all to the 'ideological blizzard' of the New Right.

Such confidence was, however, misplaced. The government had lost its overall majority as a result of byelection defeats and defections and had had to make a pact with the Liberal Party in order to survive.[9] More seriously, party activists were growing increasingly aggrieved that, as a result of successive expenditure cuts, wage restraint under the social contract was not being matched by compensatory increases in the 'social' wage. Eventually, in October 1978, a Labour conference rejected a further extension of the government's prices and incomes policy and, despite their affiliation to the Labour Party, the public sector unions launched their 'winter of discontent', which destroyed not only the incomes policy but also the government's chances of re-election.

This power struggle within the Labour Party had been fermenting since various changes to its constitution in the early 1970s and, with serious consequences for welfare policy, it continued to divide the Party in the early 1980s. Many moderate members left to form the Social Democratic Party in 1981 and, after Callaghan's resignation, Michael Foot's leadership became hopelessly compromised. Consequently there was no effective opposition to the Conservative Party's doctrinaire monetarism when it was at its most vulnerable in the

early 1980s; and more especially there was no effective opposition
to the Conservatives in the 1983 election. As has been remarked:
'amongst the forces ranged against the most unpopular leader of
modern times' at that election, there was 'a party that was unelect-
able' and 'a grouping that was destined merely to be a vote splitter.
No radical visionary . . . could have asked for more.'[10]

This assessment clearly identifies a major paradox in the eleven
years of Conservative government after 1979. After 1974 at least,
Margaret Thatcher certainly had a fundamentalist, radical vision. She
was also driven forward by immense energy and an 'inner conviction'
based on her certainty about what was 'right' and 'wrong'.[11] This
meant that, even during the initial crisis into which her monetarist
policies plunged the economy, she was not tempted – as had been
her Conservative predecessor – to perform a 'U turn'. To Edward
Heath the 'free market' policies which he had adopted between 1970
and 1972 were a means to an end and so expendable if they failed
to achieve their objectives. To Margaret Thatcher, however, monetarism with its eternal truths (such as the iniquity of spending more
than one earned) was an end in itself. Nevertheless she remained,
for a populist leader, remarkably unpopular both amongst the general public and, despite many ministerial reshuffles, within her own
Cabinet; and this inevitably placed a major constraint on what she
could achieve. It was not until her third election victory in 1987 that
such opposition was effectively quashed and even then, after three
years, she was to be forced by party pressure to resign.

The eleven years of Conservative government after 1979 were
divided into three administrations. During the first, between 1979
and 1983, the boldest decision in domestic policy was the introduction of the medium term financial strategy (MTFS) in the 1980 budget
(which laid down clear targets for monetary growth and thus for
public expenditure) and its retention during the subsequent economic
collapse. Between 1979 and 1981 industrial output and capital GDP
fell respectively by 16 per cent and 5 per cent, whilst inflation peaked
at 22 per cent and unemployment rose inexorably towards three
million. Despite such disasters, however, the Prime Minister warned
the 1980 Conservative Party conference in one of her few memor-
able, if manufactured, phrases that 'the lady's not for turning' and
the economic damage was duly exacerbated by a deflationary budget
in 1981. A Cabinet rebellion did then forestall a further proposed
round of cuts and a more moderate budget was secured for 1982.
Moreover a report from the Central Policy Review Staff recommend-

ing a radical restructuring of welfare policy (including the ending of
public funding for higher education and the replacement of the
NHS by private health insurance) was speedily withdrawn. Margaret
Thatcher's prestige, however, was little impaired because in the
meantime the Falklands War had been fought and won.

Margaret Thatcher's second term of office between 1983 and 1987
was, despite a parliamentary majority of over 140, surprisingly
restrained. In the mid-term there was even talk of consolidation – a
concept which had affronted her fellow radical, Aneurin Bevan, in
the late 1940s – and the notion gained credence that 'the Thatcher
style was to talk radical and to act conservative'.[12] The government
even appeared accident prone, with Michael Heseltine's resignation
in January 1986 over the Westland affair portraying the Prime Minister in the unaccustomed light of being unpatriotic, incompetent and
dishonest. There were, however, notable successes. The miners were
decisively beaten in March 1985 after a year-long strike and high-
spending metropolitan counties, in particular the Greater London
Council, were abolished. More positively there were continuing cuts
in income tax (so that the top rate eventually fell from 83 per cent
to 40 per cent and the standard rate from 33 per cent to 25 per cent);
an escalation in the sale of council houses; and the successful launch
of a shareholder democracy with the privatisation of British Telecom
and British Gas.[13]

The first set of achievements reassured those who had been concerned for law and order in the 1970s. The last created a distinct
client group that was likely in the near future to vote Conservative.
The true key to another sweeping election victory in 1987 (albeit
with a reduced majority) was, however, the sustained recovery of the
economy. This did not represent a triumph of the MTFS, officially
abandoned as impractical by its architect (Nigel Lawson) in the 1985
budget. Nor did it signify a decrease in unemployment which, despite
a doctoring of the figures, remained relentlessly over three million.[14]
Rather it reflected the successful containment of inflation below 5
per cent and the achievement of a high and sustained rate of growth
which increased real earnings by 14 per cent.

A third election victory revived Margaret Thatcher's radicalism
and led her to 'vow vengeance' on those who had earlier obliged her
to abandon strict monetarism and forego favoured reforms (such as
the privatisation of water and the cancellation, after the 1986 social
security review, of state earnings-related pensions).[15] A determined
attempt, as will be seen, was at last made radically to restructure

social policy. Even more significant, however, was the introduction
of a new system of local government finance – the community charge
or 'poll tax'. It proved to be extremely unpopular and, combined
with renewed anger at Margaret Thatcher's 'presidential' style, her
negativism towards the EEC and, above all, a deterioration of the
economy, it provided a pretext for her enforced resignation in November 1990.

How effectively was the classic welfare state destroyed by this
sequence of political and economic events? Clearly a major casualty was
the postwar commitment to 'full' employment, which Beveridge had
seen as essential for both the maximisation of individual welfare and
the solvency of social insurance. As Callaghan's speech to the 1976
Labour Party conference illustrated, the monetarist contention was
accepted that there was a 'natural' rate of unemployment and that,
in the long term, counter-cyclical Keynesian demand management
could reduce it only by injecting ever larger doses of inflation into
the economy.[16] The role of government consequently reverted to what
it had been before the war: the discharge of an indirect responsibility
for employment, through the provision of the conditions in which
the market should work with optimum efficiency. This entailed cuts
in both direct taxation and public expenditure and the removal of
impediments to competition imposed in particular by trade unions.

As the abandonment of the MTFS in 1975 showed, doctrinaire
monetarism proved in the real world to be as impractical as Keynesian demand management (see Chapter 5.2). The use of fiscal policy
to manipulate demand also remained irresistible, especially before
elections. After 1979, however, the government showed no undue
urgency to reduce the level of unemployment below 5 per cent,
which had been Keynes's own definition of 'full' employment. The
public appeared uninterested and electoral success was no longer
adjudged to depend on the eradication of unemployment. This was
a true measure of the cultural and political revolution that was
effected in the 1980s.

Another major casualty was corporatism. The 1974–9 Labour
governments, with their social contract and their ambition to restructure industry through the National Enterprise Board, remained committed to corporatism. Margaret Thatcher, however, was rigidly
opposed to trade unions (whose legal immunities were curtailed by
a succession of employment acts) and corporatist industrialists (to
whom she immeasurably preferred self-made entrepreneurs in the
mould of Lord King, who successfully rationalised British Airways).

After the 1983 election the TUC tried to rebuild bridges with a policy of 'new realism', thereby vindicating the 'softly, softly' approach of Margaret Thatcher's first secretary of state for employment and her principal opponent within Cabinet (James Prior). Reconciliation, however, was deliberately sabotaged by the banning of trade unions in a government defence establishment (GCHQ); and having crossed the threshold of Number 10 Downing Street only three times since 1979, the TUC general secretary (Len Murray) opted for early retirement. Disaffected industrialists likewise launched a despairing attack on government in 1985.[17]

It was not, moreover, only the leading participants in corporatism who felt the full force of Margaret Thatcher's disdain, but also those institutions which broadly supported it. The higher civil service was a principal victim. Its cause was not noticeably advanced when, at a party in 1980 designed to achieve greater understanding, the Prime Minister issued a clarion call for a coordinated attack on 'the system'. 'But', replied the head of the civil service rather lamely, 'we are the system.'[18] The Church of England was another victim, especially after the publication in 1985 of *Faith in the City*, which questioned the government's emphasis on individual rather than collective responsibility. So too was academia, which was denied its accustomed privileged access via royal commissions to policymaking. It replied with sustained attacks on government policy (such as the letter signed by 364 economists in opposition to the 1981 budget strategy) and token gestures of defiance (such as the denial to Margaret Thatcher of an honorary Oxford degree).

Throughout this carnage, however, the social services remained largely unscathed. Successive cuts in central and local budgets did reduce projected increases in social expenditure and, as will be seen, there were certain structural changes within each of the major services. Nevertheless, despite the explicit commitment of Conservative governments after 1979 to 'roll back' the state, to end the 'dependency culture' and to reduce taxation, public expenditure steadily rose in real terms between 1979–80 and 1986–7 (see Table 12.1). Expenditure on social policy likewise only suffered one real cut (in 1977–8), remained especially buoyant in election years under the Conservatives and, as a percentage of GDP, did not fall until the end of the 1980s (see Table 12.2). Moreover, to finance this expenditure, the percentage of GDP taken in both direct and indirect taxation rose from 33.5 per cent in 1978 to 36.7 per cent ten years later.[19]

Table 12.1 Public expenditure, 1974/5–1989/90

Fiscal year	£bn	Percentage of GDP
1974–5	180.2	48.75
1975–6	180.2	49.25
1976–7	175.8	46.75
1977–8	167.1	43.25
1978–9	175.4	44.00
1979–80	181.1	44.00
1980–1	184.3	46.50
1981–2	187.0	47.25
1982–3	192.0	47.50
1983–4	195.3	46.50
1984–5	200.3	46.75
1985–6	200.2	45.00
1986–7	203.2	44.00
1987–8	203.1	41.75
1988–9	198.2	39.25
1989–90	203.0	39.50

£ at 1989–90 prices.
Source: A. Cairncross, *The British Economy since 1945* (1992) pp. 205, 246.

Table 12.2 Social expenditure, 1975/6–1987/8

	Year on year change (%)	Percentage of GDP
1975–6	2.5	25.4
1976–7	3.7	25.5
1977–8	−4.7	23.7
1978–9	1.5	23.2
1979–80	1.1	22.9
1980–1	1.0	24.0
1981–2	1.1	24.3
1982–3	1.9	24.2
1983–4	4.9	24.5
1984–5	1.2	24.3
1985–6	1.4	23.7
1986–7	4.4	24.0
1987–8	1.0	23.2

£ at 1987–8 prices.
Source: J. Hills (ed.), *The State of Welfare* (Oxford, 1990) p. 339.

There were certain technical reasons for this resilience. As Beveridge had warned, the abandonment of 'full' employment sharply raised the cost of unemployment insurance and other related benefits. By increasing unemployment, therefore, monetarism ironically increased social expenditure. Demographically the number of elderly people requiring pensions and expensive health care increased (although admittedly the number of school children did fall in the 1980s by 10 per cent). In a period of inflation, the relative price of labour-intensive services also rose disproportionately. Expenditure, in other words, had to increase simply to maintain a given level of service. Public expenditure also did not decline automatically in line with the withdrawal of the state provision of services (as the increased cost of tax subsidies to owner-occupiers demonstrates).

The principal safeguard of social expenditure, however, was not technical factors such as these but the political and popular support it enjoyed. Within Cabinet, as has been seen with the defeat of the 1982 Central Policy Review Staff Report, radical reform was successfully thwarted until the 1987 election. This was due in part to the Prime Minister's lack of overall strategy. As has been argued, for instance:

She was not by habit a strategist. Although she had pictures in her mind of the kind of place she would like Britain to become . . . the common experience of those who worked closely with her was that she did not instinctively relate present problems to some grand conceptual plan. Because of her . . . emphatic way of speaking, she was usually depicted otherwise. . . . But this was propaganda, put about not so much by her staff as by an adoring press.[20]

In the main, however, it was due to the rather more positive reasons that a majority of Cabinet ministers considered the existing social services to be functionally necessary, relatively efficient and, above all, electorally popular.

This latter perception was undoubtedly correct, if the evidence of public polls is to be believed. Popular support for the social services was by no means uncritical. Measures designed purely to engineer greater equality of income and wealth were widely opposed. So too were certain cash benefits for 'undeserving' minority groups. Hence the renewed attack upon 'scroungers'. Support for the 'core' services, however, was not restricted to the poor or to those civil servants responsible for their implementation but was expressed openly by relatively prosperous non-manual and manual workers in the private sector who, on New Right assumptions, should have vigorously opposed the 'dependency culture'. Nevertheless they were only too aware of the true market cost of catering for ill-health and old age.

In addition they were themselves often dependent on state subsidies for the attainment of a desired level of housing (through tax relief on mortgage repayments) and of higher education (through state funding of tuition fees and maintenance grants).[21] For selfish if not for altruistic reasons, therefore, there was – in relation to social as opposed to economic policy – widespread popular resistance and even a rejection of Margaret Thatcher's attempted cultural revolution.

Rejection is certainly the impression to be gained from the opinion polls. Between 1979 and 1989, for instance, Gallup consistently enquired whether tax cuts or improved government services were favoured, on the explicit understanding that the former would mean a cut in services and the latter an increase in taxation. In 1979 opinion was equally divided; but by 1989 only 10 per cent favoured tax cuts while 73 per cent supported improved services. Gallup also registered between 1983 and 1987 a 20–25 per cent swing away from the belief that 'people should help themselves' and that 'government should be tough, not caring'. Similarly in 1989 MORI found that only 30 per cent of those polled favoured 'private interest and the free market', whilst 62 per cent favoured 'the public interest and a managed economy'. Surprisingly opinion amongst Conservative voters was equally divided. Many qualifications can of course be made about such findings.[22] Above all changes over time may reflect attitudes to a changing *status quo*. Nevertheless the findings do suggest that in relation to the 'core' social services, the emphatic opinion of the general public (as of a majority of Cabinet ministers) was that – to quote Margaret Thatcher wholly out of context – there was no alternative.

Despite the abandonment of both the commitment to 'full' employment and corporatism, therefore, the social services remained relatively unscathed after 1976. Under the continuing influence of egalitarian thinking, they were initially earmarked for expansion by the Labour government but such plans were hit hard by the world economic crisis. There was then a gradual relaxation in the later 1970s, but any hope of significant expansion was again hit hard by the blunt weapon of monetarist policy. Owing to widespread political and popular support, however, it was not until after the 1987 election that either their expenditure or their structure was seriously threatened by the sharper weapon of radical reform. Consequently it was not until 1988 that 'the dog finally barked'; and, even then, the muzzle was partially replaced by 1990.[23] This is the broad chronological framework in which the evolution of individual policies needs to be studied.

12.2 SOCIAL SECURITY AND THE PERSONAL SOCIAL SERVICES

The two services which were potentially most vulnerable to radical economies and reform after 1976 were ironically the first and the last to be restructured under the classic welfare state – social security and the personal social services. The former was by far the most expensive and the latter the fastest growing social service. Both were perceived essentially as services for the poor and therefore not only responsible for the growth of a 'dependency culture' but also (with the exception of pensions) of little direct appeal to the middle-class electorate.[24] Worse still the personal social services were the responsibility of local government, with which Conservative governments were embattled throughout the 1980s. Despite these potential handicaps, however, neither service suffered radical cuts or restructuring. Real expenditure on both increased and such reforms as were implemented, at least until the late 1980s, were largely incremental.

The enhancement of social security had been one of the principal objectives of the Labour government during the initial implementation of the social contract and, as a result, three major acts had been passed in 1975: the Social Security Act (which placed all social insurance contributions on an earnings-related basis); the Social Security Pensions Act (which guaranteed everyone an inflation-proof flat-rate and earnings-related pension);[25] and the Child Benefit Act (which gave mothers an inflation-proof weekly payment for all their children, with additional benefits for single parents). The common purpose behind this legislation was to reduce means-testing and to redistribute resources in favour of the low-paid and women. For instance the provision of earnings-related benefits, guaranteed to retain their real value over time, maintained Beveridge's principle – albeit in a manner of which he would have disapproved – that all claimants should have an automatic right to an 'adequate' benefit. The terms of the pensions legislation (such as the determination of the size of the earnings-related pension by the best, not the last, twenty years of a worker's earnings) favoured those who – like manual workers – enjoyed their peak earnings when young. Women were also credited with contributions for the years they spent at home bringing up children and, above all, benefited from the increased value of child benefit – financed by the withdrawal of child tax allowances, which had been enjoyed largely by fathers.

These reforms were, however, expensive and after the economic crisis of 1976 both Labour and Conservative governments fought to contain their immediate and future cost. Under Labour the principal objective was to husband scarce resources not just through administrative economies but also through the better 'targeting' of those in greatest need. This, as the 1978 Supplementary Benefit Review made explicit, meant a renewed emphasis on means-tested benefits.[26] Under the Conservatives there was an additional political motivation. High public expenditure, as has been seen, was deemed to divert resources from investment and to foster a 'dependency culture', thereby compounding the very problem it was supposed to resolve. On both economic and social grounds, therefore, reductions in social security expenditure were thought to be justified.

Conservative governments followed three strategies. The first was to reduce the real value of benefits and the number of people claiming them. Thus earnings-related supplements to all short-term benefits (such as unemployment pay) which had been introduced in 1966 were cancelled – although earnings-related *contributions* were retained. The annual uprating of benefit in line with inflation was frozen (as with child benefit in 1981 and 1988), delayed or only partially implemented. Thus between 1981 and 1983 short-term benefits were increased by 5 per cent less than prices; and this reduction was only restored once benefits had been made taxable (thereby saving £400 million per annum on unemployment insurance alone, a sum equivalent to one-tenth of payments to the unemployed).[27] Stricter rules for eligibility and tighter administration also excluded many from benefits. In a reversion to the 1930s, for example, a 'genuinely seeking work' test was introduced in unemployment pay which particularly affected part-time women workers; and in 1984 a major inquiry was launched into social security abuse, which once again largely failed to substantiate its authors' preconceptions.

The Conservatives' second strategy was to simplify and thereby reduce the cost of administration. The most significant change here was the requirement, after 1982 and 1986 respectively, that employers – rather than civil servants – should administer the payment of sickness and maternity benefit, with the costs being recovered via deductions from their tax and national insurance returns. Finally, increased emphasis was put on the targeting of those in need by the replacement of universal by selective benefits. Hence one of the main consequences of the much-vaunted Fowler review of social security between 1984 and 1986 was the withdrawal of certain universal benefits (such as maternity and death grants), the freezing of others (such as child benefit) and the concentration of resources on a streamlined system of means-tested benefits.[28] Supplementary benefit was renamed 'income support'; all its 'additional' payments, by which benefit had been adjusted to the particular needs of individuals or groups of claimants, were replaced by grants from a 'social fund', 70 per cent of which had to be repaid by claimants; and the various subsidies to meet housing costs and family need were consolidated, respectively, into a single system of 'housing benefit' and 'family credit'. To underline the change in the relative importance of universal and selective benefit, the Treasury's social insurance contributions (which had been intended by Beveridge to match employer and employee's contributions) was also withdrawn in 1988.

The number of reforms was therefore considerable, but their combined impact was neither radical nor – when judged by their declared intentions – very effective. Far more radical innovations had at various times been promised. For example, it had been intended fully to privatise sickness pay and pensions, to withdraw child benefit (to concentrate help on the poorest families) and to merge the benefits and tax system (as unsuccessfully attempted in the early 1970s). However, owing to the refusal of private insurance companies to bear the risks, only the administration of sickness pay was privatised and state earnings-related pensions (SERPS) were only reduced in value, not abolished. Likewise, because of public pressure, child benefit was frozen rather than withdrawn and a benefit-tax merger was rejected once again as impractical.[29]

In the absence of a consistent (let alone a radical) strategy, the danger then arose that the reforms would be incremental and conflict either with each other or with other government policies. Measures designed to secure long-term economies indeed incurred immediate short-term costs. The change to means-tested benefits, for example, greatly increased the cost of administration;[30] and the transfer between 1986 and 1989 of about one million contributors from SERPS to more generous private pension schemes greatly reduced government income (thereby providing perhaps a final argument against the total abolition of SERPS). Other alterations to social security regulations in the early 1980s also had the unintended consequence of greatly increasing the cost to central government of subsidies to housing and the residential care of the elderly. Such services had previously been financed by local government but, again unintentionally, rate-capping had restricted its ability to pay. The Fowler review was hastily instructed to repair the damage but its new housing benefit produced a further anomaly by rapidly decreasing ('tapering') benefit in line with increasing income and thereby condemning over half a million claimants to the 'poverty trap'.[31] Consequently instead of increasing the incentive to work – which was the fundamental purpose behind all Conservative reforms – it actually discouraged certain claimants from earning more.

The most surprising anomaly, however, was that after so many years of retrenchment real expenditure on social security continued to rise from an estimated £33.5 billion in 1978–9 to £46.6 billion in 1987–8 (at 1987–8 prices). This was not due to an increasing number of claimants because, had the number remained constant, there would still have been an estimated rise from £29.6 billion to £34.2 billion. Moreover each category of claimant – even the unemployed – enjoyed an increase in the absolute rate of their benefit, although in terms of rising earnings its relative value did fall.[32] The Conservatives could, and duly did, claim much credit for this achievement; but it was an accidental, rather than a deliberate, result of policy.

The development of the personal social services followed a remarkably similar course. Real expenditure upon them had doubled between 1970 and 1974 and national targets were for the first time set for each major client group.[33] After the 1976 economic crisis, however, this momentum was lost and the targets abandoned. Real expenditure fell so sharply in 1977–8 that it did not regain its former level until 1980–1 and there were further falls in 1981–2 and 1987–8. The cuts in the early 1980s would in fact have been even more severe had government policy been fully implemented, but many local authorities opted to maintain the existing level of their services out of their own resources. This contributed directly to the growing confrontation between central and local government which resulted in 1975 in the rate-capping of 'overspending' councils.

The initial motivation behind the cuts was largely economic but, as with social security, the Conservative government after 1979 added an extra political dimension. Ministers, like many members of the public, doubted the competence and were highly suspicious of the underlying motives of social workers. Was their principal purpose to encourage their clients to conform to or to challenge conventional norms? Were they seeking ultimately to support or to supplant the family and voluntary care? The fundamentalist Conservative instinct, moreover, was that the proper agency for the care of the individual was not state bureaucracy but the family and charitable organisations (supported perhaps by tax concessions) and the market (with its greater sensitivity, in theory at least, to changing individual needs). Consequently, community care – the apparently common objective of the 1970s and 1980s – underwent a subtle change of meaning after 1979. It came to mean the release of patients from large national institutions (such as geriatric hospitals) not into residential accommodation (provided in the community) but into non-residential accommodation (supplied largely by families).[34]

When such fundamentalist instincts came to be translated into practical legislation, however, anomalies began to appear. In the increasingly sensitive area of child abuse for example, was the family to be treated as the solution or the cause of the problem? When parents were wrongly accused (as in the 1987 Cleveland 'scandal') government and the public were quick to condemn social workers; and the major consolidating piece of legislation, the 1989 Children Act, clearly placed the 'prime responsibility' for the care of children on parents rather than on local government. However, when a tragedy did occur (as in 1985 with Jasmine Beckford), both government and the public were equally swift to criticise the failure of social workers to take the initiative and act more quickly. The disadvantages – as opposed to the advantages – of placing ultimate power and legal responsibility on the parent had yet to be resolved.

A similar anomaly arose in community care. If care was to be increasingly provided by families and voluntary agencies, who in each locality should actively encourage and coordinate it? The Seebohm Report had clearly assigned this responsibility to the social service department of each local authority; and this, surprisingly, was also the solution advanced in 1988 by Sir Roy Griffith after he had been asked to provide a radical blueprint for reform. He proposed that, within a three-year rolling programme, social service departments should be given both the power and the resources to assess the needs of individual clients, to design the appropriate 'care arrangements' and to oversee their implementation.[35]

Such a proposal, reluctantly incorporated into the 1990 National Health Service and Community Care Bill, directly contradicted past practice whereby rate-capping had deliberately restricted the political and financial independence of local government. It also reversed a surreptitious (if not wholly intended), drift to centralisation whereby, as has been seen, a tenth of the services previously funded by local government had come by the late 1980s to be financed by supplementary benefit (which itself was directly controlled from Whitehall).[36] The Griffith proposals did nevertheless mark one major break with the 1970s. Local government was no longer to provide but to supervise and coordinate community care (whilst itself being rigorously monitored by the Audit Commission and a new, central Social Service Inspectorate). This in turn acknowledged the most radical development in service provision during the 1980s: the dramatic increase in the number of elderly people cared for not by public institutions or by their families, but in private residential accommodation.[37]

The final anomaly was that, despite rate-capping and certain temporary falls, real expenditure on the personal social services – as on social security – rose in the 1980s. Taking 1973–4 as a base year, it has been estimated that real expenditure in 1987–8 was 40 percentage points higher than in 1977–8 (and 15 points higher than the peak of expenditure in 1976–7); and in relative terms it also rose from 0.8 per cent to 1 per cent of GDP.[38] All client groups and especially the victims of traditional neglect, the mentally ill and the handicapped, were beneficiaries. As with social security, however, these broad conclusions need some qualification. The personal social services were extremely labour-intensive and, at a time of rapidly accelerating labour costs, considerable increases in real expenditure were needed simply to maintain a given level of service. Moreover, it had been calculated in the 1970s that, as a result of demographic change, the personal social services needed to increase their annual expenditure by 2 per cent in order to satisfy rising need. Increasing real expenditure, therefore, may have achieved little more than the protection of existing standards of care.

For both social security and the personal social services, as has been seen, it is extremely difficult to establish statistical evidence by which to measure the input and output, let alone the final outcome, of policy. There are many omissions (such as the number of abused children), inconsistencies (especially in the measurement over time of the unemployed) and imponderables (such as the differential rate of inflation in each service). On the best evidence available, however, it is clear that the radical ideals of both the 1970s and the 1980s were disappointed. After 1976 there were neither the economic resources nor the popular support to realise the egalitarian objectives implicit in the social contract. As Donnison has remarked:

Already in the late seventies, Labour Ministers were aware that, although they could never satisfy their critics in the poverty lobbies, the government's aims were generally far more progressive than the electorate's. Their Conservative successors more brutally recognised that the lobby was electorally naked . . . 'They are not leaders of a movement', said a Cabinet Minister . . . soon after the election. 'They're crickets in the field.'[39]

The radical intentions of the Conservatives themselves, however, were also to be frustrated. Public opinion remained hostile to significant cuts, either out of altruism or self-interest; the market was reluctant to bear unknown risks; and there remained serious doubts about the administrative practicality of many proposed reforms.

This frustration of policy objectives, together with a constant flow of administrative adjustments, tended to demoralise those who were responsible for policy. This in turn threatened the quality of service. Nevertheless, the standard of provision would appear to have been maintained and, despite all the later rhetoric, increases in real expenditure were achieved. Against such positive achievements, however, must be placed a fall in the relative living standards of many claimants and the continuing struggle of the personal social services to expand in line with increases in both need and public expectations.

12.3 HEALTH CARE, EDUCATION AND HOUSING

The fortunes of the three remaining 'core' social services appeared to diverge dramatically after 1976. The NHS continued to command widespread public support and consequently an increasing share of the real resources. Education, with its emphasis on vocational training, suffered a slight cut in its budget in the late 1970s but then enjoyed stable, and eventually increased, funding. In contrast, housing – administered largely by local government and with council tenants as its most visible beneficiaries – suffered such severe cuts that between 1976–7 and 1988–9 its expenditure collapsed from 4.1 per cent to 1.6 per cent of GDP.[40]

These differences were, however, more apparent than real and were, in the main, the product of public accounting conventions and differential demographic change. In fact the development of each policy (with certain exceptions in the case of housing) followed a broadly similar pattern. There was an initial period of enhanced expenditure followed by one in which plans for expansion had to be shelved. Thereafter each service experienced incremental change until, after 1987, it became the focus for more radical reform. As with community care, the objective of this reform was not so much a reduction in real expenditure but a separation of public finance from public provision – the creation, in other words, of 'quasi-markets' in which reduced bureaucracy and increased consumer choice would ensure greater efficiency.

The mid 1970s were a period of innovation within the NHS. In order to remedy the organisational weaknesses of the old tripartite system its administration was thoroughly overhauled; and a determined attempt was made both to withdraw Bevan's enforced concessions to the medical profession (such as pay-beds) and to correct, at last, the geographical inequalities inherited from the war. The new administrative structure was the first to be attacked. The Royal Commission on the National Health Service, reporting in 1979, generally endorsed the underlying principles of the service, but condemned its excessive bureaucracy.[41] As a result, one administrative tier (the Area Health Authorities) was abolished in 1982 and responsibility for the planning and implementation of policy was entrusted to Regional and District Health Authorities alone. At the same time both of these authorities were required to appoint general managers to balance medical with administrative criteria in the allocation of scarce resources.

This requirement proved to be a prelude to a far more extensive reorganisation in 1990. Then, in an attempt to create an even more cost-effective service, an NHS Policy Board and Management Executive was established in Whitehall; family practitioner committees were brought under the control of Regional Health Authorities; and, in order to clarify lines of managerial communication, representatives of local government were excluded from District Health Authorities. Simultaneously larger hospitals were encouraged to become independent trusts and to compete with each other for patients and resources. GPs were also encouraged to accept independent budgets in the hope that they would thereby become more cost-conscious. Under what was essentially a more centralised system, therefore, hospital consultants and GPs were given a direct interest in the maximisation of patient care at the minimum cost. In the implementation of policy, it was thus hoped, the 'discipline' of the market would achieve a more cost-effective and socially responsive service.

These organisational changes appeared radical at the time and the medical profession duly opposed the 'break-up' of the NHS as vehemently as it had once opposed its creation. The proposals were, however, far less radical than many earlier ones. In 1982, for instance, the CPRS Report had proposed a reversion to social insurance (as practised on the continent) or even to private health insurance (as in the USA), but throughout the 1980s well over 80 per cent of NHS expenditure continued to be funded directly from taxation. Privatisation was also largely forestalled – with a few minor exceptions such as the reintroduction of tax allowances for private insurance (which had been withdrawn in 1975), the contracting-out of certain non-medical services (such as catering) and the eventual retention of pay-beds.[42] Most significantly of all, however, real expenditure was not cut after 1979 but consistently rose so that – regardless of any 'efficiency' gains – it remained well in line with conventional measures of rising need. In other words, if only because of public pressure, the NHS was safe in the hands of the Conservative government.

As a result of increased expenditure, both the quality of individual services and health standards improved between 1979 and 1990. Much public criticism at the time was levelled at individual services and in particular at increased charges and hospital waiting lists. Most notoriously, charges were introduced in 1989 for eye tests and dental check-ups – a move reminiscent of the Labour government's econ-omies in 1951 and justly condemned as a counterproductive attack on preventive medicine (which the government was simultaneously encouraging GPs to expand). In the 1980s prescription charges were also increased, contrary to explicit commitments in the 1979 election, by some 540 per cent.[43] However, even in these politically sensitive areas, the picture was not wholly black. The prescription charge, for instance, still only covered one-half of the cost of the relevant drugs and the number of patients exempted rose from 60 to 82 per cent. Moreover, in sharp contrast to public belief, the average waiting time for in-patient hospital treatment – after a slight increase in the late 1970s – remained stable at 17 weeks. As for the overall record of the NHS, there was a continuing improvement in basic health indicators (such as the mean age of death) and, even more signifi-cantly, a reduction in the differences of health standards between social classes and geographical regions.[44] Indeed, the redirection of resources to under-provided regions, by means of a formula devised in 1976 by the Resources Allocation Working Party, was a major triumph of policy – until it too fell victim to the 1990 reorganisation.

Why, given these achievements, did the widespread popular conviction remain that the NHS was in crisis? There are four main reasons. First, there was the continuing temptation to measure performance against an unattainable ideal (the full potential of medical advance) and the added realisation after 1976 that some patients in more prosperous countries were receiving treatment unavailable on the NHS. Secondly, after two years of exceptionally high spending between 1974 and 1976, expectations were slow to adjust to a new era in which health expenditure would grow only in absolute terms and not in relation to GDP. The gap between increasing resources and need, in other words, gradually narrowed. Thirdly, there was – perversely – the success of the NHS in diverting resources to underprovided regions. This was inevitably at the expense of other regions where, especially in the south-east of England, there were articulate vested interests. Finally, the medical profession as a whole was at last, and with some reluctance, being made fully aware through devolved budgeting of the real economic constraints on health care (which had earlier been obscured by slogans such as 'universalising the best'). Each of these factors fuelled popular dissatisfaction and they were magnified, rather than mollified, by government action. Doctors and patients alike were antagonised by the continuous stream of incremental changes to which, in the absence of a clear strategy, the NHS was subjected before 1987. Thereafter there were genuine doubts about the underlying objectives, efficiency and equity of 'quasi-markets'. Did they represent 'privatisation by stealth'? Would they, like real markets in the USA, increase administrative costs out of all proportion to the gains in efficiency which greater competition might achieve? Moreover, as in real markets, would not the needs of minority groups and the inarticulate be ignored? Only time would tell.

In education policy the full extent and significance of expenditure trends was obscured by the channelling of money through new agencies (such as the Manpower Services Commission (MSC), set up by the Labour government in 1974) and a demographic decline in demand for school places (as a result of the fall in the birthrate after the mid 1960s). On the whole, however, it would appear that policy followed the common pattern. Real expenditure remained broadly in line with changing needs and, as conventionally measured, educational standards improved. However, in relation to the ambitious expansion targets of the early 1970s (ironically contained within Margaret Thatcher's 1972 white paper, *Education: a framework for expansion*), these achievements were disappointing.[45] So too were policy developments in the 1980s in relation to the ideals of the New Right (which were again endorsed by Margaret Thatcher in her new guise as a radical visionary). Only in 1988 was a thorough reorganisation of the whole education system finally attempted.

The primary objective of policy in the mid 1970s, as has been seen in Chapter 8.2, was the raising of educational standards. It was somewhat surprising, therefore, that the opening of Callaghan's 'great debate' was marked by a real fall in educational expenditure. Primary and secondary schools, however, were little affected and at this level standards (as measured by exam passes, the number of children staying on at school after 16 and entry into higher education) continued to improve. Differences of attainment between the sexes, classes and ethnic groups also narrowed.[46] Moreover, owing to the work of the Technical and Vocational Education Initiative (TVEI) in state schools and the establishment of city technology colleges in 1986, the long-demanded emphasis on vocational training was at last seriously attempted.

There were, however, notable blemishes. Capital expenditure, which (it has been estimated) needed to double between 1976 and 1990, was actually halved. Serious doubts were raised about the quality of vocational training subsidised by the MSC and the city technology colleges were blighted by the continuing apathy of industrialists. There was, moreover, a serious shortage of resources for those over eighteen – the sector of education in which both demographic demand and economic returns were at their highest. This affected not only élite institutions such as universities, but also programmes of advanced technical training, such as day-release schemes, at which the Germans excelled and for which the county colleges of the 1944 Education Act had been designed. These blemishes all stored up problems for the future. Current achievements also fell far short of past ambitions. To decrease inequality, for example, Mrs Thatcher's ambition in 1972 had been to provide within ten years nursery education for the majority of three and four year olds. To enhance economic performance, the number of eighteen year olds in higher education was also to have risen from 14 per cent to 22 per cent. As late as 1990, however, the figures were only 44 per cent and 14 per cent of the relevant age groups.[47]

After 1979 the principal focus of policy changed to the raising of

Manpower Services Commission

educational standards through organisational change. Radical
reforms, such as the introduction of education vouchers (which
would have enabled parents to buy whatever type of education they
preferred) and the ending of public funding for higher education (as
suggested by the 1982 CPRS Report), were eschewed. Nevertheless
a sustained attack was launched on those vested interests which
had so dominated policy since 1945. This involved a simultaneous
reinforcement of the power of parents and of central government.
Parental 'choice' was widened through the lifting of the statutory
order to close grammar schools (imposed in 1976) and the withdrawal
of the threat to the charitable status of public schools.[48] 'Assisted
places' were also financed by government in private schools. In the
state sector parental 'power' was enhanced by a further series of
reforms such as the statutory provision of more information about
individual schools, an increased obligation on local authorities to
allocate children to the school of their choice and greater representation on governing bodies which, eventually, were to be given full
responsibility for the implementation of the curriculum.

These reforms greatly restricted the power of both the teaching
profession and local government. The former had won a final battle
for 'equality' in 1986 with the creation of the GCSE examination
through a merger of the academic GCE with the less prestigious
CSE, but in the mid 1980s it had antagonised the government, and
possibly the public, by regular strikes. In consequence, it was
deprived of both its right to national pay bargaining (enshrined in the
1944 Act) and, more dramatically, of its control over the curriculum.
Defying a century of tradition, and bringing Britain in line with other
European countries, the 1988 Education Reform Act imposed on all
maintained schools a national curriculum – complete with tests at
the ages of seven, eleven, fourteen and sixteen.

The principal victim of Conservative policy, however, was local
government. An attack on its financial independence had been
launched in the early 1980s with the allocation of a specified part of
its grant to staff development. Its administrative authority was then
eroded by the increased rights and powers of both parents and school
governors. The final onslaught came in the 1988 Act. This granted
devolved budgeting to the governors of state schools and colleges of
higher education. It also permitted schools to opt out of local authority control and to receive funding, like the old direct grant schools
(abolished in 1975) and the new city technology colleges, direct from
central government. Likewise polytechnics were removed altogether

from local government control. In future, they were to be financed by a central funding council, as were universities which – with some justice – feared that the demise of the UGC signified a major reduction in their traditional autonomy (see Chapter 8.4).

These radical changes might be viewed as a commendable attempt to remedy long-standing weaknesses in the education system and to extend consumer choice. At last the government – with considerable courage – was exercising the power to 'control and direct' with which it had been entrusted by the 1944 Act. The reforms also had an implicit logic. As in community care, local government was being asked to exchange an executive for a strategic role – supervising and regulating a broad mix of schools, from which parents would have almost as much freedom to choose as under a system of education vouchers. The trouble with such an argument, however, is that – at the time – this logic was obscured by a lack of clear strategic planning and a ceaseless flow of amending, and often contradictory, regulations. The 1988 Act itself was, indeed, a prime example of such improvisation. Its guiding principles seemed to be, in the words of one commentator, 'action before words, decision before debate, the presumption of guilt exceeding all possibility of innocence in the previous way of doing things'.[49] This was no way to win the minds and respect of those responsible for the implementation of policy – and thus for its ultimate success. Nor did such 'policy on the run' offer any hope of a resolution of the inherent tension between greater decentralisation (in the form of devolved budgeting and increased parental power) and greater centralisation (in the form of a national curriculum). Government, as the leading paymaster, had always enjoyed considerable influence over the content and nature of education. Now it was assuming direct administrative power which, many feared with some justice, would seriously undermine academic freedom.

In contrast to health and education, housing policy appears to provide incontrovertible proof that, after 1976, the government was seeking not only to restructure the delivery of welfare policy but also to withdraw from its postwar welfare commitments. As has already been noted, expenditure on housing (as conventionally defined) fell between 1976–7 and 1988–9 from 4.1 per cent to 1.6 per cent of GDP; and so dramatic was the fall in capital expenditure that the annual number of council houses built plummeted from 163 000 to 30 000. Simultaneously there was a sharp rise in the number of homeless and of families living in temporary housing (most notoriously bed and breakfast accommodation).

However, the decline in both public expenditure and housing standards was to an extent illusory. The recorded fall in current expenditure, for instance, represented not so much an absolute fall but merely, as John Hills has argued, a new system of finance – 'a switch from public funding through subsidies towards a mixture of public and private funding (through rent and housing benefit) of gross public *provision*, which . . . actually *increased* in real terms over the period'.[50] In other words the general housing subsidy from central to local government (which conventional public accounts recorded) fell as local authorities were encouraged and then obliged to charge full market rents. However, neither the income nor the eventual subsidisation of local government fell because it was in receipt of higher rents from its tenants, 60 per cent of whom were subsidised by housing benefit (borne by the social security rather than the housing budget). In addition the cost of debt-servicing fell (as inflation eroded the real value of past debts) and so local government was actually able to increase real spending on the management and repair of all its properties by over 4 per cent a year. The corresponding fall in capital expenditure, although real, was also less dramatic than it appeared. A 90 per cent reduction in net expenditure (the difference between outgoings and income) in fact represented only a 37 per cent reduction in the actual volume of expenditure. There were three main reasons for this. First, the sizeable receipts from the sale of council houses reduced the need to raise money on the open market. Secondly, the relative price effect for once actually worked in favour of a social service: building costs actually fell. Thirdly, and even more significantly, there was – as heralded in 1968 – a switch from house building to the more cost-effective policy of renovation. Thus whilst council house completions may have plummeted, renovations soared from 75 000 in 1976 to 234 000 in 1988.

This improvement in the quality of council stock was not atypical, but reflected a more general rise in the quality of housing. The actual shortage of housing, for instance, declined from over 1.5 million in 1971 to just over 0.5 million in 1986; and the number of properties lacking one of the five basic amenities simultaneously decreased from 17.4 per cent to 2.5 per cent, whilst those with central heating rose from a very small base to 75 per cent.[51] Moreover, in the public sector these improvements were not – despite contemporary impressions to the contrary – accompanied by a significant rise in rent. As part of the social contract, council rents were frozen after 1974 and fell in real terms. There was consequently a compensatory rise of almost 50 per cent between 1979 and 1981. The percentage of average income consumed by rent in 1986 (7.8 per cent) was, however, lower than it had been in 1973.

The trend in housing expenditure, therefore, did not diverge as much as might appear from that of other social policies; and the principles behind policy were even more consistent, anticipating the later sustained attack on local government and the attempt to separate public funding from public provision. The most dramatic development, which was to epitomise 'Thatcherism' (but which, as has been seen, Margaret Thatcher initially opposed in 1974) was the sale of council houses. Sales had been permitted since the 1950s but it was not until 1980 that tenants were given the explicit right to buy, with the inducement of sizeable discounts amounting by 1990 to as much as 70 per cent of the house's market value. Annual sales exceeded 100 000 throughout the 1980s, and a total of 1.2 million properties (one sixth of local government housing stock) had been sold by 1987. Local authority autonomy was also restricted by severe controls over capital expenditure (imposed by the Labour government in 1977) and the right of its remaining tenants to opt for different landlords. After 1986 other bodies could also assume control of council property.[52] Therefore, not only was the virtual monopoly of local government over the rented housing market challenged in the 1980s but its freedom to manage its own property was also severely curtailed.

The essential purpose behind this attack on local government was once again the transformation of its responsibilities from the executive to the strategic. Rather than being a property developer and owner itself, its role was to be the planning and monitoring of three other forms of housing tenure. Predominant amongst these was owner-occupancy which – as has been seen in Chapter 9.2 – had come to be favoured by all political parties. Accordingly, it was supported by a wide range of subsidies, the most visible of which (tax relief on mortgage interest payments, at £5.2 billion in 1988–9) cost the government as much as all other forms of current housing expenditure. By 1988 it accounted for two-thirds of all dwellings.[53] The second was rented accommodation owned by non-profitmaking housing associations which, because of their small size, government regarded as the most responsive form of public housing. Subsidies to these associations for construction exceeded those paid to local government for the first time in 1986–7 and furthermore enabled properties to be rented below their full market cost. By the end of the 1980s, however, housing associations were still only responsible for 2.6 per cent of dwellings. The final form of tenure was private rented accommodation, which the Conservative government again tried to expand by two new forms of lease: assured tenancies (which guaranteed tenants security and owners a 'market' rent) and short-hold tenancies (which guaranteed tenants a 'fair' rent and owners repossession). As in the 1950s, however, the private market did not revive and by the late 1980s it was responsible for only 7 per cent of dwellings. Housing in other words had convincingly been exposed as so expensive a good that intending purchasers, even on above-average earnings, had to be supported by subsidies. The 'free' market was imperfect and thus state intervention a necessity.

As with social security and the personal social services, therefore, there was no significant 'rolling back of the state' in health care, education or even housing policy. Expenditure may have declined marginally as a percentage of GDP and in relation to need. A sustained, if at times ill-conceived, attempt was also made to separate public finance from public provision. However, real expenditure (except in the case of housing) continued to increase; a corollary of 'quasi-markets' was a greater centralisation of power; and with the expansion of tax expenditure, especially in housing, the 'dependency culture' was increased rather than decreased. A strengthening of the power of central government and an increased dependence on the state by the better-off were indeed as much a characteristic of Conservative policy in the 1980s as privatisation and the sale of council houses.

12.4 CONCLUSION

After 1976 there was unquestionably an historic break in the development of Britain's postwar welfare state. The commitment to 'full' employment was abandoned. So too was corporatism. Expenditure on the five major social services (to which by the 1990s the term 'welfare state' had come exclusively to refer) also declined in relation to GDP and each service was radically restructured. Did such changes, however, represent a fundamental break with the past? In two ways they certainly did. The abandonment of the goal of 'full' employment significantly reduced the direct responsibility of government for individual welfare; and the rejection of corporatism symbolised a growing intolerance of opposition and thus a greater centralisation of power. Nevertheless real expenditure on the major social services (with the exception of housing) increased. There was no reversion to the prewar conception of minimum standards. Moreover, as widely agreed at the time, administrative restructuring was long overdue. Therefore, in the social services at least, the essential purpose of the radical reforms after 1976 might be portrayed as an attempt to revive – and not to replace – the objectives of the 1940s.

These reforms were not, however, very successful. The Labour government's drive to engineer greater equality was halted by a deceleration in the rate of economic growth and innate popular resistance. The mission of Margaret Thatcher to eradicate the 'dependency culture' was then frustrated by four main factors: the lack of a clear, consistent strategy; the dependence on the state by those on above, as well as below, average incomes; the relative inefficiency of the market in such areas as health and housing; and a popular dislike of centralisation. Consequently there was, after 1976, no adequate resolution to the continuing political dilemma of how to maximise individual welfare in the most cost-effective, equitable and democratically accountable way.

It had been just such a dilemma that the original founders of the welfare state had faced and, in relation to the 1930s, they had solved it with considerable success. By the 1970s, however, the momentum behind their reforms had been dissipated and so the challenge was renewed. This time it was not met so successfully; and the apprehension thereby aroused lay at the heart of the reasons for Margaret Thatcher's enforced resignation. Without doubt it will continue to lie at the heart of British domestic politics throughout the 1990s.

12.5 FURTHER READING

There are few balanced histories, but many good insider accounts, of the 1974–9 Labour governments. Of the former, perhaps the best is D. Coates, *Labour in Power? A study of the Labour government, 1974–79* (1980). Of the latter, three are particularly valuable: J. Barnett, *Inside the Treasury* (1982), B. Donoughue, *Prime Minister: the conduct of policy under Harold Wilson and James Callaghan* (1987), and D. Healey, *The Time of My Life* (1989). Pre-eminent amongst the biographies of Margaret Thatcher is H. Young, *One of Us* (2nd ed., 1991). This may be supplemented by D. Kavanagh, *Thatcherism and British Politics: the end of consensus?* (2nd ed., Oxford, 1990); D. Kavanagh and A. Seldon (eds), *The Thatcher Effect: a decade of change* (Oxford, 1989); and, from a Marxist perspective, A. Gamble, *The Free Economy and the Strong State: the politics of Thatcherism* (1988).

The most accessible introduction to economic policy in the 1970s and 1980s is A. Cairncross, *The British Economy since 1945: economic policy and performance, 1945–1990* (Oxford, 1992), which has a good bibliography. This may be enlivened by the well-informed commentaries of W. Keegan: *Mrs Thatcher's Experiment* (1984) and *Mr Lawson's Gamble* (1989). On social policy, a good introduction is provided by S. P. Savage and L. Robins (eds), *Public Policy under Thatcher* (1990) but by far the most authoritative analysis is contained within J. Hills (ed.), *The State of Welfare: the welfare state in Britain since 1974* (Oxford, 1990). It too contains an excellent bibliography and is well supported for the earlier period by P. Jackson (ed.), *Implementing Government Policy Initiatives: the Thatcher administration, 1979–1983* (1985). Books on individual areas of policy, cited in earlier chapters, are also of value.

Appendix:
The Cost of Welfare Policy

To provide a framework within which to study welfare policy, three relatively straightforward questions need to be answered. How much of the total output of the economy is spent by government? How much of government expenditure is consumed by welfare policy as a whole and by individual policies? Finally, how have proportions changed over time?

The answers to these questions were made potentially more easy by the establishment of the Central Statistical Office during the Second World War. It helped to revolutionise the collection of official statistics and consequently detailed estimates of national income and expenditure, together with their various components, have been published since 1950 in a standardised form. The answers, nevertheless, remain anything but straightforward. There are practical problems with the collection of relevant data, so that estimates can never be more than informed guesses and are open to constant revision (as anyone seeking to construct a consistent historical series will find). This has the important consequence, for historical analysis, that the statistics used 'objectively' to analyse past policy may not be the same as those to which policymakers at the time were responding. There are also conceptual problems over the definition of, and the relationship between, the various aggregate figures. For example, the definition of 'public expenditure' used by the CSO in its major publication, *National Income and Expenditure*, differs from that used by the Treasury in white papers on public expenditure. Moreover, in the 'fiscal crisis' of the mid 1970s the Treasury suddenly changed both its definition of public expenditure and the means of expressing it as a percentage of the total output of the economy. Comparisons over time and between countries – which continue to use different definitions of public expenditure and economic output, despite the attempts of bodies such as the UN and the OECD to standardise practice – are, therefore, extremely hazardous.

1.1 ESTIMATES OF THE NATIONAL PRODUCT

The aggregate output of the economy can be estimated in one of three ways: through the *output* of each sector of the economy, such as industry and agriculture; through the *income* accruing to each economic activity, such as employment and profits; and through various categories of *expenditure*, such as that by consumers and public authorities. There are major practical problems in collecting the relevant information in each of these three ways and inevitably the three estimates differ considerably.

There are also three different ways in which the statistics can be presented. Gross Domestic Product (GDP) includes broadly all the income and wealth generated within Britain. Gross National Product (GNP) also includes income from British investment overseas and excludes the profits of foreign-

331

owned enterprises in the UK. Net National Product (NNP) excludes capital consumption or depreciation. To complicate matters still further, these three estimates may be calculated at market prices or at factor cost. The latter excludes taxes on expenditure (such as VAT) but adds subsidies. In most cases, therefore, it is lower than the market price.

The choice of which measure to use is not purely academic; it can be of considerable political and analytical importance. In 1976, for instance, the respective estimates of the total output of the economy were as follows:

GNP at market prices: £123 891 million
GDP at market prices: £122 576 million
GNP at factor cost: £110 814 million
GDP at factor cost: £109 499 million
NNP at factor cost: £ 97 370 million

There was thus a £26 521 million or a 21 per cent difference between the largest and the smallest estimate; and the same measure of public expenditure could legitimately be presented as consuming 61.4 per cent or 47 per cent of total output, depending on the estimate used. Those who wish to control or attack public expenditure naturally contrast it with the lower estimates. Thus until 1977 the Treasury used estimates of GDP at factor cost and the New Right have conventionally used NNP. The generally accepted measure now taken is GDP at market prices.

1.2   DEFINITIONS OF PUBLIC EXPENDITURE

Public expenditure, as the differing practice of the CSO and the Treasury illustrates, is open to as many definitions as national output. At minimum it consists of the *consumption* by central and local government ('general government') of goods and services – the capital costs, for example, of building and equipping hospitals and the current cost of maintaining them and paying the staff. If estimates of public expenditure are to be set against those of national output to determine what percentage of national resources government consumes, this is strictly the only measure that should be used (see Tables A.2, and A.3 line 10).

Public expenditure, however, has conventionally included *transfer payments*. These are cash payments, such as pensions and supplementary benefit, which redistribute (or transfer) resources between individuals. They do not actually consume any resources – except in their administrative costs – and so are excluded from calculations of national output. Consequently to include them in the estimates of public expenditure and then to contrast those estimates with, for example, GDP will give a very distorted picture of the amount of national resources being 'consumed' by government – especially as between 1957 and 1977 they accounted for approximately 43–45 per cent of public expenditure. They continue to be included, however, because they illustrate the power of government – as opposed to the market – to influence distribution of resources.

Conversely there are certain types of government expenditure which are not included in the conventional calculations. The most important is *tax expenditure*, or the revenue which government forgoes through the granting of tax relief. Tax expenditure is synonymous with transfer payments in that government is, in effect, collecting taxation and then paying it back to the same individual to cover certain types of approved expenditure, such as the payment of mortgage interest. If transfer payments are included in estimates of public expenditure, then so should tax expenditure; but this has rarely been the case. The practical explanation is that the full cost cannot be identified in public accounts (even when the government privately has made such calculations). The cultural one is that individuals' right to retain their own income does not feel like public expenditure. The cost, nevertheless, is considerable. In 1973–4, it has been calculated, the revenue from income tax would have been 40 per cent higher but for tax relief.

A final component to public expenditure is the *cost of public corporations*, and particularly of nationalised industries. Before 1977 Britain was exceptional in that all the costs of nationalised industries were included within estimates of public expenditure. The removal of all such costs (except direct government loans) together with all interest payments on public debts (except those which could not be covered by trading revenue) enabled the government overnight to reduce its calculation of public expenditure for 1975–6 from 58.5 per cent to 51.5 per cent of GDP (see Table A.2).

Such a recalculation underlines the considerable political and analytical importance that the choice of a given definition of public expenditure can have. In Britain the Treasury has traditionally taken the broadest possible definition of public expenditure (bar tax expenditure) together with a narrow definition of the national product. This has given the impression of high public expenditure and served the Treasury well in its battle to control government spending. This was especially true during the 'fiscal crisis' of the mid 1970s, but once the priority had changed to that of convincing international financiers – and in particular the IMF – that the necessary remedial action had been taken, it was to the government's advantage to adopt different definitions. To do so was not necessarily dishonest, because it brought Britain more into line with European practice.

1.3   TRENDS IN WELFARE EXPENDITURE

Welfare policy is also difficult to define. All government policy, including defence expenditure, might be said to enhance individual well-being; and, as argued in Chapter 2, economic policy should certainly be included in any broad definition of welfare policy. Hence the statistics for expenditure on economic services are included in Tables A.1, A.3 and A.5. However, it is conventional to concentrate attention on the five 'core' social services, as in Table A.4, where social spending is divided by services, by economic category (current and capital expenditure) and by spending agency (central and local government, and public corporations). More detailed statistics for individual services have been provided in earlier chapters.

There are many pitfalls in the interpretation of these figures. Over the years many services have changed heads, the most notable being the transfer of local authority health expenditure to the NHS in 1971. Arbitrary decisions have also been taken on where to place other services. Should the training of nurses and doctors, for example, come under health or education expenditure? In a traditional British compromise, nurses have been placed under health and doctors under education – because their essential training is, respectively, in hospitals and universities. Finally, an increase in the relative or absolute size of social expenditure should not automatically be equated with an improved service or a change in the policy. The rate of inflation is likely to be higher than average in the social services because they tend to be labour intensive. They are therefore less able than other sectors of the economy to benefit from productivity resulting from technological innovation. The phenomenon is called 'the relative price effect' and means that the relative cost of the service often has to increase over the years simply to sustain the same standard. Demographic and economic change (such as an increase in the number of pensioners or a rise in unemployment) can also automatically increase the cost of social expenditure without any change in policy.

As in the rest of the industrialised world, social expenditure has risen dramatically since 1945 so that, by whatever measure taken, it represented over 50 per cent of government spending and 25 per cent of national output by the mid-1970s (Table A.1). By then, expenditure on social security, health and welfare, and education individually exceeded that on the two items that had dominated public expenditure until the 1950s – defence and interest on the national debt (Table A.3). Expenditure on housing would also have done so, had not its true size been disguised by 'tax expenditure'. The relative rise in expenditure was slow in the 1950s and then accelerated in the 1960s. There was no explosion until 1972–5 – and that explosion was the common experience of most industrial nations, not a phenomenon unique to Britain. The dominant trend in welfare expenditure between 1945 and 1975 was, therefore, its steady balanced growth (Table A.5).

1.4   EMPLOYMENT IN THE PUBLIC AND WELFARE SECTORS

An alternative measure of the relative importance of public and welfare expenditure is the amount of human, as opposed to financial, resources they consume. This attracted particular attention in the 1970s when it was widely felt that public employment was adversely affecting the economy by attracting labour away from 'productive' employment and, through the strength of public sector unions, fuelling wage-inflation.

Inevitably the choice of statistics is again controversial. What, for instance, constitutes the 'public sector'? One measure is the 'extended public sector', which includes all institutions which have tax-raising powers, have executives appointed by government (such as nationalised industries), or receive most of their finance from government (like universities). This definition has been simultaneously attacked for being too restrictive and too extensive. On the one hand it excludes all those working in the private sector (such as in the defence and construction industries) whose employment is dependent on government contracts. On the other hand it includes the NHS and nationalised industries, which are usually excluded from other countries' definitions.

There is also the recurrent problem of how to count part-time workers, who were increasing steadily in the public sector as in the labour market as a whole. Should they be counted individually or conflated into 'full-time equivalents'? Finally, how should the underlying significance of the figures be assessed? The importance of aggregate public employment, it could be argued, depends not so much on its mere size as on other factors, such as whether it is absorbing skilled manpower in a tight labour market or unskilled workers who would otherwise be unemployed – and who, as in the case of part-time female labour, might not otherwise even be regarded as part of the labour force.

Figures for the 'extended public sector' confirm certain trends apparent in financial expenditure. Employment jumped from 10 per cent of the labour force to 27 per cent between 1938 and 1951, but then slowly declined to 24 per cent by the mid 1960s before accelerating to 30.5 per cent in 1976. During this period labour was shed in the defence and nationalised industries but increased dramatically in the welfare sector – by 166 per cent in education, for example, and 142 per cent in the NHS. By conventional international measures, public employment exceeded most European countries (but not the USA) until the mid 1960s, when it was calculated at approximately 16 per cent of the total labour force. Its rate of growth was then comparatively fast, reaching approximately 21 per cent by 1977.

1.5 FURTHER READING

A full range of expenditure statistics can be found in the *Annual Abstract of Statistics* and in *Social Trends*, first published in 1970. *Social Trends* changed the basis of its tables from the CSO to the Treasury definition of public expenditure in 1976, which accounts for the slight discrepancy for the final date used in certain statistical tables in this appendix and in Part II of this book. Another exhaustive source for both expenditure and manpower statistics is P. Flora, *State, Economy and Society in Western Europe* (1983), from which Table A.1 has been extracted. Its first volume represents a bold attempt to collate, in a standardised form, statistics relevant to the development of welfare policy throughout Western Europe over the past century. Inevitably it presents these statistics in a somewhat unconventional form and, in column 2 of Table A.1, Flora's figures of public expenditure as a percentage of GDP are contrasted to the standardised figures of the OECD. The standard work on public expenditure is D. Heald, *Public Expenditure* (1983); on social expenditure, A. Walker (ed.), *Public Expenditure and Social Policy* (1982); and on public employment, R. Parry, *U.K. Public Employment* (1980).

Table A.1 Government expenditure, central and local, 1945–75

	£(m)	% of GDP (2)	Major categories as % of GDP					Major categories as % of total expenditure					Central g'ment expend. as % total (13)
			Defence (3)	Admin/ justice (4)	economic environment (5)	Social services (6)	Residual (7)	Defence (8)	Admin/ justice (9)	Economic environment (10)	Social services (11)	Residual (12)	
1945	5779	58.4	–	–	–	–	–	–	–	–	–	–	90.6
1946	4530	45.5	–	–	–	–	–	–	–	–	–	–	84.7
1947	4130	38.8	–	–	–	–	–	–	–	–	–	–	78.0
1948	4215	36.0	–	–	–	–	–	–	–	–	–	–	76.6
1949	4423	35.6	–	–	–	–	–	–	–	–	–	–	77.2
1950	4539	35.1	6.5	2.0	5.2	16.2	5.3	18.4	5.6	14.7	46.1	15.1	76.6
1951	5208	36.1	9.0	1.8	5.5	15.5	4.4	24.8	4.9	15.2	42.9	12.2	77.2
1952	5777	37.0	10.5	1.7	4.8	15.6	4.4	28.4	4.6	13.0	42.2	11.9	76.7
1953	6048	36.2	10.3	1.7	4.5	15.5	4.3	28.5	4.6	12.3	42.8	11.8	75.7
1954	5976	33.8	9.6	1.6	3.7	14.8	4.0	28.5	4.8	11.1	43.7	11.9	74.8
1955	6143	32.1	8.4	1.6	3.7	14.3	4.1	26.1	4.8	11.6	44.6	12.8	75.0
1956	7054	34.3	7.9	1.4	7.5	14.4	5.4	21.6	3.9	20.4	39.3	14.7	75.0
1957	7652	35.3	7.3	1.5	8.1	14.4	5.3	20.0	4.0	22.2	39.4	14.3	75.5
1958	8001	35.4	6.8	1.5	7.9	15.0	5.5	18.6	4.1	21.4	41.0	14.9	75.8
1959	8539	35.8	6.6	1.8	8.0	15.4	5.4	17.7	4.8	21.5	41.3	14.7	75.5
1960	9001	35.3(32.6)	6.3	1.5	8.3	15.3	5.7	17.0	4.1	22.3	41.3	15.2	75.0
1961	9893	36.4(33.4)	6.4	1.7	8.9	15.8	5.7	16.6	4.3	23.1	41.1	14.9	73.9

1962	10442	36.7(34.2)	6.5	1.7	8.9	16.2	5.5	16.7	4.5	23.0	41.6	14.2	72.6
1963	12427	41.0(35.6)	6.3	1.6	8.7	16.8	5.3	16.3	4.1	22.4	43.5	13.6	74.7
1964	12042	36.4(33.9)	6.1	1.5	8.9	17.1	5.0	15.7	3.8	22.9	44.4	13.1	69.7
1965	13376	37.7(36.4)	6.0	1.5	9.1	18.2	5.0	15.0	3.8	22.9	45.7	12.7	69.3
1966	14532	38.4(35.6)	5.9	1.6	9.5	18.4	5.0	14.5	3.9	23.5	45.6	12.4	69.1
1967	16764	42.0(38.5)	6.1	1.7	11.3	19.6	5.2	13.9	3.8	25.8	44.7	11.9	69.6
1968	18393	42.6(39.6)	5.7	1.8	11.5	20.1	5.3	12.8	4.0	26.0	45.3	11.9	70.0
1969	19083	41.4(41.5)	5.0	1.8	10.8	20.0	5.3	11.6	4.2	25.1	46.7	12.3	69.1
1970	20857	41.1(39.3)	4.9	2.0	10.9	20.3	5.1	11.3	4.5	25.3	47.1	11.8	68.1
1971	23358	41.1(38.4)	4.9	2.1	11.2	20.0	4.8	11.4	4.8	26.0	46.7	11.2	68.7
1972	26571	42.3(40.0)	4.9	2.3	10.4	21.2	4.7	11.3	5.2	24.0	48.7	10.8	68.2
1973	30491	42.4(41.1)	4.7	2.1	11.0	21.6	5.2	10.6	4.7	24.7	48.4	11.7	65.9
1974	39108	47.7(45.2)	5.0	1.9	9.5	24.9	6.4	10.5	4.1	19.9	52.2	13.3	67.4
1975	51495	49.9(46.9)	5.0	2.1	11.1	25.7	6.0	10.1	4.2	22.3	51.5	11.9	68.0

N.B. Columns 3–12 are calculated on a slightly different basis from columns 1–2.
Administration and Justice: administration, foreign affairs, judiciary, police.
Economic and Environmental: agriculture, industry and commerce, transport and communication.
Social services: social insurance and assistance, other social transfers, health, housing, education and science.
Residual: national debt.
Source: P. Flora, *State, Economy and Society*, vol. 1 (1983) pp. 345–6, 440–2.

Table A.2 Public expenditure by economic category, 1955–76 (percentage of GDP)

	Treasury definition		Public consumption	Public investment	Transfer payments
	Pre 1977	1977			
1955–9	41.1	–	18.9	7.6	14.7
1960–4	42.9	–	19.0	7.9	16.0
1965–9	48.2	40.5	20.2	9.8	18.5
1970–1	50.6	–	21.0	9.7	19.8
1971–2	50.0	–	21.2	9.5	19.2
1972–3	50.1	–	21.5	8.7	19.9
1973–4	51.1	–	21.2	9.2	20.3
1974–5	57.3	–	22.9	10.1	24.3
1975–6	58.5	51.5	–	–	–

Source: M. Wright, 'Public expenditure in Britain', *Public Administration*, vol. 55 (1977) pp. 143–69.

Table A.3 Public expenditure, 1951–75, selected services

	1951 £(m)	%	1961 £(m)	%	1966 £(m)	%	1971 £(m)	%	1975 £(m)	%
Social services:										
1. Social security	707	12.1	1628	15.8	2577	16.8	4309	17.8	8918	16.4
2. Welfare services	96	1.6	158	1.5	262	1.7				
3. NHS	498	8.4	930	9.0	1395	9.1	2784	11.4	6707	12.3
4. Education	398	6.8	1013	9.8	1768	11.6	3023	12.4	6840	12.5
5. Housing	404	6.9	555	5.4	968	6.3	1240	5.2	4291	7.9
6. Other environmental services*	135	2.3	379	3.8	652	4.3	1179	4.8	2405	4.4
Other:										
7. Commerce and industry	850	14.6	1203	11.7	1759	11.5	3180	13.1	7825	14.4
8. Defence and external relations	1411	24.2	1859	18.0	2512	16.4	3164	13.0	5876	10.8
9. Debt interest	687	11.8	1261	12.2	1558	10.2	2213	9.1	4513	8.3
10. Government expenditure on goods and services as percentage of GNP (factor cost)		28.8		26.3		29.2		31.0		34.6

* Includes such local services as public health, recreation, water supply, sewerage etc.
Source: Social Trends (1970, 1976).

Table A.4 Social expenditure, 1951–77

	1951–2		1956–7		1961–2		1966–7		1971–2		1976–7	
	£(m)	%	£(m)	%	£(m)	%	£(m)	%	£(m)	%	£(m)	%
1. Total public expenditure on social services	2135	100	3011	100	4396	100	7198	100	11790	100	32145	100
Individual service:												
2. Social security	702	32.8	1068	35.5	1674	38.1	2642	36.7	4578	38.8	11575	36.0
3. Personal social services	33	1.5	44	1.5	67	1.5	123	1.7	324	2.7	1243	3.9
4. School meals, milk and welfare food	73	3.4	99	3.3	102	2.3	148	2.1	149	1.3	470	1.5
5. NHS	494	23.1	639	21.2	928	21.1	1446	20.1	2362	20.0	6249	19.4
6. Education	416	19.5	671	22.3	1057	24.0	1827	25.4	3023	25.6	7438	23.1
7. Housing	417	19.5	490	16.3	567	12.9	1012	14.1	1354	11.5	5170	16.1
8. Current expenditure	1694	79.3	2478	82.3	3714	84.5	5938	82.5	10058	85.3	27652	86.0
9. Capital expenditure	441	21.7	533	17.7	682	15.5	1260	17.5	1732	14.7	4493	14.0
10. Central government*	1309	61.3	1833	60.9	2821	64.2	4423	61.4	7692	65.2	21444	66.7
11. Local government	805	38.7	1146	38.1	1550	35.2	2715	37.7	4098	34.8	10701	33.3
12. Public corporations	21	1.0	32	1.0	25	0.6	60	0.8	–		–	

* Excludes grants to local authorities.
Source: Annual Abstract of Statistics (1964, 1969, 1979).

Table A.5 Social expenditure, annual growth relative to growth of GDP, 1950–77

	1950–60	1960–70	1970–4	1974–7
1. Total social spending	1.10	1.40	1.50	0.98
2. Social security	1.25	1.42	1.17	1.25
3. Personal social services	1.13	2.24	2.20	1.14
4. NHS	0.91	1.21	1.43	1.05
5. Education	1.37	1.46	1.27	0.99
6. Housing	0.58	1.42	2.61	0.37
7. Defence	0.96	0.60	1.07	0.95
8. Industry and Trade	3.03	2.40	0.17	–
9. Employment services	0.62	2.11	1.56	2.54

A ratio of increase greater than one signifies that expenditure on a given programme was increasing faster than GDP.
Source: F. Gould and B. Roweth, 'Public spending and social policy: the UK 1950–77', *Journal of Social Policy*, vol. 9 (1980) pp. 349–50.

Notes and References

1 Introduction

1. Labour Party, *Report of the 75th Annual Conference* (1976) p. 188.
2. Cmd 6404 (1942) para. 440.
3. Cmd 6527 (1944) Foreword.
4. B. Donoughue, *Prime Minister* (1987) p. 187.
5. Speech to the Institute of Economic Studies in New York, 15 September 1975.
6. P. Taylor-Gooby, *The Politics of Welfare* (1985) Ch. 5.
7. P. Kavanagh, *Thatcherism and British Politics* (2nd ed., 1990) p. 311.
8. The term 'classic' welfare state was coined in Anne Digby, *British Welfare Policy* (1989).
9. Historians themselves have a vital role to play in the testing against empirical evidence, and hence the refinement, of abstract theory.

2 The Nature of the Welfare State

1. P. Flora and A. J. Heidenheimer (eds), *The Development of Welfare States in Europe and America* (1980) p. 19.
2. See H. Pelling, *The Labour Governments 1945–1951* (1984) pp. 117–18. T. H. Marshall used the phrase in his famous lecture *Citizenship and Social Class* delivered in February 1949 (Cambridge, 1950) p. 42.
3. P. Addison, *The Road to 1945* (1975) p. 168. See also p. 216 for the coining of the term 'social security'.
4. Ironically Beveridge himself disliked the identification of his Report with the term 'welfare state'. He feared that, by emphasising the state's obligation to its citizens but not the citizen's reciprocal obligations, it gave the state a role like Santa Claus. This fear was directly realised in Britain in the 1970s when some politicians, with electoral considerations in mind, opposed any restructuring of the social services on the ground that 'You can't shoot Santa Claus'. See J. Harris, *William Beveridge* (1977) p. 448, and D. Kavanagh, *Thatcherism and British Politics* (1987) p. 133.
5. N. Furniss and T. Tilton, *The Case for the Welfare State* (1979) pp. 14–21.
6. V. George and P. Wilding, *Ideology and Social Welfare* (1985) p. 62.
7. 'The scheme proposed here is in some ways a revolution, but in more important ways it is a natural development from the past. It is a British Revolution.' The Beveridge Report, Cmd 6404, para 31.
8. T. H. Marshall, *Social Policy* (1975) p. 99, 84.
9. A. Briggs, 'The Welfare State in historical perspective', *European Journal of Sociology*, vol. 2 (1961) p. 228.
10. Cmd 9663, paras 94–8.

11. R. Lowe, *Adjusting to Democracy* (1986) ch. 1; R. Middleton, *Towards the Managed Economy* (1985) p. 176. It is because of this interpretation of the welfare state as an inevitable feature of advanced capitalism that Flora and Heidenheimer have suggested that Germany (as the institutional innovator) rather than Britain (as the exceptional propagator of the idea) should be taken as a model against which to judge the international development of welfare states. See *The Development of Welfare States in Western Europe*, ch. 1.

12. R. Rose and R. Shiratori (eds), *The Welfare State East and West* (1986) ch. 4.

13. R. F. Harrod, *The Life of John Maynard Keynes* (1951) p. 436.

14. W. H. Beveridge, *Why I am a Liberal* (1945) p. 9. Too great a conflation of the views of Beveridge and Keynes is, however, dangerous. See J. Harris, 'Political ideas and the debate on state welfare, 1940–5', in H. L. Smith (ed.), *War and Social Change* (Manchester, 1986) pp. 233–63.

15. Cmd 6404, para 9.

16. For a contemporary justification, see T. E. Utley, *Not Guilty* (1957).

17. One was hesitantly provided by backbenchers, but never officially endorsed, in the pamphlets *One Nation* (1950) and *The Responsible Society* (1959).

18. T. H. Marshall, *Citizenship and Social Class and Other Essays* (1950) pp. 58, 40, 84.

19. B. Abel-Smith and K. Titmuss (eds), *The Philosophy of Welfare* (1987) p. 14.

20. C. A. R. Crosland, *The Future of Socialism* (1956) pp. 518, 63, 194. The following quotations are from pp. 20–1, 61.

21. D. Donnison, *The Politics of Poverty* (1982) pp. 20–1.

22. The phrase is Hugh Stephenson's.

23. K. Joseph, *Stranded on the Middle Ground* (1976) p. 57.

24. IEA, *Choice in Welfare* (1965) p. 7. The 'public choice' school, which accredits the expansion of the state to the self-interest of politicians and bureaucrats, is best represented by W. A. Niskanen, *Bureaucracy: Servant or Master?* (1973).

25. F. A. Hayek, *The Road to Serfdom* (1943) p. 84. The following quotations are from pp. 153, 101, 10.

26. Ibid, p. 90.

27. IEA, *Choice in Welfare* (1965) p. 58.

28. C. Ham, *Health Policy in Britain* (1982) ch. 7.

29. K. Middlemas, *Power, Competition and the State*, vol. 1 (1986). Another general treatment is T. Smith, *The Politics of the Corporate Economy* (1979) which admitted Britain was not yet a corporate state, but claimed corporatism was the 'central tendency' in politics (p. xiv). It was written before Margaret Thatcher became prime minister.

30. C. A. R. Crosland, *The Future of Socialism* (1956) ch. 1, 3, 8.

31. R. Miliband, *Capitalist Democracy in Britain* (1982).

32. See B. Jessop, *The Capitalist State* (Oxford, 1982).

33. See, for example, S. Hall, *The Hard Road to Renewal* (1988).

34. J. O'Connor, *The Fiscal Crisis of the State* (New York, 1973); I. Gough, *The Political Economy of the Welfare State* (1979).
35. C. Offe, 'Some contradictions of the modern Welfare State', *Critical Social Policy*, 2 (1982) 11.
36. J. Dearlove and P. Saunders, *Introduction to British Politics* (1984) p. 319.
37. E. Wilson, *Women and the Welfare State* (1977) p. 148. As a pioneering critique of the British welfare state, this book is itself 'crudely ideological' and therefore eminently quotable. A more balanced summary of feminist views, albeit not of the early history of the welfare state, is E. Pascall, *Social Policy* (1986).
38. Cmd 6404 (1942) para 114. However, for a summary of the practical benefits Beveridge sought for married women, see J. Harris, *William Beveridge* (1977) pp. 402–7.
39. B. Abel-Smith and K. Titmuss (eds), *The Philosophy of Welfare*, p. 92.
40. The succeeding examples are from R. Broad and J. Fleming (eds), *Nella Last's War* (1981) p. 227; PEP, *Family Needs and the Social Services* (1961) p. 39; M. Young and P. Wilmott, *Family and Kinship in East London* (1957) p. 15.
41. See in particular L. Doyal, *The Political Economy of Health* (1979) ch. 6 and C. Ungerson (ed.), *Women and Social Policy* (1985).
42. See Chapter 7.3 for a further discussion of this issue.
43. T. Skocpol, 'Political response to capital crisis', *Politics and Society*, 10 (1980–1) 157.
44. R. Lowe, *Adjusting to Democracy* (1986) pp. 246–7.
45. R. M. Titmuss, *Problems of Social Policy* (1950) p. 434.

3 The Nature of Policymaking

1. Cmd 9663 (1956) para. 733 (2).
2. R. Harris and A. Seldon, *Choice in Welfare* (1965) p. 58.
3. Bureaucracy has a multitude of meanings from 'rule by officials' in its classical sense to 'inefficiency' in popular usage. A masterly summary of these definitions and the theories relating to bureaucracy is M. Albrow, *Bureaucracy* (1970).
4. G. Roth and C. Willich, *Max Weber. Economy and Society*, vol. 3 (New York, 1968) pp. 983–5.
5. T. E. Borcheding, *Budgets and Bureaucrats* (North Columbia, 1977) p. 61; W. A. Niskanen, *Bureaucracy: servant or master?* (1973) p. 23.
6. Cmnd 3638 (1968); R. H. S. Crossman, *The Diaries of a Cabinet Minister*, vols. 1–3 (1975–7).
7. Cmd 9663 (1956) paras 699–703. For informed criticism of the Ministry of Health, see C. Webster, *The National Health Service Since the War*, vol. 1 (1988) pp. 186, 238–9.
8. B. Castle, *The Castle Diaries 1974–6 (1980)* p. 170; R. H. S. Crossman, *The Diaries of a Cabinet Minister*, vol. 1 (1975) pp. 21–39, 614–28.

9. See in particular, C. Webster, *The National Health Service Since the War*, vol. 1 (1988) p. 222.
10. H. Macmillan, *Tides of Fortune* (1969) ch. 13. Macmillan had to side-step his permanent secretary (Sir Thomas Sheepshanks) who significantly had been the official in charge of the detailed, and somewhat dispirited, implementation of the Beveridge Report in 1943.
11. J. Harris, *William Beveridge* (1977) pp. 422–3.
12. B. Castle, *The Castle Diaries 1974–6* (1980) p. 209.
13. M. Kogan, *The Politics of Education* (1971). The ministers were Boyle (1962–4) and Crosland (1965–7).
14. See R. Lowe, 'Bureaucracy triumphant or denied? The expansion of the British civil service', *Public Administration*, vol. 62 (1984) p. 291.
15. C. Ham, *Health Policy in Britain* (1982) ch. 5.
16. M. Hill, *The Sociology of Public Administration* (1972) ch. 4.
17. K. Mannheim, *Freedom, Power and Democratic Planning* (1951) p. xvii.
18. Cmnd 1432 (1961) para. 23.
19. S. Charles and A. Webb, *The Economic Approach to Social Policy* (1986) p. 66.
20. See S. Gorovitz, 'John Rawls: a theory of justice' in A. de Crespigny and K. R. Minogue (eds), *Contemporary Political Philosophers* (1975) pp. 272–89.
21. Sir A. Cairncross, *Essays in Economic Management* (1971) p. 63.
22. N. Barr, *The Economics of the Welfare State* (1987) p. 421.
23. For a full analysis of the relative efficiency of insurance in relation to health, see N. Barr, *The Economics of the Welfare State* (1987), in particular pp. 296–9.
24. See A. Maynard and A. Ladbrook, 'Budget allocation in the NHS', *Journal of Social Policy*, 9 (1980) 289–312.

4 The Historical Context

1. D. Donnison, *The Politics of Poverty* (1982) p. 20.
2. C. Feinstein, *National Income, Expenditure and Output of the United Kingdom* (1972), table 58.
3. Sir A. Cairncross, 'The postwar years', in R. Floud and D. McCloskey (eds), *The Economic History of Britain since 1700*, vol. 2 (1981) p. 376. The apparent incompatibility between the overall and the quinquennial rates is explained by the different base years taken.
4. For Beveridge's figures, see Cmd 6404, p. 91. From 1951 to 1971 women increased their relative superiority, with their life expectancy at birth rising from 71.2 to 75.2 years, and at 65 from 79.4 to 81.3. The number of people over 75 (on whom expenditure per head was highest) increased only from 1.8 to 2.6 million.
5. Those over 75 tend to require more care since dementia becomes a more common problem and there is an increasingly disproportionate number of women, who typically have fewer resources. However, the burden of an 'ageing' population was not as great as had been feared

before 1939, mainly because the elderly enjoyed better health and greater resources in terms of both national and family support. They even became major providers of care themselves. See P. Thane, 'The debate on the declining birth-rate in Britain: the "menace" of an ageing population, 1920s–1950s', *Continuity and Change*, 5 (1990) 283–305; and 'The growing burden of an ageing population?', *Journal of Public Policy* 7 (1987) 373–87. See also Chapter 6.4.

6. The succeeding figures are largely taken from A. H. Halsey (ed.), *British Social Trends since 1900* (1988) ch. 2.

7. J. F. Ermisch, *The Political Economy of Demographic Change* (1983) p. 45.

8. In the early 1960s the trade unions insisted on the retention of clause 4 either in response to their increasingly militant members or, purely defensively, to retain the historical link between the various factions of the Labour movement. See V. Bogdanor, 'The Labour party in opposition, 1951–1964', in V. Bogdanor and R. Skidelsky, *The Age of Affluence 1951–64* (1970).

9. Public Record Office, CAB 124/1016.

10. K. Morgan, *Labour in Power, 1945–1951* (1984) p. 186.

11. T. Utley, *Not Guilty* (1957) p. 156.

12. Public Record Office, CAB 130/139, GEN 625; *The Right Road for Britain* (1949) p. 14. See also R. Lowe, 'Resignation at the Treasury: the Social Services Committee and the failure to reform the Welfare State, 1955–57', *Journal of Social Policy*, 18 (1989) 505–26.

13. The following quotations are from *One Nation* (1950) p. 72. and *The Responsible Society* (1959) p. 41. See also I. Macleod and E. Powell, *The Social Services: Needs and Means* (1954).

14. D. Kavanagh, 'The Heath Government, 1970–1974', in P. Hennessy and A. Seldon, *Ruling Performance* (Oxford, 1987) p. 234.

15. Estimates for defence expenditure may be underestimates. The initial cost of developing the atom bomb in the 1940s was kept secret from Cabinet and from Parliament through its funding from the Civil Contingencies Fund. Similarly, in the 1970s the cost of the 'Chevaline' updating of the Polaris submarine was presented to Cabinet as £24 million, whereas its full cost was over £1000 million.

16. See especially C.A.R. Crosland, *The Conservative Enemy* (1962) p. 123; also, R. Lowe, 'The Second World War, consensus and the foundation of the Welfare State', *Twentieth Century British History*, 1 (1990) 152–82.

17. Cmnd 3638, ch. 1, paras 17 and 12.

18. D. Marquand, *The Unprincipled Society* (1988) p. 26; A. Booth, ' "The Keynesian revolution" in economic policy making', *Economic History Review*, 36 (1983) p. 118; P. Hennessy, *Whitehall* (1989) p. 235.

19. This and the next quotation are from P. Hennessy, *Whitehall* (1989) pp. 88 and 135.

20. Cmnd 1432, *Report on the Control of Public Expenditure*.

21. A major failure of the British Treasury was the refusal to discuss the constructive relationship between social and economic policy and the social consequences of taxation when the opportunity arose between

1955 and 1957. See R. Lowe, 'Resignation at the Treasury', *Journal of Social Policy*, 18 (1989) 520–3.

22. K. Newton and T. Karran, *The Politics of Local Expenditure* (1985) p. 52. For local government income, see R. Jackman, 'Local government finance', in M. Loughlin *et al.* (eds), *Half a Century of Municipal Decline* (1985) ch. 7.

23. A. G. Geen, 'Educational policy-making in Cardiff, 1944–70', *Public Administration*, 59 (1981) 85–104. M. Kogan (ed.), *The Politics of Education* (1971) p. 48.

24. Cmnd 4040, para. 96.

25. Ibid, para. 85. In England and Wales in 1945 there were, in urban areas, 83 county boroughs and, in rural areas, 61 counties with 309 non-county boroughs, 572 urban districts and 475 rural districts. In addition there was the London County Council with 28 boroughs. After 1974 there were six metropolitan authorities divided into 36 districts, and 47 counties divided into 333 districts. In addition there was the Greater London Council (founded in 1964 and disbanded in 1986, both by Conservative governments) with 32 boroughs. There was a parallel reorganisation in Scotland, which was divided by 1974 into nine regions and 53 districts, and in Northern Ireland which had 26 borough or district councils.

26. Ibid, para. 243.

27. The quotations are taken from one of the best introductions to the enquiries: the 'oral history' symposia reported in *Contemporary Record*, vol. 2/2 (1988), vol. 2/6 (1989), and vol 3/1 (1989).

28. Cmd 6527, foreword. R. M. Titmuss, *Problems of Social Policy* (1950) p. 434.

29. P. Addison, *The Road to 1945* (1975) p. 15.

30. Public Record Office, CAB 134/459, meeeting of the ministerial Information Services Committee, 25 February 1949; Political and Economic Planning, *Family Needs and the Social Services* (1961) p. 33; R. Harris and A. Seldon, *Choice in Welfare* (1965) p. 58.

31. See for instance D. E. Butler and A. King, *The British General Election of 1964* (1965) chs 4–5.

32. D. Butler and D. Stokes, *Political Change in Britain* (1974) p. 297.

33. The surveys are summarised in P. Taylor-Gooby, *Public Opinion, Ideology and State Welfare* (1985) ch. 2, on which the succeeding analysis is based. Rather than encouraging altruism, welfare policy could create resentment, such as that of owner-occupiers against council tenants and of small or childless families against large families in receipt of family allowances.

34. The survey was carried out in 1963–4 and its results published in J. Goldthorpe *et al.*, *The Affluent Worker*, 3 vols (Cambridge, 1968–9). The quotation is from vol. 3, p. 170.

35. In the periods 1960–8 and 1969–73, unofficial strikes accounted respectively for 57 and 50 per cent of all working days lost. That government in 1960 started to collect statistics which distinguished between official and unofficial strikes was a measure of its concern. See J. W. Durcan *et al.*, *Strikes in Post-War Britain* (1983) pp. 110, 149.

36.	M. Pinto-Duschinsky, 'Bread and circuses? The Conservatives in office, 1951–1964', in V. Bogdanor and R. Skidelsky, *The Age of Affluence* (1970) p. 77.
37.	See R. Lowe, 'The Second World War, consensus and the foundation of the Welfare State', *Twentieth Century British History*, 1 (1990) 178–9.
38.	As reported to Macmillan in Public Record Office, PREM 11/2421.
39.	Public Record Office, T171/478, memo 25 for the 1957 budget.
40.	D. Marquand, *The Unprincipled Society* (1988) p. 224.

5 Employment Policy

1.	Cmd 6527. The following quotations are from paragraphs 41 and 66.
2.	See G. C. Peden, 'Sir Richard Hopkins and the "Keynesian Revolution" in employment policy, 1929–45', *Economic History Review*, 36 (1983) 281–96.
3.	It was the Treasury (conscious of interwar hardship) which wished to bring 'work to the workers', whilst the 'progressive' Keynesians (confident that general reflation would soak up local unemployment) insisted on labour mobility regardless of its social cost.
4.	One reason for non-implementation was the incompatibility of the economic need to vary contributions with the social and political need to maintain the 'actuarial' relationship between insurance contributions and benefits. Variations in contribution would for example have exploded the reality, or the myth, that increased benefits could only be financed through increased contributions. See Chapter 6.1.
5.	The 'disinterested' nature of policymaking is well illustrated by a note from the Minister of Reconstruction (Lord Woolton) to Churchill on 16 May 1944: 'Sir William Beveridge has been working for some time on a plan for maintaining employment after the war, and his book on this subject is now with the printer. The Reconstruction Committee are unanimous that we ought not to allow him to get the credit for being the first to put before the country a policy for full employment; and we have been striving to get ahead of him.' Public Record Office, PREM 4/96/6.
6.	J. Tomlinson, *Employment Policy* (Oxford, 1987) p. 68. The following quotations are from Sir W. Beveridge, *Full Employment in a Free Society* (1944) pp. 261, 273.
7.	The comment in 1952 of Churchill's far from moderate adviser, Lord Cherwell, was conclusive: 'it is no good looking back to Victorian times . . . the people will not accept mass unemployment.' (Public Record Office, T236/3242). So was Sir Keith Joseph's confession in *The Times* of 6 September 1974: 'We were dominated by the fear of unemployment. It was this which made us turn back against our own better judgement.'
8.	The examples cited in this paragraph are taken from P. D. Balacs, 'Economic data and economic policy', *Lloyds Bank Review*, 104 (1972)

35–50; S. Brittan, *Steering the Economy* (1971); and C. D. Cohen, *British Economic Policy, 1960–1969* (1971).

9. The calculations are even more complicated in relation to national insurance, where increased benefits are matched by increased contributions – and where the increased employer's contribution will gradually feed through into increased prices. In the 1960s it was calculated that the direct effect on demand would be an increase equivalent to 90 per cent of the increased benefit rate and a decrease equivalent to 85 per cent to 90 per cent respectively of the employee's and employer's increased contribution rate. Hence, if benefits went up by £300 million, financed by a £175 million and £125 million increase respectively in employer's and employee's contributions, the net increase in real demand would be £185 million. See C. D. Cohen, *British Economic Policy, 1960–1969* (1971) p. 57.

10. S. Brittan, *Steering the Economy* (1971) p. 423.

11. The statistics in this paragraph are taken from Sir Alec Cairncross, 'The postwar years, 1945–77', in R. Floud and D. McCloskey, *The Economic History of Britain since 1700*, vol. 2 (Cambridge, 1981) pp. 370–416 and J. F. Wright, *Britain in the Age of Economic Management* (Oxford, 1979).

12. Cmnd 1432, paras 22 and 23.

13. A common criticism of the Report is that it was over-technocratic and ignored the political reality of policymaking. Such reality was well-recognised by the civil servant credited with the original concept of PESC, who later reflected: 'The essential contribution of PESC remains this. Cabinets take their decisions on public expenditure in much the same way as they take decisions on anything else – push and pull, threats and cajolery, bluff and counter-bluff, the day-to-day battle of the Cabinet room. PESC can't change this at all, for this is the nature of political life. But with PESC they are now talking and bargaining about the right questions . . . making real choices and not artificial ones. . . . This is the real gain.' Sir R. Clarke, *Public Expenditure, and Management and Control* (1978) p. xviii. The best introduction to PESC is D. Heald, *Public Expenditure* (1983) ch. 8, and another insider's view is provided in L. Pliatsky, *Getting and Spending* (1982).

14. N. Rollings, 'British budgetary policy, 1945–54: a "Keynesian revolution?" ', *Economic History Review*, 41 (1988) 283–98.

15. *The Economist*, 19 February 1954; R. A. Butler, *The Art of the Possible* (1971) p. 160; Public Record Office, T230/295; P. M. Williams, *Hugh Gaitskell* (1979) p. 217.

16. To encourage long-term investment and to combat international competition, industrial concentration was found to be frequently desirable. This legislation consequently had a greater effect on retailing rather than manufacturing, especially after the outlawing of price fixing by the 1964 Resale Price Maintenance Act – which helped to propel Heath to the leadership of the Conservative Party and, more permanently, encumbered him with the nickname of 'grocer'.

17. See S. Young and A. V. Lowe, *Intervention in the Mixed Economy* (1974) part 1. Prices and incomes policies were amongst these other

measures and, through their concessions to the low paid, had their own
direct social influence.

18. Cmnd 1337.
19. *European Cooperation. Memoranda Submitted to OEEC relating to
    Economic Affairs in the period 1949 to 1953* (Cmd 7572, 1948). The
    document, more conveniently known as the long-term plan, was pre-
    pared as a condition of Marshall Aid, which was ironic because earlier
    plans had been modified for fear that their 'socialist' implications would
    offend the US government.
20. A. Shonfield, *Modern Capitalism* (1965) p. 88.
21. S. Young and A. V. Lowe, *Intervention in the Mixed Economy* (1974)
    p. 28. The book is a case study of the IRC.
22. A. Shonfield, *Modern Capitalism* (1965) p. 160. Industrial resistance
    is well documented in A. A. Rogow, *The Labour Government and
    British Industry, 1945–51* (Oxford, 1955).
23. J. Leruez, *Economic Planning and Politics in Britain* (Oxford, 1975)
    p. 280; Sir R. Clarke, *Public Expenditure, Management and Control*
    (1978) pp. 74–5.
24. National Enterprise Board, *Annual Reports and Accounts, 1978* (1979).
25. A. Shonfield, *Modern Capitalism* (1965) p. 94.
26. Sir W. Beveridge, *Full Employment in a Free Society* (1944) p. 182.
27. See in particular the 1958 memorandum by senior officials on the
    'United Kingdom's interests abroad', in Public Record Office, PREM
    11/2321.

6 Social Security

1. Cmd 6404, para. 451; F. A. Hayek, *The Road to Serfdom* (1944) pp.
   89–90.
2. Cmd 6404, para. 8. The Treasury's desire for secrecy is noted in J.
   Harris, *Beveridge* (Oxford, 1977) p. 383.
3. Cmd 6404, para. 17. When the principles were described at greater
   length in paragraphs 303–9, the principle of 'comprehensiveness' was
   revealed to embrace the controversial assumption of universalism:
   benefits should be 'comprehensive in respect both of persons covered
   and of their needs'. They were also to be adequate in amount and 'in
   time'.
4. Ibid., para. 273. The quotations in the following paragraph are from
   para. 296.
5. A small part of the cost of the health service was to be financed through
   insurance contributions (ibid., para. 437). Beveridge himself admitted
   in para. 415 the self-imposed financial limitation: 'flat insurance contributions are either a poll-tax or a tax on employment, justifiable up to
   certain limits, but not capable of indefinite expansion'.
6. Ibid., para. 19(v). The 'housewives' charter' is unveiled in paras 107–17
   and 339–48.
7. Beveridge made both suggestions to reinforce the work ethic, but the
   Coalition government rejected them. Simultaneously it rejected the

proposal that unemployment benefit should be limitless, thus ending the principle that insurance benefits should be adequate in amount and 'in time'.

8. Ibid., paras 294, 375–84. Foreign practice is examined in Appendix F and rejected in paras 304–5. One form of voluntary insurance which Beveridge did want to end, because he adjudged it highly inefficient and exploitative, was industrial assurance – essentially the high-pressure door-to-door sale of policies to cover funeral expenses and life assurance by firms such as the Prudential. The insurance scheme was to provide a death grant and his hope was that assurance companies would be nationalised (paras 181–92, Appendix D).

9. Ibid., para. 29.

10. The most explicit criticism of the Report can be found in the following documents at the Public Record Office: CAB 87/3, RP(43)5, memorandum by the Chancellor of the Exchequer on 'the financial aspects of the social security plan', 11 January 1943; RP(43)6, report of the Official Committee on the Beveridge Report, chaired by Sir Thomas Phillips, 14 January 1943; and T273/57, the Treasury's major policy file on the draft Report, July-December 1942.

11. Public Record Office, ED 136/229, note by R. A. Butler, 14 September 1942, p. 221. Conservative Party opposition mirrored that of the Treasury, as revealed by the report of a secret backbench committee, chaired by Ralph Assheton. See P. Addison, *The Road to 1945* (1975).

12. Cmd 6404, para. 447.

13. Ibid., paras 240, 420. The final cost of Beveridge's proposals was only one-fifth of that of his ideal programme – see J. Harris, 'Enterprise and Welfare States', *Transactions of the Royal Historical Society*, vol. 40 (1990) 187. Keynes's comment, and his estimate that the Treasury was already committed to extra annual expenditure of £40–50 million, is in Public Record Office, T273/57, 9 December 1942.

14. T. Cutler *et al.*, *Keynes, Beveridge and Beyond* (1986) p. 16.

15. Cmd 6404, para. 459. For the relative cost of the new scheme, see paras 275–99.

16. See in particular H. D. Henderson, 'The Principles of the Beveridge plan' in Public Record Office, T273/57, 4 August 1942 and the report of the Phillips Committee, cited in Note 10. Beveridge, it should be noted, did not explicitly defend, or indeed use, the term 'universalism'. It was subsumed in the principle of 'comprehensiveness', see Note 3 above.

17. Cmd 6404, para. 196; unpublished paper by J. H. Veit-Wilson, 'The genesis of confusion'. Thus Beveridge's subsistence income was equivalent to only two-thirds of Rowntree's contemporary estimates and the government reduced benefit even further below this 'irreducible minimum'.

18. *Social Insurance, Part 1* (Cmd 6550, 1944) para. 13. In 1966 a Ministry of Social Security was belatedly established, but this change in terminology hardly represented a delayed victory for Beveridge. National assistance was simultaneously renamed *supplementary* benefit.

19. See Cmd 6404, para. 27. Beveridge also stated in 1942 that 'the

standard of minimum subsistence adopted by Mr Rowntree in 1899 was rejected by him a generation later as too low, and would be rejected decisively by public opinion today'. Public Record Office, CAB 87/79, SIC (42)3, para. 6.

20. A. Bullock, *The Life and Times of Ernest Bevin*, vol. 2 (1967) p. 242.
21. Cmd 6404, para. 449.
22. K. G. Banting, *Poverty, Politics and Policy* (1979) p. 68; A. Deacon and J. Bradshaw, *Reserved for the Poor* (1983) p. 61.
23. B. R. Rowntree, *Poverty: a study in town life* (1901) pp. 295–8; P. Townsend, *Poverty in the United Kingdom* (Harmondsworth, 1979) p. 31.
24. P. Townsend, 'The meaning of poverty', *British Journal of Sociology*, vol. 13 (1962); G. C. Fiegehen *et al., Poverty and Progress in Britain, 1953–73* (1977) p. 131.
25. P. Townsend, *Poverty in the United Kingdom* (Harmondsworth, 1979) ch. 11.
26. B. Abel-Smith and P. Townsend, *The Poor and the Poorest* (1965) p. 17.
27. G. C. Fiegehen *et al., Poverty and Progress in Britain, 1953–73* (1977) pp. 36–48. In some respects Rowntree (with his seeming obsession with the value of garden produce) and the assumption underlying the much-hated 'household' means test (that relations would support those in need) provided a more accurate picture of *actual* living conditions than statistics derived from government surveys.
28. A. B. Atkinson, *Poverty in Britain and the Reform of Social Security* (Cambridge, 1970) p. 35. Another source of bias, identified by Abel-Smith and Townsend in 1965, is that reported income tends to be understated by 10 per cent (because irregular earnings, for example, are omitted), whilst expenditure is overstated by 5 per cent (because, for example, respondents want to impress).
29. B. S. Rowntree and G. R. Lavers, *Poverty and the Welfare State* (1951); A. B. Atkinson *et al.*, 'National Assistance and low incomes in 1950', *Social Policy and Administration* 15 (1981) 19–31; B. Abel-Smith and P. Townsend, *The Poor and the Poorest* (1965); I. Gough and T. Stark, 'Low incomes in the United Kingdom', *Manchester School*, 36 (1968); A. B. Atkinson, *Poverty in Britain and the Reform of Social Security* (1969) and 'Poverty and income inequality in Britain' in D. Wedderburn, *Poverty, Inequality and Class Structure* (Cambridge, 1974); P. Townsend, *Poverty in the United Kingdom* (Harmondsworth, 1969); G. C. Fiegehen *et al., Poverty and Progress in Britain, 1953–73* (Cambridge, 1972); W. Beckerman and S. Clark, *Poverty and Social Security in Britain since 1961* (Oxford, 1982); R. Layard *et al., The Causes of Poverty* (1978); R. Berthoud and J. Brown, *Poverty and the Development of Anti-Poverty Policy in the U.K.* (1981).
30. A. B. Atkinson *et al.*, 'National Assistance and low incomes in 1950', *Social Policy and Administration*, 15 (1981) 24. This article provides the best comparison of the surveys of Rowntree and Abel-Smith and Townsend and, in particular, argues that generalisation from York is dangerous since it did not have a full range of low-paid industries. On

the 'scientific' basis of the sample, Rowntree and Lavers wrote: 'We took a list of all the streets in York and a man who has lived in the city for more than half a century . . . marked on our list every street where working-class families live' (*Poverty and the Welfare State*, p. 2).

31. The level of insurance contributions had been based on an anticipated rate of 8.5 per cent unemployment, whereas the actual rate was under 3 per cent. The cost of unemployment benefit in 1955, at 1948–49 prices, which had been estimated by Beveridge at £123 million, was only £11.3 million. See A. W. Dilnot *et al.*, *The Reform of Social Security* (Oxford, 1984) pp. 14–15.

32. L. Hannah, *Inventing Retirement* (Cambridge, 1986) p. 53. By 1955 the real cost of retirement pensions was almost 50 per cent higher than Beveridge's prediction and by 1965 it was 100 per cent higher. See A. W. Dilnot et al., *The Reform of Social Security* (Oxford, 1984) pp. 14–15.

33. R. Lister, *Social Security: the case for reform* ((1975) p. 67.

34. The phrase was coined by D. Piachaud in the *New Statesman*, 3 December 1971. Contemporary estimates are provided in J. C. Kincaid, *Poverty and Equality in Britain* (Harmondsworth, 1973) pp. 118–24.

35. R. Hemming, *Poverty and Incentives* (Oxford, 1984) p. 81.

36. A. W. Dilnot *et al.*, *The Reform of Social Security* (Oxford, 1984) p. 28.

37. Ibid., p. 45 and R. Hemming, *Poverty and Incentives* (Oxford, 1984) p. 81.

38. Ibid., p. 49 and A. B. Atkinson, *Poverty in Britain and The Reform of Social Security* (Cambridge, 1970) p. 58.

39. D. Donnison, *The Politics of Poverty* (1982) pp. 43–4, 92; A. Deacon and J. Bradshaw, *Reserved for the Poor* (Oxford, 1983) p. 111. The system grew more complicated with a change in clientele. The number of unemployed and one-parent families (who typically left and rejoined the register frequently) increased, whilst the number of pensioners (who tended to stay constantly on the register) declined. Discretionary payments, which had fallen after the 1966 reforms, also accelerated with inflation. In 1976, 49 per cent of claimants were in receipt of regular 'exceptional circumstances' payments, mainly to cover the cost of heating, whilst 27 per cent were in receipt of one-off 'exceptional needs' payments, mainly to cover clothing needs. See S. Macgregor, *The Politics of Poverty* (1981) pp. 39–40.

40. Two good, critical summaries of these schemes are A. B. Atkinson, *Poverty in Britain and the Reform of Social Security* (Cambridge, 1970) ch. 9, and P. Alcock, *Poverty and State Support* (1987) ch. 11.

41. For a succinct summary, see A. Deacon and J. Bradshaw, *Reserved for the Poor* (1983) ch. 4.

42. Cmd 6404, paras 258–64, 347.

43. Trade union dissatisfaction with industrial injury benefit had been the pretext for establishing the Beveridge Committee. To the unions' dismay, Beveridge recommended that the benefit should become contributory, but it was administered from a different fund and paid

at a higher rate. It was fully amalgamated with national insurance in 1973.

44. The rise of scroungermania is documented in A. Deacon, 'Unemployment and politics in Britain since 1945', in B. Showler and A. Sinfield, *The Workless State* (Oxford 1981) pp. 59–88.

45. The discrepancy between the two sets of figures illustrates not only the sensitivity of all calculations to marginal changes in the poverty line but also the large number of children living close to the poverty line, however defined.

46. See especially, J. C. Kincaid, *Poverty and Equality in Britain* (1973) pp. 118–24.

47. Cmd 6404, paras 410–25. The large cash increases in 1968 only restored family allowances, briefly, to their real value in 1945.

48. Admittedly low-paid families benefited from certain other measures, such as rent and rate rebates, and family income supplement, but the take-up of those benefits was low. See A. W. Dilnot *et al.*, *The Reform of Social Security* (Oxford, 1984) p. 51. The unpopularity of family allowances is noted *inter alia* in PEP, *Family Needs and the Social Services* (1961) p. 38 and P. Taylor-Gooby, *Public Opinion, Ideology and State Welfare* (1985) ch. 2.

49. Cmd 6404, para. 236.

50. L. Hannah, *Inventing Retirement* (Cambridge, 1986) ch. 9; S. Harper, 'The impact of the retirement debate on postwar retirement trends', in T. Gorst *et al.*, *Postwar Britain* (1989) pp. 95–108. In the early 1950s the retirement age in Canada and Sweden, for example, was 70 and 67 respectively, but it was soon reduced.

51. Cmd 9333, *Report of the Committee on the Economic and Financial Problems of the Provision for Old Age* (1954) para. 214. The committee had the same chairman, Sir Thomas Phillips, as the one in 1943 which had rejected Beveridge's principle of adequacy.

52. However, a certain number of non-claimants (from 20 per cent of couples to 38 per cent of single women) insisted that they were 'managing all right', and this may well have been true because, as seen in Chapter 6.2, official figures for entitlement disregarded certain income as well as help in kind from relatives. A. B. Atkinson, *Poverty in Britain and the Reform of Social Security* (Cambridge, 1970) ch. 3.

53. Public Record Office, CAB 129/89/C(57)208, 16 September 1957. The statistics in this paragraph are taken from L. Hannah, *Inventing Retirement* (Cambridge, 1986) ch. 4 and p. 145.

54. PEP, *Family Needs and the Social Services* (1961) p. 192.

7 Health care

1. R. J. Wybrow, *Britain Speaks Out, 1937–87* (1989) pp. 25–6; IEA, *Choice in Welfare* (1965) appendix A; PEP, *Family Needs and the Social Services* (1961). The latter recorded: 'the attitude of mothers towards the social services was enthusiastic rather than critical, but

there was not much doubt that this attitude is governed by their enthusiasm for the health services' (p. 39).

2. Beveridge commissioned Nuffield College, Oxford to survey public opinion towards the social services prior to the drafting of his Report. It found that reform of the health services was accorded top priority. See J. Harris, 'Did British workers want the welfare state?', in J. Winter (ed.), *The Working Class in Modern British History* (Cambridge, 1983).

3. All the general texts cited at the end of this chapter have an introductory chapter on the interwar period. See in particular R. Klein, *The Politics of the National Health Service* (1983) ch. 1.

4. Not all these doctors would have been practising because, once registered, doctors were removed from the register only on death or evidence of malpractice. Details of salaries are provided in H. Eckstein, *The English Health Service* (Cambridge, USA, 1958) pp. 76–8.

5. For details of dentists and opticians, see C. Webster, *The Health Services Since the War*, vol. 1 (1988) ch. 9.

6. H. Eckstein, *The English Health Service* (Cambridge, USA, 1958) p. 75. Not all areas saw incipient warfare between local authority and voluntary hospitals. Birmingham, Liverpool and Manchester were notable exceptions.

7. Cmd 6502. From the start the white paper was regarded as a consultation document, rather than a serious blueprint for the service.

8. The best introduction to the local authority health service is J. Lewis, *What Price Community Medicine?* (Brighton, 1986).

9. In addition doctors claimed that salaries would discourage initiative, diminish their sense of responsibility and encourage mediocrity. In contrast Ministry of Health officials claimed commercial competition was 'undignified' for such a profession and that the battle for patients encouraged the overprescribing of medicine and lax certification (such as sick notes). The Ministry of Health, as the department responsible for local government, had an 'obsessive desire for the municipal control' of the NHS. See F. Honigsbaum, *Health, Happiness and Security: the creation of the National Health Service* (1989) p. 213.

10. Among those dismayed was the former leader of the LCC, Herbert Morrison, who was the Labour Party's deputy leader from 1945 to 1956.

11. Cmd 6502, p. 20. One of those directly responsible for the Act admitted that it was very difficult to find in the original structure of the NHS 'much evidence of the democratic control and public participation which had been so strongly emphasised as desirable in the early planning'. See J. Pater, *The Making of the National Health Service* (1981) p. 168. By 1952 the percentage of manual workers on RHBs was 3 per cent, HMCs 6 per cent and Boards of Governors 2 per cent.

12. Health centres are claimed by Webster to 'symbolise the distinction between the socialist and non-socialist conception of the health service'; but despite the 1946 Act's imposition on each local authority of the 'duty' to provide such centres, only one wholly new one was built

before 1952 (and a mere 18 before 1964). See C. Webster, 'Conflict and consensus', *Twentieth Century British History*, I (1990) 139.

13. For the pre-eminence of hospital consultants in the USA, see D. M. Fox, *Health Policies, Health Politics* (Princeton, 1986). For British public opinion, see R. J. Wybrow, *Britain Speaks Out, 1939–87* (1989) p. 25 and PEP, *Family Needs and the Social Services* (1961) p. 113.

14. Even here Bevan would seem to have been overgenerous. Honigsbaum has estimated that fair compensation for the loss of the right to sell practices was £2700, not the average £4700 paid. See *Health, Happiness and Security* (1989) p. 101.

15. Quoted in B. Watkin, *The National Health Service* (1978) p. 21. Pater's succinct comment was that 'a little more statesmanship from *both* sides might have produced better results', see *The Making of the National Health Service* (1981) p. 179.

16. Quoted in F. Honigsbaum, *Health, Happiness and Security* (1989) p. 146. In 1942 the interim report of the BMA's Medical Planning Commission appeared to support salaries and health centres but this was due, it is now argued, to the temporary influence on the BMA of a group of left-wing doctors, the Socialist Medical Association.

17. R. Klein, *The Politics of the National Health Service* (1983) p. 21. The number of beds per 1000 people was 4.9 compared to London's average of 10.2.

18. The criticism was Gaitskell's, quoted in P. Williams, *Hugh Gaitskell* (1979) p. 248.

19. The EMS, under which all hospital resources were pooled between 1939 and 1945 (initially in anticipation of heavy air-raid casualties) not only exposed the poor condition of voluntary hospitals but also encouraged the regionalisation and rationalisation of the whole hospital service. It also accustomed consultants to salaried employment.

20. Except when stated, the following account is based on C. Webster, *The Health Services Since the War*, vol. I (1988) ch. 5; P. M. Williams, *Hugh Gaitskell* (1979) ch. 8 and the records of the Cabinet Committee on the National Health Service preserved in the Public Record Office, CAB 134/518–9. The last provides a good example of the ill-feeling Bevan created. Its meetings consisted, recorded its secretary, 'of a series of episodes in which the Minister of Health says his piece and is then contradicted by the others' (CAB 21/2027).

21. The Guillebaud Report on the NHS (1956), Cmd 9663, paras 544–7. The number of prescriptions increased from 71.5 million to 227 million and their average cost from 8p to 20p (paras 466–70). Manpower costs were increased, for example, by the 1947 Nurses Act which established national pay scales and qualifications for the first time.

22. Quoted in C. Webster, *The Health Services Since the War*, vol. I (1988) p. 162 and R. Klein, *The Politics of the National Health Service* (1983) p. 34. In 1949 he also proclaimed that prescription charges were 'a very small aspect indeed . . . what we are considering is not a considerable retreat', see P. Williams, *Hugh Gaitskell* (1979) p. 263.

23. Quoted in C. Webster, *The Health Services Since the War*, vol. I (1988) p. 150.

24. Public Record Office, CAB 128/17, CM(20)17, 3 April 1950.
25. The most bitter attack came on 20 April in the left-wing paper, *Tribune*, which – in an unseemly deal – was being subsidised by Lord Beaver-brook (Churchill's right-wing adviser and patron of left-wing MPs, including Bevan). See P. Williams, *Hugh Gaitskell* (1979) p. 257. Such associations might seem to confirm the widespread view that Bevan was his own worst enemy, to which Ernest Bevin's classic retort was 'not while I'm alive, he ain't'.
26. Gaitskell's concessions included a rise in the cash limits for the NHS and a two-year limit on charges.
27. See C. Webster, *The Health Services Since the War*, vol. I (1988) p. 392.
28. C. Webster, *The Health Services Since the War*, vol. I (1988) p. 209. The Conservative Party had voted against the 1946 National Health Service Act in Parliament, but on rather different grounds. The Act, it argued, 'discourages voluntary effort and association; mutilates the structure of local government; dangerously increases ministerial power and patronage; appropriates trust funds and benefactions in contempt of the wishes of donors and subscribers; and undermines the freedom and independence of the medical profession'.
29. B. Watkin, *The National Health Service* (1978) p. 36; T. E. Chester, 'The Guillebaud Report', *Public Administration*, 34 (1956) 207. For a summary of the committee's research findings, see B. Abel-Smith and R. M. Titmuss, *The Cost of the National Health Service in England and Wales* (Cambridge, 1956).
30. Cmd 9663, para. 733(3). A survey of its recommendations on adequacy and charges are in paras 730(7) and 732(5).
31. For Cabinet discussions and Treasury objections, see Public Record Office, CAB 128/30 part 2, CM(57)2 and T227/485. The prescription charge was an alternative means of persuading doctors to prescribe and patients to behave 'responsibly'; and after Guillebaud's rejection of a proscribed list of drugs, the government also persuaded drug companies to obey a voluntary code of practice on pricing to limit NHS costs.
32. See D. Allen, 'An analysis of factors affecting the development of the 1962 hospital plan', *Social Policy and Administration*, 15 (1981) 3–18. The minister of health was restored to the Cabinet in 1962. The Hospital Plan was Cmnd 1604 (1962), whilst the complementary white papers on the development of community care were Cmnd 1973 (1963) and 3022 (1966).
33. Quoted in B. Watkin, *The National Health Service* (1978) p. 71. Changing attitudes were of course justified by the changing nature of illness, which permitted planners to reduce between 1948 and 1962 the ideal ratio of beds for acute illness from 6 to 3.1 per 1000 people. For Powell's own later misgivings, see *Medicine and Politics* (1966) ch. 5.
34. Cmnd 5055 (1972), *National Health Service Reorganisation: England*, para. 13. To reinforce public accountability, a health service commissioner (ombudsman) was also to be appointed to hear complaints. R. Klein, *The Politics of the National Health Service* (1983) p. 99.

35. For a faithful summary, see B. Watkin, *The National Health Service* (1978) chs 3 and 7.
36. A. Bevan, *In Place of Fear* (1961 ed.) p. 110. For the rest of the paragraph, see F. Honigsbaum, *The Division in British Medicine* (1979) part 8.
37. P. Hall 'The development of health centres', in P. Hall *et al., Change, Choice and Conflict in Social Policy* (1975) pp. 299–310.
38. See A. H. Halsey, *British Social Trends Since 1900* (1988) ch. 11, and *Inequalities in Health* (Harmondsworth, 1988) which reprints the 1980 Black Report.
39. Tobacco-smoking was the largest self-inflicted cause of disease and might have been officially discouraged earlier than 1957 since the link with cancer was first identified in 1950. Delay was occasioned by the lack of conclusive scientific proof and fears about infringing personal liberty. The tobacco companies also contributed generously to Conservative Party funds and the tobacco tax to government revenue. 'We all know' remarked Macleod as minister of health in 1956 'that the Welfare State and much else is based on tobacco smoking' (Public Record Office, MH55/1011).
40. Nurses gained greatly from shorter hours, increased pay and relaxed discipline, but the status of women within the NHS suffered from the reduction in status of the hospital matron who, as head of nursing and housekeeper, had traditionally attended governors' meetings.
41. See E. Powell, *Medicine and Politics* (1966) pp. 48–9.
42. A. Bevan, *In Place of Fear* (1961) p. 109.
43. E. Powell, *Medicine and Politics* (1966) p. 16.

8   Education

1. Public Record Office: RG23/71, Social Survey report on public attitudes towards the Education Act, 1945.
2. There were, of course, a wide range of 'educative' influences outside the formal education system – such as reading and television (which increased with affluence), the family and the neighbourhood (which educationalists came to accept as more powerful influences on children than schooling) and other institutions (such as the Army Bureau of Current Affairs, which was held to have radicalised conscripts' opinions during the Second World War).
3. B. Simon, 'The Tory government and education, 1951–1960', *History of Education*, 14 (1985) 283.
4. C.A.R. Crosland, *The Future of Socialism* (1956) p. 258; Cmd 9703, *Technical Education* (1956) p. 4.
5. Crosland's views are expressed in *The Future of Socialism* (1956) ch. 12; Eccles's are in a letter to Eden preserved in the Public Record Office, PREM 11/1785 (June 1955). For the 1944 *Employment Policy* white paper, see Ch. 5.1.
6. H. C. Dent, *The New Education Bill* (1944); B. Simon, 'The 1944

Education Act: a Conservative measure?', *History of Education*, 15 (1986) 41.
7. Cmd 6458, *Educational Reconstruction* (1943) para. 48.
8. The requirement was reduced by 25 per cent in 1959 and 20 per cent in 1969. Only 500 Church of England schools were expected to opt for 'aided' status, but eventually 3000 did.
9. The authority of central over local government was made explicit in section 68 of the second part of the Act. The extent to which this authority was qualified by the requirement that pupils should be 'educated in accordance with the wishes of their parents' (section 76 of part four) has never been fully resolved.
10. The one exception was direct-grant schools. Since 1926 certain prestigious schools such as Manchester Grammar School had received subsidies directly from central rather than local government, and against Butler's better judgement they were permitted to continue charging fees. The Attlee Government reduced their number from 232 to 164. See Chapter 8.4.
11. This did not signify the administrative unification of the whole formal education system, as later friction was to prove. The Ministry of Labour retained responsibility for industrial training, and the University Grants Committee (answerable to the Treasury and then, after 1962, to the Ministry of Education) for universities. Greater local democracy was permitted with the devolution of power from county councils and boroughs to 'district committees', but these committees were explicitly the agent of the larger authorities.
12. Cmd 6458 (1943) paras 2 and 47.
13. Cmd 6458 (1943) para. 28. The Spens Committee had been appointed in 1933 to report on 'secondary education with special reference to grammar schools and technical high schools'.
14. C. Barnett, *The Audit of War* (1986) p. 275.
15. Public Record Office: ED 136/181.
16. C. Barnett, *The Audit of War* (1986) p. 284; J. Harris, 'Enterprise and Welfare States', *Transactions of the Royal Historical Society*, 40 (1990) 192.
17. C. Barnett, *The Audit of War* (1986) p. 291.
18. In the terminology of the time a multilateral school was one in which children (who would otherwise have been divided according to perceived aptitude between grammar, technical and 'modern' schools) were taught within three different streams on the same site. Comprehensive schools also provided education for all children of a given locality on one site, but with a minimum of streaming.
19. P. H. Gosden, *Education in the Second World War* (1976) pp. 247, 256. The philosophy underlying the tradition of 'education for leadership', and its articulation by Norwood, is best described in G. McCulloch, *Philosophers and Kings* (Cambridge, 1991).
20. This paragraph is based on P. H. Gosden, *Education in the Second World War* (1976) chs 11 and 14. The quotation is from p. 334.
21. A. Howard, *RAB. The Life of R. A. Butler* (1987) p. 115.
22. The defeat was made an issue of confidence and reversed the following

day. On the issue of equal pay, see P. Thane, 'Towards equal opportunities? Women in Britain since 1945', in T. Gourvish and A. O'Day,
Britain since 1945 (1991) pp. 183–4.

23. C. Knight, *The Making of Tory Education Policy in Postwar Britain,
1950–86* (1990) p. 11.

24. The increased number of children in specialist primary schools also
reflected the decrease in children in all-age schools from 1.1 million in
1946 to 636 246 in 1954.

25. The number of school meals rose from under half a million in 1941 to
2.7 million in 1948 (53 per cent of all school children) and, having
fluctuated around 50 per cent in the 1950s, peaked at 70 per cent in
1975. It had been promised that they would be free (providing one
reason for keeping family allowances below Beveridge's minimum) but
there was always a charge, initially to cover the cost of the food but
not administration. There was an immediate 90 per cent take-up of
free milk. It was withdrawn from secondary schools by Labour in the
1960s and, notoriously, from eight to eleven year olds in 1971 by
Margaret 'milk-snatcher' Thatcher.

26. In the Hutting Operation for the Raising of the School Leaving Age,
4162 classrooms, 2195 practical rooms and a quarter of a million chairs
and desks were provided by 1949. Ellen Wilkinson is quoted in P.
Gosden, *The Education System since 1944* (1983) p. 5.

27. Public Record Office: ED 136/890, Butler to Horsbrugh, 7 October
1953. The economies are detailed in T227/401. The low priority
accorded to education was illustrated by Churchill's offer of the Ministry to the Liberal leader, in the hope of forming a coalition, and its
exclusion from Cabinet until 1952.

28. Public Record Office: PREM 11/1785, Eccles to Eden, 6 June 1955.
The white paper was Cmnd 604.

29. Its report in 1963 was Cmnd 2154. There was, as will be seen, a deluge
of reports and white papers on education, details and abstracts from
which can most conveniently be found in J. S. Maclure, *Educational
Documents* (5th edn, 1986) and R. Rodgers, *Crowther to Warnock*
(1980). Reference, where practical, will be made to these sources rather
than the originals.

30. Roy Lowe, *Education in the Postwar Years* (1988) p. 200.

31. P. Gosden, *The Education System since 1944* (1983) p. 32. On the
Labour Party, see B. Simon, 'The Tory Government and Education,
1951–60', *History and Education*, 14 (1985) 289.

32. J. S. Maclure, *Educational Documents* (1986) pp. 302, 333. The Plowden Committee is covered on pp. 308–23.

33. B. Simon, *Education and the Social Order, 1940–90* (1991) p. 262.
Robbins is quoted on p. 251.

34. Legal compulsion was adjudged necessary to galvanise 14 LEAs which
had declined to respond to Crosland's request and was finally introduced in 1976. For the succeeding figures, see B. Simon, *Education
and the Social Order, 1940–90* (1991) pp. 420–30.

35. H. Young, *One of Us* (1989) pp. 69–70. Margaret Thatcher's permanent
secretary has argued conversely that the Open University was saved

because 'their degrees cost only half of Oxbridge's', see B. Simon, ibid., p. 464. Iain Macleod, as chancellor, had expressed his determination to close the Open University, but died within a month of taking office.

36. Two contrasting interpretations of the educational backlash can be found in B. Simon, ibid., ch. 8 and C. Knight, *The Making of Tory Education Policy in Postwar Britain, 1950–86* (Brighton, 1990) chs 1–5.

37. The statistics in this paragraph are taken from H. Glennester and W. Low, 'Education and the Welfare State: does it all add up?', in J. Hills (ed.) *The State of Welfare* (Oxford, 1990) pp. 28–87. In 1947 the number of candidates for School Certificate and Higher School Certificate was 107 000 and 26 000 respectively. By 1975 the number for the equivalent GCE 'O' and 'A' level was 865 000 and 251 000. See Department of Education and Science, *Educational Statistics* (1978) vol. 2, p. 4.

38. Quoted in P. Lewis, *The Fifties* (1978) p. 172.

39. Boyle's view was expressed in the foreword to the Ministry of Education, *Half Our Future* (1962) – the Newsom Report. For its time it was radical since it assumed children's intelligence was not genetically determined, as asserted by educational psychologists such as Burt, but could be 'acquired'.

40. See O. Banks, *Parity and Prestige in English Secondary Education* (1975) pp. 135–8.

41. See M. Sanderson, *Educational Opportunity and Social Change in England* (1987) p. 85: 'The 1870s unequal treatment of equals was as unjust as the 1970s equal treatment of unequals. . . . Anti-egalitarians would regard English education as having swung from one form of injustice to another. They would see the just equilibrium in that arc as the late 1940s and the 1950s.'

42. B. Simon, *Education and the Social Order* (1991) p. 215. Girls had to score higher marks than boys to qualify for entry into grammar schools.

43. *Educational Reconstruction*, for instance, had stated that it would be 'wrong to suppose' that the three types of education would 'necessarily remain separate and apart' (Cmd 6458, para. 31). However, in their general guide to the implementation of the Act, *The Nation's Schools* (1945) and their specific instruction to LEAs, circular 144/1947, officials (with the sanction of the Labour government) made their preference explicit.

44. Several comments favourable to comprehensive education in the draft of *Secondary Education for All* were, however, censored. See B. Simon, *Education and the Social Order* (1991) p. 219.

45. Central government gave higher maintenance grants to grammar schools and local government found ways of paying grammar school teachers higher wages for special qualifications and 'responsibilities'.

46. M. Sanderson, *Educational Opportunity and Social Change in England* (1987) p. 55. All the examples in the following paragraph are taken from chapter 3 of this book, unless otherwise stated.

47. A. Yates and D. E. Pidgeon, *Admission to Grammar Schools* (1958); Roy Lowe, *Education in the Postwar Years* (1988) p. 117. The initial

errors of reallocation were compounded by the failure to transfer more than 2–3 per cent of children per annum between schools after the age of eleven.

48. For a summary of this research, particularly that by Floud, Halsey, Martin and Jackson, see H. Silver (ed.), *Equal Opportunity in Education* (1973).

49. The early age of selection had also concerned Conservative ministers such as Butler and Eccles, who commented with characteristic bluntness: 'Eleven plus is too early to show your paces if you come from a dumb or a bad home' (Public Record Office, ED 147/207). Norwood had also favoured a common curriculum for all children between the age of eleven and thirteen to facilitate late transfers.

50. *Educational Reconstruction* (1943) para. 17; Public Record Office, ED 12/479, 10th meeting of the Norwwod Committee, October 1942.

51. See P. Gosden and P. R. Sharp, *The Development of an Education Service* (1978) p. 166. It had been a principal objective of the 1938 Spens report to discourage children with high IQs from automatically opting for an academic rather than a practical training.

52. D. Thom, 'The 1944 Education Act', in H. L. Smith, *War and Social Change* (1986) p. 108. See also B. Evans and B. Waites, *IQ and Mental Testing* (1981) ch. 3. The irony is all the greater since IQ tests had been used to exclude fee-paying middle-class children from grammar schools, and thereby to raise their academic standards. See O. Banks, *Parity and Prestige in English Secondary Education* (1955) ch. 5.

53. Quoted in B. Simon, *Education and the Social Order* (1991) pp. 235–6. See also P. E. Vernon, *Secondary School Selection* (1957).

54. The concept of general intelligence, let alone its measurability, is today seriously questioned. There are, some psychologists have argued, many different kinds of intelligence controlled by different parts of the brain. There is now also general agreement that exceptional ability is not usually transferred from one generation to the next ('regression to the mean').

55. P. Summerfield, *Women Workers in the Second World War* (1984) ch. 4: *Educational Reconstruction* (1943) para. 8. Summerfield sees the history of nursery education as a major failure in 'collective provision for women's benefit' (p. 119).

56. The 1972 Halsey Report on *Educational Priority*, quoted in R. Rodgers, *From Crowther to Warnock* (1980) ch. 8. Unlike the practice in other European countries, however, the age of entry into full-time primary education was five not six.

57. Quoted in B. Simon, *Education and the Social Order* (1991) p. 364. Progressive educational methods had been facilitated by courses such as 'new maths' pioneered by the Nuffield Foundation.

58. See K. G. Banting, *Poverty, Politics and Policy* (1979) ch. 4. The incidence of streaming is recorded in Simon, ibid., p. 346.

59. B. Simon, 'The 1944 Education Act', *History of Education*, 15 (1986) 33.

60. T. C. Worsley, *The End of the Old School Tie* (1941) p. 11; C.A.R.

Crosland, *The Future of Socialism* (1956) p. 264; Roy Lowe, *Education in the Postwar Years* (1988) p. 121.

61. Tax relief on gifts to minors and on loans was removed in 1962 and 1969 respectively although, crucially, public schools still retained their charitable status. Public schools were also made subject to inspection after 1957.

62. Public Record Office: ED 147/211. The official view of the virtues of private schooling is documented in P. Gosden, *Education in the Second World War* (1976) ch. 14.

63. H. Glennerster and W. Low, 'Education and the Welfare State', in J. Hills (ed.), *The State of Welfare* (1990) p. 51. These figures cover children in preparatory as well as public schools. A further reason for the popularity of public schools was their success with eleven-plus 'failures'. In the 1950s, 70 per cent of those 'failures' attained five or more 'O' levels, and 25 per cent two or more 'A' levels.

64. Roy Lowe, *Education in the Postwar Years* (1988) p. 111.

65. In Yorkshire, for example, parents were reported to be 'almost frantic' that their children should not be allocated to secondary moderns. See P. Gosden and P. R. Sharp, *The Development of an Education Service* (1978) p. 174.

66. Quoted in P. Gosden, *The Education System since 1944* (1983) p. 68.

67. For a lively debate on the education record of the 1945 Labour government, see *History Workshop Journal*, vols 9–10 (1980–1). The NUT, it should be noted, did not vote in favour of comprehensive education until 1965.

68. Quoted in B. Simon, *Education and the Social Order* (1991) p. 281. The essentially negative purpose behind Labour's plans for comprehensives can be caught in Harold Wilson's slogan 'grammar school education for all'. Later he claimed that grammar schools would be abolished only over his dead body – a challenge to which there was surprisingly little response.

69. See especially, P. Gosden and P. R. Sharp, *The Development of an Educational Service* (1978) ch. 7. The West Riding pioneered the concept of the 'middle school' which, by dividing children at thirteen, permitted some rationalisation of existing school buildings.

70. See Chapter 8.2. The nine CATs, which gained university status in 1965, were Aston, Bath, Bradford, Brunel, City, Heriot-Watt, Loughborough, Salford and Surrey. Higher education was provided by other institutions, but students largely worked for university external degrees.

71. Founded in 1919, the UGC initially represented the views of individual universities to government but was later entrusted with coordination and planning. Until 1962 it reported directly to the Treasury. Universities were also perceived to encourage inequality. Through their control of the GCE examination, for example, they imposed on secondary schools the specialist curricula which discouraged many working-class pupils. The cost of educating undergraduates, who were largely middle class, was equivalent to that of ten years' education in state schools. See B. Abel-Smith 'Whose Welfare State?', in N. Mackenzie (ed.), *Conviction* (1958) p. 57.

72. C. Chitty, 'Central control of the school curriculum, 1944–87', *History of Education*, 17 (1988) 324.
73. Quoted in ibid., p. 330. For the establishment and record of the Schools Council, on whose governing body teacher representatives were in the majority, see B. Simon, *Education and the Social Order, 1940–1990* (1991) pp. 311–4.
74. W. A. C. Stewart, *Higher Education in Postwar Britain* (1989) pp. 74, 132.
75. *Technical Education* (Cmd 9703). The Hives Committee later became the Council for National Academic Awards which validated all degrees outside universities. Lord Cherwell did encourage the foundation of Churchill College, Cambridge, in an unsuccessful attempt to create a British MIT.
76. S. J. Prais, 'Vocational qualifications of the labour force in Britain and Germany', *National Institute Economic Review* (1982); M. Sanderson, *Educational Opportunity and Social Change in England* (1987) p. 124. The enquiries into missing scientists were the 1968 Dainton and Swann Committees (Cmnd 3541 and 3760). See also M. Sanderson, 'Social equity and industrial need: a dilemma of English education since 1945' which is included in T. Gourvish and A. O'Day, *Britain since 1945* (1991) pp. 159–82.
77. *Educational Reconstruction* (1942) para. 29.
78. Cmd 9703, ch. 5. Employers were abetted in their conservatism by trade unions which (out of a historic fear of unemployment) remained suspicious of any attempt to increase the number of, or to modernise, apprenticeships.

9 Housing

1. M. Foot, *Aneurin Bevan* (vol. I, 1962), p. 473. Eden first used the phrase 'property-owning democracy' at the Conservative Party conference in 1946.
2. R. J. Wybrow, *Britain Speaks Out, 1937–87* (1989) p. 17. The other quotations in this paragraph are from PEP, *Family Needs and the Social Services* (1961) p. 37 and *The Economist*, 5 June 1954.
3. Conservative Political Centre, *One Nation* (1950) pp. 30–1.
4. Cmd 6153 (1940) para. 428.
5. Cmd 6378 and 6386 (1942). On account of the detailed legal issues involved, both Scott and Uthwatt were high court judges.
6. As Macmillan was characteristically to remark, the methods were 'more suitable to an oriental bazaar than to the traditions of the British revenue system'. *Tides of Fortune 1945–1955* (1969) p. 423.
7. Cmd 6537 (1944) p. 2. The white paper used the term 'betterment', as it is used in this chapter, to cover the increase in value of both undeveloped land granted planning permission (strictly its 'development' value) and of developed land resulting from adjacent improvements.
8. In 1947 and 1975 the tax was levied on the developer. In 1967 land

was purchased from the owner at 60 per cent of its development value and therefore an effective tax of 40 per cent was imposed.

9. This and the succeeding paragraph are based on A. Cox, *Adversary Politics and Land* (Cambridge, 1984).

10. Hence the 100 per cent betterment tax was designed in 1947 not by ministers to achieve socialist ends but by the Treasury to prevent the Land Commission from raising any money. In 1967 it clawed back all – and in 1975 40 per cent of – the revenue from betterment and the sale of land. The constitutional objections also resulted in local government rather than a central Land Commission being responsible for the execution of policy in 1975.

11. S. Merrett, *State Housing in Britain* (1979) p. 81. The property boom drove Edward Heath to coin the phrase 'the unacceptable face of capitalism', whilst the seriousness of the credit crisis was illustrated by the rare collapse of a bank (the 'secondary' bank, London and Home Securities).

12. J. R. Short, *Housing in Britain* (1982) p. 214; S. Merrett, *State Housing in Britain* (1979) p. 79. The parks were the Brecon Beacons, the Pembrokeshire Coast and Snowdonia; Dartmoor and Exmoor; Northumberland, the North Yorkshire Moors and the Yorkshire Dales; the Lake District and the Peak District.

13. J. R. Short, *Housing in Britain* (1982) p. 87. The secrecy of planners became so notorious that after 1968 they were obliged by law to prove that they had taken account of public opinion in the drafting of plans.

14. Except where specified, housing in this section refers not just to houses but also to 'dwellings', that is, parts of buildings (such as flats) which provide structurally separate living quarters.

15. Economic historians have widely criticised the diversion of resources from industry to housing. Corelli Barnett's comment is typical: 'instead of starting with a new workshop to become rich enough to afford a new family villa, John Bull opted for the villa straightaway – even though he happened to be bankrupt at the time.' *Audit of War* (1986) pp. 246–7.

16. Partly under Churchill's influence, 160 000 prefabs (each of which could be erected in a day) were built between 1946 and 1948. Like the experiment with prefabricated building in the early 1960s, they proved to be more expensive and of lower quality than conventional housing. They were also urged on government by wartime contractors with spare capacity. They were, in short, 'an object lesson in the failure of centralist planning'. See O. Gay, 'Prefabs: a study in policy-making', *Public Administration*, 65 (1987) 407–22.

17. Quoted in M. Foot, *Aneurin Bevan* (vol. 2, 1973) p. 82.

18. See M. Sissons and P. French, *Age of Austerity, 1945–1951* (Harmondsworth, 1964) pp. 44–8.

19. The 300 000 target was one of the very few policy decisions forced by a Conservative conference on the Party's leaders. For the details see A. Seldon, *Churchill's Indian Summer* (1981) p. 248.

20. Public Record Office: T273/91, Macmillan to Butler, 21 Dec. 1951. For his antics, which the head of the civil service condemned as 'ridiculous

and underhand', see H. Macmillan, *Tides of Fortune 1945–55* (1969) ch. 13.

21. There were 2500 housing associations and they attracted criticism because they were too small to reap economies of scale and, as non-elected bodies, consumed much public money. They were, however, human in scale and extremely flexible. For a brief and critical summary, see J. R. Short, *Housing in Britain* (1982) pp. 188–93.

22. Cmnd 2838 (1965) p. 8. Bevan had of course opened the way for greater municipalisation through the Housing Act of 1949, which empowered local government for the first time to provide accommodation for all members of the community, not just 'the working classes'.

23. Cmnd 3602 (1968).

24. One analyst in 1969 calculated that it would cost annually £600 million to construct 200 000 local authority houses, but only £230 million to improve 230 000 homes. See P. N. Balchin, *Housing Policy: an introduction* (2nd ed, 1989) p. 75. This book provides the best brief introduction to rehabilitation.

25. The statistics in this paragraph are taken from S. Merrett, *State Housing in Britain* (1979) p. 115 and J. R. Short, *Housing in Britain* (1982) p. 59.

26. The Labour government did flirt with a few radical alternatives and briefly revived council house building, but after the economic crisis of 1976 it reverted to more traditional policies, as demonstrated by the 1977 consultative document, *Housing Policy* (Cmnd 6851), which reaffirmed that owner-occupation was a 'basic and natural desire' (p. 50).

27. Nevertheless in 1967 the powerful television documentary on homelessness, *Cathy Come Home*, inspired the creation of the highly successful housing pressure group, Shelter.

28. Ministry of Housing and Local Government, *Homes for Today and Tomorrow* (1961) para. 7. The later quotation is from para. 10.

29. D. Donnison and C. Ungerson, *Housing Policy* (1982) p. 187. The statistics are taken from A. H. Halsey (ed.), *British Social Trends since 1900* (2nd edn, 1988) table 10.13 and P. N. Balchin, *Housing Policy* (2nd edn, 1985) p. 90. The proportion of households in England and Wales lacking a fixed bath and lavatory fell respectively between 1951 and 1971 from 37 per cent to 9 per cent and from 8 per cent to 4 per cent.

30. *One Nation* (1950) p. 26. A masterly analysis of high-rise building is provided by P. Dunleavy, *The Politics of Mass Housing in Britain, 1945–75* (Oxford, 1981), upon which this and the succeeding paragraph are based. Its conclusion is that there was a 'sacrifice of previously maintained design and amenity standards to the overriding imperatives of production' (p. 20).

31. S. Merrett, *State Housing in Britain* (1979) p. 131. Half of all public dwellings constructed between 1962 and 1972 were flats, and at the peak in 1964 half of all flats were in blocks of 15 storeys or more. Ibid., p. 128.

32. Central government could also vary the cost of local government bor-

rowing. Thus cheap loans were provided through the Public Works Loan Board until 1955, after which local authorities had to pay the full market rate. In 1967, however, the Labour government sought to combat inflation by agreeing to pay any interest over 4 per cent. This quickly quadrupled the cost of subsidising a house. See J. R. Short, *Housing in Britain* (1982) p. 57.

33. To encourage home ownership by non-taxpayers, who would not benefit from these concessions, the government introduced 'option mortgages' at especially low rates of interest. Local authorities or building societies, which administered the scheme, were reimbursed for any difference in the proceeds from these and ordinary mortgages which enjoyed tax relief. Until inflation brought most people above the tax thresholds, option mortgages accounted for about a fifth of all mortgages. Ibid., p. 56.

34. See M. Daunton, *A Property-Owning Democracy?* (1987) p.x. Policy was regressive because not only did subsidies go exclusively to those who could afford to buy their homes, but also the largest subsidies went to those who took out the highest mortgages and received relief from the highest tax rates.

35. Public Record Office: T230/312, EC(S)(56)2, Economic Section discussion paper on rent control, 1956.

36. For an analysis of the Milner-Holland Report (which found that only 1 per cent of tenants were abused and, at most, only 5 per cent were 'completely dissatisfied' with their landlords) and the Rachman scandal, see K. G. Banting, *Poverty, Politics and Policy in Britain in the 1960s* (1979) pp. 14–65.

37. The criterion for a 'fair rent' was 'the likely market rent assuming no scarcity' – a concept as impossible to measure as the price of land under the Land Commission in the 1940s.

38. Cmnd 2838 (1965) p. 15. The 1972 Act, it should be noted, broke new ground by introducing rent allowances for the poorest tenants in private rented accommodation – the first direct subsidy this sector of the housing market had received.

39. For an account of popular resistance, see S. Merrett, *State Housing in Britain* (1979) ch. 7. For the relative costs of rent and mortgages, see A. H. Halsey (ed.) *British Social Trends Since 1900* (2nd ed 1988) table 10.33.

40. Quoted in J. Hills (ed.), *The State of Welfare* (Oxford, 1990) p. 137.

41. Enoch Powell, *The Welfare State* (1961) p. 13.

10 The personal social services

1. Cmnd 3703. The term 'personal social services' was coined for this committee.

2. The ultimate objectives of the personal social services have been alternatively defined as social integration (for those who would otherwise be marginalised) and social control. The latter includes the protection of society from the respective danger, embarrassment and distress

368Notes and References

which might arise, for instance, from juvenile delinquency, the behaviour of the mentally-ill or from the knowledge that elderly people were living in squalor. See M. Evandrou *et al.*, 'The personal social services', in J. Hills (ed.), *The State of Welfare* (Oxford, 1990) p. 209.

3. Lord Beveridge, *Voluntary Action: A report on methods of social advance* (1948). For a critique, see K. and J. Williams, *A Beveridge Reader* (1989) ch. 5.

4. Battles were also fought with professionals in other services and especially the NHS. Within hospitals, almoners (renamed 'medical social workers' in 1963) long resisted the attempt to transform them into medical auxiliaries helping doctors, among other things, to process more patients by finding alternative sources of care in the community. They preferred the far more challenging role of identifying possible social causes of illness, such as anxiety or family breakdown. Accordingly in 1973 they left the NHS to join the local authority social service departments. GPs unwisely ignored the Seebohm Committee and thus lost the chance to become 'senior social workers' promoting community medicine (see Chapter 7.3).

5. See E. Younghusband, *Social Work in Britain, 1950–1975* (vol. 1, 1978) p. 39.

6. Quoted in B. Rodgers and J. Dixon, *Portrait of Social Work* (Oxford, 1960) p. 163. The book provides the best survey of social work practice in the 1950s.

7. The best, and extremely influential, account of the remaining Poor Law 'warehouses' is P. Townsend, *The Last Refuge* (1965).

8. The initial objective was that of the 1930 Poor Law Act; the latter was articulated by the report of the Curtis Care of Children Committee (Cmd 6922) and confirmed by the 1948 Act. This Act was also progressive in that it projected a large number of women for the first time into senior positions within local government.

9. J. Parker, *Local Health and Welfare Services* (1965) p. 108. The Act introduced charges, and thus means tests, for services in order to distinguish them from 'free' but stigmatising Poor Law services.

10. E. Younghusband, *Social Work in Britain, 1950–1975* (vol. 1, 1978) p. 35.

11. An exhaustive report on training was completed in 1959 by the Younghusband working party on social workers in local authority health and welfare services.

12. Cmnd 3703, para. 1. There was a parallel reappraisal in Scotland, resulting in the 1968 Social Work (Scotland) Act. This Act was more radical than Seebohm, imposing on local government the 'duty to promote social welfare' and placing the probation service within the social work departments.

13. Ibid., para. 32. The Home Office did successfully use its experience to prevent any discussion of the division of administrative responsibility in Whitehall and the inclusion of the probation service within the social services department, as well as excluding from the Committee's membership leading academics, fieldworkers and consumers of the service.

14. The successive quotations are from paras. 111, 478, 516 and 473. Approval of appointments of directors of social services by the secretary of state (a recommendation which split the Committee) was sought essentially to ensure that successful candidates would have social work qualifications and were not, as had happened in certain combined health and welfare committees in London, medical officers of health. In the event, of the 174 appointees in 1971 only five had medical qualifications, whereas 58 were former children's officers and 79 former welfare officers. In a predominantly female profession, only 21 were women. See E. Younghusband, *Social Work in Britain, 1950–1975* (vol. 1, 1978) p. 240.

15. Cmnd 3703, para. 454. The Report was equally vague about the content and nature of professional training. Crossman, as the responsible minister, dismissed the report as 'boring and unconvincing' and its adoption was only assured once Baroness Serota had become one of his junior ministers. Characteristically Crossman claimed he was unaware she was a member of the Committee whose report he wished to jettison. See P. Hall, *Reforming the Welfare* (1976) p. 92.

16. R. Pinker, 'Social work and social policy in the twentieth century', in M. Bulmer *et al.*, *The Goals of Social Policy* (1989) p. 98.

17. Cmnd 3703, paras 477–81.

18. Fears on this score were exaggerated because although the Report wanted each case to be the responsibility of one social worker, that worker could be the most appropriate specialist. Hall notes that specialisation was a major subject of disagreement within the Committee, as was the balance between central and local government, and the relationship with the Ministry of Education over pre-school education. *Reforming the Welfare* (1976) ch. 4.

19. See E. Younghusband, *Social Work in Britain, 1950–1975* (vol. 1, 1978) p. 30.

20. Ibid., p. 45. This figure was equivalent to 7.2 per 1000 children under the age of eighteen. 29 400 were in foster care, 15 600 remained at home and the others were in residential care.

21. Ibid., p. 51. For details of the tragedies, see J. Packman, *The Child's Generation* (1975), especially pp. 168–76.

22. J. Hills (ed.), *The State of Welfare* (1990) p. 232.

23. Age Concern, *The Attitudes of the Retired and Elderly* (Mitcham, 1974). In the 1940s local authorities could only provide home helps (a service originally designed for young mothers). It was made mandatory in 1968. Other services were made permissive – such as chiropody in 1959 and meals-on-wheels in 1962 – and became mandatory in 1971 together with additional concessions such as the provision of telephones.

24. Cmnd 3703, para. 319. In 1944 a much-vaunted Disabled Persons (Employment) Act had been passed which was designed to reserve jobs for the physically disabled. In time it came largely to be ignored. See especially H. Bolderson, 'The origins of the disabled persons employment quota', *Journal of Social Policy* 9 (1980) 169–86.

25. Both documents were published by the DHSS, not as command papers. The quotation is from p. 14 of the second report.
26. Voluntary provision existed in all the main welfare services (for example, parents' fund-raising for schools and the 'friends' of hospitals) but was particularly prevalent in areas covered by the personal social services, owing to their nature and underdevelopment.
27. See chapters 7.1 and 6, note 8. By 1947 it was estimated that 72 per cent and 41 per cent of households respectively subscribed to industrial assurance and private health care (Public Record Office, RG23/138).
28. PEP, *Family Needs and the Social Services* (1961) p. 130; M. Evandrou et al., 'The personal social services', in J. Hills (ed.), *The State of Welfare* (Oxford, 1990) pp. 215, 269. For the difficulties in measuring the value of informal care, see Chapter 3.2.2.
29. The best, if somewhat over-romanticised, accounts of working-class self-sufficiency, forged in poverty and based on a 'reciprocal flow of services' between mothers and daughters, are two books by M. Young and P. Wilmott: *Family and Kinship in East London* (1957) and *Family and Class in a London Suburb* (1960). Redevelopment did not reduce but changed the nature of informal care, to the disadvantage of the elderly.
30. The most thorough review of informal care is G. Parker, 'Who Cares? A review of empirical evidence from Britain', in R. E. Pahl (ed.), *On Work* (Oxford, 1988). It concludes that responsibility within the family is usually concentrated on one person, and that that person is a woman.
31. Quoted in B. Watkin, *The National Health Service* (1978) p. 18. For a definition of the political and functional roles of the welfare state, see Chapters 2.1 and 3.2.1.
32. Quoted in M. Brasnett, *Voluntary Social Action* (1969) p. 170.
33. The concept of 'community action' radically changed between the 1930s and the 1960s. In the 1930s middle-class philanthropy had largely sought to recreate a sense of community based on middle-class values. In the 1960s, as the Seebohm Committee explicitly admitted, the object was again 'social control' (Cmnd 3703, para. 477). Control was to be achieved by peer pressure from within a community, however, rather than imposed from outside by another class – although, of course, the role of the social worker, as a professional worker ultimately responsible to government, was highly ambivalent.
34. *The Future of Voluntary Organisations* (1978) p. 26. The terms of reference for the Wolfenden Committee were to examine 'the role and function of voluntary organisations'. It was financed by the Rowntree Memorial and the Carnegie Trusts.
35. The Citizens' Advice Bureaux and the Samaritans, which could respectively call on 7000 and 14 600 volunteers in 1971, represented the two extremes of the spectrum. The former were almost wholly financed by government, the latter hardly at all.
36. *The Future of Voluntary Organisations* (1978) p. 27. The succeeding quotation is from Cmnd 3703, para. 496.
37. Volunteers within the social services tended to be middle-aged. As part of the 1960s revolution, the young were increasingly recruited by

agencies such as Community Service Volunteers (founded in 1962) and Task Force (founded in 1964).
38. Cmnd 3703, para. 498. The Aves Report was published under the title *The Voluntary Worker in The Social Services*.
39. E. Younghusband, *Social Work in Britain, 1950–1975* (vol. 1, 1978) p. 264. An indication of the extent of local initiatives in the 1970s is provided by J. Hatch, *Outside the State: voluntary organisations in three English towns* (1980).
40. For a good survey, see R. Means and R. Smith, *The Development of Welfare Services for Elderly People* (1985) ch. 6.
41. *The Future of Voluntary Organisations* (1978) p. 20; M. Brenton, *The Voluntary Sector in British Social Services* (1985) p. 37.
42. This paragraph is based largely on E. Younghusband, *Social Work in Britain, 1950–1975* (vol. 1, 1978) ch. 18. NACRO is described as the 'outstanding example of the new voluntary organisations started in the 1960s which could look questioningly at the present and future, unfettered by past assumptions' (p. 263). Much of the most innovative research was also financed by such philanthropic trusts as the Gulbenkian, Leverhulme, Nuffield and Joseph Rowntree Foundations.
43. For the full statistical details, see A. Webb *et al.*, *Voluntary Social Services: manpower resources* (1976) and J. Unell, *Voluntary Social Services: financial resources* (1979).
44. E. Younghusband, *Social Work in Britain, 1950–1975* (vol. 1, 1978) p. 35.
45. The description of the DHSS document, *Priorities for Health and Personal Social Services in England*, is in J. Hills (ed.), *The State of Welfare* (Oxford, 1990) p. 234.

11 The achievement

1. V. George and P. Wilding, *Ideology and Social Welfare* (1985) p. 62.
2. P. M. Williams (ed.), *The Diary of Hugh Gaitskell* (1983) p. 542; *One Nation* (1950) p. 75. See also Chapters 2.2.1–2.2.3 and 8.2.
3. This assumption was confirmed by the 1951–5 Royal Commission on the Taxation of Profits and Income which observed that 'not merely progressive taxation, but a steep gradient of taxation, is needed in order to conform with the notions of equitable distribution that are widely, almost universally accepted'. See Cmd 9105 (1954) para. 108. The government's chief economic adviser in 1957 also defined 'the foundations of the Welfare State' as 'the provision of social services and . . . progressive direct taxation'. (R. Hall in Public Record Office: T171/478, memo 25).
4. H. Phelps Brown, *Egalitarianism and the Generation of Inequality* (Oxford) p. 350. Admittedly the recorded income and wealth of the very rich did decline, but the benefits accrued largely to those who were already well-off.
5. Public Record Office, T171/427. Memorandum by A. Cockfield, 4 February 1950, para. 9. In 1942 Keynes had planned a 'social policy

budget' designed to redistribute income as well as raise taxation (T171/360) but in 1975 the Central Policy Review Staff was still calling, in *A Joint Framework for Social Policies*, for regular calculations to be made.

6. F. Field *et al.*, *To Him Who Hath* (Harmondsworth, 1977) p. 20.
7. To avoid too great a surge in taxation, 55 per cent of goods had initially to be zero-rated for VAT, a percentage which has steadily shrunk.
8. In 1952, for example, the first £100 of taxable income was taxed at 12 per cent, the next £150 at 22 per cent and a further £150 at 28 per cent. Only when taxable income reached £400 was it taxed at the full 47.5 per cent. See F. Field *et al.*, *To Him Who Hath* (Harmondsworth, 1977) pp. 38–42.
9. Ibid., pp. 32, 41. The figures in the following paragraph are taken from p. 53.
10. Reprinted in R. M. Titmuss, *Essays on 'The Welfare State'* (1958) ch. 2.
11. A Sinfield, 'Poverty, privilege and welfare', in P. Bean and D. Whynes, *Barbara Wootton* (1966) p. 112. One of the first tax allowances to be granted, in 1909, was the child allowance, which taxpayers continued to enjoy until 1976 in addition to the cash family allowances. Those sufficiently rich to pay tax therefore received considerably more child support than the poor. This explains in part the lack of protest against the falling real value of family allowances; and indeed one of the most serious objections to fiscal welfare is that it undermines the mutual interest in state welfare which universalism was designed to foster.
12. The share of the total tax paid by the top 10 per cent of taxpayers fell between 1959 and 1976–7 from 65 per cent to 40 per cent. See Cmnd 7595, the Royal Commission on the Distribution of Income and Wealth, *Report* no. 7 (1979) para. 7.2.
13. Public Record Office; CAB 128/29, CM (55) 45, para. 6(2), Cabinet meeting of 6 December 1955. The following quotations are from H. Phelps Brown, *Egalitarianism and the Generation of Inequality* (Oxford, 1988) pp. 331–2.
14. B. Abel-Smith, 'Whose welfare state?', in N. MacKenzie (ed.), *Conviction* (1958) p. 57.
15. J. Le Grand, *The Strategy of Equality* (1982) p. 3. Attempts were made to equalise provision, such as Education Priority Areas, Housing Action Areas, and the work of the Resource Allocation Working Party in health care. Each, however, has been adjudged a failure.
16. The first analyses were published in *Economic Trends* vol. 109 (1962) and 124 (1964). A more recent analysis has established that in the late 1960s an average family lost 38 per cent of its income in taxation and received 21.2 per cent back in benefit. Its conclusion was that 'the imbalance between activity and effect is a central criticism of the operation of the British welfare state'. See R. Parry, 'UK', in P. Flora (ed.), *Growth to Limits. The Western European Welfare States since World War II*, vol. 2 (Berlin, 1986) p. 201.
17. For a summary of the inadequacy of statistics relating to wealth, see

Cmnd 6171, the Royal Commission on the Distribution of Income and Wealth, *Report* no. 1 (1975) paras 324–35.

18. For a full discussion of the problems in calculating and presenting statistics relating to income, see respectively N. Barr, *The Economics of the Welfare State* (1987) ch. 6 and H. Phelps Brown, *Egalitarianism and the Generation of Inequality* (Oxford, 1988) ch. 9.

19. C. A. R. Crosland, *The Future of Socialism* (1956) p. 347. This book provides the most powerful contemporary perspective of the equalisation of economic and political power in postwar Britain (part one) as well as an agenda for further change (part four).

20. See Chapter 2.2.2. Marshall had of course argued that universal welfare policy was the means by which the capitalist need for incentive (and hence unequal money incomes) could be reconciled with the democratic need for equality.

21. Public Record Office: T171/478, memo. 25.

22. K. and J. Williams, *A Beveridge Reader* (1987) p. 155.

23. W. D. Rubinstein, *Wealth and Inequality in Britain* (1986) p. 54.

24. P. M. Williams (ed.), *The Diary of Hugh Gaitskell* (1983) p. 542. The succeeding quotations are from R. H. S. Crossman, *Socialism and Planning* (1967) p. 80 and T. Utley, *Not Guilty* (1957) p. 87.

25. R. Parry, 'U.K.', in P. Flora (ed.), *Growth to Limits* (Berlin, 1986) p. 204. This article is a leading example of the use of the framework to examine the efficiency of welfare policy after 1945, whilst some of the conceptual issues it raises are discussed in J. Hills (ed.), *The State of Welfare* (Oxford, 1990) ch. 1.

26. N. Barr, *The Economics of the Welfare State* (1989) p. 358.

27. R. Parry, 'U.K.', in P. Flora (ed.), *Growth to Limits* (Berlin, 1986) p. 209. The relative cost of the NHS is summarised in R. M. Page, 'Social welfare since the war', in N. F. R. Crafts and N. Woodward (eds), *The British Economy since 1945* (Oxford, 1991) p. 472.

28. See R. M. Page, op. cit., pp. 446–7, and R. Lowe, *Adjusting to Democracy* (Oxford, 1986) pp. 217–8.

29. E. Powell, *Medicine and Politics* (1966) p. 16.

12 The welfare state under threat

1. Crosland was, symbolically, the Labour minister most closely identified with the belief that government should use the increased wealth generated by economic growth to create painlessly a more just and efficient society (see Chapter 2.2.2). His audience was important, since local government was still responsible for one-third of public expenditure.

2. David Owen, quoted in H. Young, *One of Us* (1989) p. 294. See also Chapter 8.2.

3. R. Parry, 'U.K.', in P. Flora (ed.), *Growth to Limits*, vol. 2 (Berlin, 1986) p. 169. In the same decade the total number of public employees increased from 6.2 million to 7.8 million, or from 24.3 per cent to 31.5 per cent of the total workforce.

4. Quoted in T. Raison, *Tories and the Welfare State* (1990) p. 91.

5. Neo-Marxists have described the purpose of the 'authoritarian populism' of Thatcherism as being 'to force-march . . . society, vigorously, into the past'. See S. Hall and M. Jacques (eds), *The Politics of Thatcherism* (1983) pp. 10–11.

6. J. Le Grand in J. Hills (ed.), *The State of Welfare* (Oxford, 1990) p. 350.

7. Between 1979 and 1984 Britain's rate of growth had been less than half that of other OECD countries, whereas between 1984 and 1989 it was 20.4 per cent compared to 18.8 per cent. See A. Cairncross, *The British Economy since 1945* (1992) p. 228.

8. J. Barnett, *Inside the Treasury* (1982) p. 23.

9. The defection of the former Cabinet minister, Reg Prentice, to the Conservatives in October 1977 was symbolic of the attraction Mrs Thatcher's blend of strong leadership and traditional values held for many social democratic academics and politicians with strong local interests.

10. H. Young, *One of Us* (1989) p. 298. In 1981 Gallup recorded support for Margaret Thatcher amongst only 25 per cent of those polled. Her average rating of 39 per cent between 1979 and 1987 was lower than that for any other prime minister. See D. Kavanagh, *Thatcherism and British Politics* (Oxford, 2nd ed, 1990) p. 269.

11. As she confided to a journalist: 'I am in politics because of the conflict between good and evil, and I believe in the end good will triumph' (*Daily Telegraph*, 18 September 1984).

12. H. Young, *One of Us* (1989) p. 498. The temporary support for the Social Democratic Party, which polls regularly recorded at over 30 per cent of the electorate, was a major political constraint on radical action.

13. By 1990 the number of private shareholders had risen from three to nine million and there were over one million new home-owners.

14. The official basis for the calculation of unemployment was constantly tightened with, for example, its restriction to those claiming unemployment benefit; stricter qualification rules for benefit; and the creation of various temporary employment and training programmes. By the traditional definition, the figure for 1986 would have been nearer 3.8 million than 3.1 million. See G. D. N. Worswick, *Unemployment* (Cambridge, 1991).

15. H. Young, *One of Us* (1989) p. 504.

16. See Chapter 1. The conclusion of his principal policy adviser was that Callaghan was not 'a doctrinal monetarist, but he was instinctively conservative . . . his basic position being that monetary laxity was nearly always wrong'. The IMF agreement 'formally entrenched monetarism in Labour's economic policy-making although it really only made public what was already happening in Whitehall'. B. Donoughue, *Prime Minister* (1987) pp. 82, 100.

17. Margaret Thatcher unilaterally vetoed a compromise at GCHQ based on a 'no-strike' agreement, although the unions had admittedly provoked such intransigence by selecting this key security installation for strategic strikes (which had resulted in the loss of 10 000 working days between 1979 and 1981). The industrialists' attack was launched,

somewhat symbolically, in the House of Lords Select Committee Report on Overseas Trade of October 1985.

18. H. Young, *One of Us* (1989) p. 231.
19. See A Cairncross, *The British Economy since 1945* (1992) p. 276.
20. H. Young, *One of Us* (1989) p. 367.
21. For a summary of the polls, see D. Kavanagh, *Thatcherism and British Politics* (Oxford, 2nd ed, 1990) pp. 244–306; for a more detailed analysis, see P. Taylor-Gooby, *Public Opinion, Ideology and State Welfare* (1985); and for an interesting historical perspective, see the introduction to P. Baldwin, *The Politics of Social Solidarity* (Cambridge, 1990). The failure of the Thatcherite cultural revolution raises questions about the existence of the new 'hegemonic bloc', identified by S. Hall and M. Jacques in *The Politics of Thatcherism* (1983) chs 1–2.
22. Two conventional qualifications are respondents' lack of understanding ('civic illiteracy') and a readiness to state what they feel is expected of them, rather than their own opinions. A 'cultural revolution', it could also be argued, is necessarily a long process and can best be identified in the opinions not of the general public but of the young.
23. J. Le Grand in J. Hills (ed.) *The State of Welfare* (Oxford, 1990) p. 351.
24. The whole electorate had an interest in social insurance, although most of its services – especially pensions – were increasingly supplemented by private schemes. Means-tested benefits and the personal social services were exclusively the preserve of the 'undeserving' minority.
25. The earnings-related pension was indexed against price rises, the flat-rate pension against increases in prices or earnings (whichever were the higher). The alteration of the criteria for indexation was a favourite method of economising in the 1980s.
26. See M. Hill, *Social Security in Britain* (Aldershot, 1990) p. 52.
27. N. Barr and F. Coulter, 'Social security', in J. Hills (ed.), *The State of Welfare* (Oxford, 1990) p. 284.
28. There were four white papers in 1985 covering the recommendations and implementation of the Fowler review, all entitled *The Reform of Social Security*: Cmnd 9517–9 and 9691.
29. A new minister, John Moore, was appointed to implement Fowler and thereby to end the 'dependency' culture. Instead his career ended. So too did his ministry, which was divided into two separate departments (those of Health and Social Security). The requirement after 1981 that family credit and housing benefit should consider income net of tax has led some to argue that progress has been made towards a merger of the tax and benefit systems. The claim is disputed in M. Hill, *Social Security in Britain* (Aldershot, 1990) chs 5, 9.
30. Full details are provided in N. Barr and F. Coulter, 'Social security', in J. Hills (ed.), *The State of Welfare* (Oxford, 1990) pp. 336–7. The administrative cost of supplementary benefit in 1986–7 was equivalent to almost 12 per cent of the benefit paid; that of child benefit 2.2 per cent.
31. Ibid., p. 329.
32. Ibid., pp. 288–91. The real value of benefit was calculated in terms of

the retail price index, but there is evidence to suggest that the price of goods typically bought by the poor rose faster. Were this true for the 1980s, their absolute living standards would have risen less slowly or even fallen. It should also be noted that, consistent with the policy to encourage the work ethic, the difference between the benefit and former earnings of the average unemployed worker ('the replacement rate') increased at this time. Ibid., pp. 316–7.

33. See Chapter 10.1, 10.3.
34. See, for example, *Growing Older*, Cmnd 8173 (1981) para. 1.9.
35. *Community Care: agenda for action* (1988). Margaret Thatcher specifically opposed the strengthening of local government, but she was forced to concede when the subsidisation of the personal social services by supplementary benefit spiralled out of control (see M. Evandrou *et al.*, 'The personal social services', in J. Hills (ed.), *The State of Welfare* (Oxford, 1990) p. 254). The more radical proposals such as a ministry for community care and, in child care, a Family Court were nevertheless rejected; and in both cases the lack of any clear financial commitment raised questions about the practicality of reform.
36. M. Evandrou *et al.*, 'The personal social services', in J. Hills (ed.), *The State of Welfare* (Oxford, 1990) p. 226.
37. Ibid., p. 250. Between 1974 and 1986 the proportion of elderly people accommodated in private homes rose from 13 per cent to 37 per cent.
38. Ibid., p. 218. These figures exclude the cost of supplementary benefit and special tax allowances for 'carers', the elderly and the handicapped.
39. D. Donnison, *The Politics of Poverty* (Oxford, 1982) p. 132.
40. The figures for real expenditure on the three services are taken from J. Hills (ed.), *The State of Welfare* (Oxford, 1990), in particular pp. 38, 95, 147.
41. Cmd 7615. The 1989 reforms were announced in *Working for Patients* (Cm 555).
42. Private health insurance increased by 26 per cent in 1980 and covered 9 per cent of the population by the late 1980s. See J. Le Grand, 'The National Health Service', in J. Hills (ed.), *The State of Welfare* (Oxford, 1990) p. 106. On the efficiency of the service, see ibid., p. 100.
43. For the statistics in this paragraph, see ibid., pp. 103–4.
44. Improved health standards may of course have reflected improvements outside the NHS and, in particular, a rise in living standards in the 1960s and 1970s. The long-term health costs of high unemployment in the 1980s, if any, have yet to be felt. Were true regional equality to be achieved, the health budgets of Scotland and Wales would have to have been reduced respectively by 19 per cent and 27 per cent in favour of England. Ibid., p. 120.
45. Cmnd 5174 (1972).
46. For a review of the evidence, see H. Glennerster and W. Low, 'Education and the Welfare State', in J. Hills (ed.), *The State of Welfare* (Oxford, 1990) pp. 55–75. With falling rolls, primary school expenditure per pupil actually increased in the 1980s.
47. In 1986 19 per cent of primary schools also had classes over the intended maximum of 30.

48. The most valuable concession enjoyed by public schools was exemption from VAT, which accounted for approximately four-fifths of the total tax concession of £190 million they are estimated to have enjoyed in 1982–3. Numbers did increase marginally to 6.4 per cent of all secondary school pupils by the mid 1980s, but this was well short of the total in the 1930s of 10 per cent. See H. Glennerster and W. Low, 'Education and the Welfare State', in J. Hills (ed.), *The State of Welfare* (Oxford, 1990) pp. 50–3. The number of 'assisted places' had risen to 33 200 by 1987–8.

49. H. Young, *One of Us* (1990) p. 521. Policy on higher education particularly attracted muddled thinking. Wider access was sought for example, but a dramatic fall in the real value of student grants (and their gradual replacement by loans) actively discouraged applications from poorer students. An attempt to introduce a quasi-market – by requiring polytechnics and universities to bid competitively for a certain percentage of funded places – also descended into costly farce and was withdrawn.

50. J. Hills, 'Housing', in J. Hills (ed.), *The State of Welfare* (Oxford, 1990) p. 154. This book again is the principal source of the statistics in the following paragraphs.

51. As explained in Chapter 9.2, figures for a national housing surplus or deficit are hard to establish. The figures cited make allowance for unfit property and 'concealed households' (those who would move to separate housing were it available). They do not allow for 'second' homes or vacant properties.

52. Centralisation was complete by 1988. The housing budgets of local government were 'ring-fenced' so that rents could not be subsidised by the rates nor other policies financed from, for instance, the sale of council houses. Areas deemed 'run-down' could also be transferred to unelected Housing Action Trusts.

53. Apart from tax relief on mortgage interest payments, owner-occupiers benefited from other tax concessions such as the exemption of house sales from capital gains tax and VAT. Certain restrictions were placed upon them in the 1980s, such as a ceiling on mortgage tax relief at £30 000 (a limit which, as the result of the explosion in house prices, one-third of borrowers were exceeding by the late 1980s). It has also been estimated that state subsidies covered only one quarter of their full housing costs compared to one-half of council tenants. Owner-occupiers were, however, being assisted to acquire a private capital asset. See J. Hills, 'Housing', in J. Hills (ed.), *The State of Welfare* (Oxford, 1990) pp. 161–2.

Index

Abel-Smith, Brian   135–6, 140–1, 156, 180, 287
Acts, Parliamentary (select)
Child Benefit (1975)   313
Children: (1948)   264–5, 269; (1989)   317
Children and Young Persons: (1963)   265; (1969)   269
Chronically Sick and Disabled Persons (1970)   47, 270
Contracts of Employment (1963)   81
Commonwealth Immigrants (1962, 1968, 1971)   75
Education (1944)   88, 193, 196–204, 207–8, 210–13, 215, 223, 227, 232, 282, 323–5
Education Reform (1988)   324–5
Employment Training (1973)   229
Housing Finance (1972)   254, 257–8
Industrial Training (1965)   113, 229
Local Government (1972)   90
Mental Health (1959)   190
National Assistance (1948)   47, 142, 265
National Insurance: (1946)   141; (1959)   143, 159–60
National Parks (1949)   242–3
New Towns (1946)   242–3
Redundancy Payments (1965)   81
Rent (1957)   248, 257
Social Security (1975)   146, 313
Town and Country Planning (1947)   240, 243
Amis, Kingsley   96, 210
Atlantic Charter (1941)   11, 122, 131
Attlee, Clement   10, 79, 84, 178

Bevan, Aneurin   21, 76–8, 203, 245–7, 250, 307, 357 n25
and NHS   28, 40, 65, 167, 172–9, 181, 184, 187, 190, 271–2, 356 n20
Beveridge Report (Social Insurance and Allied Services, 1942)   1–4, 13, 17, 33, 99, 122–36, 141–51, 155–62, 166, 182, 188, 238, 266, 282, 285, 291, 310, 315
reception   11, 34, 44, 92, 290
Beveridge, William   16–17, 39, 72, 203, 342 n4

and economic policy   66, 103, 109, 119, 302
and voluntary insurance   262, 271–2, 274, 291
Boyle, Sir Edward   45, 211
Burt, Cyril   211, 217
Butler, R.A.   16–18, 81, 95, 112–13, 196, 200, 202–4, 220, 231, 247
see also Acts: Education (1944)

Callaghan, James   1, 99, 210, 227, 301, 305, 308, 323, 374 n16
Castle, Barbara   43, 45
Central Policy Review Staff (CPRS)   88, 307, 311, 321, 324
Child benefit   see Family allowances
Child Poverty Action Group (CPAG)   145, 275, 319
Children   70–4, 92, 138, 154, 156–7, 163–4, 189, 193, 264, 266, 268–9, 274–5, 311
infant mortality rate   164, 188–9
see also under Acts; families, one-parent; family allowances
Churchill, Winston   11, 45, 82, 91, 129–31, 202
Civil service   29, 30, 41–8, 85–8, 117, 241, 247, 263, 302, 309, 335
see also individual departments
Commission and Committee Reports (under chairman)
Barlow (Scientific Manpower, 1946)   228–9
Beveridge (Social Insurance and Allied Services, 1942)   see Beveridge Report
Bullock (A Language for Life, 1975)   211
Crowther (15 to 18, 1959)   206, 227
Diamond (Distribution of Income and Wealth, 1974–9)   288–9, 297
Fleming (Public Schools and the General Education System, 1944)   202, 207, 220
Fowler (Reform of Social Security, 1975)   315–16
Fulton (Civil Service, 1968)   42–3, 86–8, 90, 96

378